Texas REAL ESTATE Agency

Seventh Edition

Minor Peeples III,
Donna K. Peeples,
A. Sue Williams

This publication is designed to provide accurate and authoritative information in regard to the subject matter covered. It is sold with the understanding that the publisher is not engaged in rendering legal, accounting, or other professional advice. If legal advice or other expert assistance is required, the services of a competent professional should be sought.

President: Dr. Andrew Temte
Chief Learning Officer: Dr. Tim Smaby
Vice President, Real Estate Education: Asha Alsobrooks
Development Editor: Julia Marti

TEXAS REAL ESTATE AGENCY, SEVENTH EDITION
©2012 Kaplan, Inc.
Published by DF Institute, Inc., d/b/a Kaplan Real Estate Education
332 Front St. S., Suite 501
La Crosse, WI 54601

All rights reserved. The text of this publication, or any part thereof, may not be reproduced in any manner whatsoever without written permission from the publisher.

Printed in the United States of America
12 13 14 10 9 8 7 6 5 4 3 2 1
ISBN: 978-1-4277-3825-7 / 1-4277-3825-4
PPN: 1560-0508

Contents

About the Authors viii
Acknowledgments ix
Preface x

CHAPTER 1
Agency Concepts 1
What Is Agency? 2
Roles People Play in Agency Relationships 3
Client or Customer? 4
Why Study Agency? 4
The Real Estate License Act, the Texas Real Estate Commission, and the Licensee 8
Summary 9
Key Points 9
Suggestions for Brokers 10
Chapter 1 Quiz 11

CHAPTER 2
Basic Agency Relationships, Disclosure, and Duties to the Client 13
Agency Defined 14
Classifications of Agency 14
Fiduciary Duties and Responsibilities 17
Summary 30
Key Points 30
Suggestions for Brokers 31
Chapter 2 Quiz 32

CHAPTER 3
Disclosure and Duties to Third Parties 35
Duties to Others (Third Parties) 36
Avoiding Disclosure and Misrepresentation Problems 36
Material Facts 43
Stigmatized Properties 46
Liability for Misrepresentation 52
Summary 54
Key Points 54

Suggestions for Brokers 55

Chapter 3 Quiz 56

CHAPTER 4
Creation and Termination of Agency 58

How and When Agency Is Created 59

Important Issues 66

How Agency Is Terminated 70

Duties of Agency that Continue 74

Summary 74

Key Points 75

Suggestions for Brokers 75

Chapter 4 Quiz 76

CHAPTER 5
Seller Agency 78

Express and Implied Agreements 79

Listing Agreements 80

Benefits of Seller Agency Relationships 96

Approaches to Representing Sellers 98

Exclusive Seller Agency 98

Nonexclusive Seller Agency 105

Disclosure Issues 105

Summary 107

Key Points 107

Suggestions for Brokers 108

Chapter 5 Quiz 109

CHAPTER 6
Buyer Agency 112

Deciding to Represent the Buyer 114

The Creation of Buyer Agency 115

Benefits of Buyer-Agency Relationships 124

Fee Arrangements 129

Written Notification of Compensation to Broker 136

Procuring Cause 137

Purchase Agreement 137

Buyer's Broker Disclosures 142

Summary 144

Key Points 144

Suggestions for Brokers 145

Chapter 6 Quiz 146

CHAPTER 7
Representing More Than One Party in a Transaction: Intermediary Brokerage 149

The Path from Dual Agency to Intermediary Brokerage 150

Representation of More Than One Party in a Transaction 151

Former Statutory Dual Agency Rules in Texas 153

Intermediary Brokerage 155

Concerns Related to Intermediary Practice 166

Nonresidential Intermediary Applications 168

Intentional versus Unintended Dual Representation 169

Summary 177

Key Points 178

Suggestions for Brokers 179

Chapter 7 Quiz 180

CHAPTER 8
Nonexclusive Single Agency 183

Practicing Nonexclusive Single Agency 184

Counseling Sessions Prior to Engagement 186

Advantages and Disadvantages 188

Summary 188

Key Points 189

Suggestions for Brokers 189

Chapter 8 Quiz 190

CHAPTER 9
Clarifying Agency Relationships 192

Disclosure Policy 193

Developing a Company Policy 201

Summary 203

Key Points 204

Suggestions for Brokers 205

Chapter 9 Quiz 206

CHAPTER 10
Employment Issues 209

Employment Relationships between Brokers and Principals 210

Employment and Compensation of Personal Assistants 216

Employment Relationships between Brokers and Subagents 216

Other Compensation Issues 217

Summary 218

Key Points 218

Suggestions for Brokers 219

Chapter 10 Quiz 220

CHAPTER 11
Agency, Ethics, and the Law 222

Current Environment 223

Distinctions between Law, Ethics, and Morals 224

Federal and State Law Relating to Conduct 226

TRELA and Rules of the Commission 227

Professional Codes of Ethics 227

A Practical Guide for Everyday Practice 242

When Enough Is Not Enough—Minimum Ethical Standards 246

The Bottom Line on Ethics 247

Summary 247

Key Points 247

Suggestions for Brokers 248

Chapter 11 Quiz 249

CHAPTER 12
Deceptive Trade Practices and Consumer Protection Act 251

Applicability: Real Estate Broker and Salesperson Exemption from the DPTA: SB 1353 252

Fraud versus Misrepresentation 253

Deceptive Trade Practices and Consumer Protection Act 254

Damages 266

Defenses 267

Ethical and Legal Concerns 269

Summary 269

Key Points 270

Suggestions for Brokers 270

Chapter 12 Quiz 271

CHAPTER 13
Putting It All Together 274

Preventive Brokerage 275

First Contact: The Broker Working for/with the Seller 276

First Contact: The Broker Working for/with the Buyer 280

Other Considerations 281

Using Rehearsed Dialogue 285

Risk Management 287

Summary 289

Key Points 289

Suggestions for Brokers 290

Chapter 13 Quiz 291

APPENDIX A
Texas Occupations Code 294

APPENDIX B
Questions and Answers Regarding Disclosure of Agency and Intermediary Practice 334

APPENDIX C
Agency Cases from 50 States 346

Chapter 2. Basic Agency Relationships, Disclosure, and Duties of the Client 346

Chapter 4. Creation and Termination of Agency 362

Chapter 6. Subagency 365

Chapter 8. Representing More Than One Party in a Transaction: Intermediary Brokerage 369

APPENDIX D
Web Site Resources 372

Glossary 373

About the Authors

Donna K. Peeples (Katy), PhD, is an associate professor of management at Texas A&M Corpus Christi and previous co-owner of the Real Estate Institute of Corpus Christi. She is licensed as a real estate broker in Texas, holds a BBA in finance, an MBA from Texas A&M University at Corpus Christi, and a PhD from Texas A&M University at College Station. Her real estate designations include the GRI, CRB, and the Texas Real Estate Teachers Association's (TRETA) CREI designation. Katy is a frequent public speaker on topics relating to business and real estate. Katy is a coauthor of *Prepare for the Texas Real Estate Exam* with Dr. Johnnie Rosenauer and Dr. Minor Peeples III, PhD.

Minor Peeples III, PhD, is cofounder, previous owner, and former CEO and principal instructor of the Real Estate Institute of Corpus Christi, Inc. Minor is a Texas real estate broker with extensive experience in the real estate business and has served as a content expert for various editions of the Texas real estate examination and as a member of the TREC MCE content committee. He is a coauthor of *Prepare for the Texas Real Estate Exam* with Dr. Johnnie Rosenauer and Dr. Katy Peeples. His educational background includes a BA in economics from Texas A&M at College Station, an MBA from Texas A&M-Corpus Christi, and a PhD from Texas A&M at College Station. Currently, Dr. Peeples offers consulting services to real estate brokerage companies and expert witness services in the area of agency law and is a frequent speaker at professional real estate meetings throughout south Texas.

A. Sue Williams, MS, GRI, served for over 20 years in the U.S. Navy in myriad assignments ranging from associate professor of computer science at the U.S. Military Academy in West Point, New York, to commanding officer of the fleet ballistic missile (FBM) submarine base in Holy Loch, Scotland. She has been licensed as a real estate broker since 1996 in Texas and holds a BA in English from Texas State University in San Marcos and an MS in computer science from the Naval Postgraduate School in Monterey, California. Sue has been affiliated with the Real Estate Institute of Corpus Christi since 1994, serving full time as an instructor and writer of prelicensing and continuing education courses. She then stepped up to the position of executive director for several years before retiring in December 2010. She continues to author and teach mandatory continuing education (MCE) courses throughout the Coastal Bend and often contributes to the review and editing of real estate textbooks for Dearborn Real Estate Education, including previous editions of *Texas Real Estate Agency* and *Texas Real Estate Exam Prep, Third Edition*, and the writing of exam and chapter quiz rationales for *Modern Real Estate Practice in Texas, 13th Edition*. Sue is a member of the Texas Real Estate Teachers Association (TRETA) and the Real Estate Educator's Association (REEA).

Acknowledgments

The authors and publisher wish to thank the following individuals for their valuable contributions to this edition: Terri Macaluso, broker/manager, Ebby Halliday REALTORS®, Frisco Texas, and associate faculty, Collin College; Ken Combs, professor (retired, Del Mar Junior College, Corpus Christi, Texas), GRI, CREI, MBA, Ken Combs Realty, Corpus Christi, Texas.; Cheryl Nance, EdD, DREI, CREI, author of *Modern Real Estate Practice in Texas*; Edd Price, owner, Century-21 Hallmark, Corpus Christi, Texas; James Wiedemer, BA, JD, DREI, CREI, State Bar Real Estate Forms Committee and author of several real estate text books.

The authors and publisher wish to thank the following reviewers for their valuable contributions to previous editions: Harold E. Grimes, Tyler Real Estate College; Nanci Hawes, previous owner of Leonard-Hawes Real Estate School, now Kaplan Professional Schools; Phillip G. (L.) Schöewe, CREI, DREI, JD, adjunct professor San Jacinto College, managing broker HomeIndex, Int'l REALTY; Bob Reynolds, San Antonio College; Kenneth West, Tarrant County College; Patricia Banta, Collin County Community College; Dave Garcia, The Academy of Real Estate; James E. George, EdD, Professional Development Institute, University of North Texas (North Denton); Rick Knowles, Capital Real Estate Training; Randy McKechnie, RLM Consulting, Inc.; Joe C. Pickett, Academy of Real Estate (El Paso); Thomas E. Powell, Lee College; John Wesley Tomblin, J. Wesley Tomblin & Associates (Austin).; and Cheryl Nance, EdD, DREI, CREI, author of *Modern Real Estate Practice in Texas*.

Preface

Knowledge of agency relationships is vital to a licensee's survival and ultimate success in the field of real estate. As clients and customers become more aware of their rights, real estate licensees are often expected to increase their level of service and are being held to higher standards of practice. In addition, because agency law is an evolving law, the practitioner must keep abreast of its changes. Many issues, such as those involving intermediary brokerage, buyer agency, or recent changes to the Texas Deceptive Trade Practices Act continue to evolve and be interpreted by the courts. The explanations in this text are consistent with the Texas Real Estate Commission's interpretations, but as more case law develops, these interpretations are subject to change.

This book is designed to help students seeking a real estate license and real estate practitioners understand relationships that are created in real estate transactions. Agency is a course of study required by The Real Estate License Act (TRELA) for all persons seeking a real estate license. This edition therefore focuses on all statutory topics and ethical standards required by TRELA for a prelicensing core course in agency law.

This seventh edition of *Texas Real Estate Agency* retains many examples from previous editions to help students understand some of the new agency laws that have been enacted. Cases, used as learning tools, are meant to bring the real world into the study of agency and to give students the benefit of seeing how the courts interpret these issues.

Many references to TRELA and the rules of the Texas Real Estate Commission are included in the text to remind the reader that the law dictates much of our basic practice. Students who have a clear understanding of the basis of practice will usually have a clearer understanding of how and why certain practices exist.

While this text covers agency issues and may be used in Law of Agency core courses offered by colleges, universities, and proprietary level real estate schools, it is not intended to replace competent legal counsel. Each real estate transaction is unique; therefore, this text cannot be the source of law for any particular transaction. General direction that will guide a licensee's practice can be gained from study of the materials in this text; the licensee's sponsoring broker and legal counsel, who is retained to give advice, will decide specific practices.

CHAPTER 1

Agency Concepts

Few real estate topics receive more attention than that of agency. Even the use of the term can be confusing because in Texas, there are two categories of license holders: salespersons and brokers. The entry level license is that of a salesperson who is prohibited from working independently. All salesperson licensees must be associated with a licensed broker. Although salespeople are "agents" of their broker, under agency law, only a broker is an agent of the buyer/seller or tenant/landlord. Yet we refer to brokers as agents, to salespeople as agents, and to our brokerage offices as real estate agencies. It is not surprising that the public mistakenly considers all licensees to be agents.

In addition, numerous court cases have demonstrated that the public, as well as brokers and sales licensees, are often unclear about the various roles that the broker may be playing while assisting in a real estate transaction and about the duties those different roles may impose on the broker. For example, a broker may be an agent (because agency is consensual); a sales licensee holding an active license is *always* an agent of the sponsoring broker (because salespersons have a fiduciary relationship with their sponsoring broker); a principal may be a client or a customer of the broker; and thus a broker may be working with one principal and for another. Confusing? Indeed. It will be helpful to remember that for a licensee to be an agent for a principal, there must be a principal-client relationship. That is, brokers work for clients but with customers.

It is critical today for real estate professionals to be well grounded in the fundamentals of agency law in order to perform the duties expected of them. Brokers must have a good understanding of the principles of agency law so that they may train their sales and broker associates properly. Licensees associated with a broker must likewise be able to communicate the principles of agency information to prospective customers and clients—both buyers/tenants and sellers/landlords—in order to make informed decisions about the relationship that should be established with the broker that will best serve the consumers interests. This chapter introduces you to some basic agency concepts that will help you understand the larger, more complex issues introduced in succeeding chapters.

■ LEARNING OBJECTIVES

This chapter addresses the following:

- What Is Agency?
- Roles People Play in Agency Relationships
- Client or Customer?
- Why Study Agency?
    - Increased Litigation against Real Estate Licensees
    - Confusion Regarding Whom the Licensee Represents
    - Public Perceptions
    - Emotional Aspects
    - Complexity
    - Greater Consumer Expectations
    - Use of More Than One Broker
    - Greater Licensee Professionalism
    - State Agency Disclosure Laws
    - Required Topic of Study for Potential Licensees
- The Real Estate License Act, the Texas Real Estate Commission, and the Licensee

■ WHAT IS AGENCY?

Agency, in its most basic form, occurs when one person, the agent, acts on behalf of another, the principal (client). This can be as simple as neighbors authorizing you to accept a postal package for them or as complex as a business transaction involving millions of dollars. Agency relationships are not unique to real estate; they are an essential part of many business arrangements and are controlled by the principles of business law. The laws governing agency are drawn from both common law and statutory law. Common law is law that has evolved by custom or by court decisions (case law), and it is contrasted with statutory law, which is enacted by legislatures. You should know that such legislative law is often specifically intended to contradict and supersede the common law.

For centuries, people have engaged others to represent them in all types of situations. They may grant others the authority to act on their behalf in a single activity, in a specified group of activities, or in the ongoing operation of a business. Some agency relationships, like those in real estate, involve money and/or property and create a fiduciary relationship, in which one party is bound to act in the best interest of another. A fiduciary handles money or property for the client; therefore, special duties are created. (These special fiduciary duties are discussed in detail in a later chapter.) In any event, agents must at all times act in the best interest of the parties they represent. Today, a licensee must know what the priorities are—especially when a fiduciary relationship is coupled with an agency activity such as a real estate transaction.

ROLES PEOPLE PLAY IN AGENCY RELATIONSHIPS

In this book, we use many terms that describe the relationships created as a result of real estate transactions. The following list of terms will help you understand the roles real estate licensees play and the terminology used in this book and in the real estate industry. You will notice that the terms may overlap at times, and several terms may apply to a single participant in a transaction.

- **Licensee (active)**—A person licensed by the Texas Real Estate Commission (TREC) to act as a broker or a salesperson in a real estate transaction.
- **Licensee (inactive)**—A person licensed by the Texas Real Estate Commission (TREC) but not authorized to conduct business as a broker or salesperson until the license is converted to active status.
- **License holder**—A broker or salesperson licensed by TREC.
- **Agent**—(1) A broker who represents a seller, a landlord, a buyer, or a tenant. (2) Salespersons or broker licensees who represent the broker with whom they are associated. (All references in the text to the broker's duties and responsibilities to the principal also apply to salespersons or broker associates in the firm.)
- **Subagent**—A license holder not sponsored by or associated with the client's broker but who is representing the client through a cooperative agreement with the client's broker. Also called the other broker.
- **Broker licensee**—An individual holding a broker's license issued by TREC. Brokers may act independently in conducting real estate transactions or may engage other broker or salesperson licensees to represent them in the conduct of their real estate business.
- **Sponsoring broker**—The broker through whom the salesperson's active license is issued and who assumes responsibility for the real estate brokerage activities of that salesperson.
- **Fiduciary**—As defined by the rules of the Texas Real Estate Commission (§ 531.1), the duties of a fiduciary include (1) representing the interests of the agent's client; (2) being faithful and observant to the trust placed in the agent; (3) being scrupulous and meticulous in performing the agent's functions, and (4) placing no personal interest above that of the agent's client.
- **Salesperson licensee**—An individual holding a salesperson's license issued by TREC, an agent of the sponsoring broker. Salesperson licensees may conduct business only through their sponsoring broker.
- **Broker associate**—A broker associated with and conducting business as an agent of another broker who accepts responsibility for the broker associate's brokerage activities.
- **Sales associate**—A salesperson licensee associated with and conducting business as an agent of the sponsoring broker.

- **Seller's agent**—A broker representing the seller in a real estate transaction. Also called seller's broker, listing broker, or listing agent.
- **Buyer's agent**—A broker representing the buyer in a real estate transaction. Also called buyer's broker, selling broker, selling agent, cooperating broker, or other broker.
- **Intermediary**—An agency alternative permitting the broker to act as an agent for both a buyer-client and a seller-client in the same transaction.
- **Landlord's agent**—A broker representing a landlord in a real estate transaction.
- **Tenant's agent**—A broker representing a tenant in a real estate transaction.
- **Client**—A person, sometimes called a principal, who engages services that include the professional advice and advocacy of another, called an agent, and whose interests are protected by the specific duties and loyalties of an agency relationship.
- **Customer**—A person who receives limited brokerage services without establishing an agency relationship. Specifically, advice, advocacy, and fiduciary relationships are not included in customer services.

The agency relationships that the above individuals can enter into are discussed in detail in the following chapters. As you study the subject of agency, it is important that you pay close attention to the relationships that are created and begin to understand how these relationships affect the way you will relate to the person or entity you are working with in your real estate transactions. You cannot be all things to all people.

CLIENT OR CUSTOMER?

It is important that a licensee have a clear understanding of the difference between a client and a customer. The extent of services that a licensee can offer is determined by the relationships established with individuals.

Clients are represented by licensees who are acting as agents. Customers represent themselves. A licensee works for a client, providing services that include advice, opinions, and advocacy while carrying out the instructions of the client. The licensee works with a customer, giving limited services such as touring available properties, discussing financing options, and per the seller's instructions, relaying information from the seller (e.g., the condition of the property and acceptable price and terms). The licensee does not assist the customer in negotiations by offering advice or opinions regarding price or negotiation strategy or in any way acting as an advocate of the customer.

WHY STUDY AGENCY?

Increased Litigation against Real Estate Licensees

There are many good reasons to study agency law, but a key explanation for increased interest in agency is increasing litigation in this area of real estate practice. A real estate lawsuit usually results from something other than agency issues, such as breach of contract, misrepresentation, or a decision by one of the contracting parties to rescind a contract. After most lawsuits are filed, however, the issue of who represented whom frequently becomes the focal point. Licensees may not have adequately discussed or disclosed whom they represent. Therefore, a lawyer seeking to set aside a transaction may search for an undisclosed, often unintended agency relationship. For example, a lawyer interviewing a buyer-client before filing a misrepresentation action might ask the buyer:

- "How were you treated by the licensee who represented you?"
- "Did you think that the licensee was your agent?"
- "Did you sign a written agreement whereby the licensee agreed to represent you?"
- "Did you know that the licensee with whom you were working was really the legal agent of the seller?"
- "How do you feel about that now?"

An undisclosed or inadequately disclosed agency relationship might result in the licensee's representation of both parties without their permission to do so—a circumstance strictly prohibited by law. Such undisclosed relationships can be grounds for not paying a brokerage commission or may be used as a basis to rescind a purchase contract between a buyer and a seller. Many potential problems, even lawsuits, may be avoided by adherence to timely agency disclosure requirements.

Confusion Regarding Whom the Licensee Represents

As implied in the introduction to this chapter, what at first may appear quite simple can be complex and confusing to the participants in a real estate transaction. In some transactions, the buyers and the sellers (and licensees as well) are not sure whether a licensee is an agent for the seller, the buyer, both, or neither. Why? Because it is the nature of a real estate licensee to be solicitous, friendly, and service driven. This behavior can be misconstrued as implying an agency relationship to a customer. In an effort to reduce the confusion regarding agency relationships, TREC has produced the Information About Brokerage Services form shown in Figure 9.1 (voluntary in format, but mandatory in content), which provides consumers with information relating to the differences when a broker represents a seller or a buyer or acts as an intermediary. This statutory language is critical to the consumers' understanding of the various roles that the broker may play in a transaction and must be delivered to buyers or sellers before any substantive discussions begin. In addition to timely delivery, the information must be presented in an understandable and meaningful way to the consumer. The TREC form referenced in this paragraph is discussed in more detail in Chapter 9, "Clarifying Agency Relationships."

The question of whether an agency relationship in a real estate transaction has been created is a question of fact—that is, one a judge or a jury might be called on to determine. The particular circumstances of each case must be examined to determine whether the agent represents the buyer, the seller, or both. Because of the ease with which agency relationships may be created and in the absence of any required formalities or written agreements, a real estate licensee may be held to be an unwitting agent in a so-called unintended or accidental agency. In essence, if you act as the advisor for any party, you may find that you have unintentionally become the "agent" for that party. William D. North, past executive vice president of the National Association of REALTORS® (NAR), stated, "It's often hard to tell which party the broker represents, and both the buyer and seller are apt to visualize the broker as their broker."

A jury might find that the conduct of both the licensee and the consumer demonstrated that the consumer authorized the licensee to act on the consumer's behalf and that the licensee did so, thus creating a principal-agent relationship. Such a finding has serious legal, economic, and ethical consequences to brokers, salespersons, sellers, and buyers because the Texas Real Estate Commission tends to hold the professional licensee responsible should consumers misunderstand the role the licensee played in the transaction. (TRELA 1101.652(b)(7))

Public Perceptions

Perhaps you have noticed the way the media portray real estate licensees. The image is often one of greedy, fast-talking salespersons whose primary purpose is to line their pockets with commissions while showing little regard for buyers and sellers. Granted, some licensees richly deserve such an image; however, many more try their best to be honest, knowledgeable professionals who make every effort to conduct their business in an ethical manner. An understanding of agency law is the foundation for sound business practices that will guide real estate professionals in their daily activities and help in changing public perceptions about the real estate industry.

Emotional Aspects

Unlike the purchase or sale of many items, a real estate transaction is frequently charged with emotion. Buyers, hopeful of realizing a part of the American dream through home ownership, are also faced with the prospect of a fearfully large financial obligation. Sellers, perhaps eager to improve their lifestyle, are sometimes struck with the prospect of leaving behind years of memories attached to the home they are selling. As a result of these high emotions, a small issue may blossom into a major event between the parties. Licensees who fail to understand and accommodate these emotional aspects will frequently lose the trust and confidence of the principals and have a difficult time becoming successful in the real estate business. Understanding the roles that licensees play also helps the professional maintain a clear sense of purpose and direction during such emotional periods.

Complexity

Buying a home is an investment decision, as well as a practical consideration. Transactions are becoming increasingly more complex in terms of property disclosures, inspection issues, land surveys, mineral interests, and of course financing. Today many consumers buy, sell, and buy again. Each time increases the consumer's understanding of the importance of receiving sound, objective advice and opinions, in addition to accurate information about the property under consideration. These repeat buyers and sellers recognize the distinction between advice and information, especially with so much money at stake. Many less experienced consumers, however, do not understand that as customers, they are entitled to any accurate, relevant information the licensee might possess, but as clients they are additionally entitled to advice and opinions, such as suggested negotiating strategies in light of the other party's marketing position.

Greater Consumer Expectations

Buyers seek representation more frequently in today's market because consumer education has led to their understanding the benefits of the agency relationship. Both the buyer and the seller increasingly have come to expect professionalism and competence from real estate licensees. After all, state licensing requirements demand a higher knowledge and competency level for brokers and salespersons than for the average person. A judicial trend has emerged, away from the tradition of caveat emptor (let the buyer beware) and toward greater consumer protection and professional accountability on the part of the real estate licensee. Frequently, real estate licensees are the most visible experts in the transaction, and both the buyer and the seller tend to defer to the judgment and skill of the real estate professional. Seasoned real estate professionals are acutely aware of their importance and wisely know when to defer to another professional a matter not within the licensee's area of responsibility or expertise.

Use of More Than One Broker

A Federal Trade Commission (FTC) study on national residential brokerage practices noted that 66 percent of the home sales studied involved two brokers or salespersons, and more than half involved the services of two brokerage firms. With two brokers participating in one transaction, each working a different side of the transaction, it is not surprising that buyers and sellers sometimes question whom the participating brokers really represent. To some, it seems a natural division of labor for the listing broker to represent the seller and the other broker, the buyer. In practice, however, many buyers are surprised to learn that the salesperson they regard as "theirs" actually represents the seller. The surge in buyer brokerage is, no doubt, due in part to better information regarding the services available from brokers and more complete disclosure of agency relationships.

Greater Licensee Professionalism

In the past, the listing broker was hired primarily to find a buyer for the seller's property. Today, it is likely that another broker will find the buyer. Sellers look to listing brokers to protect their best financial interests in the form of professional advice and opinions as to the soundness of a buyer's offer. Buyers usually look to the licensees who introduce them to the property to provide the same service.

Many licensees now emphasize the variety and quality of services they offer rather than their salesmanship and matchmaking skills. Real estate licensees promote themselves as advisers, problem solvers, and data interpreters rather than solely as information providers. Licensees are expected to be generally knowledgeable in such areas as taxation, law, mortgage planning, contract preparation, investment analysis, finance, appraisal, and property management. The law and the industry itself are demanding higher standards of skill, care, and due diligence from brokers in promoting clients' best interests, in furnishing required disclosures, in treating everyone honestly, in spotting potential problems, and in recommending the use of experts when necessary.

State Agency Disclosure Laws

Nearly every state, including Texas, has passed legislation requiring real estate licensees to disclose whom they represent in each transaction. Some state laws permit simple oral disclosure; other laws mandate the use of specific disclosure forms. In all cases, the licensee faces the likelihood that the buyer or the seller will want to know what the licensee's role will be. Licensees who are not comfortable discussing their role may find the prospective client or customer seeking a more competent real estate licensee.

Required Topic of Study for Potential Licensees

For some, the most compelling reason to study agency law is the educational requirement mandated by the Texas legislature in 1993. The law, as implemented by TREC, requires that all applicants for licensure show evidence that a minimum of 30 clock hours (2 semester hours) in Law of Agency has been completed from an acceptable source of study.

■ THE REAL ESTATE LICENSE ACT, THE TEXAS REAL ESTATE COMMISSION, AND THE LICENSEE

To deal with the issues regarding agency relationships and other laws pertinent to real estate, the Texas legislature passed the first law governing the activities of real estate professionals in 1939. As we know it today, The Real Estate License Act (TRELA) has been amended numerous times. TRELA is the law that establishes the duties of real estate licensees in their dealings with the public; it provides the legal framework within which each licensee operates. The law regarding agency relationships, as it pertains to real estate licensees, is carefully detailed in the act. Each person licensed in Texas is obligated to be familiar with the act and to conduct real estate transactions in strict accordance with the act.

The Texas Real Estate Commission (TREC) was established by TRELA in 1949. In 2011, TREC became a self-directed, semi-independent agency no longer subject to the legislative budget and appropriations process at the state legislature. Instead, TREC conducts business using the licensing fees it collects, which exceed the agency's expenditures. TREC's mission, however, has not changed. It remains the official agency in Texas for administering rules and regulations that govern real estate licensing.

TREC is responsible for the administration of TRELA. TREC consists of nine members—six brokers and three public members—who serve staggered terms of six years each. The governor, with approval of the senate, appoints three replacement members every two years.

The commissioners may appoint an administrator and an assistant administrator who oversee the day-to-day operations of the commission. From a real estate licensee's perspective, some of the key functions of the TREC are

- ■ enforcing TRELA in a manner that protects the public,

FIGURE 1.1	Real estate professionals in Texas are governed by both The Real Estate License Act and Title 22 of the Texas Administrative Code. Examples of both are provided below.
Statutes versus Rules	*Example of statute (TRELA) versus rule (22 TAC):* ■ TRELA § 1101.652(b)(13) states that TREC may suspend or revoke a license if the licensee "solicits, sells or offers for sale a real property by means of a lottery." ■ 22 TAC § 535.149 defines and gives specific examples of what does and does not constitute a lottery.

- overseeing the licensing process, and
- monitoring and controlling the educational activities of approved providers of real estate education.

If the commission receives a complaint about the practice of a licensee who has violated TRELA, it may investigate the complaint and take the appropriate action, which could result in fines and/or suspension or revocation of the license. The wise practitioner never forgets that TREC is a consumer protection agency.

TRELA provides that the commission is authorized to establish rules and regulations necessary to administer the act (TRELA § 1101.151(b)). Typically, each legislative session results in new and revised statutes that affect real estate practice. Following the legislative session, the commission is then empowered by the Texas Administrative Code (TAC) to adopt the necessary rules and regulations resulting in the implementation of the legislation. The new provisions are then published at Title 22 of the TAC. These rules and regulations allow the law to be interpreted and enforced (*see* Figure 1.1). Throughout this text, the authors will reference specific sections of TRELA as well as the Rules of the Texas Real Estate Commission, as passed under the provisions of the TAC.

■ SUMMARY

From the most basic residential real estate transaction to the most complex commercial contract, it is important to understand whom the licensee represents and what services can or cannot be provided in accordance with Texas law. There exists an increased interest in clarifying agency issues, precipitated by agency disclosure laws, the growth in buyer agency, and the expanded professional liability suits against real estate licensees.

By developing a positive, and applied, awareness of agency relationships, the real estate professional, when acting as an agent, will be able to adapt to consumer demands for greater representation in today's real estate marketplace.

■ KEY POINTS

- An agent is one who acts on behalf of another—the principal or client.
- The Real Estate License Act (TRELA) is the law that establishes the duties of real estate licensees in Texas. The Texas Real Estate Commission (TREC) administers TRELA empowered by the Texas Administrative Code (TAC).

- The real estate licensee may work for a client in a principal-agent relationship, or the licensee may work with a customer in a nonagency relationship. A client has a legal right to expect accurate information, advice, informed opinions, and advocacy. A customer has a legal right to expect fair treatment, accurate information, referral to sources when advice or advocacy is demanded, and the seller's honest disclosure of the property's condition.
- An undisclosed, underdisclosed, or accidental agency relationship may create an unauthorized representation of more than one party, and could result in a lawsuit for rescission, forfeiture of commission, money damages, loss of license, or disciplinary action.
- The study of agency is important because of misunderstandings among the public and licensees regarding agency issues, the complexities of real estate transactions, the presence of more than one broker in transactions, the growing demand for buyer representation, state disclosure laws, and the escalation of lawsuits involving real estate transactions.

■ SUGGESTIONS FOR BROKERS

Develop a written company agency disclosure policy that emphasizes awareness of the various agency situations salespersons will encounter in daily practice. Establish training programs within your firm that will allow your sales staff to become comfortable in understanding and disclosing whom they represent (or don't represent), consistent with your established company policy. The lack of a clear company agency policy may easily lead to unlawful actions by the associated licensees of the broker. (The TREC holds the broker responsible for the professional acts of all licensees associated with the broker.)

CHAPTER 1 QUIZ

1. Agency is
   a. a real estate brokerage.
   b. the operation of a business.
   c. one person acting on behalf of another.
   d. one person giving advice to another person.

2. An agent works on behalf of
   a. the customer.
   b. the client.
   c. both the customer and the client.
   d. neither the customer nor the client.

3. TRELA
   a. enforces the License Act.
   b. may appoint an administrator for the TREC.
   c. is the law that establishes the duties of real estate licensees.
   d. is the law established by the TREC.

4. The Texas Real Estate Commission
   a. does not hold the broker accountable for the actions of sponsored associates.
   b. holds the broker accountable for the professional actions of sponsored associates.
   c. holds buyers or sellers accountable for the acts of their real estate brokers and salespeople.
   d. holds the public accountable for the acts of real estate licensees.

5. A broker is representing Jim Smith, a buyer. In this transaction, Smith is considered a(n)
   a. customer.
   b. fiduciary.
   c. client.
   d. agent.

6. People who engage an agent to represent their interests in a transaction are called principals, or
   a. customers.
   b. sellers.
   c. buyers.
   d. clients.

7. A key distinction between the services given to clients versus those given to customers is that
   a. advice, opinions, and advocacy are given to clients, not customers.
   b. more advice and opinions are offered to the customer.
   c. customers get advice and opinions free, while clients must pay.
   d. clients must have a contract to receive services, while customers do not.

8. A licensee NOT associated with the listing broker who represents the seller through the listing broker is known as a(n)
   a. buyer's agent.
   b. intermediary.
   c. seller's agent.
   d. subagent.

9. One of the BEST ways a broker might protect against agency problems is to
   a. never represent buyers.
   b. never discuss agency issues with the parties.
   c. always treat both parties as valued customers.
   d. develop a clear, written office policy regarding agency issues.

10. A key reason to study agency today is
    a. to better represent customers.
    b. the increased litigation against agents.
    c. to be able to settle legal disputes between buyers and sellers.
    d. that commissions are greater to the agent when agency law is followed.

DISCUSSION QUESTIONS

1. What types of services does the typical buyer expect of a licensee?
2. What types of services does the typical seller expect of a licensee?
3. What are some of the emotions that a buyer and a seller may experience in a real estate transaction?
4. What are some of the reasons for the increased interest in agency?
5. What is the essential difference between a client and a customer?

CHAPTER 2

Basic Agency Relationships, Disclosure, and Duties to the Client

In real estate transactions, a variety of agency relationships may be created. For this reason, agency relationships must be clearly defined and recognized so they don't become a source of confusion and misunderstanding to buyers, sellers, real estate salespersons, brokers, lawyers, and judges. Preconceived notions about the right to representation and misapplied terminology often create roadblocks to greater understanding.

■ **LEARNING OBJECTIVES** *This chapter addresses the following:*

- Agency Defined
- Classifications of Agency
  - Universal Agency
  - General Agency
  - Special Agency
  - The Flow of Authority
- Fiduciary Duties and Responsibilities
  - Reasonable Care and Diligence
  - Obedience
  - Loyalty

- Disclosure
- Confidentiality
- Accounting
- Minimum Service Requirements

AGENCY DEFINED

As we learned in the previous chapter, agency occurs when one person, the agent, acts on behalf of another person, the principal or client. The basic doctrines of agency are common to all businesses.

In real estate practice, a licensee can be an agent for a broker; a broker also can be an agent for the buyer/tenant or seller/landlord, or both. Because of the many opportunities for confusion, it is necessary to understand the general classifications of agency to determine the scope of authority to act for the client.

It is worth noting here that real estate brokers or licensee associates should not be referred to as agents until an actual expressed agency relationship has been established. After an agency relationship has been established with the broker, the broker is called the agent of the client and the licensee associates are called agents of the broker. As agents of the broker, licensee associates (real estate salespersons or broker associates) have the same duties to the broker's principal as the sponsoring broker.

The agency relationship is established between the real estate broker and the broker's client/principal. All licensees in that office, as agents of the broker, are obligated to recognize that agency relationship and have the same duties to the principal as the broker.

CLASSIFICATIONS OF AGENCY

Agency is typically classified into three categories: universal, general, and special. Each has its own unique set of duties, responsibilities, and liabilities for both the principal and the agent. It is important for licensees to understand the scope of each type of agency so that they can understand and comply with the duties and obligations that are expected to be carried out in the course of conducting business.

Universal Agency

Universal agency gives a very broad and general scope of power to the agent to act for the principal. With this type of agency, the agent is empowered to conduct every type of transaction that may be legally delegated by a principal to an agent. Such agency power may include acquisition and disposal of assets, expenditure of the principal's funds, and entering into contracts on behalf of the principal. This type of agency would hold a principal accountable for virtually any action by the agent. Universal agency is not very common in typical real estate transactions. An example of universal agency is an adult son or daughter who has been empowered by an elderly parent to conduct all personal and business transactions on the parent's behalf. In this case, the parent is accountable for the actions of the son or the daughter in conducting the parent's affairs.

General Agency

The scope of authority in general agency is more restricted than in universal agency. The agent is authorized to conduct an ongoing series of transactions for the principals and can obligate them to certain types of contractual agreements. General agency is the relationship that most often exists between a broker and the broker's associates (broker licensees and sales licensees). Brokers authorize associates to act as broker's agents in the course of the brokerage operations. These agents are authorized to act for their brokers in any number of activities that are typical for a brokerage firm. Some of the most frequently performed activities are

- obtaining listings from sellers;
- conducting marketing activities for properties listed by the company;
- entering into buyer-representation agreements;
- showing properties to prospective buyers;
- preparing, presenting, and negotiating offers to purchase properties; and
- maintaining and transferring a complete singular file of each transaction completed or otherwise terminated.

Considerable authority may be given to the agent by the broker. For example, an agent of the broker (such as an associate broker or a sponsored salesperson) can obligate the broker to a listing contract with a seller or to a buyer-representation contract with a buyer. As with universal agency, the broker assumes a considerable amount of liability for the agent's actions. For example, if a broker's agent engages in inappropriate or illegal conduct while acting for the broker, the broker is held responsible for those actions. In addition to liability under general agency law, The Real Estate License Act also holds brokers accountable for the actions of their agents while acting within the scope of the general agency authority that was granted to them (§ 1101.803; 22 TAC § 535.2(a)).

In rule 22 TAC § 535.2, TREC lays considerable responsibility on the broker for the conduct of their business activities. Because of this extensive responsibility, brokers are usually concerned about engaging conscientious associated licensees and training them to make good decisions and take actions that are not only within the scope of the law but also are honest and ethical. Just one poorly trained or unethical associate who commits an illegal act can jeopardize a broker's entire business. For this reason brokers must satisfy themselves as to the character and integrity of licensees who would like to be associated with the brokerage firm.

Another general agency relationship that frequently occurs in real estate practice is when a broker acts as a property manager for an owner. In most cases, the broker conducts a number of transactions for the owner, such as negotiating and signing lease contracts, contracting for maintenance, and initiating eviction lawsuits on behalf of the owner. Frequently, the owner is unwilling or unable to perform these functions; therefore, it is necessary to confer on the broker the full authority to carry out these activities.

Special Agency

Special agency, sometimes known as limited agency, authorizes the agent to perform only those acts permitted by the principal. Real estate agents are most frequently called limited or special agents; their scope of authority usually does not extend beyond the terms of a listing agreement or a buyer-representation or tenant-representation agreement. A well-written listing agreement defines the duties of the broker and the client, and it uses distinct, well-defined terms rather than the broad, sweeping language of general agency agreements.

A listing agreement authorizes the broker to represent the seller in the marketing of the seller's property. The listing broker is authorized to find a ready, willing, and able buyer. Generally, the broker has no authority to sign contracts for the seller, to initial changes to an offer, to accept offers (even for the full purchase price) on behalf of the seller, or to permit early occupancy by a potential buyer or tenant. In exceptional cases, the broker may be appointed as attorney-in-fact under a separately granted power of attorney. Brokers are usually hesitant to accept a power of attorney because of potential conflicts or the appearance of impropriety that can arise because of the broker's interest in a transaction. Frequently a family member, a business associate, or an attorney will be granted the power of attorney when buyers or sellers are unable to be present to act in their own behalf.

A buyer-representation or tenant-representation agreement authorizes the broker to represent the buyer as an agent in purchasing or leasing a property. The agent seeks properties that meet the buyer's or the tenant's requirements and then will help negotiate the best contract terms and conditions for those parties. As when representing sellers, the agent generally has no authority to sign contracts unless a power of attorney has been established.

■ **EXAMPLE** In *Joseph v. James*, 2009 WL 3682608 (Tex. App. Austin 2009), the buyers had their agent fax an offer for $1,875,000 to the sellers' agent to purchase Joseph's home. The sellers' agent verbally informed the buyers' agent that the seller would not accept an offer for anything less than $2 million. The buyers' agent, after consulting with the buyers, changed the sales price to $2 million by crossing through the sales price on the contract and then, without obtaining the buyers' initials on the change, faxed the counteroffer to the sellers' agent. The sellers countered with several changes, including raising the sales price to $2,195,000. Each change was initialed by the sellers. The buyers' agent again altered the sales price, this time changing the total price to $2.1 million. Again, the buyers did not initial the changes. The buyers' agent attached the contract to an e-mail, along with a comment that the buyers loved the home and were countering at $2.1 million. The sellers' agent communicated a verbal counter from the sellers offering $2,125,000 and that the seller would leave several items of personal property. Hearing nothing back from the buyers, the sellers signed and initialed the latest written offer from the buyers' agent (for $2.1 million) and, without the knowledge of the seller's agent, asked the selling agent's assistant to send an e-mail acknowledging receipt and acceptance of the buyers' latest offer of $2.1 million.

When the transaction did not go forward, the buyers' agent apologized for the confusion, admitted he did not have the buyers' permission to make the changes and that the counteroffer of $2.1 million had been transmitted by mistake. The sellers sued for breach of contract and fraud (Texas Business and Commerce Code § 27.01. Fraud in Real Estate and Stock Transactions.)

■ **DISCUSSION** The sellers argued that the buyers' agent had the authority to sign on behalf of the buyers. By sending the counteroffer, the buyers' agent therefore bound the buyers to the purchase contract. The court, however, granted summary judgment to the buyers, relying on a long line of Texas cases confirming the special agent relationship held in the typical real estate transaction. The sellers were unable to show that the buyers had signed or initialed the last counteroffer of $2.1 million, thus no contract had been created. A licensee, without a power of attorney, has no authority to bind a principal to a transaction. In the heat of negotiation, licensees feel pressured by their clients to expedite the negotiation by making verbal offers/counteroffers. In this case, the buyers' agent attempted to simply make the change to the contract and fax the form without the buyers' initials. Without signatures and initials by the actual parties to the contract, according to the Texas statute of frauds (Texas Business and Commerce Code Section 26, Statute of Frauds), there is no binding contract.

■ **EXAMPLE** In the similar *Mushtaha v. Kidd*, 2010 WL 5395694 (Tex. App. Houston [1 Dist.], 2010) a seller directed his agent to mark through the price offered by a buyer and substitute a higher price, which the broker did, and then initialed and delivered it to the buyer's broker. The seller then received a higher offer from a second buyer. Realizing a higher offer was on the table, the first buyer quickly signed the seller's counteroffer. The seller, however, signed the contract accepting the offer from the second buyer. The court ruled that no binding contract existed between the first buyer and the seller, again citing that the special agency relationship of a broker did not include the right to bind the owner.

Licensees must make clear to the parties that verbal offers and counteroffers are simply not binding on the other party. Furthermore, licensees should never attempt to sign contracts or initial changes on behalf of their clients without benefit of a power of attorney.

The Flow of Authority

As shown in Figure 2.1, a typical real estate transaction commonly consists of two levels of agency. One level of agency exists between the associated licensee and the sponsoring broker, and another level exists between the broker and the buyer or the seller. Real estate licensees associated with a broker have a general agency relationship with their broker for the operation of the brokerage firm, and brokers have a special agency relationship with buyers or sellers for the purchase or sale of property. Because these relationships can be complex and carry legal obligations, it is important that every principal and agent understand the concepts that surround agency relationships.

■ FIDUCIARY DUTIES AND RESPONSIBILITIES

Today the broker may play many roles—agent for a seller or a landlord, agent for a buyer or a tenant, subagent of a seller or a buyer, or intermediary. These roles are discussed in detail in later chapters, but for the moment, it is important to know

FIGURE 2.1

The Flow of Authority in Agency Relationships

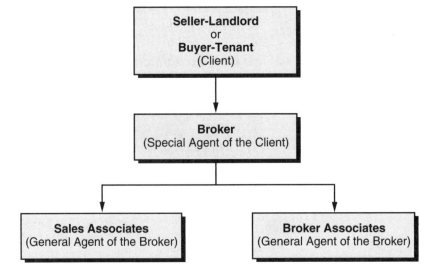

that, regardless of the agency role assumed by the broker, a clear understanding of duties to the client is critical.

If an agency relationship exists, the real estate agent is held to be a fiduciary. In classic terms, a fiduciary responsibility implies a position of trust or confidence in which one person—the fiduciary—is usually entrusted to hold or manage the assets (in real estate, the property) of another—the principal or the client. Common examples of fiduciaries are trustees, executors, and guardians. In real estate terms, the client relies on the real estate agent, as a fiduciary, to give skilled and knowledgeable advice and to help negotiate the best price and terms for the client in dealings with a third person (the customer).

Restatement (Second) of Agency, a widely accepted legal authority on the law of agency authored by the American Law Institute, states the following:

Fiduciaries are held to the highest amount of good faith, are required to exclude all selfish interest, are prohibited from putting themselves in positions where personal interest and representative interest will conflict and must, in any direct dealing with the principal, make full disclosure of all relevant facts and give the latter an opportunity to obtain independent advice.

In lay terms, fiduciaries have special skills and expertise that place them in a position of advantage over their principals. An important aspect of this relationship is that trust and confidence are on one side (the principal's), and superiority of knowledge and influence are on the other (the agent's). This is why the fiduciary has special obligations to the principal. The most important obligations a fiduciary owes to a principal can be remembered by using the "OLD CAR" memory device:

- Obedience
- Loyalty
- Disclosure
- Confidentiality
- Accounting
- Reasonable care and diligence

It is important to note that the real estate licensee, when acting as an agent on behalf of either party in the transaction, owes these fiduciary duties *in* addition to whatever duties are specified in the listing contract with the seller, the buyer-representation or tenant-representation agreement, property management agreement, TRELA, and the TREC Rules.

Many licensees elect to join trade associations that provide specialized services and support to licensees in the industry. The largest is the National Association of REALTORS® (NAR), which was founded in 1908. In turn, NAR is composed of state (i.e., Texas Association of REALTORS® [TAR]) and local associations. While the public tends to use the term REALTOR® synonymously with real estate agent, only a member of NAR may be called REALTOR®. All other licensees must be referred to as real estate licensees or agents.

In addition to the Canons of Professional Ethics and Conduct to which all Texas licensees are bound (22 TAC § 531), a licensee who is a REALTOR® owes additional ethical duties outlined in the REALTORS® Code of Ethics. The NAR Code of Ethics is generally recognized as representing reasonable and acceptable standards of conduct for any real estate licensee, REALTOR® or otherwise. These two ethical codes are discussed in more detail in Chapter 11.

Reasonable Care and Diligence

An agent is hired to do more than merely locate a property or find a ready, willing, and able buyer, and an agent's obligations extend beyond simply selling or locating a property. Real estate agents are held to a standard of care that requires, among other things, that they be knowledgeable concerning the land, the title, and the physical characteristics of the property being sold.

The agent must use reasonable care and diligence in

- guiding the seller-client to arrive at a reasonable listing price;
- advising the buyer-client to accept a reasonable purchase price in light of the current market values;
- making reasonable efforts to sell the property, such as holding open houses, advertising, listing with a multiple listing service (MLS), if customary; and using whatever marketing and advertising means proven to be effective in the specific market area;
- making properties available that meet the buyer's purchasing objectives;
- affirmatively discovering relevant facts and disclosing these facts to the client;
- investigating the material facts related to the sale and asking the seller questions (the duty to question) that will clarify the seller's needs and protect his or her best interests (e.g., "Does your roof leak?");
- preparing and explaining the provisions of the listing form, buyer-representation agreement, purchase contract, and other relevant legal documents;
- recommending that the client seek independent expert advisers such as attorneys, inspectors, appraisers, and accountants, when appropriate; and
- helping the principals meet deadlines and closing dates.

Agents must exercise care by knowing the laws, financing options, and most importantly the level of knowledge and expertise the client possesses. An inexperienced client requires vast amounts of information to make the best choices, while clients who have previously bought or sold properties usually are more aware of the basic concepts of ownership. It is important for agents to give their clients the information they need to make informed decisions regarding the purchase or sale of real estate.

Suppose an agent sells a home one week after the listing is signed. Initially, the seller is thrilled. Later, however, the seller may complain that the agent lacked skill and care because the listing price was set too low or that the agent failed to obtain better financing terms (this is not meant to suggest that homes that sell quickly are necessarily underpriced). The seller may become angry after discovering that the agent assisted the buyer-customer in obtaining financing that resulted in the seller's paying higher discount points when lower-discount-point options were available. Likewise, a seller who unwittingly closes a transaction a few days before becoming eligible for favorable tax benefits could well complain that the agent failed to exercise reasonable skill by not informing the seller that an early closing would cost thousands of dollars in avoidable taxes.

Similarly, an agent who represents a buyer must exercise reasonable care and diligence on the buyer's behalf. This duty extends beyond giving honest information to a customer—it extends to rendering sound advice and advising the buyer to obtain assistance from experts when appropriate. At the very essence of the fiduciary concept is the fact that a true agent is an equity preserver for the client. A buyer's agent preserves equity for the buyer-client by using all the agent's specialized skills and knowledge in negotiating the least possible price with the best terms.

Agents do not have to meet the high standard of legal knowledge required of attorneys; however, agents do need a basic knowledge of real estate law to qualify for state licenses. Courts impose on agents a duty to know and to explain, in basic terms, the practical effects of key financing terms, contingency clauses, holding title, restrictions, and routine contract provisions. In short, agents must spot common problem areas and direct their clients to expert help when the clients require specific advice.

Unlike attorneys, agents do more than act as fiduciaries. Typically, agents are hired to market property. Sometimes these dual responsibilities—marketing and advising—create practical and ethical dilemmas not normally experienced by other fiduciaries. Recognizing that the agent's income usually depends on a sale, the unprofessional agent could easily justify holding back information, based on the likelihood that the sale will proceed and that certain information would only cloud the client's decision. Nevertheless, the agent must disclose information to the client as part of the fiduciary duty required by law and ethics.

A practical test applied by courts to decide whether an agent has used reasonable skill and care in a given case is, "Would a reasonably efficient broker in the community in a like situation use more care to protect the best interests of the client?" If the answer by the trier of fact (judge or jury) is yes, the agent has been negligent.

■ **EXAMPLE** Salesperson Jane has just returned from a three-month vacation in Barbados. She immediately contacts her client, John, to see whether he is ready to list his property for sale. He informs her that his company has just finalized his transfer and that he needs to sell his property as soon as possible. She lists his property for $270,000, using her vast list of prior sales in the neighborhood to determine property value. A full-price contract is submitted by a buyer's broker the same day the property is listed, and the seller eagerly signs the offer.

After signing the contract, John talks with a neighbor, Al, who is also under contract to sell his home. Their homes are very similar in style, amenities, and condition, so they compare their selling prices. Al's contract is for $295,000, with basically the same terms and conditions as John's, and he received his offer about ten days after the property was listed.

■ **QUESTIONS** 1. Why do you think the sales price for John's home is $25,000 less than Al's? 2. What is Jane's liability, if any? 3. Would you do anything different if you were Jane? What? Explain.

Obedience

The agent has an obligation to follow the lawful instructions of the client. The agent frequently is asked to obtain a survey, obtain an appraisal, or arrange for an inspection for the client. It is important that the client make decisions about who will provide the services. The agent then can arrange for the services to be performed. Because the agent cannot act without the client's approval, doing such things as extending closing dates or loan approval dates is not allowed without authorization by the client before the changes are made.

Under no circumstances is an agent allowed to violate the law. Frequently, clients are unaware that a request is illegal. If the client requests an unlawful act, the agent should explain that the request is against the law and that all agents are required to adhere strictly to the law. If the client continues to insist upon the illegal act, the agent should withdraw from the transaction.

■ **EXAMPLE** Jane has been asked by her good friend, Cecil, to list his property. Jane is delighted to take this listing because the home is in a great neighborhood, close to schools, in wonderful condition, and should have an excellent chance of selling quickly at the price and terms that Cecil desires.

After the listing agreement has been signed and Jane is preparing to leave, Cecil clears his throat and says, "Of course, you know how I feel about selling my home to a minority. I would like you to do whatever is necessary not to show my home to any of 'those folks.'"

At first Jane is stunned. She had no idea that Cecil would make this request. She would really like to take this listing; however, she knows that what he is asking is against the law. Jane has no experience in dealing with this type of situation, and she is very unsure how to proceed.

■ **QUESTIONS** 1. What should Jane do? 2. What could she say to convey her point and still be able to maintain the listing?

Loyalty

Agents must always act in the best interest of their clients and must be loyal to the trust placed in them. Once an agreement has been reached between an agent (broker) and a client, all the associates of the firm, whether licensed as salespersons or brokers, will represent the client through the broker. Thus, all licensees associated with the firm will have the same obligations as the broker and must represent the best interests of the client. This means striving to

- obtain the best price and terms possible to satisfy the client's needs;
- investigate and explain all offers;
- obtain as much relevant information about the other party as possible; and
- above all, exert maximum effort for the client's benefit.

The agent who acts otherwise is not acting in the best interests of the client. This is a requirement of Texas common law and the Texas Administrative Code (TAC), under the Rules of the Texas Real Estate Commission (22 TAC § 535.2(b), 535.156(a), (b), and (c)). Disloyalty to the principal or the client is not only unethical and unprofessional, it is forbidden under the law governing real estate licensees. Disloyalty may be grounds for forfeiture of commission, loss of the license to practice, lawsuit for damages incurred by the client, and possible rescission of the sales or lease contract itself.

■ **EXAMPLE** Broker Nancy and her friend, George, owned homes in the same subdivision. Nancy listed George's home when George was transferred to Alaska. Nancy also placed her home on the market about the same time she listed George's home for sale. Nancy showed both her home and George's home to buyer Alicia. Alicia fell in love with George's home and expressed an immediate desire to purchase it for cash. Nancy then persuaded Alicia to purchase her own home instead.

■ **QUESTIONS** 1. Has Nancy breached her fiduciary duty of loyalty to George? 2. How could Nancy have avoided any question of a breach of her fiduciary duty?

Disclosure

A key point related to loyalty is the obligation of the agent to make a full, fair, and timely disclosure to the client of all known facts relevant or material to the transaction. A material fact is one that a reasonable person might feel is important in choosing a course of action. Recent changes to the Texas Deceptive Trade Practices Act (DTPA) clarify that real estate brokers are not subject to liability under that act unless the licensee has committed a misrepresentation of material facts, an unconscionable act, or a failure to disclose. The intent in the change to the DTPA, however, is that licensees should not be held liable under DTPA for innocent acts of omission as long as the licensee can show that there was no attempt to defraud or deceive. The licensee continues to be at risk for even innocent acts of omission or commission under TRELA, the TREC Rules, and ethical standards dictated by various trade associations.

Important disclosures by an agent to a client include

- the relationship between the client's agent and other parties to the transaction,

- the existence of other offers and the status of the earnest money deposit (22 TAC § 535.156(a) and § 535.159(b)),
- the buyer's financial condition,
- the agent's true opinion of the property's value (22 TAC § 535.16(c)),
- any commission split between a listing broker and another broker,
- the meaning of factual statements and business details contained in the contract, and
- all known facts that might affect the status of title to real estate.

Clearly, an agent who has actual knowledge of a property defect is liable to both the client and the customer if the defect is not disclosed (§ 1101.652(b)(2)-(3); 22 TAC 535.156(a)). In addition, under TRELA and TREC Rules, liability may exist if agents fail to disclose facts that they should have known within the range of expertise expected of agents. Thus, a case can be made that in addition to disclosure of known material facts, the agent may have a duty of reasonable discovery and a duty to investigate the many aspects of the transaction as they affect the client's decision making. Texas courts, however, have held that the real estate agent is not liable for physical inspection of the property for defects. This is the realm of licensed inspectors, not of brokers and salespersons (*Kubinsky v. Van Zandt Realtors*, 811 S.W.2d 711 [Tex. 1991]).

On the other hand, important facts affecting a client's decision fall within the broker's domain. In one case, a buyer offered a seller a property as part of the down payment in the purchase of the seller's property; however, the listing broker failed to verify the appraised value of the property offered by the buyer. As a result, the broker was held liable for failure to disclose information that was important to the seller in making a decision to accept the buyer's offer.

Full disclosure relating to the property. Full disclosure to the client is required, regardless of whether the fact is favorable or unfavorable, whether the fact is found before or after the purchase contract is signed, or whether disclosure might prevent the successful completion of the sale. Not only is the client entitled to know the same facts that the agent knows, but the client is generally assumed, by law, to know what the agent knows. The duty of disclosure is greater to a client than to a customer. A customer is not entitled to facts about the client or the broker's opinion of value; however, the customer is entitled to information regarding material facts about the property, such as

- property defects,
- defects in the title,
- problems relating to the survey,
- floodplain information,
- rights of parties in possession (such as tenants), and
- environmental issues and/or property conditions that would affect the health or safety of occupants.

A client is entitled to all the items listed plus full disclosure of information relating to the transaction and the other party to the transaction, such as

- the broker's opinion of the value of the property,
- possible negotiating strategies or options available to the client,
- motivation of the other party to buy or sell, and
- financial condition of the other party.

It is important that an agent clearly understand the disclosure issues as they relate to a client or a customer. A key distinction is that the interest of the client is paramount, although the customer must, at the same time, be treated honestly and fairly. It should be noted that treating the customer honestly and fairly is usually in the best interest of the client.

Full disclosure of relationships. The real estate agent must disclose to the client any special relationship that might exist between the broker and any of the broker's associates and the other parties in the transaction. Because the client may rely on the agent's loyal advice and counsel, it is important to know what interest any agent involved in the transaction may have in the other party's decision. The agent must disclose in writing, for example, whether the prospective buyer or seller is a relative or close friend of one of the broker's salespersons (§ 1101.652(a)(3); 22 TAC § 535.144), whether the broker has an agreement with the buyer or the seller to be compensated if and when the property is resold, or whether the broker is loaning money to the buyer for the down payment.

The agent also must disclose whether any compensation is to be received from the referral of business to companies controlled by the broker or others, such as appraisal, termite control, lender, title, escrow, home warranty, or property inspection services (22 TAC § 535.148). Many brokers offer a number of these services in their offices, thus providing buyers and sellers with "one-stop shopping." When these services are discussed with the client or the customer, the agent must disclose that use of the broker-controlled services is optional.

Full disclosure of other offers. Unless instructed otherwise by the seller, the listing agent should continue to present all offers until the transaction is closed. For rental property, the agent should continue to submit offers until the tenant takes possession of the premises. The agent must submit, or at least communicate, all offers and counteroffers to the client, even those that are believed to be too low or too high to warrant serious consideration. The offers may be oral or in writing or may or may not be accompanied by earnest money. The listing agent should disclose all offers presented after the acceptance of an offer to purchase or lease because the seller or the landlord may want to negotiate these offers as secondary contracts. This decision is for the seller or the landlord to make.

Although TREC Rule 22 TAC § 535.156(a) states that the licensee has no duty to submit offers to the principal after the principal has accepted an offer, the contract forms promulgated by TREC over the years have routinely provided that "the seller may continue to show the property and receive, negotiate, and accept back up offers" unless expressly prohibited by the written contract between the parties. The buyer can object to this provision and attempt to negotiate with the seller to remove the property from the market. If the seller continues to offer the property for sale, it is recommended that the agent warn the seller to handle all subsequent offers strictly as secondary contracts to avoid the danger of lawsuits for breach of contract or for interfering with existing contracts. The buyer has acquired equitable title to the property once a contract has been agreed to by all parties. Equitable title is the right of the buyer to expect to complete the sale and receive title to the property once all the requirements of the contract are met.

Full disclosure of information. Because the licensee's relationship with the client is that of a fiduciary, licensees must always place the interest of the client above that of their own interest, even if doing so directly or indirectly impacts on the agents' ultimate commission. Sellers' agents must disclose all information that would help sellers develop the best selling strategy, which means disclosing information that agents have about a buyer's level of price resistance or motivation to purchase. For instance, if a seller's agent is aware that a buyer is under pressure to complete a purchase in a short period, that information should be disclosed to the seller (22 TAC § 535.156).

Full disclosure regarding status of earnest money deposits. Many listing agreements authorize the seller's broker to accept an earnest money deposit from the buyer. If the deposit is a postdated check or a promissory note, the broker must inform the seller. Otherwise, if the buyer defaults and the seller cannot collect on the note, the broker could be liable to the seller for the amount of the deposit to which the seller normally would be entitled.

According to the TREC-promulgated contract forms, the buyer, not the broker, is responsible for depositing the earnest money with an escrow agent on final signing of the contract by all parties. In practice, in residential sales, it is common for the licensee delivering the contract of sale to the title company to also deliver the earnest money check because the title company is the most common holder of earnest money. For transactions involving other types of earnest money arrangements, it is incumbent on the seller's agent to check periodically with the escrow agent named in the contract to determine the status of the earnest money check and to keep the seller informed of all findings.

If the buyer asks the seller's broker to postpone the deposit of the earnest money check, the seller's broker should disclose this request to the seller and obtain written agreement between the parties to delay the deposit. Otherwise, the licensee holding the earnest money has one of two options: (1) to deposit it according to the contract or (2) to deposit it within a reasonable time, which is defined as "the close of business of the second working day after the execution of the contract by the principals" (22 TAC § 535.159(i)).

Full disclosure of buyer's financial condition. Frequently, a seller will make a decision to accept or reject a buyer's offer based on the buyer's financial standing. The seller's agent must disclose to the seller all information, good or bad, regarding the buyer's financial condition. This information is usually obtained directly from the buyer or the agent working with the buyer. The only exception is information that a licensee gains during the course of an agency relationship. For example, suppose the buyer had been represented by agent A in another transaction, and during this association A came to know the buyer's financial condition. This information was gained in confidence and cannot be disclosed to the seller, even though the seller is now A's client.

Normally, the seller should make an independent evaluation of the buyer's finances on the basis of data collected from the buyer. Prudent sellers' agents or subagents will inform sellers that because they are not lenders or arrangers of credit, they are not in a position to verify or interpret the financial information supplied by the prospective buyer; however, they will use all possible skill to obtain such information for the seller's evaluation.

Because of the fiduciary relationship between the seller's agent, any subagents, and the seller, the seller's agent or subagents must disclose

- any negative information that the agent has concerning the prospective buyer's financial situation. This is especially true when the seller is asked to carry a note for the buyer or allow an assumption of an existing loan that requires that the seller remain liable for repayment of the loan to the lender;
- facts that the buyer states or that the agent has learned independently—for instance, that the buyer has other property that must be sold before closing on the seller's property; and
- any information that affects the buyer's ability to obtain financing or gives the buyer an option to terminate the offer if financing is not obtained.

A buyer's agent has no duty to communicate negative information concerning the buyer's financial strength to the seller. Instead, the buyer's agent has a duty of confidentiality to not communicate to the seller the financial strength of the buyer's position unless given permission or direction to do so by the buyer-client. This does not mean the buyer's agent can misrepresent the buyer's financial strength by giving false or misleading information, only that information must not be disclosed unless the buyer gives specific permission.

Full disclosure of property value. Disclosure of property value is a very important part of an agent's fiduciary duty to the client. Real estate agents have a duty to inform their clients of their opinion of the value of the real estate being listed or shown. Real estate licensees employ many of the same techniques for valuing property as professional appraisers do. Yet a real estate licensee may not perform an actual appraisal of real property unless also licensed or certified as an appraiser under Section 1103 of the Texas Occupations Code. Instead, when providing an opinion of value, real estate licensees are actually providing a broker price opinion (BPO) or a comparative market analysis (CMA) to a consumer. That written opinion must include the statutory language indicating that the real estate licensee's opinion is not an actual appraisal (22 TAC § 535.17(b)). The opinion of a property's value is arrived at through studies of the sales of properties similar to the subject property, the value of the land and improvements, and/or the value of the income the property might be expected to produce.

The agent is also liable for disclosure of sales prices of all comparable properties that the agent should have known through a reasonable review. An agent can be held liable to the client and customer for rendering a false opinion of value because the agent is obligated to keep informed on market conditions. An agent is also liable for giving a wrong opinion of value to a client or customer if the opinion was negligently based on inaccurate comparisons or inaccurate application of a broker price opinion or comparative market analysis methods (TRELA § 1101.652(b)(1); 22 TAC § 535.156(d); DTPA § 17.46(b)(5),(6),(7)). These duties and the law are especially relevant in cases in which the seller directs the listing agent to underprice or overprice a property to achieve the seller's objectives. For example, the seller may want a particularly fast sale and may suggest that the property be placed on the market for less than market value to achieve this goal. The listing agent should document this request to avoid future problems.

When a seller's agent learns of factors that change the value of the property after the listing is signed, disclosure of such factors must be made as soon as possible and certainly before the seller-client decides to accept or reject an offer. The price and terms of the listing may have to be adjusted in accordance with such changed conditions (TRELA § 1101.652(b)(2); TAC § 535.156(c),(d)).

An agent does not have the obligation to give an opinion of value to a customer. Customers will usually form their opinions about the value of a particular property by comparing it with other properties they have seen for sale. Offers that customers submit generally reflect their perception of value based on all the properties they have seen. Seller's agents have an obligation to encourage buyers to submit offers that are favorable to the seller.

Occasionally, agents wish to purchase a property they have listed for a client. According to the rules of TREC, the agent must have given the seller-client an opinion of property value at the time of listing. If the seller's agent later attempts to negotiate an offer to purchase the seller-client's property for the agent's own account, it is particularly important to inform the seller of any change in the property's value. It may be particularly advisable for the seller or the broker to obtain an appraisal in these circumstances (22 TAC § 535.16 (c)).

Full disclosure of commission split. The listing agent must disclose to the seller the existence of any fee-sharing arrangement with a cooperating broker (also known as the other broker). Although the exact amount of any split does not have to be revealed, it is better to disclose fully to the client the amounts to be split, with the rationale for doing so. This disclosure should be in writing, preferably in the listing agreement. (Note: It is a violation of TRELA § 1101.652(b)(11) for a broker to pay a commission or fees to or divide a commission or fees with anyone (including attorneys) not licensed as a real estate broker or a salesperson for compensation for services as a real estate agent; however, a broker is not prohibited from reducing a brokerage fee to either principal—buyer or seller.)

Full disclosure of contract provisions. Before signing (executing) any document that is intended to be legally binding, the licensee is obligated to discuss the provisions of the contract with the client (22 TAC § 537.11(h)) and suggest that the client seek competent legal advice. Competent legal advice is especially important when there are unusual matters or areas of confusion that can best be handled by an attorney. In fact, where it appears that an unusual matter should be resolved by legal counsel or that the document is to be acknowledged and filed for record, the licensee is required, by Texas law, to advise both parties in the transaction to seek legal counsel. Failure to do so is grounds for loss of license (TRELA § 1101.654; 22 TAC § 537.11(b)).

Although licensees should not practice law or give legal advice, they are permitted to

- explain the provisions of contracts,

- disclose all pertinent facts of which the licensee has knowledge, and
- explain the meaning of factual or business details (22 TAC § 537.11(c)–(h)).

Of course, licensees who are also licensed attorneys would be allowed to give legal advice. However, rendering legal advice in a transaction where the attorney is also participating as a real estate licensee might create a conflict of interest within the Texas State Bar Association's Code of Ethics.

■ **EXAMPLE** Buyer Brown is considering writing an offer to purchase a property that fits his idea of a perfect home. While reviewing the purchase contract, Brown asks agent Allen whether he will be obligated to purchase the property if he cannot obtain the financing he has asked for in the contract. Allen explains the meaning of the paragraphs regarding financing and asks whether Brown would like to seek legal advice for further inquiries.

■ **QUESTIONS** 1. Did the agent practice law by explaining the terms relating to financing to the buyer? 2. Under what circumstances would the agent be practicing law?

Confidentiality

The duty of loyalty requires that the agent keep confidential any discussions, facts, or information about the principal that should not be revealed to others. This is similar to the privileged information concept of a lawyer-client or doctor-patient relationship. The duty of confidentiality owed to a client extends to an affirmative responsibility to withhold from an unrepresented party such confidential information as the client's bargaining position, motivations for selling or buying, opinions of value, marketing and negotiating strategies, the seller's lowest acceptable price, or the buyer's highest price, and the client's financial position (unless the client is aware of and consents to the disclosure of such information). Licensees are prohibited from disclosing any confidential information gained during an agency relationship even after the relationship has been terminated.

■ **EXAMPLE** Agent Maxwell has been working with buyer-customer Taylor for three weeks. Finally, they find the perfect property for Taylor's business, and he is ready to offer $215,000 for the property, which is $15,000 less than the seller is asking. Maxwell believes that the owner would be happy to accept $195,000 and informs Taylor of his opinion.

■ **QUESTIONS** 1. Has Maxwell breached his duty of confidentiality? 2. If so, what should Maxwell have done to avoid a breach?

There are limits to the duty to maintain confidentiality. Laws and ethical standards prohibit a licensee from withholding information regarding the condition of the property, the condition of the title, and other material facts that any prudent person would need to make an informed decision to purchase. The duty of confidentiality is thus modified by a greater duty to the public.

Licensees have a legal requirement and duty to be honest and fair to the customer. For instance, it would be fair and honest for the seller's agent to reveal to the buyer any known hazardous conditions, such as the presence of lead-based paint.

The customer has the right to pertinent information about the property but not to personal information about the seller.

Accounting

Money received by a broker as a result of transactions such as purchase contracts or property management agreements are trust funds and are frequently held by the broker for the benefit of the principal. The funds must be held in an account that is separate from the broker's own account(s)—one that does not pay interest unless specifically authorized by the parties. Brokers who hold both their own funds and trust funds in a single account are considered to be commingling funds. Commingling is strictly forbidden by TRELA and is grounds for suspension or revocation of the broker's license (§ 1101.652(b)(10)). To lessen the risk of unintended commingling, brokers might consider having separate trust accounts for sales and for rentals.

Once a contract has been fulfilled or terminated, the broker must deliver the trust funds to the principal or the appropriate party. If the funds have not been transferred within a reasonable time after a valid demand has been made, the broker may be subject to license revocation or suspension by TREC. In the event of a contract default, however, the broker or any other entity acting as escrow agent for earnest money may require that all parties sign releases before the earnest money is paid to either party. TREC addresses the details of setting up of and disbursement of funds from trust accounts at 22 TAC § 535.159.

As a general practice in Texas, most brokers in residential real estate sales do not hold earnest money in their own trust accounts. Instead, they insist that the principals in the transaction agree on a neutral escrow agent to hold the earnest money. Generally, the escrow agent is the same title company that will close the transaction and provide the title insurance.

Minimum Service Requirements

The preceding discussions address the general duties owed to the client in an agency relationship. TRELA § 1101.557 reinforces that a broker who represents a party in a real estate transaction is that party's agent. Therefore, once the licensee accepts the responsibility of agency, the licensee has a fiduciary duty to provide certain defined minimum services to their client, services that cannot be passed to the other broker in the transaction.

For example, TRELA § 1101.652(b)(22) provides that a broker may not negotiate a transaction directly with a consumer if the broker knows that the consumer is already subject to an exclusive agency relationship with another broker. The amendment to Section 1101.557 clarifies however that the mere delivery of an offer by one broker to the client of another broker would not violate TRELA. Thus, while a listing broker may not instruct a buyer's broker to deliver and negotiate the offer directly with the seller, the simple delivery of the offer to the seller would not violate TRELA as long as the buyer's broker did not also attempt to negotiate directly with the listing broker's seller.

Specifically, TRELA § 1101.557(b) states that a broker representing a party or listing real estate for sale is that party's agent and

1. "may not instruct another broker to directly or indirectly violate § 1101.652(b)(22);
2. must inform the party if the broker receives material information related to the transaction to list, buy, sell, or lease the party's real estate, including the receipt of an offer by the broker; and
3. shall, at a minimum, answer the party's questions and present any offer to or from the party."

■ SUMMARY

In any given transaction, the decision to represent the seller exclusively, the buyer exclusively, or both of them at the same time is a serious matter. Agents must understand their fiduciary responsibilities to clients and their general duties of fairness, honesty, and good faith to customers. It is easy for salespersons in an automobile showroom to know whom they work for (client-employer) and whom they work with (customer). It is a more complex question in real estate, when salespersons can show a buyer in one day a property listed by their firm, an MLS listing, a for-sale-by-owner (FSBO) property, or even the salesperson's own home. The various relationships must be understood by all participants in the transaction. One way to understand is to recognize how and when agency relationships are created.

■ KEY POINTS

- Agency occurs when one person, the agent, acts on behalf of another person, the principal (or client).
- There are a variety of agency relationships for agents, buyers, and sellers to consider in every transaction.
- There are three general categories of agency: universal, general, and special. Each category has a unique set of duties, responsibilities, and liabilities for the principals.
- A general agency relationship is common between a broker and sponsored sales associates but uncommon between a broker and a client in a typical sales transaction.
- A general agency relationship is common in property management situations.
- A special agency relationship is common between the seller or the buyer and the broker for the purchase or sale of property.
- The agent owes the client the fiduciary obligations of obedience, loyalty, disclosure, confidentiality, accounting, and reasonable care and diligence (OLD CAR).
- As a fiduciary, a real estate agent owes greater duties to a client than to a customer, and thus the risk of liability is greater.
- A fiduciary for one party still owes a duty of fairness and honesty to the party for whom the agent is not a fiduciary.

- Principals and licensees are not liable for unknown misrepresentations of other parties.
- A real estate licensee may not perform an appraisal of real property unless the licensee is licensed or certified as an appraiser under TOC § 1103.

SUGGESTIONS FOR BROKERS

Company training programs should stress the implications of agency relationships and the fiduciary duties imposed on the licensee acting as an agent. The broker's associates must understand that unless care is exercised, the firm may become an agent of a principal when agency relationship was not intended. The associate should be instructed on the type of agency relationships promoted by the firm as well as the scope of authority when acting in those agency capacities. Brokers should be ever mindful that they are ultimately responsible for the acts of any broker or sales associate when those associates are acting within the scope of authority given to them by the broker.

CHAPTER 2 QUIZ

1. An example of a general agency relationship would be one that exists between the
   a. seller and the broker.
   b. buyer and the broker.
   c. sales associates and the broker.
   d. selling broker and the listing broker.

2. Special agency occurs when
   a. the principals give an agent a limited authority to act on their behalf.
   b. the principals give an agent authority to act for them in the operation of a business.
   c. a person operates a real estate brokerage business.
   d. a person operates a special real estate brokerage business.

3. Brokers can buy a property listed with them under which of the following conditions?
   a. If a family member secretly purchases the property for more than the asking price
   b. Under no circumstances
   c. Only if the property is listed under an open listing
   d. Only if full disclosure is made to the seller of the broker's involvement as a purchaser

4. Which statement is TRUE of listing agents?
   a. They must present every written offer to the seller.
   b. They may refuse to present an offer if it is too low.
   c. They must tell the buyer the seller's lowest acceptable price.
   d. They may tell the buyer the terms of a counteroffer the seller made yesterday.

5. A salesperson owes all of the following fiduciary duties EXCEPT
   a. inform the broker and the seller of material facts.
   b. be loyal to the best interests of the client.
   c. prepare a power of attorney for the buyer.
   d. obey the lawful instructions of the broker.

6. A listing agent tells a buyer-customer that the seller is under pressure to sell because of a pending divorce and possible foreclosure. Such disclosure is
   a. acceptable if it results in a sale.
   b. acceptable if no details of the foreclosure are disclosed.
   c. unacceptable because of the fiduciary duty owed the owner.
   d. unacceptable because the listing broker is the agent of the buyer.

7. Sally, as an agent for the seller, listed and subsequently sold George's town house. She did not tell George that a major zoning change in progress would allow business use in the area, thus increasing property values. Which statement is TRUE?
   a. Sally was not required to disclose the change because George never asked her.
   b. Sally was not required to disclose the change if George received his full asking price.
   c. Sally was required to disclose the change because it was a material and pertinent fact.
   d. Sally was required to disclose the change because the zoning laws require notice to all interested persons.

8. Which is NOT a fiduciary obligation owed to a client?
   a. Obedience
   b. Confidentiality
   c. Accounting
   d. Inspection

9. A material fact is one that
   a. the client considers important.
   b. the customer considers important.
   c. a reasonable person might feel is important.
   d. the listing broker considers important.

10. A customer is entitled to all of the following material facts EXCEPT
    a. the broker's opinion of value.
    b. the type and age of an existing roof.
    c. the lease termination date of the current occupant.
    d. repairs completed to correct the drainage problems.

DISCUSSION QUESTIONS

1. What are the main duties a fiduciary owes to the principal?

2. As a broker, would you prefer to act for a client as a universal agent, general agent, or a special agent? Why?

3. Although brokers are permitted to act as escrow agents and maintain trust accounts, many choose not to do so. List some of the pros and cons of maintaining trust accounts.

4. If you act for the listing broker or as a subagent of the listing broker, how much information can you disclose to the buyer before you begin to act contrary to the best interests of your seller?

5. If you act for the buyer as a buyer's agent, how much information can you disclose to the seller or the sellers' agents before you begin to act contrary to the best interests of your buyer?

CHAPTER 3

Disclosure and Duties to Third Parties

In the previous chapter, we discussed fiduciary duties to clients, those parties the agent represents. The broker and the client (buyer or seller) are the parties to the agency contract; however, for the agency to be functional, a third party must be involved. A third party is the party to a transaction who is not represented by the agent. For example, if the licensee is representing a seller, the third party is the buyer. Conversely, if the licensee represents the buyer, the seller is the third party. In some transactions, both principals engage their own agent to represent their individual interests. In this case, the agent representing the seller would consider the buyer the third party. Likewise, the agent representing the buyer would consider the seller the third party. In any event, even though third parties are not clients, they are due certain duties by the licensees.

■ **LEARNING OBJECTIVES** *This chapter addresses the following:*

- Duties to Others (Third Parties)
- Avoiding Disclosure and Misrepresentation Problems
- Material Facts
  - Physical Material Facts
  - Material Facts Relating to Title Issues
  - Material Facts Relating to Survey Issues
- Stigmatized Properties
  - Purely Psychological Stigmas
  - Physical Stigmas

- Guidelines for Disclosure of Stigmatized Properties
- Prohibited Disclosures to Third Parties
- Liability for Misrepresentation
  - Element of Reliance
  - Watch What Is Said

DUTIES TO OTHERS (THIRD PARTIES)

Although a broker owes specific fiduciary duties to the client, under Texas Law the broker also owes general duties of honesty and fairness to all parties in a transaction. A great deal of confusion concerns the use of the word *fairly*, which remains in the Texas law. Perhaps more to the point for licensees, TREC rules specify that while the primary duty of the agent is to the client, the licensee "shall treat other parties to a transaction fairly" (22 TAC § 531.1(1)). Remember, *fairly* does not mean *equally* in the context of comparative duties owed to a client versus those owed to a customer. However, when *fair* or *fairly* is used in discussing the treatment of—and comparative duties owed to—one customer versus another customer, the concept of equal treatment is much more relevant. This is particularly germane when applying federal fair housing laws to the required treatment of members of protected classes.

Likewise, the listing broker has responsibilities to both seller and buyer, although it is clear that the responsibilities to each are different. The listing broker owes a buyer-customer duties of honesty, fairness, competency, good faith, and disclosure of all material facts. While these duties are nonfiduciary in nature, they are strong duties under Texas law.

Moreover, the listing broker and any seller's subagent broker owe the buyer certain statutory duties and other duties under TREC rules of fairness, such as promptly presenting all offers and avoiding misrepresentation and false promises. The fact that the buyer is represented by a broker does not diminish the duties of the listing broker to the buyer through the buyer's broker.

The duties of fairness to customers are not clearly defined—except where specifically mandated in federal or state laws, such as in fair housing law. Nevertheless, a licensee must be honest at all times and levels when dealing with clients and customers.

AVOIDING DISCLOSURE AND MISREPRESENTATION PROBLEMS

The most common complaint of buyers against brokers relates to misrepresentation by brokers or the brokers' associates. The National Association of REALTORS® (NAR) reports that nearly two-thirds of all complaints against members result from misrepresentation issues.

Misrepresentations may occur when a licensee makes a false statement to a potential buyer or when a licensee fails to disclose to the buyer important facts about the property. Licensees have a duty to disclose material facts affecting the value and desirability of a property. A buyer frequently asks a broker to describe a property and make representations in connection with a sale. The most common complaint concerns a listing broker's failure to point out material defects the broker knows of—or should have known. In California, for instance, court rulings have identified "red flags" that should put the broker on notice that a problem exists—and should be brought to the buyer's attention. Such red flags include evidence of recent mudslides, obvious building code violations, and drainage and soil settlement problems. In Texas, the broker, even if licensed as a real estate inspector, is neither expected nor even allowed to function as both broker and inspector in the same transaction. The licensee is, moreover, always responsible for revealing to a prospective buyer important negative facts about a property.

In most cases of liability, a threshold issue concerns the materiality of the issue and whether statements were facts or opinions. The materiality of the issue is based on misrepresentations of factual matters and whether such matters are important to reasonably prudent homebuyers in deciding to purchase.

Generally, statements of opinion are not considered appropriate grounds for a misrepresentation or fraud suit by a buyer or a seller. This is based on the belief that most buyers or sellers will not rely on a licensee's opinion as the basis for a decision to purchase or sell. Nevertheless, a licensee must take considerable care to clarify whether a statement is merely an opinion or a fact. For example, a licensee's opinion regarding easily verifiable factual matters such as property boundaries could be interpreted by the buyer as a statement of fact. Should the statement prove incorrect, the licensee may be held liable. The licensee is well advised to never give opinions about factual matters. Furthermore, when giving opinions about nonverifiable matters, the licensee should make it unequivocally clear that the statement is an opinion, not based on fact. A licensee must be especially careful when dealing with a topic that might be a primary purchasing or selling factor to the principals. In such cases, the licensee should suggest employing a professional, licensed if appropriate, and should not become the source of information outside the scope of real estate licensure or expertise of the licensee.

■ **EXAMPLE** Sally's client asks her about the local school district, and she responds by stating that the ratings that have been published by state education authorities. She goes on to say that her children attend a school in the district and that she believes it to be a good district. She then suggests that the buyers visit the school authorities in order to have the opportunity to explore any areas of concern or interest with them.

■ **QUESTIONS** 1. Was Sally's statement regarding the district rating fact or opinion? 2. How would you classify Sally's statements about her experience with the district?

■ **DISCUSSION** This example is typical of questions raised by buyers. If Sally raved about the district's rating and quality and later the buyer's children do not do well in school, Sally might be exposed to some liability. Although Sally is free to express her opinion based upon her experience, it is extremely important to support factual statements with proof (documentation from the state rating agency, in this case) and further suggest that the buyers personally visit the school officials to satisfy specific needs or questions.

To provide better disclosures to buyers, Section 5.008 of the Texas Property Code (TPC) requires a written seller's disclosure notice for most residential resales.

Specifically TPC § 5.008 states:

> *A seller of residential real property comprising not more than one dwelling unit located in this state shall give to the purchaser of the property a written notice as prescribed by this section or a written notice substantially similar to the notice prescribed by this section which contains, at a minimum, all of the items in the notice prescribed by this section.*

TREC has produced a form for licensees to help sellers meet the requirements under the Texas Property Code (see Figure 3.1). The form is called Seller's Disclosure of Property Condition, and while not a promulgated form, it is widely used by licensees. Because the TPC indicates the form used by the seller must only read "substantially similar" to the TPC wording, members of the Texas Association of REALTORS® routinely use a modified version of the TREC form provided by that trade association. According to TREC, this form "provides a vehicle for disclosure of defects or items in need of repair." Conditions such as the presence of lead-based paint, termite damage, and flooding are also addressed. The form is frequently revised during Texas legislative sessions. The most recently added disclosures to the form include those relating to the presence of smoke detectors, carbon monoxide alarms, emergency escape ladders, the previous use of the premises for manufacture of methamphetamines, liquid propane gas, blockable drains in pools, hot tubs, or spas, and rainwater harvesting systems. If the notice is not given before the effective date of the contract, the purchaser may terminate the contract for any reason within seven days after receiving the notice. TREC contract forms help facilitate compliance with the law. Consistent and proper use of this form gives buyers better information about the property and can help prevent lawsuits against the broker, who is also tasked with disclosing material facts about properties to consumers.

A review of Figure 3.1 will reveal that most of the listed items involve physical conditions of the property. The mistake made by many sellers and real estate licensees, therefore, is to presume that only items shown on the Seller's Disclosure of Property Condition need be addressed by the seller. Yet liability under the Texas Deceptive Trade Practices Act can accrue to a seller of property for failure to disclose any "material" (see Chapter 12 for the DTPA "laundry list") fact that would influence a reasonable buyer's decision to purchase. That includes both physical defects and nontangible facts or "psychological stigmas" which will be discussed later in this chapter. Remember, TPC § 5.008 states that the items listed on the form represent the "minimum" items required for a seller to identify in writing. As will be discussed more in Chapter 12, once the facts are known, the licensee is also liable for a cause of action under DTPA.

Another difficulty is that additional statutorily mandated disclosure issues can only be addressed during a legislative session (every other year in Texas). Because ongoing litigation frequently results in disclosures of new information the courts

FIGURE 3.1

Seller's Disclosure of Property Condition

APPROVED BY THE TEXAS REAL ESTATE COMMISSION (TREC)　　09-01-2011

SELLER'S DISCLOSURE OF PROPERTY CONDITION

CONCERNING THE PROPERTY AT _____
(Street Address and City)

THIS NOTICE IS A DISCLOSURE OF SELLER'S KNOWLEDGE OF THE CONDITION OF THE PROPERTY AS OF THE DATE SIGNED BY SELLER AND IS NOT A SUBSTITUTE FOR ANY INSPECTIONS OR WARRANTIES THE PURCHASER MAY WISH TO OBTAIN. IT IS NOT A WARRANTY OF ANY KIND BY SELLER OR SELLER'S AGENTS.

Seller ☐ is　☐ is not occupying the Property. If unoccupied, how long since Seller has occupied the Property? _____

1. The Property has the items checked below [Write Yes (Y), No (N), or Unknown (U)]:

___ Range	___ Oven	___ Microwave
___ Dishwasher	___ Trash Compactor	___ Disposal
___ Washer/Dryer Hookups	___ Window Screens	___ Rain Gutters
___ Security System	___ Fire Detection Equipment	___ Intercom System
	___ Smoke Detector	
	___ Smoke Detector-Hearing Impaired	
	___ Carbon Monoxide Alarm	
	___ Emergency Escape Ladder(s)	
___ TV Antenna	___ Cable TV Wiring	___ Satellite Dish
___ Ceiling Fan(s)	___ Attic Fan(s)	___ Exhaust Fan(s)
___ Central A/C	___ Central Heating	___ Wall/Window Air Conditioning
___ Plumbing System	___ Septic System	___ Public Sewer System
___ Patio/Decking	___ Outdoor Grill	___ Fences
___ Pool	___ Sauna	___ Spa ___ Hot Tub
___ Pool Equipment	___ Pool Heater	___ Automatic Lawn Sprinkler System
___ Fireplace(s) & Chimney (Woodburning)		___ Fireplace(s) & Chimney (Mock)
___ Natural Gas Lines		___ Gas Fixtures
___ Liquid Propane Gas:	___ LP Community (Captive)	___ LP on Property

Garage:　___ Attached　　___ Not Attached　　___ Carport

Garage Door Opener(s):　___ Electronic　　___ Control(s)

Water Heater:　___ Gas　　___ Electric

Water Supply:　___ City　　___ Well　　___ MUD　　___ Co-op

Roof Type: _____　Age: _____ (approx)

Are you (Seller) aware of any of the above items that are not in working condition, that have known defects or that are in need of repair? ☐ Yes　☐ No　☐ Unknown　If yes, then describe. (Attach additional sheets if necessary): _____

_____

_____

TREC No. OP-H

Texas Real Estate Agency, Seventh Edition

FIGURE 3.1

Seller's Disclosure of Property Condition (continued)

Seller's Disclosure Notice Concerning the Property at _____ Page 2 09-01-2011
(Street Address and City)

2. Does the property have working smoke detectors installed in accordance with the smoke detector requirements of Chapter 766, Health and Safety Code? ☐ Yes ☐ No ☐ Unknown If the answer to this question is no or unknown, explain. (Attach additional sheets if necessary): _____

* Chapter 766 of the Health and Safety Code requires one-family or two-family dwellings to have working smoke detectors installed in accordance with the requirements of the building code in effect in the area in which the dwelling is located, including performance, location, and power source requirements. If you do not know the building code requirements in effect in your area, you may check unknown above or contact your local building official for more information. A buyer may require a seller to install smoke detectors for the hearing impaired if: (1) the buyer or a member of the buyer's family who will reside in the dwelling is hearing impaired; (2) the buyer gives the seller written evidence of the hearing impairment from a licensed physician; and (3) within 10 days after the effective date, the buyer makes a written request for the seller to install smoke detectors for the hearing impaired and specifies the locations for the installation. The parties may agree who will bear the cost of installing the smoke detectors and which brand of smoke detectors to install.

3. Are you (Seller) aware of any known defects/malfunctions in any of the following? Write Yes (Y) if you are aware, write No (N) if you are not aware.

   ___ Interior Walls   ___ Ceilings   ___ Floors
   ___ Exterior Walls   ___ Doors   ___ Windows
   ___ Roof   ___ Foundation/Slab(s)   ___ Basement
   ___ Walls/Fences   ___ Driveways   ___ Sidewalks
   ___ Plumbing Sewers/Septics   ___ Electrical Systems   ___ Lighting Fixtures
   ___ Other Structural Components (Describe) _____

   If the answer to any of the above is yes, explain. (Attach additional sheets if necessary): _____

4. Are you (Seller) aware of any of the following conditions? Write Yes (Y) if you are aware, write No (N) if you are not aware.

   ___ Active Termites (includes wood destroying insects)   ___ Previous Structural or Roof Repair
   ___ Termite or Wood Rot Damage Needing Repair   ___ Hazardous or Toxic Waste
   ___ Previous Termite Damage   ___ Asbestos Components
   ___ Previous Termite Treatment   ___ Urea-formaldehyde Insulation
   ___ Previous Flooding   ___ Radon Gas
   ___ Improper Drainage   ___ Lead Based Paint
   ___ Water Penetration   ___ Aluminum Wiring
   ___ Located in 100-Year Floodplain   ___ Previous Fires
   ___ Present Flood Insurance Coverage   ___ Unplatted Easements

TREC No. OP-H

FIGURE 3.1

Seller's Disclosure of Property Condition (continued)

Seller's Disclosure Notice Concerning the Property at _____ Page 3 09-01-2011
(Street Address and City)

____ Landfill, Settling, Soil Movement, Fault Lines   ____ Subsurface Structure or Pits

____ Single Blockable Main Drain in Pool/Hot Tub/Spa*   ____ Previous Use of Premises for Manufacture of Methamphetamine

If the answer to any of the above is yes, explain. (Attach additional sheets if necessary): _____

*A single blockable main drain may cause a suction entrapment hazard for an individual.

5. Are you (Seller) aware of any item, equipment, or system in or on the Property that is in need of repair? ☐ Yes (if you are aware)
   ☐ No (if you are not aware)   If yes, explain. (Attach additional sheets if necessary): _____

6. Are you (Seller) aware of any of the following? Write Yes (Y) if you are aware, write No (N) if you are not aware.

   ____ Room additions, structural modifications, or other alterations or repairs made without necessary permits or not in compliance with building codes in effect at that time.
   ____ Homeowners' Association or maintenance fees or assessments.
   ____ Any "common area" (facilities such as pools, tennis courts, walkways, or other areas) co-owned in undivided interest with others.
   ____ Any notices of violations of deed restrictions or governmental ordinances affecting the condition or use of the Property.
   ____ Any lawsuits directly or indirectly affecting the Property.
   ____ Any condition on the Property which materially affects the physical health or safety of an individual.
   ____ Any rainwater harvesting system connected to the property's public water supply that is able to be used for indoor potable purposes.

   If the answer to any of the above is yes, explain. (Attach additional sheets if necessary): _____

7. If the property is located in a coastal area that is seaward of the Gulf Intracoastal Waterway or within 1,000 feet of the mean high tide bordering the Gulf of Mexico, the property may be subject to the Open Beaches Act or the Dune Protection Act (Chapter 61 or 63, Natural Resources Code, respectively) and a beachfront construction certificate or dune protection permit may be required for repairs or improvements. Contact the local government with ordinance authority over construction adjacent to public beaches for more information.

_____ _____   _____ _____
Signature of Seller   Date   Signature of Seller   Date

The undersigned purchaser hereby acknowledges receipt of the foregoing notice.

_____ _____   _____ _____
Signature of Buyer   Date   Signature of Buyer   Date

TREC No. OP-H

deem important to reasonable purchasers under the common law, it is argued that the TREC form lacks provisions of timely notice and may be less effective in avoiding litigation than the disclosure form prepared by the Texas Association of REALTORS® (TAR) for its members, which contains such language. TAR may add items to its seller's disclosure form at any time the organization deems appropriate.

The listing agent will most likely obtain a complete factual statement from the seller by explaining the purpose and importance of the Seller's Disclosure of Property Condition form. The seller (not the agent) should complete the form, and the agent should carefully explain each section of the form to ensure complete compliance with the law. Generally, a good transaction starts with a good listing presentation and full disclosure of all material facts regarding the property. The following case illustrates the importance of the seller's disclosure statement, as well as the issue of facts versus opinions.

■ **EXAMPLE** In *Kessler v. Fanning*, 953 S.W.2d 515 (Tex.App., Fort Worth 1997), the Fannings purchased a property after having received the proper Seller's Disclosure of Property Condition form, which indicated that there were no drainage problems. The Fannings had the property inspected, and no drainage problems were detected, even though it was raining at the time of the inspection. However, after moving into the property, the Fannings discovered drainage problems and sued the sellers, claiming violations of the Texas Deceptive Trade Practices Act (DTPA) for failing to disclose a material fact. The Fannings further claimed that they would not have purchased the home had they known of the drainage problems.

Although other issues had to be decided by the court, a key issue was whether the statements by the seller constituted misrepresentations or merely statements of opinion. The TREC disclosure form used by the sellers states that the form "is not a substitute for inspections or warranties" and that it contains "representations made by the owner(s) based on the owner's knowledge." The sellers claimed that the statements contained in the disclosure form were merely opinions and not statements of fact.

The court found, however, that the statements by the sellers met the three requirements for determining whether a statement is a fact rather than opinion in that

- the statements were specific rather than vague,
- the parties did not possess the same knowledge, and
- the representations pertained to past rather than future conditions.

As statements of fact, the representations contained in the disclosure form were considered deceptive and misleading. The court found in favor of the buyers.

■ **QUESTIONS** 1. Why was the broker not also found liable in this case? 2. The buyers had their own property inspector who indicated no drainage problems. Why was the seller not able to claim that the buyers relied on the inspector rather than on their statements?

■ **DISCUSSION** This case illustrates the importance of having the seller write a detailed disclosure of property condition. The broker was able to show that the statements were those of the seller and that the broker did not know about—nor was it reasonable that he would have known about—the drainage problems.

The argument that the buyer relied on the inspection report rather than on the seller's disclosure statements may be a defense under some circumstances when no fraud has occurred. Nevertheless, the law states that an independent inspection that might have uncovered fraud does not prevent the recovery for fraudulent misrepresentations.

MATERIAL FACTS

One of the more vexing issues for licensees is determining what is, or is not, a material fact relating to a transaction. Why? Because the listing broker has a fiduciary responsibility to make clear to their principal that addressing only the items shown on the Seller's Disclosure of Property Condition does not absolve the seller from disclosing other material facts that may be of importance to a reasonable buyer's decision to purchase. Furthermore, once known, the licensee is considered to know the material fact and has legal and ethical responsibilities to disclose as well.

In the fifth edition of *The Language of Real Estate*, John W. Reilly defines and discusses a material fact as follows:

> [A material fact] is any fact that is relevant to a person making a decision. Agents must disclose all material facts to their clients. Agents must also disclose to buyers material facts about the condition of the property, such as known structural defects, building code violations, and hidden dangerous conditions. Brokers are often placed in a no-win situation of trying to evaluate whether a certain fact is material enough that it needs to be disclosed to a prospective buyer, such as the fact that a murder occurred on the property 10 years ago or the fact that the neighbors throw loud parties. It is sometimes difficult to distinguish between "fact" and "opinion." The statement "real property taxes are low" is different from "real property taxes are $500 per year." Even though brokers act in good faith, they may still be liable for failure to exercise reasonable care or competence in ascertaining and communicating pertinent facts that the broker knew or "should have known."

Physical Material Facts

Generally, the physical aspects of the property that may require disclosure are easier to identify than the nonphysical issues. Physical issues may relate to any negative condition of the property itself, such as

- foundation;
- previous flooding;
- roof problems;
- termite infestation or damage;
- electrical;
- plumbing;
- heating, ventilation, and air conditioning (HVAC);
- well water;
- septic;
- lack of smoke detectors/carbon monoxide alarms;
- propane gas tanks;
- rainwater harvesting systems; and
- blockable drains in pools/hot tubs/spas.

Obviously this list could include virtually any physical component of the property. When licensees know of problems in a property relating to these types of issues, disclosures must be made. As mentioned, the seller in the Seller's Disclosure of Property Condition should reveal the negative condition of any of these types of matters; nevertheless, a buyer should be advised not to rely solely on these disclosures and hire licensed property inspectors and/or other professionals to inspect the property carefully. Further, the buyer should know that such inspections are not warranties and that they verify only that the inspected equipment was or was not functioning adequately at the time of inspection. The buyer should be informed that warranties are available through residential service companies that must be registered through TREC to offer such services in Texas.

Material Facts Relating to Title Issues

As important as disclosure of the physical issues that have been described are disclosures relating to the type and quality of title to be conveyed by the seller to the buyer. Types of title may include fee simple, defeasible fee, and life estate. Each of these types of ownership has a different value, and the persons acquiring the property should be fully informed about them.

In addition to the type of title a purchaser receives, there are concerns regarding the quality of the title. Licensees in Texas must advise buyers to determine the quality of the title by obtaining either an attorney's opinion of title, based on an abstract, or a policy of title insurance.

Abstracts of title are condensed versions of all records relating to the subject property, beginning with the initial transfer from a sovereign government forward to the present owner. The abstract contains a chronology of all instruments filed into the property records; this may include taxes, judgments, releases, and so on. Although abstractors make no judgments relative to the condition or quality of title, they are liable for failing to include or properly record all pertinent data. The abstract is then examined in detail by an attorney who evaluates the facts and submits a written report (opinion of title) on the condition of the title to the purchaser. The report is considered evidence of title for the current owner.

Because both abstractor and attorney have liability for mistakes, purchasers often believe that title insurance is not necessary. Purchasers should know, however, that the liability is only for mistakes made to properly filed, truthful records. For example, documents might have been forged, unrecorded claims might exist, unknown heirs might surface—in these instances, the property owner would have no recourse. If a purchaser seeks protection from such possibilities, the purchaser should obtain insurance.

Title insurance is a contract between the insurance carrier and the policyholder to indemnify the holder for defects in title up to the policy limits. Note that the insurer does not guarantee continued ownership, only compensation for losses up to the policy limits. Title insurance companies are regulated by the Texas Board of Insurance and are authorized to issue standard Texas policies. As a result of the 2007 80th Texas legislative session, title insurance companies may also offer protection against defects in title for items of personal property, such as boats, RVs, automobiles, etc. The extension of coverage to personal property is particularly applicable in commercial real estate and farm and ranch, where lack of clear title and/or undisclosed liens to items such as office furnishings and equipment could be quite costly to the purchaser. The coverages, available endorsements, and exceptions relating to standard Texas policies that should be disclosed to buyers are shown in the following lists.

Standard coverage includes the following:

- Defects found in public records
- Forged documents
- Incompetent grantors
- Incorrect marital statements
- Improperly delivered deeds
- Lack of access to and from land
- Lack of good and indefeasible title

Standard exceptions in Texas policies are as follows:

- Deed restrictions or covenants
- Existing liens listed in policy
- Unrecorded title defects
- Governmental rights of limitation and eminent domain
- Shortages in area or discrepancies in boundaries, encroachments, or overlapping of improvements
- Issues relating to bankruptcy
- Taxes for the current and subsequent years

Additional coverage (endorsements) may be purchased to include the following:

- Property inspection
- Rights of parties in possession (such as tenant's rights)
- Examination of survey
- Unrecorded liens not known of by policyholder
- Environmental Protection Agency (EPA) lien endorsement (concerning claims relation to EPA violations)
- Homestead or community property or survivorship rights
- Tax liability due to changes in land usage (rollback taxes)
- Title defects relating to personal property

Mortgagee's (lender's) title insurance. Title coverage for the lender is available and usually required when the purchaser secures a new loan on the purchased property. This sometimes is confusing when buyers who have negotiated title policies to be furnished by sellers are charged for a mortgagee's title policy at closing. This policy is a separate policy to ensure that the lender has a valid lien against the property. The amount of coverage is for the original loan amount, and coverage decreases as the loan balance decreases, while the owner's title policy is for the sales price and remains constant. For these reasons, as well as the fact that the research is only required once, the price of a mortgagee's policy is considerably less when purchased in connection with an owner's title policy.

Material Facts Relating to Survey Issues

As with defects or flaws in the title to the property, any known problems relating to the physical description of the property must be disclosed. These problems may include discrepancies in the area of the property, boundary lines, encroachments, or the overlapping of improvements from one property onto the property of another. Note that these types of problems are specifically excepted from the standard title policy as shown.

Buyers should be advised not to rely on measurements furnished by the seller, measurements of a licensee, or their own measurements, but on the measurements of a registered professional land surveyor. Additionally, a buyer should be alerted that previous surveys, perhaps furnished by the seller, should not be relied on; the buyer should obtain a new survey. Surveys are generally required when

- conveying a portion of a given tract of land,
- obtaining a mortgage loan,
- government entities acquire land through condemnation procedures,
- showing the location of new or existing improvements, and
- determining legal descriptions of properties.

STIGMATIZED PROPERTIES

Another type of disclosure issue involves material facts related to stigmatized properties. Stigma refers to a perception of conditions or events (real or imagined) related to a property that reduces the marketability or value of the property. Stigmas may be classified as purely psychological stigmas or physical stigmas.

Purely Psychological Stigmas

Purely psychological stigmas are those that occur as a result of real or imagined events, at the property, that have no actual physical impact on the property or the occupants. An example of this type of stigma is a death occurring on the property as a result of natural causes, accident, murder, suicide, or an AIDS-related illness.

A stigma may also arise from a notorious event or individual associated with the property. Highly publicized and negatively stigmatized properties include the apartment building in which the serial killer Jeffrey Dahmer housed his victims; the California home where Andrew Luster, the great-grandson of cosmetics magnate Max Factor and heir to a fortune, allegedly drugged and raped women; and the home of former football star O.J. Simpson in Buckingham Estate. The Dahmer and the Simpson houses were ultimately demolished because of severe stigma. In 2003, the Luster house finally sold for more than 20 percent below its nonstigmatized market value. Yet in none of the cases were the buildings physically impacted by the events. In the O.J. Simpson case, the alleged murder of his former wife and her friend did not even occur on the Buckingham property, but rather the stigma arose from the fact that Simpson, the accused murderer, lived in the house.

Curiously, one person's stigma can be another person's selling point! For example, after his shooting death on the steps of his own property, fashion designer Gianni Versace's mansion ultimately sold for $19 million, the highest price ever paid for a house in Miami-Dade County. Jacqueline Kennedy Onassis's apartment on Manhattan's Fifth Avenue, even though she died in the apartment, sold in 1995 for $9.5 million and listed as recently as 2006 for $32 million. So while the value of one property may be negatively impacted by horrific events (the Luster house), another property may represent the ultimate in glamour and style (Kennedy) to the purchaser.

It is important for licensees to accept that whether potential buyers will be concerned about death or horrific events on a property frequently relates to whether the previous owner was celebrated or disgraced, how long ago the event occurred, and the impact of the event on the public conscience. Furthermore, highly publicized stories such as the Dahmer, Versace, or Kennedy stories produce buyers who are fully aware of the property's reputation and know exactly what they are getting. But when deaths are private, buyers caught unaware tend to call their broker or attorney wanting to know: "Shouldn't we have been told this?"

So purely psychological stigmas raise a number of issues for licensees, including materiality, fact or fiction, duration of the stigma, and laws relating to disclosure of certain events. Suppose it is rumored that satanic rites have been performed in a property by a previous occupant, or that a murder occurred at a property ten years ago, or that a previous occupant had an AIDS-related illness—would these issues require disclosure? The answers to some of these questions may be found in Texas law. In 1993, the Texas legislature passed certain statutes relating to disclosure, later incorporated into The Real Estate License Act:

> § 1101.556. DISCLOSURE OF CERTAIN INFORMATION RELATING TO OCCUPANTS. *Notwithstanding other law, a license holder is not required to inquire about, disclose, or release information relating to whether:*
> *(1) a previous or current occupant of real property had, may have had, has, or may have AIDS, an HIV-related illness, or an HIV infection as defined by the Centers for Disease Control and Prevention of the United States Public Health Service; or*
> *(2) a death occurred on a property by natural causes, suicide, or accident unrelated to the condition of the property.*

It should be noted that on the issue of AIDS-related disclosures, TRELA does not prohibit disclosure; rather, it merely relieves the licensee of a duty to disclose. It is important, however, to note that TREC rules actually prohibit such disclosures (22 TAC § 531.19) under the Canons of Professional Ethics and Conduct for Real Estate Licensees. Further guidelines on this issue may be found in the 1988 Fair Housing Amendment Act, which added persons with handicaps as a protected class. AIDS-HIV–related illnesses are included in the definition of a handicap. As a result, statements by the Department of Housing and Urban Development (HUD) make it illegal for licensees to make disclosures regarding an occupant or prior occupant with problems related to AIDS-HIV. In addition, HUD advises that licensees not respond to direct questions relating to these matters even if the licensee has actual knowledge that an occupant or prior occupant has, or has had, an AIDS-HIV–related illness. Although HUD has not produced an acceptable statement, the National Association of REALTORS®, in its Legal Liability Series relating to property disclosures, recommends the following response when their members are asked questions relating to these issues:

> *It is the policy of our firm not to answer inquiries of this nature one way or the other since the firm feels that this information is not material to the transaction. In addition, any type of response to such inquiries by me or other salespeople of our firm may be a violation of the federal fair housing laws. If you believe that this information is relevant to your decision to buy the property, you must pursue this investigation on your own.*

In relation to the four classifications of causes of death—natural causes, accident, suicide, and homicide—Texas law, as quoted here, requires that only a homicide be affirmatively disclosed. However, it is reasonable to believe that many buyers might be affected negatively if any type of death has occurred at the property. Remember that any type of death (or other issue) may be disclosed with permission of the client. A licensee who is concerned about such matters should discuss the issue with the seller and, if not satisfactorily resolved, should consider refusing the listing.

Under 22 TAC 535.156, the licensee is tasked with conveying to the client any information that would impact the client's decision to make, accept, or reject offers. Further, 22 TAC 535.2(b) obligates the agent to convey to the client "all information of which the agent has knowledge and which may affect the client's decision." It can therefore be reasonably argued that properties can be stigmatized by happenings not on but within the vicinity of the subject property that would also be material to a reasonable buyer's decision to purchase.

Nearby activities that might concern a reasonable purchaser include

- persistent criminal activity,
- drive-by shootings,
- planned rezoning of vacant lot,
- large airport considering extending its flight path over the neighborhood,
- numerous pet disappearances/killings,
- planned sewage treatment plant, and
- noisy, obnoxious neighbors.

Physical Stigmas

Physical stigmas arise when some negative or detrimental physical or environmental condition exists that may not directly affect the property but may affect the health or safety of the occupants. These conditions may have real or imagined health-related problems, but in either case the property suffers a loss in marketability or value. Problems in this area may include asbestos, lead hazards, electromagnetic fields (EMFs), radon, chlorofluorocarbon emissions, hazardous waste disposal, underground storage tanks, soil or groundwater contamination, and previous use of premises for manufacture of methamphetamines.

Although there is much conjecture regarding the true health risks of many of these problems, property values may be impacted when the public becomes aware of such a condition. In her article "When Bad Things Happen to Good Properties" (*Tierra Grande*, April 1999), Jennifer Hoffman cites the asbestos scare of the 1970s as an example:

> *The fibrous material was commonly used in the construction industry for decades until studies began to demonstrate that the asbestos fibers could infiltrate the lungs—a potentially fatal condition. Hitting the papers, this news caused a near panic in some real estate markets. "Many properties containing asbestos were stigmatized, becoming unmarketable virtually overnight," says Guntermann.*
>
> *With more scientific information available, public fear and concern in the real estate community dissipated and became more narrowly focused on a smaller sample of properties than originally suspected.*

Although today the presence of asbestos requires disclosure to potential buyers, the stigma is much reduced due to better knowledge and understanding of remedies.

Guidelines for Disclosure of Stigmatized Properties

The National Association of REALTORS®, in its Legal Liability Series, offers members the following guidelines in the publication *Property Disclosures—What You Should Know*:

- ***Determine whether the information is fact or fiction.*** *Investigate the validity of the information by checking sources such as newspaper accounts or reports from state or local agencies. Separate rumor from reality. If the stigma is based on rumor and not on facts that can be confirmed, there may be no obligation to disclose. If, on the other hand, the stigma turns out to be factual (e.g., there was in fact a murder on or near the property) you should proceed to the next step.*
- ***Check state law.*** *In Texas the law requires disclosure of all physical facts regarding the property. With nonphysical matters, the requirement to disclose will hinge on the materiality of the matter.*
- ***Determine materiality.*** *To analyze the materiality of a set of facts that may produce a stigma, one must determine whether knowledge of those facts would affect the willingness of a reasonable person in deciding whether to buy the property or the amount of money to offer or pay for the property. Most stigmatized property cases involve stigmas that are less sensational than, for example, a multiple murder on the property. Less sensational stigmas may or may not impact the market value of the property. Whether or not the problem is a high-profile one, however, it is necessary to assess how reasonable persons would react to the information and if they are less likely to desire to purchase the property.*
  Alternately, one should consider how the "market" would judge such a property and whether it can be objectively concluded that the market value of the property is less because of the property's history. If this analysis results in the conclusion that the facts and stigma may have an impact on the buying decision of prospective purchasers, the facts creating the stigma are probably material and should be disclosed.
- ***Discuss disclosure with the sellers.*** *A listing agent who concludes that the physical or psychological stigma-producing facts are material and need to be disclosed should also discuss with sellers the basis for his conclusions and his intended course of action. The sellers need and deserve to understand the salesperson's analysis and why the particular facts may affect the marketing and sale of their property and, thus, must be disclosed. Often sellers can*

understand the problem better if they are asked to consider themselves in the position of a prospective purchaser and whether or not they would want the factual information before deciding to purchase or what to offer for the property. Discussing the matter with the sellers up front avoids objections and controversy later about why the particular facts were disclosed to prospective purchasers.

If the sellers refuse to agree to disclose what the listing broker (or a subagent working with the listing broker) has determined to be a material factor regarding the property, the agents should strongly consider terminating the listing or other involvement in the transaction.

Although such guidelines are helpful, the licensee should seek competent legal counsel whenever there is doubt regarding disclosure issues. Members of the Texas Association of REALTORS®, for example, may contact the TAR legal hotline for guidance. The following case illustrates the difficulty of determining the materiality of facts regarding stigmatized property.

■ **EXAMPLE** In *Sanchez v. Guerrero*, 885 S.W.2d 487 (Tex. App.—El Paso, 1994), the Guerreros purchased a VA-foreclosed property through broker Sanchez. After closing, the Guerreros discovered that a prior occupant of the property had been accused (although acquitted) of child molestation in the property. Upon learning this information, the new buyers moved out and later sold the property at a loss. The Guerreros then sued Sanchez, alleging that the broker was aware of the circumstance and willfully withheld the information in order to induce them to buy the property. The suit brought under the Texas Deceptive Trade Practices Act was won by the Guerreros, finding that the broker took advantage of the buyer's lack of knowledge of real estate to a grossly unfair degree and supported a claim for mental anguish as well as damages. The jury awarded the Guerreros $120,000 in actual damages, $20,000 for closing costs, and $100,000 for mental anguish.

■ **QUESTIONS** 1. What implication does this have for licensees regarding disclosure of events that may not have happened but apparently created a stigmatized property? 2. What types of crimes that may or may not have occurred on the property must be disclosed? 3. Would the broker be exposed to a potential libel suit from the acquitted defendant for disclosing this information to the Guerreros?

■ **DISCUSSION** Unfortunately, this case raises more questions than it resolves. The fact that a prior occupant had been accused of a notorious crime, even though acquitted, was sufficient to create a stigma that would have required disclosure by the broker. The broker admitted knowledge of the circumstances surrounding the property but felt that the alleged crime had no direct or physical impact on the property and therefore did not need to be disclosed. Further, the defendant argued that as the accused had been acquitted, it would have been inappropriate and potentially libelous to make such a disclosure. The court disagreed on the basis that the information was public knowledge and that the story had been reported in the media. All in all, a very troubling case for Texas brokers.

Megan's Law. An issue related to *Sanchez v. Guerrero* is the federal law concerning the registration of individuals convicted of child molestation and other dangerous sex crimes. The federal government now requires states to develop and implement registration procedures for released sex offenders living in their communities. The federal law requiring such registration is commonly known as Megan's Law.

Current Texas law enacted as a result requires a released sex offender to register with local law enforcement agencies and be photographed and fingerprinted. This information must be submitted to superintendents of public schools and to the administrators of private primary and secondary schools in the district where the offender resides. Additionally, enforcement officials must publish in a local newspaper information regarding the offender, including the name, age, and gender, a brief description of the offense, the street name, zip code, and municipality of residence, and the person's risk level, generally. If the individual is determined to be high risk (level 1), then notices must be mailed by the Texas Department of Safety to each residential address within three blocks in a subdivided area, or within one mile in an area that is not subdivided.

Some states, including Texas, have given specific exemptions to some real estate licensees from any requirement to disclose such matters, leaving the issue to law enforcement. The Texas rule exempts owners of single-family residences and real estate agents from a duty to disclose information relating to sex offenders to prospective buyers or tenants.

Although the law does not require agents to make a sex offender disclosure, many licensees feel compelled to do so on ethical grounds. Further, it may be implied that when representing a buyer, a duty of care to the buyer would include disclosure of a released offender living in near proximity to a property being considered for purchase. When representing a seller who requests that such information not be disclosed, the broker should consider the advisability of offering brokerage services to the seller.

In any event, such disclosures should be approached with great care, citing the source of information and warning that the information may be incorrect or incomplete. A licensee is cautioned from making any related statements based on rumor or hearsay.

Even when a licensee has no specific knowledge that a sex offender lives in close proximity, it may be advisable to add this issue to a general checklist of items that may concern prospective buyers, including guidance on where to obtain such information. Such sources include local law enforcement agencies and lists published on Web sites. In Texas, sex offender information may be found at the Texas Department of Public Safety Web site, www.dps.texas.gov.

Prohibited Disclosures to Third Parties

Licensees should take care during disclosure to avoid volunteering information about or responding to questions relating to protected classes under federal, state, or local fair housing laws. Prohibited disclosures relate to race, color, religion, sex, national origin, familial status, or handicap. Such questions may be asked by buyers in relation to specific owners and/or properties, or neighborhoods in general. If the potential buyers have concerns relating to these matters, they should be advised to seek information through their own independent investigations.

In addition to the matters described, care must be taken not to volunteer to the buyer so much information that the client's negotiating position is compromised. Suppose the licensee knows that the sellers are anxious to sell because they have just completed the purchase of another home. If the broker discloses this information and the prospective buyer chooses to offer substantially less than the listing price, the seller can claim that the listing broker acted contrary to the seller's best interests and cancel the listing. The buyer obviously would like to know that the seller is considering a price reduction, but the buyer is not entitled to disclosure of this information.

What if the seller orders the listing broker not to disclose a material fact, such as a basement that floods? If such an order is given early in the listing period, the broker should decline the listing and refuse to work with this seller. But if the order comes two days before closing, after the broker has fully performed all obligations, should the broker disregard the instruction, make the disclosure, and protect the earned commission, even if the disclosure prevents the sale? Whenever full and fair disclosure of a material fact is not made, the real estate agent is at risk. The broker has an independent duty to the buyer to take reasonable steps to avoid giving the buyer false information or concealing material facts. Seek immediate legal counsel in these situations. It is not a good idea to continue to market the property until you have resolved the problem.

LIABILITY FOR MISREPRESENTATION

Under the Texas Deceptive Trade Practices Act (Chapter 12), to file a successful misrepresentation claim against a broker, the plaintiff must prove that the

- broker made a misstatement (oral or written) to the buyer or failed to disclose a known material fact to the buyer,
- broker either knew or should have known that the statement was not accurate or that certain undisclosed information should have been disclosed,
- buyer reasonably relied on such statement, and
- buyer was damaged as a result.

Element of Reliance

Courts have held that the buyer is entitled to relief if the representation was a material inducement to the contract, even though the buyer may have made efforts to discover the truth and did not rely wholly on the representation. Also, agency is no defense; that is, it is generally not a defense that the broker merely passed along information that the seller provided—for example, the amount of taxes or the connection to the sewer system. The seller has a duty not to misrepresent, and the broker's duty stems from the seller's duty.

In fixing liability or in applying remedies, TRELA and various ethical codes make no distinction between whether the misrepresentation was intentional or negligent. Under changes made to the Texas Deceptive Trade Practices Act (DTPA) (Chapter 12) during the 82nd legislative session, however, legislators decided that licensees should not be held liable for innocent acts of misrepresentation. The difficulty arises when licensees are unable to prove they did not know or could not have known of the material fact.

Revisions to the DTPA in the 82nd Legislature (2011) also exclude the rendering of professional services from the purview of that act, meaning that a licensee's advice, opinion, or judgment cannot serve as a cause of action. However, the courts have not set precedence as to the meaning of "advice, opinion, or judgment" in the case of real estate licensees. Unfortunately, dissatisfied consumers tend to later remember a licensee's statement as being one of "fact" rather than "opinion," particularly if the decision to purchase was based on the statement and it turns out to be incorrect information.

Under a successful cause of action filed under the DTPA, plaintiff remedies include

- monetary damages,
- rescission of the contract, and
- forfeiture of the broker's commission.

Under TRELA, enforcement actions against licensees include the following:

- Criminal Prosecution (§ 1101.756)
- State Civil Penalty (§ 1101.753)
- Administrative Penalty (§ 1101.701)
- Court Injunctions (§ 1101.751)

Watch What Is Said

Brokers must carefully consider their statements to consumers. The broker is considered the real estate expert; therefore, consumers rely on what the broker says, even when the broker is not acting as their agent. Following is a short list of broker statements that should never be made:

- No need to get a title search. I sold this same property last year, and there was no title problem.
- Don't worry, the seller told me by phone I could sign the contract for her.
- If it helps you make up your mind about the price to offer on my listing, the seller countered a $230,000 offer last week with $235,000.
- I won't be able to present your offer until the seller decides on the offer submitted yesterday.
- I can't present your offer yet. We have a contract working.
- I can't/won't present your offer with that type of contingency clause in there.
- Go ahead and make an offer. If you can't get financing, you don't have to buy anyway and you'll still get your earnest money back.
- I can't submit your offer without earnest money. It's not legal.
- Trust me. I can word a contingency clause in such a way that you can back out whenever you want.
- You don't have to disclose anything that is not listed on the "Seller's Disclosure of Property Condition."

SUMMARY

In addition to the fiduciary duties owed to a client, a licensee must be aware of duties to third parties to the agency transaction. These duties include honesty, fairness, and a duty to disclose material facts regarding the property.

Material facts are important facts that may affect the decision to purchase or the price to offer. These facts may relate to physical attributes and title and survey problems, as well as certain stigmas that may have been attached to the property. These stigmas may be purely psychological, stemming from events that may have occurred in the property but that do not directly affect the structure, such as a death on the property. Other sources of stigma are physical psychological issues relating to environmental or other conditions surrounding the property that may affect the health or safety of the occupants, such as electromagnetic fields or radon gas.

Licensees should be constantly alert for circumstances or conditions that require disclosure and ensure that such disclosures are made in writing. In matters where the licensee is unsure of a disclosure issue, the licensee should consult a competent attorney.

KEY POINTS

- An agency contract is a two-party agreement in which clients engage an agent to represent their interests; however, agency becomes functional due to a third party, the party to the transaction who is not represented by the agent.
- Licensees should take considerable care in avoiding misrepresentations to clients or third parties. Misrepresentations may occur by misstatements or by the omission of important facts by the licensee.
- While duties owed to a third party are not fiduciary duties, they are strong and include a duty to treat the third party fairly and honestly. In addition, the licensee is obligated to disclose any material facts regarding the property that might affect the buyer's decision to purchase the property or the amount the buyer would be willing to pay.
- Licensees should be certain that affected residential sellers complete the Seller's Disclosure of Property Condition form in complete detail and that, whenever possible, the potential buyer receives a copy before signing an offer to purchase.
- Material facts are those facts that would affect a reasonable buyer's decision to buy, or the amount of money to be offered for the property, and include but are not limited to the following:
  — Physical condition
  — Title issues
  — Survey issues
  — Stigmatized properties
- Stigmas may be created from purely psychological sources, such as the reaction of a purchaser to a death that may have occurred on the property, or from physical conditions outside the property that may have a negative

health or safety impact on the occupants. Examples of physical stigmas are exposure to radon gas or electromagnetic fields.

The National Association of REALTORS® suggests the following guidelines when dealing with stigmatized properties:

- Determine whether the information is fact or fiction.
- Check state law.
- Determine materiality.
- Discuss disclosure with the seller.
- Although a licensee has a duty to disclose material facts to a third party, care should be exercised not to disclose confidential nonmaterial information to a third party that could be detrimental to the best interest of the client.

SUGGESTIONS FOR BROKERS

Research indicates that a key reason for complaints against licensees across the nation relates to misrepresentation or omission of important information to clients and customers. In response to this problem, brokers should encourage associated licensees to participate in continuing education efforts in this area. Further, a well-designed, ongoing legal issue program is strongly recommended as part of company training. Keep in mind that the laws governing disclosure are dynamic and must be reviewed carefully and frequently.

CHAPTER 3 QUIZ

1. Title insurance companies in Texas are regulated by the
   a. Texas Board of Insurance.
   b. Texas Real Estate Commission.
   c. Texas attorney general.
   d. U.S. attorney general.

2. Title coverage for the lender is called
   a. mortgagor's title insurance.
   b. mortgage company title insurance.
   c. title commitment.
   d. mortgagee's title insurance.

3. The buyer should only rely on measurements furnished by
   a. the seller's previous survey.
   b. the listing agent.
   c. the registered professional land surveyor.
   d. all of these.

4. On the issue of AIDS-related disclosures,
   a. TREC rules prohibit disclosure.
   b. TREC rules do not prohibit disclosure.
   c. licensees may follow their best judgment.
   d. HUD requires the licensee to respond to a direct question from the buyer.

5. Under Megan's Law, individual states
   a. may choose to ignore Megan's Law.
   b. must develop procedures for registering sex offenders.
   c. must require licensees to disclose registered sex offenders.
   d. are required to post a sign in the yard of the offender identifying the occupant as a sex offender.

6. Agents of a buyer should disclose information regarding a convicted child molester in close proximity to a subject property
   a. if they have actual knowledge.
   b. if the seller gives authorization to disclose.
   c. even if it is only rumor.
   d. only if the buyer asks.

7. A seller states that he will list his home with you only if you do not reveal to prospective buyers that the police have twice raided the house next door for suspected drug activity. You should
   a. take the listing as long as there was no conviction.
   b. take the listing but reveal the information to prospective buyers.
   c. decline the listing and refuse to work with this seller.
   d. refer the seller to another agent in your office and take a referral fee.

8. The listing agent tells the buyer that the seller installed a new air conditioner as agreed in the contract, when in fact the seller only refurbished the existing air conditioner. Under TRELA, the licensee is
   a. not liable because the misrepresentation was not intentional.
   b. not liable because the misrepresentation was not negligent.
   c. not liable because he only passed on the seller's representation.
   d. liable.

9. A property whose value or marketability has been affected by conditions or events related to the property
   a. is considered unsalable.
   b. is considered stigmatized.
   c. is considered valueless by appraisers.
   d. may not legally be sold until the condition is corrected.

10. A property whose value has been diminished by a murder occurring on the property has suffered which of the following?
    a. Physical stigma
    b. Incurable obsolescence
    c. Curable obsolescence
    d. Purely psychological stigma

DISCUSSION QUESTIONS

1. Presume that you have learned from a neighbor that a property that you are attempting to list was the site of a death that occurred by natural causes. How would you approach the seller regarding this matter?

2. List the conditions or circumstances regarding a property that you consider important in making a decision to purchase. Compare your list with others.

3. In reference to question 2, how do the comparative lists illustrate the difficulty in determining the materiality of an issue?

Creation and Termination of Agency

Few people, including many licensees, know the acts, conditions, expectations, and statements that can unintentionally turn an ordinary broker into an agent for one or more parties. It is in the best interests of all parties to a real estate transaction to understand the rules that govern agency. This is particularly important for licensees to enable them to establish when their responsibilities begin and which set of legal duties they owe—and to whom. Many professional publications, standards of professional conduct, and state licensing laws focus on the strict fulfillment of the rules of conduct for an agent. However, few offer exact determinations of when an agency relationship is created and to whom fiduciary duties are owed.

Licensees must know and understand the dynamics of agency and are responsible for strict compliance with the law of agency. This chapter introduces the concepts of how and when agency is created as well as how the relationship may be terminated. This knowledge will lay the foundation for understanding one of the most vital aspects of real estate practice today.

■ **LEARNING OBJECTIVES**   *This chapter addresses the following:*

- How and When Agency Is Created
    - Express Agency
    - Implied Agency
    - Ostensible Agency or Agency by Estoppel
    - Agency by Ratification
    - Gratuitous Agency and Compensation

- Important Issues
  - Legal Effect
  - Constructive or Imputed Notice
  - Imputed Knowledge
  - Professional and Ethical Responsibility
- How Agency Is Terminated
  - Lapse of Time
  - Actions of Principals and Agents
  - Operation of Law
- Duties of Agency that Continue

HOW AND WHEN AGENCY IS CREATED

We know that an agency relationship generally is created when one person authorizes another to act on that persons' behalf and to exercise some degree of authority and discretion while acting in this capacity. In most cases, the agreement must be mutual; that is, the principal must authorize the agent to act on the principal's behalf, and the agent must agree to do so. The agent may be empowered to do many of the things the principal could do but has chosen not to do. Typically, the agency relationship is created by some spoken or written agreement between the parties, but as will be shown, agency can be created by other, less formal means. Regardless of how or when the agency relation is ultimately created, TRELA states that a broker who represents a party in a real estate transaction acts as that party's agent (§ 1101.557(a)). Furthermore, while acting as an agent for another, the broker or salesperson acting for the broker is a fiduciary (22 TAC § 531.1).

The fact that a person licensed as a real estate broker or a salesperson performs a service for a consumer is not, by itself, sufficient to create an agency relationship. A real estate licensee's role is to give valuable service both to clients and to customers. The creation of an agency relationship requires more than just giving benefits and services. It requires consent and control. Once created, the agency relationship requires that licensees place the interest of clients above their own personal interests in the transaction (22 TAC § 531.1(3); § 535.156(b)). The licensee, as an agent, becomes an advocate of the principal/client in dealing with third parties (customers) and is obligated to protect the interests of that person.

As stated earlier, an agency relationship ideally results from mutual consent between the principal and the agent. In this case, the agent agrees to act on the principal's behalf and is subject to the principal's control. Formalities are not required, however, and an agent does not need a license, written contract, or receipt of a commission or fee for an agency relationship to exist (*see* Figure 4.1). Keep in mind the basic definition of a "broker" in Texas. Under TRELA § 1101.002(1)(A), broker means "a person who, in exchange for a commission or other valuable consideration or with the expectation of receiving a commission or other valuable consideration, performs for another person one of the following acts."

TRELA goes on to list the myriad acts that would require an individual to be licensed as a real estate agent. Licensing as a broker or a salesperson is technically not required to perform any of those activities unless compensation is either received or anticipated. Compensation can come in many forms, however, ranging from cash to barter. So an individual who routinely provided the listed brokerage services for consumers would be hard-pressed to convince any court that compensation in some form was not being received for those services. In addition, the licensing requirement does not apply to myriad other individuals specifically exempted such as Texas attorneys, on-site property managers, trustees, public officials, or individuals operating under a power-of-attorney (§ 1101.005).

While it is desirable for the agent and the principal to enter into a written agreement, nothing exists in Texas statutory or common law mandating that the agency relationship be created by written contract. Most states, however, including Texas, would require a written agreement, if the broker wants to have the option of bringing a lawsuit for a commission should the client default on the agreement (§ 1101.806(c)). Texas also requires written permission to perform specific acts, such as advertising or placing the broker's sign on the property.

Agency can be created by an oral agreement between the agent and the principal. The prudent broker will, however, establish a written contract as soon as possible. The written agreement should, at minimum, address the issues relating to the duties of the agent and principal and the expectations for compensation, and it should be sufficient to protect the interests of both parties.

Some form of authorization from the principal is needed for the agent to act on behalf of the principal in dealing with others. The principal must delegate authority to act to the agent and the agent must consent to act, or no agency exists. Licensees should be clear about their authority to act for others.

FIGURE 4.1

Elements Not Essential to Create an Agency Relationship

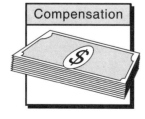

Specific authorization may come in different forms—express or implied—and by different means—words, actions, or, in some cases, by inaction. Agency may be classified as

- express agency,
- implied agency,
- ostensible agency or agency by estoppel,
- agency by ratification, or
- gratuitous agency.

It would be helpful for you to refer to Figure 4.2 during your study of these topics.

Express Agency

Express agency is the agency relationship created when principals engage or employ an agent to act for them. In legal terms, the word *express* means clear, definite, explicit, unmistakable, and unambiguous. In carrying out the duties of an express agency agreement, the agent acquires express authority to act for the principal.

In practice, this authority is created when principals authorize an agent to act for them by specifying certain acts, functions, or duties that the agent should perform. Remember that these instructions may be either written or oral. Generally, the more specific the agreement, the better for both the agent and the principal. Some states require such an agreement of representation to be in writing under both the licensing law and other laws relating to oral versus written contracts. In Texas, the authorization may be in writing or by an oral agreement between the principal and the broker. The obligations of the agent (broker) and the principal

FIGURE 4.2

How Agency Is Created

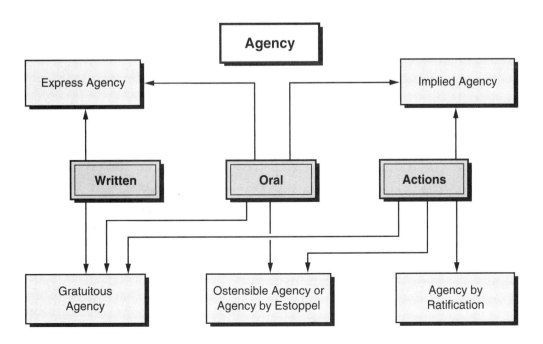

are the same, whether the agreement is in writing or is oral; however, if a broker wishes to have the right to bring a lawsuit for payment of a commission or fee for services, the agreement must be in writing. The agreement can be a simple note or memorandum that includes an agreement to compensate the broker for services performed.

The two most common express agency agreements used by brokers in sales transactions are written listing contracts and buyer representation contracts. Generically, these agreements are called broker employment agreements. In written listing contracts, the broker is authorized to represent a seller or a landlord in the sale or lease of that principal's property. The written buyer-tenant representation agreement employs the broker to represent the buyer or the tenant in the purchase or lease of a property. These written agency contracts are usually quite detailed. They attempt to clarify the rights and obligations of both the principal and the agent and include provisions for compensation when the agent's duties have been performed. These contracts will be discussed in detail later in Chapters 5 and 6.

Implied authority (not to be confused with implied agency) is a concept that is applicable to both express agency and implied agency (discussed in the next section). Implied authority is authority not specifically granted to the agent but necessary or customary if agents are to perform their agency duties, and it is implied by the principal's actions. Due to the varied functions required of real estate agents, it is unlikely that the entire scope of an agent's activities could be stated in an express written agreement such as a listing agreement. The agent, therefore, may also acquire certain authority to act for the principal by implied authority. For example, a listing contract may not specifically outline each and every tool that the agent may employ in marketing the property. However, when owners instruct agents to make their best efforts to sell their properties, it is implied that the agents have the authority to advertise, conduct open houses, distribute flyers, and so on. Note that this type of authority is created between the agent and the principal and does not require some third party's reliance or actions to become operational.

Implied Agency

Implied agency (not to be confused with implied authority) occurs when there is no express agreement that the broker will act as an agent for a party. The actions or words of the broker and the party may lead the party to believe that the broker is representing the party's interests. This often occurs when a licensee who is working with a buyer-customer with no intended representation makes statements or performs actions that lead the customer to believe the licensee has become the customer's agent.

In the past, licensees were not accustomed to discussing and confirming whom they represented when meeting with third parties. As a result, unrepresented buyers often assumed that licensees who were showing them properties were the buyer's representatives. Those buyers were unaware of the fact that the licensees legally represented the sellers.

Courts generally look to the actions of a broker and to the reliance by a buyer on a licensee to determine whether an implied agency relationship existed between broker and buyer. Because formalities are not required, courts may hold that an agency arrangement was implied, based on the intentions of the broker and the alleged principal, as shown by their actions and/or words. Even though a broker is the seller's agent, the broker could be held to be acting as the buyer's agent as well. Courts will ask the question, "Did the broker act under the alleged principal's direction and control?"

■ **EXAMPLE** Buyer Betty contacts Bay Realty, seeking to purchase a four-unit rental building. Sally, a licensee with Bay Realty, agrees to work with Betty; however, Betty signs no representation contract. Sally shows ten properties listed by her company and other real estate companies and negotiates unsuccessfully on two of those properties. During the negotiations, Sally gives advice and opinions to Betty. After the two unsuccessful attempts to negotiate a purchase, Sally tells Betty not to despair, as she is sure that she can locate the "perfect property." Sally continues to seek, and ultimately finds, a four-unit rental building that suits Betty's needs and qualifications. Sally then obtains the listing on the four-unit building from owner Harry on behalf of Bay Realty. Betty and the seller enter into a contract for the purchase of the property.

■ **QUESTIONS** 1. Did Sally represent Betty during the negotiation on the two unsuccessful contracts? If so, when did the representation begin? 2. Did Sally's actions imply to Betty that Sally represented her? If so, what actions would give this impression?

Disclosure and clarification should lessen the chances of creating an implied agency. However, a licensee who behaves like a buyer's agent, even though bound to an express written agreement to represent the seller, nevertheless will be deemed an implied agent of the buyer. Licensees must be careful of their actions, even after they disclose their agency arrangements in writing. The conduct of the parties can result in the creation of an agency relationship, even if a written agreement asserts that no agency exists or that the parties never intended for an agency relationship to exist.

Ostensible Agency or Agency by Estoppel

The word *ostensible* means "for all appearances." In agency law, ostensible agency and agency by estoppel (when a court does not allow a principal to deny that agency existed) are based on a third party's being led to believe that a licensee was acting as an agent of another party. If the actions of a principal led reasonable persons to assume that a licensee was acting on their behalf, then ostensible agency or agency by estoppel could have occurred. In that event, a court would likely prevent the principal from denying that an agency relationship existed. In effect, if a principal allows a licensee to "walk like an agent, talk like an agent, and act like an agent," third parties will reasonably be allowed to presume that the licensee is an agent for that principal.

This concept could apply either before a formal agency agreement is created or after it expires. For example, presume that the sellers allow their "former agent" to show and advertise their property after the listing contract expires. During this period of unofficial representation, a buyer purchases the property and, after closing, discovers that the licensee has made misrepresentations regarding the property. The buyer later sues the sellers, claiming misrepresentations were made by the licensee while acting as an agent of the sellers. The sellers then claim that because the listing contract had terminated, the licensee was not the sellers' agent and the buyer cannot hold the seller liable for the misrepresentations made by the licensee. Under these circumstances, the court is likely to hold that, based on the doctrine of estoppel, the sellers cannot deny the agency relationship still existed. The sellers allowed the buyer to believe that an agency relationship continued to exist between them and the licensee, and the buyers were justified in relying on that belief.

■ **EXAMPLE** In *Wilson v. Donze*, 692 S.W.2d 735 (Tex. Ct. App.—Fort Worth 1985), Ken Wilson, the owner of Ken/Car Investments, Inc., approached Anthony and Lena Donze in May asking if their home was for sale. The Donzes informed Wilson that they did not do business with brokers and did not pay commissions. Wilson said he would get the commission from the buyers if he could sell their home. The Donzes agreed to allow him to show the property and told him that they wanted $85,000 for the home.

On June 1, another real estate broker named Powers, acting with Wilson, wrote an offer from the Bullards for $100,000, telling the Bullards that it would probably take $115,000 to purchase the home. On June 2, Wilson presented a contract to the Donzes for $85,000, naming Ken/Car Investments, Inc., trustee or assigns, as the purchasers; the contract was accepted by the Donzes. Also on June 2, the Bullards were informed by Powers that their offer had been rejected and that it would indeed take $115,000 to purchase the property; they agreed.

The Donzes and the Bullards met only once after the contracts were signed and both assumed that the contract was between them, and not Ken/Car, even though Ken/Car Investments, Inc., trustee or assigns, was named as the purchaser on the Donzes' contract and Ken Wilson, trustee as the seller on the Bullards' contract. No one clarified to the Donzes or the Bullards that this was a pass-through transaction. Ken Wilson believed that he had done no wrong because the Donzes received what they wanted for the sale of the property, and the Bullards were willing to pay $115,000.

The court held that Ken Wilson was a broker for the Donzes and that he breached his fiduciary duty by not obtaining the best price for them. The jury awarded $24,900 in actual damages and $35,000 in punitive damages. The court of appeals upheld the jury's decision.

■ **QUESTIONS** 1. When did Ken Wilson become an agent for the Donzes?
2. How could Ken Wilson have avoided this problem?

Agency by Ratification

Agency by ratification occurs when a principal gains some benefit from a previously unauthorized act of an agent, and the principals, on learning of the act, do not deny that the agent had authority to perform such an act on their behalf. The principals ratify the action of the agent by accepting the benefits that come from the action. Principals have an affirmative duty to reject any unauthorized acts of an agent; otherwise the principals may be held liable for the consequences of the agent's actions. Under the ratification theory, principals are considered to have approved the agency if they accept the benefits of an agent's previously unauthorized act. This is agency after the fact. There are four elements to look for in this concept:

- The agent performs an unauthorized act.
- The principal subsequently learns of the act.
- The principal does not repudiate (deny) the agent's authority to act.
- The principal benefits from the act.

EXAMPLE Daniel, from Action Realty, tried unsuccessfully to obtain a listing on a warehouse from Harry. Daniel went to Harry one day and told him that he had a number of interested buyers, but Harry would not give him a listing. Nevertheless, Daniel showed several buyers the property. When Daniel brought an offer from a buyer, Harry accepted the offer, which contained a provision for him to pay Daniel. Harry asked Daniel to monitor the closing. Subsequently, the buyer brought a lawsuit against Harry to cancel the purchase contract because of a misrepresentation made by Daniel. Harry argued that Daniel was not his agent because he did not sign a listing agreement. A court likely would hold that Harry ratified or affirmed the agency by signing the contract of sale and asking Daniel to monitor the closing and that he is, therefore, bound by Daniel's misrepresentation.

QUESTIONS 1. What actions should Harry have taken to ensure that Daniel did not represent him? 2. What could Daniel have done to secure his position as Harry's agent?

Gratuitous Agency and Compensation

The most common notion of real estate agency has been frequently expressed as "You are the agent of the person who pays you." In the past, when asked what the determining factor was in creating an agency, most real estate licensees answered that it is payment of the fee. However, the payment of a commission is not the sole factor in creating an agency relationship. In fact, by contract, the seller could agree to pay all the buyer's broker's fee, just like the seller sometimes agrees to pay the loan discount points on the buyer's loan or the cost of the professional home inspection. Also, by contract, the buyer could agree to pay the brokerage fees and/or any of the seller's closing expenses. An agency relationship can exist without regard to who pays the fee: the seller, the buyer, both, or neither. Texas law, like most state agency disclosure laws, confirms the common-law rule that payment of the fee does not determine agency.

The agency relationship created when the agent provides brokerage services and charges no fee is known as gratuitous agency. Thus, a gratuitous agent giving free advice, perhaps to build goodwill, could be held liable when giving the wrong advice. For example, an agent working without charge could be liable for bad advice if the agent were asked for and gave an opinion about the need to obtain an inspection or title insurance. If the agent's opinion were subsequently relied on and resulted in a loss to the principal, the agent could be held liable just as though a fee or commission had been charged to render the service.

Licensees are often placed in positions where they are asked their opinions regarding real estate matters. Many licensees will say that once they obtained a real estate license, they never could go to a gathering of people without someone asking their advice about real estate. While it is flattering to be asked for advice, it is also *very risky* to offer advice without being fully informed about the situation. This is particularly true in the arena of helping a for-sale-by-owner party who "only needs a simple question answered."

Despite the fact that payment of the commission does not necessarily determine agency, prudent licensees should discuss and document whom they represent and who pays whom. A clear disclosure can dispel any notion that the licensee represented the person who paid the broker's commission when the licensee did not. If no agency documentation exists, courts will probably use the commission payment as evidence of the intended agency relationship, especially if the person paying the fee is the one claiming that an agency existed. Without clear evidence to the contrary, the broker will have difficulty proving no agency existed. Note that this could apply either to a buyer who pays the commission or to a seller who pays the commission.

■ **EXAMPLE** In *Kelly v. Roussalis*, 776 P.2d. 1016 (Wyo. 1989), John Roussalis called Gus Kelly of McNamara Realty to show him a property located on South Poplar because Gus had worked with him on several other real estate transactions. The house was listed with another firm, and the asking price was $600,000. John said that he would like to pay less and that he would need to sell his current home before purchasing another. Gus had heard that the seller was having financial problems and thought the South Poplar house might go into foreclosure. He suggested that John might be able to buy the property for less at a foreclosure sale.

Subsequently, a property in the name of the same person who owned the South Poplar property was posted for foreclosure. John asked Gus whether it was the South Poplar property that he had seen, and Gus told him that it was, without checking to verify the information.

Gus then helped John purchase the property by accompanying him to the foreclosure sale—even though Gus's company had a policy of not attending foreclosure sales. Gus bid $150,000 for John and won the final sale, obtained a check from the bank, and paid the sheriff, only to find out that the property John had been successful in buying was not the South Poplar property.

John sued Gus and McNamara Realty for negligence. Gus said he was just being a friend and not an agent. John won the suit, and Gus and McNamara Realty appealed. The state Supreme Court upheld the lower court's decision, saying that Gus did not exercise the care expected of real estate agents. The court also held McNamara Realty responsible for Gus's actions.

■ **QUESTIONS** 1. When did Gus become an agent for Roussalis? 2. How did the fact that no fee was being paid affect the outcome? 3. What steps should Gus and his broker have taken to prevent this problem?

■ IMPORTANT ISSUES

Why is it so important to determine in every case whether an agency relationship has, in fact, been created? The main reasons are legal effect, constructive or imputed notice, professional and ethical responsibility, and quality of representation.

Legal Effect

The agent stands in the shoes of the principal and carries out those duties agreed on in the agency contract. The agent speaks, listens, and acts for the principal. This is the very essence of the word *represents* when used in the context of the agency relationship.

Because the agent acts on behalf of the principal, the principal may be responsible for or bound to the agent's statements within the scope of the agency. That is, anything done to further the principal's objective to sell or purchase may be assumed to be done with the knowledge and approval of the principal. This is true whether the words or actions are fraudulent, negligent, or innocent. The statements, omissions, admissions, and misrepresentations made by the agent or the subagent may be attributed to the principal, even though the principal may be unaware of them. The reasoning behind this ruling is that principals should not be allowed to benefit from the negligent acts of their agents and subagents.

Texas contract law will not, presumably, hold principals responsible for the unauthorized acts of their agents unless they are actually aware of the acts. Likewise, there would be no liability under TRELA § 1101.805(d). There is, however, little case law to reflect how the courts interpret these changes. In any event, principals should make an informed decision regarding the agent they select for representation.

The judicial trend, however, continues to hold an agent liable in the area of negligence. Courts often base decisions on the fact that as a professional, an agent knew or should have known certain information, such as the sewer's not being connected, the roof's leaking, or the property's location in a flood-prone area. The listing agent's failure to discover obvious defects and disclose such defects to the buyer may be termed *negligence*. However, in Texas, the courts have found that agents who did not know of latent defects were not bound to the same extent as real estate inspectors, and agents are, in fact, prohibited from acting as inspectors and brokers in the same transaction. In the landmark case *Kubinsky v. Van Zandt*, the broker appropriately was found to have not known in a "should have known" situation. A few courts in the United States have held that brokers and their principals are liable for the brokers' innocent misrepresentations.

■ **EXAMPLE** Agent Charlie lists a home in an exclusive area of town. Although the property is near the shoreline and at a relatively low elevation, the property has never flooded. However, mortgage lenders require flood insurance when making loans in the area. Charlie finds a buyer, and the seller agrees to "owner finance" the property. Neither Charlie nor the seller advises the purchaser about the issue of possible flooding. Six months after the sale, the property floods after a torrential downpour. The new purchaser has not secured flood insurance, and the loss is devastating. Charlie claims no fault because he was not aware of the potential problem.

■ **QUESTIONS** 1. Is this something that Charlie should have known? 2. Is the seller obligated to disclose this type of information? 3. What should Charlie have done differently, if anything?

Constructive or Imputed Notice

During a real estate transaction, licensees are required to give notice to buyers and sellers regarding matters such as acceptance or rejection of offers to buy or sell, withdrawal of offers, or removal of a property from the market. Time is important in negotiations of offers, and proper notice may determine who is the rightful purchaser of a property—particularly when more than one offer is being negotiated.

It is important for everyone involved in a real estate transaction to know who is representing whom, so that when notifications are required, it may be determined when a legal notification actually occurred. In practice, licensees often find themselves involved in disputes over issues of notification to buyers and sellers, as well as to other licensees involved in the transaction.

Once the buyer and the seller have reached an agreement and all parties have signed the contract, it must be delivered to all principals, or their agents, to become enforceable. Most contracts have a number of details that must be completed to process the sale. Frequently, there are deadlines for the delivery of inspection reports, approval of the buyer's financing, or a title commitment.

Many licensees erroneously believe that an agent must actually tell the principal before notice is effective. In reality, the knowledge of or notice to the agent is binding on the principal, even if the information is never conveyed to the principal. Notifying the agent is regarded as actually notifying the principal. This is called constructive or imputed notice.

The following case is somewhat complex; nevertheless, it demonstrates the importance of properly notifying each party and making sure that all parties are aware of whom each agent is representing.

■ **EXAMPLE** In *Stortroen v. Beneficial Finance Company*, 736 P.2d 391 (Colo. 1987), Beneficial Finance entered into a listing agreement with Olthoff Realty Company to sell a property it owned. Olthoff placed the property in the local multiple listing service (MLS). Mary Panio, an associate with Foremost Realty, saw the listing in the MLS and subsequently showed the home to the Stortroens, who had expressed an interest in selling their home and purchasing a larger one. After touring the home, the Stortroens asked Mary to prepare and present an offer for $105,000 to the seller. Because the Stortroens needed to sell their current home before buying another one, they made the offer contingent on selling and closing the sale of their present home. The contingency also stated that Beneficial would keep the home on the market and give the Stortroens 72 hours to remove the contingency on notification that Beneficial Finance had received another acceptable offer.

Beneficial's representative, Donald Reh, reviewed the contract and instructed Olthoff to increase the sales price to $110,000 and to state in the counteroffer that acceptance by the buyer would be "evidenced by the Purchaser's signature hereon; and if seller receives notice of such acceptance on or before 9 PM 2-3-84."

While the offer from the Stortroens was being negotiated, the Carellis also toured the home and submitted an offer for $112,000 on Friday, February 3, 1984, through their agent. Olthoff informed Beneficial's Reh of the second offer and was told by him to have the Carellis' agent bring the offer directly to him. Reh reviewed the contract and told Olthoff to withdraw the counteroffer to the Stortroens and accept the offer from the Carellis.

Olthoff tried contacting Mary Panio but was unable to speak to her personally, so he left messages at her office and her home informing her that the counteroffer with Beneficial had been withdrawn. Olthoff told Reh about the messages to Panio, whereupon Reh signed the offer from the Carellis.

Before she received the messages from Olthoff, Mary Panio presented the counteroffer to the Stortroens. The Stortroens agreed to the terms of the counteroffer and signed it at about 4:10 PM on Friday, February 3. On returning to her office with the signed counteroffer, Mary received the messages from Olthoff.

On Saturday, February 4, Mary Panio obtained a withdrawal of the contingency from the Stortroens. On Monday, February 6, Mary delivered the signed offer and the withdrawal of the contingency to Olthoff. Subsequently, the Stortroens filed their contract into record at the county clerk's office—thereby placing a cloud on the title to Beneficial's property.

The Carellis moved into the home on a month-to-month lease because they didn't want to close on the property while there was a cloud on the title. The Stortroens brought suit against Beneficial for specific performance of the contract and against the Carellis to vacate the premises. The Carellis brought suit against Beneficial and a complaint against Olthoff.

The district court found in favor of Beneficial and against the Stortroens, saying that Mary Panio was acting as a representative of the buyer. Thus, when the counteroffer and the contingency were signed by the Stortroens and given to Panio, this was not considered to be notification of acceptance to Beneficial.

The state supreme court was asked to render a decision regarding whom Mary Panio was representing. They found that she was representing Beneficial Finance through the agreement of subagency (working with the buyer but representing the seller) offered through the MLS. Therefore, when the counteroffer from Beneficial was accepted and signed by the Stortroens in the presence of Mary, constructive notice to Beneficial had been officially made. This decision made the Stortroens the prevailing party.

This case illustrates how licensees can run into enormous problems when notification is required. Technically, once all parties have signed the offer, it becomes an enforceable contract, but only when all parties or their agents have received notification (thus, constructive notice). If Mary had been representing the buyers—not the seller through a subagency agreement—notice would have been considered effective only when she delivered it to Olthoff Realty.

Imputed Knowledge

In addition to imputed notice, both agents and clients should be familiar with the related legal concept of imputed knowledge. Although this term is sometimes considered the equivalent of imputed notice, it is more specific to information or facts known by the agent but not actually delivered or relayed to the client. In such cases, it may be deemed that such knowledge has been imputed, or constructively delivered to the client.

Thus, clients are considered to have the same information or knowledge that their agent has regarding a property or transaction. Because the agent has a duty to convey such information to the client, it is generally held that this has, in fact, occurred. Additionally, other parties involved in the transaction may presume that the principal has been (or should have been) made aware of this information or knowledge.

For example, a listing agent who tells the buyer's agent about a major drug raid on the property next door the previous evening has given notice of a material fact to the buyer through the buyer's agent. Once agency is established, it is the fiduciary duty of the agent to communicate material information to their client (TRELA § 1101.557(b)(2)).

Professional and Ethical Responsibility

Real estate licensees acting as agents owe general duties of good faith, fairness, and honesty to all with whom they deal. But when acting as agents and subagents, licensees owe a far greater degree of care and loyalty to a principal than they do to a third person. In general, a customer is entitled to honesty, fairness, accurate information, and material facts concerning a property. A client is entitled to accurate information, opinions, and advice about the significance of facts and information, the available alternative courses of action, and the agent's recommendations. The best interests of the client must be kept in mind at all times.

HOW AGENCY IS TERMINATED

Except in the case of an agency coupled with a broker's interest in the transaction (partial ownership), an agency relationship may be terminated at any time for any of the following reasons:

- Lapse of the time specified in the agreement
- Lapse of a reasonable time if no time is specified
- Completion of the purpose of the agency
- Mutual rescission
- Revocation by the principal
- Agent's renunciation
- Abandonment of the agreement by the agent
- Incapacity or death of either the agent or the principal
- Bankruptcy of the owner if title is transferred to the receiver
- Condemnation or destruction of the premises
- Agent's breach of duties to the principal

Lapse of Time

The Real Estate License Act (TRELA) does not specifically address the length of time appropriate for listing or buyer-tenant agency contracts. It does, however, state that an agent may not enter into these contracts without a definite termination or expiration date that requires no action on the part of the principal (there are exceptions for certain types of property management contracts). Likewise, a contract may not automatically renew itself into perpetuity (forever). Failure to provide for a definite termination date may be grounds for revocation or suspension of the agent's real estate license (§ 1101.652(b)(12)).

Although TRELA does not limit the term of these agency agreements, it is inherent in agency law that such agreements must be for reasonable periods. In practice, the length of the listing and the buyer representation contracts are negotiated between the broker and the principal. Typically, these negotiations depend on the type of property, market conditions, and motivation of the sellers or the buyers.

Actions of Principals and Agents

The actions of a principal or agent may terminate the agency in a variety of ways. These include

- accomplishment of the agency objective,
- expiration of agency agreement,
- rescission,
- revocation,
- renunciation,
- abandonment by the agent, and
- breach of the agent's duty to the principal.

Accomplishment of the agency objective. The agency agreement was entered into for a specific purpose. When that purpose has been accomplished, the agency terminates. The house is sold for the seller, or the prospective buyer client purchases a property. Neither the agent nor the principal needs to take any action for the agency to end.

Expiration of the agency agreement. Other than accomplishment of the agency objective, perhaps the most common form of agency termination occurs when the property remains unsold throughout the term of the listing agreement between the broker and the seller. This is frequently called an expired listing. Once the listing has expired, the seller may be approached by other brokerage firms and relist the property with a different broker. Typically, the broker and the seller are free of their obligations to each other under the terms of the listing agreement. Continuing obligations of the seller may include buyers who were shown the property during the listing period by the broker and registered under a protection clause, if included in the listing contract. During a protection period, if a protected buyer attempts to purchase directly from the seller after the listing expires, the seller would still be obligated to pay the broker a commission. The broker should also be aware that certain fiduciary duties may still be owed the seller after the expiration of the listing. Of primary concern would be the duty of confidentiality, which would require that all information of a confidential nature learned while acting as the agent of the seller remain confidential even after the listing terminates.

Rescission by the parties. Because these agency agreements are created by mutual consent, they may be terminated in the same way. The parties can jointly decide to rescind the agreement at any time. A seller could reasonably anticipate that the listing broker will agree to mutual rescission if the seller decides not to sell the property for whatever reason. Perhaps a job transfer fell through, family status changed, or the market value dropped below the seller's loan balance. Regardless, neither party would be held in default because of the mutual agreement to rescind.

Revocation by the principal. The agency relationship is highly personal and requires the continuing consent of the principal and the agent. Thus a principal may unilaterally, at any time, revoke the authority of the agent to represent them. Such revocation may of course create liability to the principal for any financial damages suffered by the broker. For example, if a seller revokes the broker's agency after the broker has incurred substantial expenses relating to the marketing of the property, the broker may be entitled to recovery. Likewise, although the broker has no further authority to represent the seller, should the seller sell the property within the term of the listing contract period, the seller may owe the broker a commission, depending on the terms of the original listing contract. Keep in mind, however, that in order to receive damages, the broker would be required to sue the seller and hope the court sees the broker's case favorably. Many brokers have found such suits to be impractical at best.

Regardless, the contractual agreement between the principal and the agent traditionally distinguishes between the granting of authority to act as the principal's agent, and the how, when, where, and by whom the agent will be compensated. So continuing to offer a property for sale after revocation of agency by the principal, for example, would be cause for suspension or revocation of a licensee (§ 1101.652 (b)(18)–(20)). A listing agent should therefore immediately cease all advertising, remove For Sale/For Lease signs for the property, remove the listing from the multiple listing service (MLS), and remove all information from internet postings. The listing broker may then begin deal with the matter of compensation as a separate contractual issue.

Renunciation by the broker. A broker might unilaterally choose to discontinue representation of a seller during the term of a listing or a buyer-representation contract. Again, agency is highly personal and consensual. The client cannot force an agent to continue providing agency duties once the agent has renounced. An excellent example would be a broker who renounces the relationship after the seller-client insists the broker not disclose a material property defect. Although the licensee has the duty of confidentiality to the client, that duty does not apply if the client is demanding that the licensee violate a legal responsibility.

Of course, a seller or a buyer who is damaged by such action of the broker may be able to seek damages against the broker. An example might include a broker who charges the sellers an up-front nonrefundable fee and later decides to renounce the listing before the end of the agreement. As a result, the sellers may believe that they were damaged by at least the amount of the nonrefundable fee. As with revocation by the principal, the issue of compensation is contractually separate from that of agency.

Abandonment by the broker. Although a rare claim, a buyer or a seller may terminate the agency agreement if the broker takes no action to accomplish the agency objective. Examples may include a broker who is never available to show properties to a buyer represented by the broker; a broker who, having listed a property for a sale, makes no marketing effort to sell the property; or a listing associate who fails to return phone calls from a buyer's agent seeking delivery of an offer from the buyer. Remember, a broker who agrees to represent a party has accepted responsibility to provide statutorily defined minimum services to the client, including relaying material information, answering questions, and negotiating on the client's behalf (§ 1101.557(b)). Under the rules defining broker responsibility, a broker must "promptly respond to sponsored salespersons, clients, and licensees representing other parties in real estate transactions" (22 TAC § 535.2(j)). In such cases, the principals may terminate the agency due to ostensible abandonment by the broker.

Breach of the agent's duty to the principal. This circumstance is related to the above example. When an agent breaches any duty to the principal, the principal may terminate the agency without recourse from the broker. Such a breach, particularly when associated with a fiduciary duty, may also expose the broker to legal liability in addition to the termination of the agency agreement. There are virtually no restrictions relating to a seller's right to revoke due to breaches of fiduciary duties by the broker.

Operation of Law

In addition to acts of the parties to the agency relationship, certain circumstances, such as death of a principal, incapacity, supervening law, bankruptcy, or loss or destruction of the property, will cause the agency to terminate by law.

Death of the agent or principal. Unless the agent has an ownership or contractual interest in the property (known as agency coupled with an interest), death of the agent or principal will terminate the agency relationship. In the event of the death of a broker, all the listings held by the broker will terminate, as well as cause all the licenses of the broker's associates to become inactive. The sellers must find another broker with whom to list their properties, and the associates must secure another sponsoring broker before continuing their brokerage activities. In the event of the death of the principal, the listing agreement will terminate and the property would be subject to probate under the terms of the will or the administration of the estate by the courts in the event of an intestate death (no valid will).

Incapacity of the agent or principal. Unless operating under a durable power of attorney, the incapacity of the broker or the principal will also terminate the agency agreement. The term *incapacity* refers to an individual's lack of mental or physical capabilities, which would preclude certain legal consequences to attach to their actions. For example, an individual in a coma or diagnosed with Alzheimer's has incapacity to make a binding contract. The circumstances and resolutions under the insanity provisions apply in essentially the same way as described under the death provisions.

Supervening law. Occasionally, a change in the law can result in the termination of an agency agreement. This occurs when the agency involves an activity that was legal when the agreement was entered into, but due to change of law, the activity later becomes illegal; the agency will terminate. Presume that a broker has a contract to manage a building providing adult-oriented entertainment and later a city ordinance makes the activity illegal. In this case, the management contract will terminate, provided the contract was tied to the management of the adult-oriented business.

Bankruptcy, loss, or destruction of property. Other reasons of termination by law include bankruptcy of the principal that results in the property being taken into receivership, the property being taken by the government through condemnation, or the physical destruction of the property.

DUTIES OF AGENCY THAT CONTINUE

Even though the agency relationship may have appeared to terminate by action of time, actions of the parties, or operation of law, the duty of confidentiality of information remains after the termination of the agreement. Under no circumstances can a licensee disclose confidential information that was gained during the course of the agency contract unless authorized to do so by the principal. Frequently an agent who has listed and/or sold a property for a seller subsequently is asked to show that seller other property to purchase. Whether or not the agent has a formal agency agreement with the former client, the agent cannot disclose any information gained during the previous relationship with the former client without that client's authorization.

■ **EXAMPLE** Christian from Executive Realty listed and sold one of Judy's investment homes. Three weeks after closing, Judy asks Christian to show her possible replacement properties. She does not ask to be represented by Christian. He knows that Judy has $30,000 from the sale of her other property to invest in new properties. He also knows that for personal reasons, Judy must invest this money quickly. Christian shows Judy one of his listings—one that he believes she will consider an excellent investment. She tours the property and proceeds to write an offer that is substantially below the list price.

■ **QUESTIONS** 1. Is Judy still Christian's client? 2. How much information is Christian allowed to give the seller about Judy? 3. Will Christian have to disclose his former agency relationship with Judy to the seller?

SUMMARY

Real estate licensees need to be aware of the variety of positions relative to agency that a broker can have in a real estate transaction. Because no formalities are required to create an agency relationship, one can be found to exist when none was ever intended. The existence of an agency relationship can have a significant impact on issues of liability, notice, responsibility, and quality of representation. By becoming more aware of agency issues, the real estate licensee can better define and control agency relationships, thus ensuring that working relationships intentionally created are the most effective and successful while better reducing the possibility of risk.

Subsequent chapters examine in depth each agency alternative. Brokers have to evaluate which alternative is best. Today, companies must consider many factors in developing their agency policies. One thing is certain: no perfect solution exists.

■ KEY POINTS

- The payment of a fee does not determine agency.
- An agency can be created expressly, by implication, by estoppel, by ratification, or gratuitously, with or without a written agreement.
- Regardless of how or when the agency relation is created, a broker who represents a party is a fiduciary (22 TAC § 531.1).
- Agency may be terminated by mutual agreement (rescission), unilaterally (renunciation or revocation), expiration of time, abandonment by the agent, or operation of law.
- A customer is entitled to accurate information and material facts; a client is entitled to accurate information, opinions, and advice.
- In establishing liability and responsibility, courts look at not only the documents creating agency but also the acts of the agent and the parties.
- The duty of confidentiality continues after the termination of an agency.

■ SUGGESTIONS FOR BROKERS

Develop a company policy covering which agency alternative the company prefers, which services the broker or sales and broker associates may extend to customers, and which services they must or must not provide to clients. It should be policy that any variations must be reported to the managing broker, as when a salesperson in a large, exclusively seller-agency-oriented firm attempts to represent a buyer in locating a property.

CHAPTER 4 QUIZ

1. Which is required to create an agency relationship?
   a. Compensation
   b. A contract
   c. A real estate license
   d. A belief that the relationship exists

2. Express agency
   a. is created by the principal's actions.
   b. is always in writing.
   c. can be a verbal agreement.
   d. is ambiguous.

3. Implied authority is
   a. specifically given in a listing contract.
   b. not specifically given to an agent.
   c. the same as implied agency.
   d. a part of every contract.

4. Agency based on a third party's being led to believe that a licensee was acting as an agent of another party is
   a. express agency.
   b. implied agency.
   c. ostensible agency.
   d. agency by ratification.

5. Which of the following statements is FALSE?
   a. A licensee who is not compensated for services is not liable.
   b. The broker and a consumer must enter into a written agreement to establish an agency relationship.
   c. The buyer must be personally notified of a property defect or the seller is liable for failure to disclose.
   d. All of these are false statements.

6. Which statement is TRUE regarding termination of agency for time?
   a. Unlike seller agency, a contract for buyer agency does not require a definite termination date.
   b. TRELA mandates a maximum of 180 days for residential listings.
   c. A contract for seller or buyer agency may not automatically renew itself into perpetuity.
   d. All property management contracts require a definite termination date.

7. You entered into an agency agreement with and successfully found a home for a buyer. To terminate the agency, you
   a. need take no action.
   b. must wait until closing.
   c. must notify the buyer in writing.
   d. must notify the seller in writing.

8. Which statement is TRUE regarding the determination of whom the broker represents?
   a. Whoever pays the commission is the principal.
   b. The principal must sign a written agreement for an agency to exist.
   c. It is important to decide whether the buyer or the seller is the broker's principal because the broker will owe the principal a higher standard of care and more extensive duties.
   d. The broker must be paid a commission for an agency to exist.

9. Notice to an agent that is considered notice to the principal is known as
   a. ostensible notice.
   b. constructive notice.
   c. implied notice.
   d. unintended notice.

10. Duties that continue after the termination of agency include the duty
    a. to continue to present offers to the seller.
    b. to continue to advertise the property.
    c. not to disclose confidential information.
    d. to offer advice and opinions.

DISCUSSION QUESTIONS

1. What two essential elements are necessary to create an agency relationship?
2. Compare and contrast implied and express agency.
3. When is gratuitous agency most likely to occur?

Seller Agency

Until the late 1990s, the traditional viewpoint in real estate brokerage had been that the real estate licensee, when acting as an agent in a transaction, represented the seller. In fact, until 1988, when the first written agency disclosure was required in Texas, most licensees, clients, and customers gave very little thought to who represented whom. This agency disclosure requirement had the effect of raising the awareness of both the public and the licensees. Once they recognized that they were entitled to representation, more and more buyers began to actively seek brokers who were willing to offer advocacy to the purchaser. The growth in buyer representation in turn led to conflicting loyalties when brokers found themselves trying to offer agency to either side of the transaction (or both!); this, in turn, led to a very special and complex relationship involving dual representation. Thus, with the increased awareness of the dynamics of the agency relationship comes the necessity to first adequately identify the responsibilities agents assume when they agree to represent a single party to a real estate transaction. Brokers who represent only one side of the transaction are practicing single agency; that is, they only have one client. In this chapter, we will explore the agent's responsibility to the seller, also called exclusive seller agency, and identify how these responsibilities translate into our dealings with the buyer-customer. In Chapter 6, we will deal with a similar type of single agency known as exclusive buyer agency. The more complex relationship involving brokers who elect to provide representation to either side of the transaction, or both, will also be addressed in later chapters.

LEARNING OBJECTIVES *This chapter addresses the following:*

- Express and Implied Agreements
- Listing Agreements
  - Types of Listing Agreements
- Benefits of Seller Agency Relationships
  - Agency Benefits to Seller or Landlord
  - Benefits to Seller or Landlord's Agents
- Approaches to Representing Sellers
- Exclusive Seller Agency
  - In-House Sales
  - Cooperative Sales—Subagency
  - Exclusive Seller Agency in Practice
  - Advantages and Disadvantages of Exclusive Seller Agency
- Nonexclusive Seller Agency
- Disclosure Issues
  - Disclosures of Seller's Agent to Seller
  - Disclosures of Seller's Agent to Buyer

EXPRESS AND IMPLIED AGREEMENTS

The most common and easily recognized agency relationship in real estate is that between the seller (client) and the listing broker (agent). The relationship is usually evidenced by a written agreement called a listing agreement, typically an exclusive-right-to-sell listing. (This and other types of listing agreements are discussed later in this chapter.) Listing agreements establish the working agency relationship between the seller and the broker. Although the actual listing agreement is frequently presented and signed by an associate of the broker on the broker's behalf, the agency relationship and all the rights and obligations of the agreement fall to the broker. As shown in Chapter 2, these duties flow through the broker to all the associated licensees of the broker. Additionally, if other licensees not associated with the firm are permitted to represent the seller through the listing broker, the duties of the other licensees to the seller will be the same as those of the listing broker. This arrangement, although becoming much less common, is known as subagency. Listing agreements, as well as other agency agreements, may be either oral or in writing. TRELA § 1101.806 states that "a person may not maintain an action in this state to recover a commission for the sale or purchase of real estate unless the promise or agreement on which the action is based, or a memorandum, is in writing and signed by the party against whom the action is brought or by a person authorized by that party to sign the document."

In other words, properties may be listed orally, but if the seller refuses to pay an orally agreed-on commission, the broker cannot look to the courts to compel the seller to pay. An oral listing agreement and commission entitlement may, however, be enforced against third parties who attempt to tortuously (wrongfully) interfere with them (for example, a licensee from another firm who attempts to list a property during the term of an oral listing).

Neither a written contract nor an oral agreement to pay a fee is necessary to create an agency relationship with the seller. As discussed in Chapter 4, the words and conduct of the parties may create an agency relationship. A listing created in this manner is called an implied agency, and a broker may be surprised when a court finds an agency relationship when the broker intended none. This implied agency could be a result of a previous relationship with the principal. For example, a licensee has represented a buyer in acquiring a new home and then unofficially helps the principal sell another property. Under these circumstances, it is assumed that the licensee has a close working relationship with the former client that is likely to continue after the previous contract is fulfilled or has terminated. Buyers who have been clients of a broker thus may continue to be clients when they subsequently sell a property with the unofficial help of the broker, even though no written listing agreement has been signed.

Regardless of how the agency relationship originated, once created with the seller, the law imposes a number of fiduciary duties on the seller's agent, the most important one being that the agent must protect and promote the best interests of the seller. The interests of the seller must be placed above those of anyone else, including the agent's own interests. The seller's agent owes absolute allegiance to the seller.

■ LISTING AGREEMENTS

The listing agreement between the broker and the seller creates an express agency relationship—it is essentially a broker's employment contract. Typically, this agreement is a contract that establishes the rights and obligations of both principals to the agreement—the seller and the broker. Sellers give permission and authority to the broker to act as their agent and generally agree to pay compensation (a fee or commission) for the service the broker renders. The broker agrees to represent the sellers, market the property, and place the sellers' interests above all others. Compensation is usually conditioned on the broker producing a ready, willing, and able buyer at the price and terms stated in the listing agreement.

The parties to a listing contract are the broker and the seller. The listing contract is an agreement to market the property and to seek qualified buyers; it is not a contract to "sell" the property. Once a qualified buyer has submitted a contract that meets the price and terms stated in the listing contract, the broker has fulfilled any obligation. A seller who elects not to sell technically owes the broker the stated compensation. The buyer has no recourse if the seller decides to remove the property from the market after the buyer has presented an offer but before a contract of sale is signed. Remember: The only signed contract at this point is between the listing broker and the seller—no other parties (buyers or any other brokers involved) have the right to sue under the terms of the listing agreement because they do not have a signed contract with the seller.

■ **EXAMPLE** Broker James, Precision Realty, obtained a listing contract from Joyce to sell her home for $218,000 cash or with a conventional loan. James marketed the home, and three weeks after he listed the property, a full-price cash offer was submitted by a buyer with the resources to fulfill the terms of the offer. James met with Joyce later that evening and presented the offer. After discussing the terms and projected proceeds, it appeared that Joyce was prepared to sign the offer; however, at the last moment she had a change of heart and decided not to sell the property after all.

■ **QUESTIONS** 1. Is the broker entitled to a fee or commission? 2. If this contract offer was written by another agency, could the other broker sue Joyce? 3. What, if any, legal recourse might the buyer have against Joyce?

■ **DISCUSSION** Under the terms of most listing contracts, the broker is entitled to a fee or commission once a ready, willing, and able buyer makes an offer that meets the price and terms stated in the listing contract. If the listing contract is in writing, the broker can seek the compensation and even go so far as to sue the seller, if necessary. If the contract is taken orally, the broker has no recourse.

■ **DISCUSSION** If the purchase contract were written by another agency, Precision Realty would have the same right to seek compensation as it would if the sale had been in-house. However, the broker from the other firm would have no recourse because the listing contract was between Precision Realty and the seller. The decision to pursue the seller for compensation is one that can be made only by the listing broker.

Although the listing broker may have the right to bring legal action against the seller, this may not prove to be the best solution for the broker. The time, energy, expense, and possible damage to the broker's reputation may far outweigh the potential benefits.

Because the offer to purchase was not signed, the buyer has little recourse other than to pursue the seller on the basis of fraudulent advertising. While sellers can always remove their properties from the market, questions might be raised if they later sell the property to someone else under terms similar to the first contract offer. Of particular concern would be issues of discrimination, which could arise (under the Civil Rights Act) if it could be shown that the seller's reason for rejecting the first offer was based on the buyer's being a member of a protected class.

Types of Listing Agreements

The three generally recognized types of listing agreements that brokers and sellers can enter into are

- exclusive-right-to-sell listing,
- exclusive-agency listing, and
- open listing.

The type of listing the broker and the seller select depends on the circumstances surrounding the seller's motivation to sell and the broker's policies regarding listings.

The exclusive-right-to-sell listing offers the broker the greatest amount of security and, in many cases, offers the seller the greatest amount of service. Under this agreement, the broker is entitled to the stated fee or commission no matter who sells the property—even if it is the seller. The seller also benefits by offering the maximum protection to the broker because the broker then can afford to invest time and money in promoting the property with the assurance of payment regardless of who finds the buyer. It can be very costly for a broker to market listings and to operate a general brokerage business.

Most brokers avoid listings that do not have a reasonable chance to sell or that do not fairly compensate the broker for expenses. The brokerage business is just like any other business; it must pay for operations and give its investors a fair return on their money. The exclusive-right-to-sell listing gives the broker a greater opportunity to realize those goals. Brokers holding an exclusive-right-to-sell listing usually will agree to let other brokers negotiate with the seller through them. The listing broker typically agrees to pay the other broker some part or percentage of the commission paid by the seller. When brokers agree to cooperate in this manner, sellers gain wider exposure for their properties. Figure 5.1 depicts the lines of communication and negotiation in an exclusive-right-to-sell listing, and Figure 5.2 is an example of the exclusive-right-to-sell listing agreement made available by the Texas Association of REALTORS® exclusively for use by its members.

Notice that it states "USE OF THIS FORM BY PERSONS WHO ARE NOT MEMBERS OF THE TEXAS ASSOCIATION OF REALTORS® IS NOT AUTHORIZED." Forms establishing contractual business relationships between brokers and clients are not provided by TREC for licensee use. The TAR form is provided here, however, as an example of the types of contractual provisions that should be addressed when establishing an agency relationship with the seller of a residential property. Examples of provisions that should be routinely addressed in a listing contract include the following:

- Parties to the contract (Paragraph 1)
- Legal description of the property (Paragraph 2)
- Initial listing price of the property (Paragraph 3)
- The term of the contract (beginning and ending date) (Paragraph 4)

FIGURE 5.1

Lines of Communication with an Exclusive-Right-to-Sell Listing

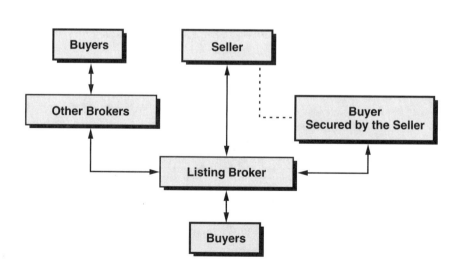

- Broker's compensation (Paragraph 5)
  — How is it calculated?
  — When is it earned?
  — When is it payable?
  — Who pays it?
  — Are there miscellaneous fees?
  — Is there a protection period?
- Listing services the broker will provide (Paragraph 6)
  — Will the broker place the listing in the MLS?
- Access to the property (Paragraph 7)
  — Are there restrictions on the access times?
  — Are lockboxes permitted?
- Cooperation/fees involving other brokers (Paragraph 8)
  — Will the seller permit cooperation with other brokers?
  — Will the seller permit licensees who are non-members of the Multiple Listing Service (MLS) to show the property?
  — Will the seller permit both cooperating buyers' agents as well as sub-agents to show the property?
- Intermediary (Paragraph 9)
  — On an in-house transaction will the seller permit the broker to also represent the buyer and if so, how does that impact on the commission earned?
  — Can the seller still receive advice and opinion?

An exclusive-agency listing allows sellers to reserve the right to sell a property themselves without the obligation to pay a commission or fee, if successful. Under an exclusive-agency listing, a seller can do this and still have the property listed by a broker. If, however, another brokerage firm secures a buyer, it must present the contract through the listing brokerage; it cannot go directly to the seller. Hence the term *exclusive agency*—indicating that another agency cannot work directly with the seller.

As with the exclusive-right-to-sell listing, listing brokers may allow other brokers to negotiate through them. Thus, if any broker finds a buyer, the listing broker is entitled to a fee that will be shared with the selling broker. Sellers should be made aware that with this type of listing, the broker may not be able to justify the same level of advertising and promotion because the sellers still may secure their own buyer. In that case, the broker would not be entitled to a commission. Figure 5.3 illustrates the exclusive-agency listing. The TAR listing agreement shown in Figure 5.2 can be easily amended to an exclusive agency agreement by adding the "Exclusive Agency Addendum" (TAR 1403 not provided).

Open listings generally entitle brokers to compensation only if they are the procuring cause (the person who secures the offer from the buyer) of the sale or lease of the property. The open listing does not give any broker the exclusive right to offer the property for sale; rather, it allows the owner of the property to give one or more brokers the same opportunity simultaneously, but only the broker who produces an accepted contract is compensated. The open listing also allows the seller to continue to seek potential buyers and to negotiate independently of the broker. If successful, the seller does not owe any broker a commission.

FIGURE 5.2

Example of Exclusive-Right-to-Sell Listing Agreement

RESIDENTIAL REAL ESTATE LISTING AGREEMENT
EXCLUSIVE RIGHT TO SELL

USE OF THIS FORM BY PERSONS WHO ARE NOT MEMBERS OF THE TEXAS ASSOCIATION OF REALTORS® IS NOT AUTHORIZED.
©Texas Association of REALTORS®, Inc. 2012

1. **PARTIES:** The parties to this agreement (this Listing) are:

   Seller: _____

   Address: _____
   City, State, Zip: _____
   Phone: _____ Fax: _____
   E-Mail: _____

   Broker: _____

   Address: _____
   City, State, Zip: _____
   Phone: _____ Fax: _____
   E-Mail: _____

   Seller appoints Broker as Seller's sole and exclusive real estate agent and grants to Broker the exclusive right to sell the Property.

2. **PROPERTY:** "Property" means the land, improvements, and accessories described below, except for any described exclusions.

   A. <u>Land</u>: Lot_____, Block_____, _____
   _____ Addition, City of_____,
   in _____ County, Texas known as _____
   _____ (address/zip code),
   or as described on attached exhibit. *(If Property is a condominium, attach Condominium Addendum.)*

   B. <u>Improvements</u>: The house, garage and all other fixtures and improvements attached to the above-described real property, including without limitation, the following **permanently installed and built-in items,** if any: all equipment and appliances, valances, screens, shutters, awnings, wall-to-wall carpeting, mirrors, ceiling fans, attic fans, mail boxes, television antennas and satellite dish system and equipment, mounts and brackets for televisions and speakers, heating and air-conditioning units, security and fire detection equipment, wiring, plumbing and lighting fixtures, chandeliers, water softener system, kitchen equipment, garage door openers, cleaning equipment, shrubbery, landscaping, outdoor cooking equipment, and all other property owned by Seller and attached to the above-described real property.

   C. <u>Accessories</u>: The following described related accessories, if any: window air conditioning units, stove, fireplace screens, curtains and rods, blinds, window shades, draperies and rods, door keys, mailbox keys, above-ground pool, swimming pool equipment and maintenance accessories, artificial fireplace logs, and controls for: (i) satellite dish systems, (ii) garage doors, (iii) entry gates, and (iv) other improvements and accessories.

   D. <u>Exclusions</u>: The following improvements and accessories will be retained by Seller and must be removed prior to delivery of possession: _____
   _____.

(TAR-1101) 03-02-12   Initialed for Identification by Broker/Associate _____ and Seller _____, _____

FIGURE 5.2

Example of Exclusive-Right-to-Sell Listing Agreement (continued)

Residential Listing concerning_____

  E. <u>Owners' Association</u>: The property ❏ is ❏ is not subject to mandatory membership in a property owners' association.

3. **LISTING PRICE:** Seller instructs Broker to market the Property at the following price: $_____ (Listing Price). Seller agrees to sell the Property for the Listing Price or any other price acceptable to Seller. Seller will pay all typical closing costs charged to sellers of residential real estate in Texas (seller's typical closing costs are those set forth in the residential contract forms promulgated by the Texas Real Estate Commission).

4. **TERM:**

  A. This Listing begins on _____ and ends at 11:59 p.m. on _____.

  B. If Seller enters into a binding written contract to sell the Property before the date this Listing begins and the contract is binding on the date this Listing begins, this Listing will not commence and will be void.

5. **BROKER COMPENSATION:**

  A. When earned and payable, Seller will pay Broker:

  ❏ (1) _____% of the sales price.

  ❏ (2) _____.

  B. <u>Earned</u>: Broker's compensation is earned when any one of the following occurs during this Listing:
   (1) Seller sells, exchanges, options, agrees to sell, agrees to exchange, or agrees to option the Property to anyone at any price on any terms;
   (2) Broker individually or in cooperation with another broker procures a buyer ready, willing, and able to buy the Property at the Listing Price or at any other price acceptable to Seller; or
   (3) Seller breaches this Listing.

  C. <u>Payable</u>: Once earned, Broker's compensation is payable either during this Listing or after it ends at the earlier of:
   (1) the closing and funding of any sale or exchange of all or part of the Property;
   (2) Seller's refusal to sell the Property after Broker's compensation has been earned;
   (3) Seller's breach of this Listing; or
   (4) at such time as otherwise set forth in this Listing.

  Broker's compensation is <u>not</u> payable if a sale of the Property does not close or fund as a result of: (i) Seller's failure, without fault of Seller, to deliver to a buyer a deed or a title policy as required by the contract to sell; (ii) loss of ownership due to foreclosure or other legal proceeding; or (iii) Seller's failure to restore the Property, as a result of a casualty loss, to its previous condition by the closing date set forth in a contract for the sale of the Property.

  D. <u>Other Compensation</u>:

   (1) <u>Breach by Buyer Under a Contract</u>: If Seller collects earnest money, the sales price, or damages by suit, compromise, settlement, or otherwise from a buyer who breaches a contract for the sale of the Property entered into during this Listing, Seller will pay Broker, after deducting attorney's fees and collection expenses, an amount equal to the lesser of one-half of the amount collected after deductions or the amount of the Broker's Compensation stated in Paragraph 5A. Any amount paid under this Paragraph 5D(1) is in addition to any amount that Broker may be entitled to receive for subsequently selling the Property.

FIGURE 5.2

Example of Exclusive-Right-to-Sell Listing Agreement (continued)

Residential Listing concerning_____

    (2) <u>Service Providers</u>: If Broker refers Seller or a prospective buyer to a service provider (for example, mover, cable company, telecommunications provider, utility, or contractor) Broker may receive a fee from the service provider for the referral. Any referral fee Broker receives under this Paragraph 5D(2) is in addition to any other compensation Broker may receive under this Listing.

    (3) <u>Reimbursable Expenses</u>: _____
_____
_____.

  E. <u>Protection Period</u>:

    (1) "Protection period" means that time starting the day after this Listing ends and continuing for _____ days. "Sell" means any transfer of any interest in the Property whether by oral or written agreement or option.

    (2) Not later than 10 days after this Listing ends, Broker may send Seller written notice specifying the names of persons whose attention was called to the Property during this Listing. If Seller agrees to sell the Property during the protection period to a person named in the notice or to a relative of a person named in the notice, Seller will pay Broker, upon the closing of the sale, the amount Broker would have been entitled to receive if this Listing were still in effect.

    (3) This Paragraph 5E survives termination of this Listing. This Paragraph 5E will not apply if:
      (a) Seller agrees to sell the Property during the protection period;
      (b) the Property is exclusively listed with another broker who is a member of the Texas Association of REALTORS® at the time the sale is negotiated; and
      (c) Seller is obligated to pay the other broker a fee for the sale.

  F. <u>County</u>: All amounts payable to Broker are to be paid in cash in _____
_____ County, Texas.

  G. <u>Escrow Authorization</u>: Seller authorizes, and Broker may so instruct, any escrow or closing agent authorized to close a transaction for the purchase or acquisition of the Property to collect and disburse to Broker all amounts payable to Broker under this Listing.

6. LISTING SERVICES:

❑ A. Broker will file this Listing with one or more Multiple Listing Services (MLS) by the earlier of the time required by MLS rules or 5 days after the date this Listing begins. Seller authorizes Broker to submit information about this Listing and the sale of the Property to the MLS.

    <u>Notice</u>: MLS rules require Broker to accurately and timely submit all information the MLS requires for participation including sold data. Subscribers to the MLS may use the information for market evaluation or appraisal purposes. Subscribers are other brokers and other real estate professionals such as appraisers and may include the appraisal district. Any information filed with the MLS becomes the property of the MLS for all purposes. **Submission of information to MLS ensures that persons who use and benefit from the MLS also contribute information.**

❑ B. Seller instructs Broker not to file this Listing with one or more Multiple Listing Service (MLS) until ___ days after the date this Listing begins for the following purpose(s): _____
_____.
(NOTE: Do not check if prohibited by Multiple Listing Service(s).)

❑ C. Broker will not file this Listing with a Multiple Listing Service (MLS) or any other listing service.

(TAR-1101) 03-02-12   Initialed for Identification by Broker/Associate_____ and Seller_____, _____

FIGURE 5.2

Example of Exclusive-Right-to-Sell Listing Agreement (continued)

Residential Listing concerning_____

7. **ACCESS TO THE PROPERTY:**

   A. <u>Authorizing Access</u>: Authorizing access to the Property means giving permission to another person to enter the Property, disclosing to the other person any security codes necessary to enter the Property, and lending a key to the other person to enter the Property, directly or through a keybox. To facilitate the showing and sale of the Property, Seller instructs Broker to:
   (1) access the Property at reasonable times;
   (2) authorize other brokers, their associates, inspectors, appraisers, and contractors to access the Property at reasonable times; and
   (3) duplicate keys to facilitate convenient and efficient showings of the Property.

   B. <u>Scheduling Companies</u>: Broker may engage the following companies to schedule appointments and to authorize others to access the Property: _____.

   C. <u>Keybox</u>: **A keybox is a locked container placed on the Property that holds a key to the Property. A keybox makes it more convenient for brokers, their associates, inspectors, appraisers, and contractors to show, inspect, or repair the Property. The keybox is opened by a special combination, key, or programmed device so that authorized persons may enter the Property, even in Seller's absence. Using a keybox will probably increase the number of showings, but involves risks (for example, unauthorized entry, theft, property damage, or personal injury). Neither the Association of REALTORS® nor MLS requires the use of a keybox.**

   (1) Broker ❑ is ❑ is not authorized to place a keybox on the Property.

   (2) If a tenant occupies the Property at any time during this Listing, Seller will furnish Broker a written statement (for example, TAR No. 1411), signed by all tenants, authorizing the use of a keybox or Broker may remove the keybox from the Property.

   D. <u>Liability and Indemnification</u>: When authorizing access to the Property, Broker, other brokers, their associates, any keybox provider, or any scheduling company are not responsible for personal injury or property loss to Seller or any other person. Seller assumes all risk of any loss, damage, or injury. **Except for a loss caused by Broker, Seller will indemnify and hold Broker harmless from any claim for personal injury, property damage, or other loss.**

8. **COOPERATION WITH OTHER BROKERS:** Broker will allow other brokers to show the Property to prospective buyers. Broker will offer to pay the other broker a fee as described below if the other broker procures a buyer that purchases the Property.

   A. <u>MLS Participants</u>: If the other broker is a participant in the MLS in which this Listing is filed, Broker will offer to pay the other broker:
   (1) if the other broker represents the buyer: _____% of the sales price or $_____; and
   (2) if the other broker is a subagent: _____% of the sales price or $_____.

   B. <u>Non-MLS Brokers</u>: If the other broker is not a participant in the MLS in which this Listing is filed, Broker will offer to pay the other broker:
   (1) if the other broker represents the buyer: _____% of the sales price or $_____; and
   (2) if the other broker is a subagent: _____% of the sales price or $_____.

9. **INTERMEDIARY:** *(Check A or B only.)*

   ❑ A. <u>Intermediary Status</u>: Broker may show the Property to interested prospective buyers who Broker represents. If a prospective buyer who Broker represents offers to buy the Property, Seller authorizes

FIGURE 5.2

Example of Exclusive-Right-to-Sell Listing Agreement (continued)

Residential Listing concerning _____

Broker to act as an intermediary and Broker will notify Seller that Broker will service the parties in accordance with one of the following alternatives.

(1) If a prospective buyer who Broker represents is serviced by an associate other than the associate servicing Seller under this Listing, Broker may notify Seller that Broker will: (a) appoint the associate then servicing Seller to communicate with, carry out instructions of, and provide opinions and advice during negotiations to Seller; and (b) appoint the associate then servicing the prospective buyer to the prospective buyer for the same purpose.

(2) If a prospective buyer who Broker represents is serviced by the same associate who is servicing Seller, Broker may notify Seller that Broker will: (a) appoint another associate to communicate with, carry out instructions of, and provide opinions and advice during negotiations to the prospective buyer; and (b) appoint the associate servicing the Seller under this Listing to the Seller for the same purpose.

(3) Broker may notify Seller that Broker will make no appointments as described under this Paragraph 9A and, in such an event, the associate servicing the parties will act solely as Broker's intermediary representative, who may facilitate the transaction but will not render opinions or advice during negotiations to either party.

☐ B. <u>No Intermediary Status</u>: Seller agrees that Broker will not show the Property to prospective buyers who Broker represents.

Notice: If Broker acts as an intermediary under Paragraph 9A, Broker and Broker's associates:
- may not disclose to the prospective buyer that Seller will accept a price less than the asking price unless otherwise instructed in a separate writing by Seller;
- may not disclose to Seller that the prospective buyer will pay a price greater than the price submitted in a written offer to Seller unless otherwise instructed in a separate writing by the prospective buyer;
- may not disclose any confidential information or any information Seller or the prospective buyer specifically instructs Broker in writing not to disclose unless otherwise instructed in a separate writing by the respective party or required to disclose the information by the Real Estate License Act or a court order or if the information materially relates to the condition of the property;
- may not treat a party to the transaction dishonestly; and
- may not violate the Real Estate License Act.

10. **CONFIDENTIAL INFORMATION:** During this Listing or after it ends, Broker may not knowingly disclose information obtained in confidence from Seller except as authorized by Seller or required by law. Broker may not disclose to Seller any confidential information regarding any other person Broker represents or previously represented except as required by law.

11. **BROKER'S AUTHORITY:**

A. Broker will use reasonable efforts and act diligently to market the Property for sale, procure a buyer, and negotiate the sale of the Property.

B. Broker is authorized to display this Listing on the Internet without limitation unless one of the following is checked:

☐ (1) Seller does not want this Listing to be displayed on the Internet.
☐ (2) Seller does not want the address of the Property to be displayed on the Internet.

Notice: Seller understands and acknowledges that, if box 11B(1) is selected, consumers who

FIGURE 5.2

Example of Exclusive-Right-to-Sell Listing Agreement (continued)

Residential Listing concerning_____

      conduct searches for listings on the Internet will not see information about this Listing in response to their search.

  C. Broker is authorized to market the Property with the following financing options:
- ❑ (1) Conventional
- ❑ (2) VA
- ❑ (3) FHA
- ❑ (4) Cash
- ❑ (5) Texas Veterans Land Program
- ❑ (6) Owner Financing
- ❑ (7) Other

  D. In addition to other authority granted by this Listing, Broker may:
    (1) advertise the Property by means and methods as Broker determines, including but not limited to creating and placing advertisements with interior and exterior photographic and audio-visual images of the Property and related information in any media and the Internet;
    (2) place a "For Sale" sign on the Property and remove all other signs offering the Property for sale or lease;
    (3) furnish comparative marketing and sales information about other properties to prospective buyers;
    (4) disseminate information about the Property to other brokers and to prospective buyers, including applicable disclosures or notices that Seller is required to make under law or a contract;
    (5) obtain information from any holder of a note secured by a lien on the Property;
    (6) accept and deposit earnest money in trust in accordance with a contract for the sale of the Property;
    (7) disclose the sales price and terms of sale to other brokers, appraisers, or other real estate professionals;
    (8) in response to inquiries from prospective buyers and other brokers, disclose whether the Seller is considering more than one offer, provided that Broker will not disclose the terms of any competing offer unless specifically instructed by Seller;
    (9) advertise, during or after this Listing ends, that Broker "sold" the Property; and
    (10) place information about this Listing, the Property, and a transaction for the Property on an electronic transaction platform (typically an Internet-based system where professionals related to the transaction such as title companies, lenders, and others may receive, view, and input information).

  E. Broker is not authorized to execute any document in the name of or on behalf of Seller concerning the Property.

12. SELLER'S REPRESENTATIONS: Except as provided by Paragraph 15, Seller represents that:
  A. Seller has fee simple title to and peaceable possession of the Property and all its improvements and fixtures, unless rented, and the legal capacity to convey the Property;
  B. Seller is not bound by a listing agreement with another broker for the sale, exchange, or lease of the Property that is or will be in effect during this Listing;
  C. any pool or spa and any required enclosures, fences, gates, and latches comply with all applicable laws and ordinances;
  D. no person or entity has any right to purchase, lease, or acquire the Property by an option, right of refusal, or other agreement;
  E. Seller is current and not delinquent on all loans and all other financial obligations related to the Property, including but not limited to mortgages, home equity loans, home improvement loans, homeowner association fees, and taxes, except_____;
  F. Seller is not aware of any liens or other encumbrances against the Property, except_____;
  G. the Property is not subject to the jurisdiction of any court;
  H. all information relating to the Property Seller provides to Broker is true and correct to the best of Seller's knowledge; and

FIGURE 5.2

Example of Exclusive-Right-to-Sell Listing Agreement (continued)

Residential Listing concerning_____

    I. the name of any employer, relocation company, or other entity that provides benefits to Seller when selling the Property is: _____.

13. SELLER'S ADDITIONAL PROMISES: Seller agrees to:
    A. cooperate with Broker to facilitate the showing, marketing, and sale of the Property;
    B. not rent or lease the Property during this Listing without Broker's prior written approval;
    C. not negotiate with any prospective buyer who may contact Seller directly, but refer all prospective buyers to Broker;
    D. not enter into a listing agreement with another broker for the sale, exchange, lease, or management of the Property to become effective during this Listing without Broker's prior written approval;
    E. maintain any pool and all required enclosures in compliance with all applicable laws and ordinances;
    F. provide Broker with copies of any leases or rental agreements pertaining to the Property and advise Broker of tenants moving in or out of the Property;
    G. complete any disclosures or notices required by law or a contract to sell the Property; and
    H. amend any applicable notices and disclosures if any material change occurs during this Listing.

14. LIMITATION OF LIABILITY:

    A. If the Property is or becomes vacant during this Listing, Seller must notify Seller's casualty insurance company and request a "vacancy clause" to cover the Property. Broker is not responsible for the security of the Property nor for inspecting the Property on any periodic basis.

    B. **Broker is not responsible or liable in any manner for personal injury to any person or for loss or damage to any person's real or personal property resulting from any act or omission not caused by Broker's negligence, including but not limited to injuries or damages caused by:**
        (1) other brokers, their associates, inspectors, appraisers, and contractors who are authorized to access the Property;
        (2) other brokers or their associates who may have information about the Property on their websites;
        (3) acts of third parties (for example, vandalism or theft);
        (4) freezing water pipes;
        (5) a dangerous condition on the Property;
        (6) the Property's non-compliance with any law or ordinance; or
        (7) Seller, negligently or otherwise.

    C. Seller agrees to protect, defend, indemnify, and hold Broker harmless from any damage, costs, attorney's fees, and expenses that:
        (1) are caused by Seller, negligently or otherwise;
        (2) arise from Seller's failure to disclose any material or relevant information about the Property; or
        (3) are caused by Seller giving incorrect information to any person.

15. SPECIAL PROVISIONS:

(TAR-1101) 03-02-12   Initialed for Identification by Broker/Associate_____ and Seller_____, _____

FIGURE 5.2

Example of Exclusive-Right-to-Sell Listing Agreement (continued)

Residential Listing concerning_____

16. **DEFAULT:** If Seller breaches this Listing, Seller is in default and will be liable to Broker for the amount of the Broker's compensation specified in Paragraph 5A and any other compensation Broker is entitled to receive under this Listing. If a sales price is not determinable in the event of an exchange or breach of this Listing, the Listing Price will be the sales price for purposes of computing compensation. If Broker breaches this Listing, Broker is in default and Seller may exercise any remedy at law.

17. **MEDIATION:** The parties agree to negotiate in good faith in an effort to resolve any dispute related to this Listing that may arise between the parties. If the dispute cannot be resolved by negotiation, the dispute will be submitted to mediation. The parties to the dispute will choose a mutually acceptable mediator and will share the cost of mediation equally.

18. **ATTORNEY'S FEES:** If Seller or Broker is a prevailing party in any legal proceeding brought as a result of a dispute under this Listing or any transaction related to or contemplated by this Listing, such party will be entitled to recover from the non-prevailing party all costs of such proceeding and reasonable attorney's fees.

19. **ADDENDA AND OTHER DOCUMENTS:** Addenda that are part of this Listing and other documents that Seller may need to provide are:
    - [X] A. Information About Brokerage Services;
    - [ ] B. Seller Disclosure Notice (§5.008, Texas Property Code);
    - [ ] C. Seller's Disclosure of Information on Lead-Based Paint and Lead-Based Paint Hazards (required if Property was built before 1978);
    - [ ] D. Residential Real Property Affidavit (T-47 Affidavit; related to existing survey);
    - [ ] E. MUD, Water District, or Statutory Tax District Disclosure Notice (Chapter 49, Texas Water Code);
    - [ ] F. Request for Information from an Owners' Association;
    - [ ] G. Request for Mortgage Information;
    - [ ] H. Information about Mineral Clauses in Contract Forms;
    - [ ] I. Information about On-Site Sewer Facility;
    - [ ] J. Information about Property Insurance for a Buyer or Seller;
    - [ ] K. Information about Special Flood Hazard Areas;
    - [ ] L. Condominium Addendum to Listing;
    - [ ] M. Keybox Authorization by Tenant;
    - [ ] N. Seller's Authorization to Release and Advertise Certain Information; and
    - [ ] O. _____.

20. **AGREEMENT OF PARTIES:**

    A. <u>Entire Agreement</u>: This Listing is the entire agreement of the parties and may not be changed except by written agreement.

    B. <u>Assignability</u>: Neither party may assign this Listing without the written consent of the other party.

    C. <u>Binding Effect</u>: Seller's obligation to pay Broker earned compensation is binding upon Seller and Seller's heirs, administrators, executors, successors, and permitted assignees.

    D. <u>Joint and Several</u>: All Sellers executing this Listing are jointly and severally liable for the performance of all its terms.

    E. <u>Governing Law</u>: Texas law governs the interpretation, validity, performance, and enforcement of this Listing.

    F. <u>Severability</u>: If a court finds any clause in this Listing invalid or unenforceable, the remainder of this Listing will not be affected and all other provisions of this Listing will remain valid and enforceable.

(TAR-1101) 03-02-12   Initialed for Identification by Broker/Associate_____ and Seller_____, _____   Page 8 of 9

FIGURE 5.2

Example of Exclusive-Right-to-Sell Listing Agreement (continued)

Residential Listing concerning_____

G. Notices: Notices between the parties must be in writing and are effective when sent to the receiving party's address, fax, or e-mail address specified in Paragraph 1.

21. ADDITIONAL NOTICES:

A. Broker's compensation or the sharing of compensation between brokers is not fixed, controlled, recommended, suggested, or maintained by the Association of REALTORS®, MLS, or any listing service.

B. Fair housing laws require the Property to be shown and made available to all persons without regard to race, color, religion, national origin, sex, disability, or familial status. Local ordinances may provide for additional protected classes (for example, creed, status as a student, marital status, sexual orientation, or age).

C. Broker advises Seller to contact any mortgage lender or other lien holder to obtain information regarding payoff amounts for any existing mortgages or liens on the Property.

D. Broker advises Seller to review the information Broker submits to an MLS or other listing service.

E. Broker advises Seller to remove or secure jewelry, prescription drugs, other valuables, firearms and any other weapons.

F. Statutes or ordinances may regulate certain items on the Property (for example, swimming pools and septic systems). Non-compliance with the statutes or ordinances may delay a transaction and may result in fines, penalties, and liability to Seller.

G. If the Property was built before 1978, Federal law requires the Seller to: (1) provide the buyer with the federally approved pamphlet on lead poisoning prevention; (2) disclose the presence of any known lead-based paint or lead-based paint hazards in the Property; (3) deliver all records and reports to the buyer related to such paint or hazards; and (4) provide the buyer a period up to 10 days to have the Property inspected for such paint or hazards.

H. Broker cannot give legal advice. READ THIS LISTING CAREFULLY. If you do not understand the effect of this Listing, consult an attorney BEFORE signing.

_____   _____
Broker's Printed Name   License No.   Seller   Date

By:_____   _____
   Broker's Associate's Signature   Date   Seller   Date

_____
Broker's Associate's Printed Name

(TAR-1101) 03-02-12   Initialed for Identification by Broker/Associate_____ and Seller_____, _____

FIGURE 5.3

Lines of Communication and Negotiation with Exclusive-Agency Listing

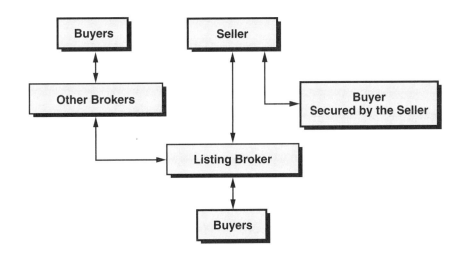

A listing generally is considered open listing unless its terms clearly indicate that both parties intend a more exclusive agreement.

Depending on the terms of a specific open listing, the broker may be entitled to a commission if the broker produces an offer from a buyer that meets or exceeds the exact terms of the listing and the owner refuses to sell. The buyer, however, has no rights under the broker's listing agreement to force the owner to sell the property, even if the buyer's offer meets or exceeds the terms of the listing agreement.

One disadvantage of the open listing is that a broker and the broker's associates may expend a great deal of energy and time advertising and showing a property, only to have another broker provide the actual buyer and receive the commission. For this reason, most brokers generally will not advertise open listings; however, they will show the properties to buyers in the course of showing other properties.

Most multiple listing service (MLS) systems refuse to take open listings because of the potential for disputes over procuring cause and commission entitlements. The only broker entitled to a commission under an open listing agreement is the one who procures the buyer. Any broker procuring a buyer for the seller who does not have an open listing agreement with that seller is merely a volunteer, as far as the seller is concerned.

While open listings are not common in residential sales, they are common in the sale of commercial properties and farm and ranch properties. Figure 5.4 shows the lines of communication and negotiation in an open listing.

Net listings relate to the way the broker is paid rather than to the type of agency agreement. Any of the agency agreements mentioned previously could be used in a net listing. With these types of listings, sellers determine the amount of money they will accept after the costs of sale; the broker receives the remainder as a commission.

FIGURE 5.4

Lines of Communication and Negotiation in an Open Listing

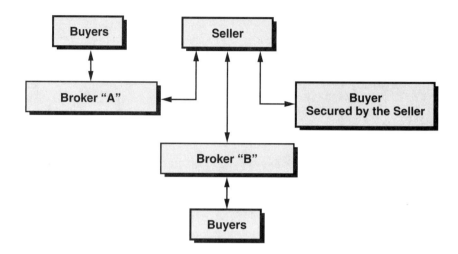

This type of listing may present some legal and ethical problems, particularly with an inexperienced seller. Net listings are not illegal in Texas. However, two specific rules of the commission are especially designed to curb potential abuse:

> 22 TAC § 535.16(b): A "net listing" is a listing agreement in which the broker's commission is the difference ("net") between the sales proceeds and an amount desired by the owner of the real property. A broker may not take net listings unless the principal requires a net listing and the principal appears to be familiar with current market values of real property. The use of a net listing places an upper limit on the principal's expectancy and places the broker's interest above the principal's interest with reference to obtaining the best possible price. If a net listing is used, the listing agreement must assure the principal of not less than the principal's desired price and to limit the broker to a specified maximum commission.
>
> 22 TAC § 535.16(c): A real estate licensee is obligated to provide a broker price opinion or comparative market analysis on a property when negotiating a listing or offering to purchase the property for the licensee's own account as a result of contact made while acting as a real estate agent.

For many years, the Texas Real Estate Commission (TREC) has warned licensees that TREC officially discourages taking net listings because of their possible manipulation and harm to the public, which TREC is designed to protect. In some cases, however, it is the broker rather than the seller who ends up with less money because of a net listing.

■ **EXAMPLE** Susan took a net listing on Gertrude's property. The asking price was $330,000, the closing costs were expected to be $15,000, and Gertrude had a loan balance of $269,000. The net listing agreement called for Gertrude to receive $23,000 in cash at closing.

After marketing the property for six months, Gertrude accepted an offer of $318,000 for her property. Susan received $11,000 as her brokerage fee because all costs of the sale ($269,000 note plus $15,000 closing costs) and the seller's agreed-on net ($23,000) were deducted before Susan's fee could be calculated. If Susan and Gertrude had agreed on the 5.5 percent commission her firm had established as its commission fee, she would have earned $17,490.

Most would agree that the broker in the preceding example should have been more careful to safeguard her position in the transaction. However, because a broker is considered to have the expertise to conduct business in a manner consistent with the desired outcomes, this transaction may have been one that met her objectives.

The situation that causes the greatest concern is one in which the broker earns an unusually large commission relative to the property being sold. The question in these cases is whether the broker took unfair advantage of a naive seller who was unaware of the real value of the property. Such actions by the broker would be regarded as clear examples of breaching the fiduciary duties owed to the client by the broker. The following example illustrates the problem that concerns most state regulators.

■ **EXAMPLE** Phillip, the broker for Action Real Estate, has been called by Elvin and Elma Jones to list their property. The Joneses have lived in their present home for 60 years and have decided to move to California to be close to their grandchildren. During the listing presentation the Joneses tell Phillip that they would like to receive $420,000 cash for their home, and if he can guarantee them that amount, they will be absolutely delighted with the sale. In fact, they are quite willing for Phillip to keep whatever amount he can obtain over the $420,000, plus closing costs and repairs. Phillip attempts to tell the Joneses that he believes that the home will sell for at least $490,000, but the Joneses are not impressed and tell him, "Just get us $420,000 to take to California and we will be very happy." The Joneses sign the listing agreement. The home subsequently sells for $495,000. At closing, the Joneses receive their $420,000, the closing costs and repairs cost $22,000, and Phillip receives $53,000! One week later, the grandchildren call and threaten to bring a lawsuit against Action Real Estate for fraud.

■ **QUESTIONS** 1. How could Action Real Estate have avoided this situation? 2. Could Phillip refuse to take the listing for Action Real Estate?

■ **DISCUSSION** This example appears to be a gross exaggeration; unfortunately, however, there have been many such situations. Action Real Estate could have avoided this problem by insisting on a percentage commission, especially because it was obvious that there was an enormous disparity between what the sellers desired to net and the potential net profit.

Action Real Estate should make sure that it has a clearly written policy regarding net listings that carefully follows TREC rules. At minimum, the broker should be notified by the associate that the sellers desire a net listing so that the final decision can be made by the broker, not the associate. If the sellers continue to insist on the net listing, the broker may refuse to enter into the agreement (knowing that a potential lawsuit is almost guaranteed) or give full disclosures that are signed by the sellers. The broker may suggest that family members enter into the discussion, although many sellers might reject this proposal, believing that it would be an unwelcome intrusion.

A one-time-showing agreement allows the terms of the agreement to apply to a specific buyer only. This frequently is used in situations where the seller is offering the property for sale by owner (FSBO) but is agreeable to allowing a licensee to show the property to a single potential buyer. If an acceptable contract of sale is entered into between that buyer and the seller, the broker will receive a commission according to the terms of the agreement.

It is important that the relationship between the seller and the agent, as well as the relationship between the buyer and the agent, be fully understood and disclosed. For example, if the licensee has no expressed oral or written agreement to represent the buyer, and FSBOs routinely represent themselves, then the licensee may be left without a clearly established agency role in the transaction. Numerous court cases have resulted from misunderstandings of who represented whom in these situations. Licensees are frequently unaware that their obligation to the seller under a one-time-showing agreement may be the same as under any other agency agreement. A license may be suspended or revoked if the licensee fails to make clear to all parties who they represent (TRELA § 1101.652(b)(7)).

■ BENEFITS OF SELLER AGENCY RELATIONSHIPS

Agency Benefits to Seller or Landlord

The following are some of the benefits to sellers and landlords who are represented by agents instead of representing themselves in a sale or leasing transaction.

Reaching buyers through broad marketing. Reaching buyers through marketing efforts has long been one of the most valuable services that real estate professionals have offered sellers. Sellers generally do not have the expertise or the funds to advertise effectively. When a broker has numerous agency contracts with sellers, advertising can be combined to give each seller's property the greatest possible exposure to the market. Brokers who are members of the MLS also market to other real estate professionals in their areas through this medium. The Internet has become a powerful means for brokers to advertise their listings. Many licensees, as well as professional real estate organizations, have begun to develop Web sites that provide valuable new conduits for advertising. Although several Internet listing services are available, the National Association of REALTORS® (NAR) site at *www.realtor.com* has received considerable attention from real estate professionals and the public since it began posting listings from local boards of REALTORS® from around the country.

Receiving advice and opinions that inform the seller or landlord. Giving advice and opinions is another of the basic services that an agent offers to the seller. Licensees are considered the "experts" in the field of real estate, and sellers and landlords are anxious to receive information about all aspects of listing and selling or leasing their properties. The information that licensees provide allows sellers to make informed decisions about their transactions. Licensees have an obligation to be knowledgeable about market conditions, financing conditions for buyers, rental information for tenants, and all other aspects of the real estate market that affect their clients.

Assistance in contract negotiations. Assistance in contract negotiations for the seller-landlord also represents another key benefit to the seller in seller representation. Sellers' agents may be able to greatly assist sellers during negotiations by giving helpful advice relating to pricing, favorable financing options, counteroffers, and other terms and conditions of a sale. Many sellers are unprepared for the many details of contract negotiations and must rely on their agents for such assistance.

Confidentiality. When agents represent the seller, they are obligated to keep confidential the negotiating position of the seller-landlord and all other information that might compromise the owner's interests—except those aspects that must legally be disclosed, such as property or title condition. If the owners are selling or renting the property themselves, and the licensee has obtained information in a manner that was not confidential, that licensee is under no obligation to withhold the information from a prospective buyer-tenant. In fact, if the buyer-tenant is a client, that licensee has an affirmative duty to disclose all information that might be relevant in the client's decision to purchase or lease.

Benefits to Seller or Landlord's Agents

The seller-landlord's agent can expect certain benefits from a seller-landlord agency that would not be available to them when owners represent themselves.

Greater understanding of the circumstances of the sale or lease. A licensee who is attempting to locate property for a buyer-customer will often show owner-listed properties. Without an understanding of the circumstance of the sale or the lease, the licensee may lose the potential sale or lease due to a lack of important information that would aid in facilitating the transaction.

Incentive to market the property. With an exclusive-right-to-sell, an exclusive-right-to-lease, or an exclusive-agency agreement, the agent will feel more comfortable marketing the property because there is a reasonable expectation that the property will sell or be leased and a commission will follow. Without some expectation of a return, as perhaps with an open listing, an agent may find it necessary to reserve scarce advertising dollars for other more promising opportunities. Sellers should be made aware of these limitations when deciding on the type of listing agreement they are entering.

No conflict of loyalties. A seller-landlord's agent will feel free to be an advocate for the seller-landlord. There should be no conflict of interest when showing buyer-customers because the agent's loyalty is strictly to the owner. The agent must always be fair and honest with the buyer, however; the owner's interests will be the primary focus of the agent during negotiations.

Limited liability for the acts of the buyer's broker. When buyers employ their own agent, the owner's agent is not responsible for the actions of that agent. This can be particularly important when a buyer's agent gives misinformation or makes a misstatement of a material fact without the knowledge of the listing agent. Texas law gives some protection from the acts of other brokers and their agents; however, when buyers employ their own agent, there may be a more clearly defined separation of liability.

APPROACHES TO REPRESENTING SELLERS

Brokers have several options when deciding on company policy regarding seller agency:

- *Exclusive seller representation*, in which brokers and associates represent sellers only, whether they are showing properties listed by their own companies (in-house sales) or properties listed by other brokers (cooperative sales)
- *Nonexclusive seller representation*, in which brokers and their associates represent sellers on all in-house transactions but may represent buyers when selling the listings of other brokers (discussed in detail in Chapter 8)
- *Subagency*, which may involve permitting brokers and associates from other firms to represent a listing broker's sellers through their firms or permitting a broker's associates to represent sellers listed by other firms through those listing brokers
- *Intermediary agency*, in which the broker may act as an agent of both buyer and seller but with reduced representation to both while negotiating a transaction between the parties (Chapter 7).

EXCLUSIVE SELLER AGENCY

Some real estate brokerage firms represent only sellers. In this situation, the seller is always the client and the buyer is always the customer. Until the increased acceptance of buyer agency, exclusive seller agency was the traditional and predominant type of practice. In Texas, some traditional brokerages have made the transition to other forms of agency representation, whereas other firms retain their commitment to represent sellers exclusively. These exclusive seller agencies encourage buyers and tenants who want representation to seek buyers' or tenants' brokers, appraisers, or attorneys. The broker usually offers to work with buyers or tenants in the purchase or lease of property as long as they realize that the broker and all licensed associates of the firm represent the interests of the sellers and the landlords.

Licensees working in firms representing sellers exclusively must be careful not to convey the impression that the buyer is being represented. A variety of situations can arise for licensees working in exclusive seller agency firms. Brokers and associates should have a clear understanding of their duties when conducting in-house sales as well as cooperative sales involving other brokers.

Many firms today find that it is beneficial to represent people generally rather than people classified by their relationship to the property in question—that is, a broker may wish to represent a person whether that person sells, buys, or leases a property. As a result, exclusive seller agency is no longer the majority practice.

In-House Sales

A large number of residential real estate transactions involve the services of two brokers in a cooperative sale. However, a significant number of sales are in-house sales, especially in those real estate firms with large market shares. In-house sales involve only one broker, although several associates from the same brokerage firm may participate. In an in-house sale, brokers and their associates offering exclusive seller agency will treat buyers as customers, not clients.

When a seller lists a property with a broker, the seller expects—and Texas law demands—that everyone associated with the brokerage firm use his or her best efforts to produce a ready, willing, and able buyer. In a firm offering exclusive seller agency, the broker, the associate taking the listing, and all associates in the firm work exclusively for the seller to find a buyer.

Many brokers prefer to sell their listings in-house because of the control they maintain over the transactions and because of the prospect of earning the full commission. Some firms offer the selling associate a greater share of the commission as an incentive for producing an in-house sale. This incentive may motivate some associates to look primarily toward in-house listings, something that may not be in the best interests of every prospective buyer.

Cooperative Sales—Subagency

Transactions usually start from two positions quite independent of each other. A buyer begins to consider buying and then starts taking action to buy. Meanwhile, a seller starts to consider selling and later starts taking action to sell. A transaction is the result of these two independent forces meeting. During the marketing of a property by the seller's broker, the buyer frequently visits the property with another broker or a licensed associate of another broker, who may be called the other broker, cooperating broker, selling broker, or buyer's broker. Who is this other broker? Whom does the other broker represent?

Because significant numbers of transactions occur between two brokerage firms, particularly in large metropolitan areas with active MLSs, licensees should understand the roles they play in cooperative sales. The roll of a cooperating broker acting as a buyer's agent will be discussed in Chapter 6. The cooperating brokers and all associates of those brokers who are working with rather than for the buyer, as buyer agents should always seek to act as subagents of the listing broker's client when selling another broker's listing. TRELA § 1101.002 (8) gives the following definition:

> (8) *"Subagent" means a license holder who:*
>
> *(A) represents a principal through cooperation with and the consent of a broker representing the principal and*
>
> *(B) is not sponsored by or associated with the principal's broker.*

In the model in Figure 5.5, notice that associates of the listing broker are not subagents. Wording in TRELA leaves room for speculation about the proper term to describe an associate of another broker when that other broker is acting as a subagent of the listing broker's client. It is clear, however, that the associate is an agent of the subagent broker and will carry out the duties of a subagent. In other words, when a broker is acting as a subagent, the associates of the subagent broker will have the same obligations to the listing broker's client as the subagent broker.

FIGURE 5.5

Agency and Subagency

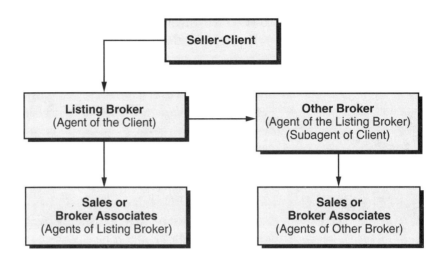

Selective offers of subagency. Like any agency relationship, the subagency relationship is created by the consent of those involved. Only when a valid subagency is created does the law impose fiduciary duties and liabilities on the subagent. Subagency may be created expressly by agreement or implicitly by words, conduct, or custom. Subagency may be created within or apart from the framework of a multiple listing service (MLS). Even within the MLS, subagency is not automatic. The seller has the option to offer subagency. On the other hand, the listing broker has the option to condition the taking of a listing on whether the seller will allow or insist on subagency or some other form of representation. Also, any other broker in the transaction can reject any offer of subagency and can elect to work for the buyer on a client basis as the buyer's agent.

Creating subagency. Subagency can be created outside the framework of an MLS. While many listing brokers are members of an MLS, thousands of listings in the small towns and rural areas of Texas have no MLS systems. Further, MLS systems do not require that certain types of properties be listed. Commercial properties, new project sales, business opportunities, long-term leases, and vacant land typically fall into this voluntary category. Still, listing brokers at the direction of the seller may work with other brokers on a selective basis to help in the search for buyers for these types of properties.

Rather than talk in terms of a formal offer of subagency, brokers may talk of cooperating in a transaction and sharing or splitting the commission. This type of informal understanding is particularly dangerous because it is often unclear as to whom the other broker represents or who is responsible for payment of compensation. In a recent case, a Texas commercial broker failed to recover a commission in a $9 million transaction because he was unable to convincingly establish whose agent he was, in whose best interests he acted, and who was supposed to pay him. Instead of the $270,000 commission he sued for, he settled for $40,000. Had the commercial broker known and practiced the principles set out by law, the outcome might have been decidedly different.

Listing brokers and the other brokers involved in a transaction often have separate commission agreements among themselves that serve as a basis for the subagency relationship. Such agreements are often silent as to agency duties and tend to cover only how commission is to be split. Brokers who work cooperatively frequently operate without any specific written or oral agreement; however, a written arrangement is preferable.

In subagency transactions, the buyer is not represented or contractually bound to any licensee and may be viewing properties with a number of brokers or salespersons and may in fact view the same property with more than one licensee. In these situations, where more than one broker works with a single nonrepresented buyer, the possibility exists that procuring-cause disputes may arise between different selling, cooperating, or other brokers, with two or more of the other brokers each claiming a right to share the commission with the listing broker. However, from the listing broker's perspective, even though subagency may be offered to multiple brokers, only the subagent who procures the sale is entitled to a share of the commission as the procuring cause.

Note paragraph 8 in Figure 5.2, Example of Exclusive-Right-to-Sell Listing Agreement. Because agency is consensual, the sellers may elect not to allow licensees from other offices to represent them in the sale of the property, particularly licensees they do not know. In which case, the listing broker would insert the elected commission to the cooperating broker in paragraph 8.A(1) and/or 8.B(1) and indicate "N/A" or "none" in the remaining blanks. Should the listing broker not offer subagency, the cooperating broker in this instance would not be able to show the property to the buyer-customer. The cooperating broker could at best contact the listing agent and obtain a written agreement for a referral fee should the buyer-customer show interest in the listing.

Fiduciary duty owed to the seller. By accepting the listing broker's offer of subagency through the MLS, the cooperating broker and the broker's associates owe complete fiduciary duties and loyalty to the seller. Any real estate agent acting as a subagent of the seller must relate to both buyer and seller exactly as if the subagent's company had taken the listing. The subagent must be careful not to act for the buyer in any manner adverse to the seller's best interests. This may be a problem if the subagent has developed close ties with the buyer. By the same token, the subagent rarely meets the seller and usually knows little about the seller's needs. The subagent's main source of information will be what is revealed in the MLS or what is discussed with the listing agent.

Liability and ethics in regard to subagency. No one can make an informed decision to choose or not choose subagency without first becoming aware of the legal and practical consequences of a subagency relationship. Often, the outcome of a court case turns on whether the other broker is found to be a subagent of the seller or an agent of the buyer. Sellers and listing brokers have at times refused subagency on the basis of potential liability created by a subagent over whom the listing broker may have no control or no knowledge. Some of these issues have recently been resolved by the Texas legislature, as shown in the following paragraphs.

TRELA addresses the concern some listing brokers have in regards to the liability that may attach to them for the acts of other parties and cooperating brokers, in this case, subagents (vicarious liability), amended as follows:

§ 1101.805 LIABILITY FOR MISREPRESENTATON OR CONCEALMENT

(a) In this section, "party" has the meaning assigned by Section 1101.551.

(b) This section prevails over any other law, including common law.

(c) This section does not diminish a broker's responsibility for the acts or omissions of a salesperson associated with or acting for the broker.

(d) A party is not liable for a misrepresentation or a concealment of a material fact made by a license holder in a real estate transaction unless the party:

(1) knew of the falsity of the misrepresentation or concealment; and

(2) failed to disclose the party's knowledge of the falsity of the misrepresentation or concealment.

(e) A license holder is not liable for a misrepresentation or a concealment of a material fact made by a party to a real estate transaction unless the license holder:

(1) knew of the falsity of the misrepresentation or concealment; and

(2) failed to disclose the license holder's knowledge of the falsity of the misrepresentation or concealment.

(f) A party or a license holder is not liable for a misrepresentation or a concealment of a material fact made by a subagent in a real estate transaction unless the party or license holder:

(1) knew of the falsity of the misrepresentation or concealment; and

(2) failed to disclose the party's or license holder's knowledge of the falsity of the misrepresentation or concealment.

Exclusive Seller Agency in Practice

In the following examples, assume that Sally is a top salesperson for Bay Realty, a multioffice firm offering exclusive seller agency.

■ **EXAMPLE** **Sally as the listing associate.** Sally successfully acquires for Bay Realty an exclusive listing of a three-bedroom town house from her friend George. At the first open house conducted by Sally, prospective buyer Betty discusses the property with Sally. Sally initially discloses to Betty that she is an agent of the seller and furnishes Betty with a written TREC statement regarding information about brokerage services. Later that night, Sally prepares an offer from Betty on George's property, which is later accepted by George.

■ **QUESTIONS** 1. Because Sally represents the seller through Bay Realty, must she suggest that Betty use another brokerage firm that would represent Betty's interest? 2. Would Bay Realty's agency role change if Betty were referred to a different licensee within the firm?

■ **DISCUSSION** In this case, Bay Realty clearly represents George only. No facts indicate that Bay Realty has become an implied agent of Betty because of any of Sally's actions. No law prohibits in-house sales or requires that Sally suggest that the buyer hire another broker to prepare the offer. Sally can show the property, explain its features, and deliver the buyer's offer without creating any implied agency with the buyer—in fact, that's her job. However, Sally must tell Betty that she is the agent of the seller and that she does not represent Betty. Also, unless Betty is represented by an agent, Sally must present Betty with a written statement regarding representation responsibilities as required by § 1101.558(c). This statement must be presented during the first substantive meeting between Sally and Betty. Otherwise, the disclosure is not timely and may fail to protect Sally in case of a later lawsuit.

■ **EXAMPLE** **Sally as the selling associate with no prior relationship with the buyer.** Bay Realty has a policy of exclusive seller representation. Sally is the licensee on duty when Bob Brown walks in and asks about available properties. Sally checks Bay Realty's listings and finds a property on Main Street listed by Carol, from a branch office of Bay Realty, and one on King Street listed by Tom, from Southside Realty on the other side of town. Sally makes appointments to show Bob both properties.

■ **QUESTIONS** 1. Because Sally is not the listing agent on the Main Street property, will she be free to represent Bob on this property? 2. When Sally shows the properties, how will her duties to Bob and to the sellers differ when she shows the Main Street property from when she shows the King Street property?

■ **DISCUSSION** Sally must remember that Bay Realty is the agent of the seller of the Main Street property and will be the subagent of the sellers of the King Street property. Even though an associated licensee other than Sally took the listing on the Main Street property, Sally is bound to act in the best interests of the seller. Because Bay Realty represents sellers exclusively, the same thing is true on the King Street property. Sally should be careful not to give Bob the impression that she can represent him in negotiations regarding any property. She can do this by giving Bob the written statement required by TRELA § 1101.558, discussing it with him, and disclosing her agency relationship with the sellers. In an exclusive seller agency firm, Sally should treat Bob as a customer, not as a client.

■ **EXAMPLE** **Sally as the selling associate with prior relationship with buyer.** Sally, as listing agent, has just negotiated a completed sales contract on George's town house. She has opened escrow by placing the contract and earnest money with the escrow agent named in the contract. George is extremely pleased with Sally's professional attitude and skills and asks her to find a suitable replacement property. Sally is well aware of George's needs and wants, as well as his financial resources and favorite bargaining techniques. Sally knows a perfect property for George, and it happens to be listed with Bay Realty through Tom, another Bay Realty salesperson.

Sally knows from experience that when satisfied clients like George sell their homes and buy replacement properties in the same locality, the client typically works with the same listing agent (Sally, in this case). It is natural for George to think that Sally is still his agent. Sally recognizes that the seller of the new home might find it useful, in negotiations, to know how much cash George will receive from his recent sale and when George is planning to move. This seller, like most sellers, wants to learn as much information as possible from the agent about the buyer, especially if the offer is contingent on financing.

■ **QUESTIONS** 1. If Sally is to represent the new seller on behalf of Bay Realty, should Sally disclose these useful facts to the seller? 2. Would such disclosure surprise George or violate any fiduciary duty to him?

■ **DISCUSSION** This in-house "turnaround" sale, so common in today's market, can present some confusing agency relationship questions. Is Bay Realty now representing two parties? Is George a client in the listing of his town house and a customer in buying the replacement property? Is it understandable for George to expect he'll continue to receive client-level services, even though his status has changed from seller to buyer?

It would be the path of least resistance for Sally to keep quiet, to avoid raising any of these questions, to simply proceed to do the best job for both parties, and to hope all goes well. This too often happens in the real world of real estate, especially with real estate licensees who regard themselves primarily as facilitators who help work out differences between buyers and sellers and bring a transaction to a successful close. The correct approach, though, is to clarify each relationship through discussion and disclosure to the buyer and the seller.

Because Bay Realty represents sellers exclusively, George must be made fully aware that in the purchase transaction he will be receiving the reduced services extended to buyer-customers and will not enjoy client status. Sally also must inform the seller of the home that George is interested in purchasing that because of a prior client relationship with George, there might be financial information known to Sally regarding George that she cannot disclose to the seller. Even with the informed consent of both parties, Bay Realty may be on shaky ground. Changing George's status from client to customer may be difficult at best.

If either George or the seller is not in agreement with Bay Realty's role in the transaction, Sally should not proceed until the agency issues are resolved. One possible alternative is to refer George to another firm offering buyer's brokerage services so he can get representation in the purchase of the home. In this scenario, Sally or any licensee within Bay Realty still would be prohibited from disclosing George's financial circumstances to the seller because that information was gained during a client relationship with George. Before continuing with the transaction, the seller must give informed consent to Sally and Bay Realty.

Advantages and Disadvantages of Exclusive Seller Agency

Some advantages of exclusive seller agency are as follows:

- It reduces chances of conflicts of interest that may arise by mixing dual representation or buyer agency in the same firm, especially if the brokerage has a considerable number of licensed associates and listings.
- Sellers receive 100 percent loyalty and confidentiality, with someone advocating their best interests and providing expert advice.
- It may be more comfortable and familiar to licensees trained as sellers' agents.
- It is a proven method of compensation in cooperating sales transactions.
- Agency lines are clarified in the in-house sale.

Some disadvantages of exclusive seller agency include the following:

- It does not satisfy the needs of qualified buyers seeking representation.
- An increased potential exists for undisclosed representation of more than one party (may be an implied buyer agency).
- The broker may lose buyers who want representation.

NONEXCLUSIVE SELLER AGENCY

Rather than choosing to represent sellers exclusively, many firms wish to represent buyers and sellers, but not in the same transaction. This means that the brokerage firm will engage buyers in representation agreements, but will show only properties listed by other brokers to their buyer clients. (Buyer representation is covered in detail in Chapter 6.) An advantage of nonexclusive over exclusive seller representation is that the broker at least can offer representation services to buyers on properties not listed by the firm. The obvious disadvantage of this form of nonexclusive seller representation is that a buyer wishing to be represented by the firm cannot be shown any property listed by that firm. This may work to the disadvantage of the buyer, the seller, and the firm. That is, the buyer may not have access to a desirable property, the seller may miss a sale, and the firm is unable to earn a commission.

In an effort to overcome the problem of not being able to show represented buyers properties listed in-house, some brokers have an understanding with buyers to show properties listed with their firms before entering into a buyer-representation agreement. If after viewing the firm's listings, a suitable property has not been found, the broker and the buyers then enter into a buyer-representation agreement in which the broker agrees to represent the buyers on all properties listed by other brokers. If such an arrangement is undertaken by the broker, the buyers must be made fully aware of the lack of representation that will occur if they choose to negotiate on any property listed by the brokerage firm. In addition, the broker who wishes to avoid situations that involve representing more than one party in a transaction must be prepared to deal with a possible dilemma if a buyer who has entered into a representation agreement later decides to negotiate on a listing held by the firm.

DISCLOSURE ISSUES

Disclosures of Seller's Agent to Seller

Before signing the listing agreement, the listing agent should provide the seller with the written statement required by TRELA § 1101.558, which describes the services that the seller may expect from a seller's agent, a buyer's agent, and an intermediary. TRELA requires that the listing agent provide this statement at the first substantive dialogue with the seller—that is, the first meeting or written communication that involves a substantive discussion relating to specific real property. In addition, the seller's agent should attempt to provide as much information to the seller as is reasonable to ensure that the seller is fully informed regarding matters such as

- general company policies regarding cooperating with other brokers;
- the fact that buyer/tenant agents represent the buyer/tenant, even if paid by the listing broker or the seller; and
- the possibility, if any, of the listing agent's acting as an agent for both the seller and a buyer.

The licensee obtaining the listing also should discuss with the seller whether an MLS will be used and whether an offer allowing other brokers to represent the seller (subagency) through the listing broker will be permitted by the seller.

TREC rules require that a real estate licensee give the seller the licensee's opinion of market value of the property at the time of negotiating a listing (22 TAC § 535.16(c)). If the licensee expects to receive compensation from more than one party or to represent buyers as well as the seller in a transaction, the source of compensation and consent to the arrangement must be expressed in writing (§ 1101.652(b)(8)). These and other disclosures can be made either in the listing agreement or in a special addendum to the listing agreement.

Disclosures of Seller's Agent to Buyer

The seller's agent must disclose to the buyer that the brokerage represents the seller, not the buyer. To facilitate this required disclosure, some firms have the buyer read and acknowledge a customer letter that outlines what the licensee can and cannot do for the buyer while acting as an agent of the seller. This letter could soften the tone of the disclosure, but it should not diminish the intent.

Early information and disclosure is the best policy. But keep in mind that state law prevails. If the buyer is not represented by an agent, the written information statement required by TRELA § 1101.558 must be provided at the first substantive dialogue with the buyer. This statement, known as the Information About Brokerage Services notice, contains state-mandated language relating to the various roles that a broker may play in a transaction. In addition, the agent must disclose to the buyer that the agent is the seller's representative at the time of the first contact with the buyer. This agency disclosure may be oral or written.

Remember, the seller's agent dealing with a buyer cannot provide advice regarding the buyer's purchase decision that may be considered adverse to the seller's best interests unless it is information that the licensee is required, by law, to supply, such as a known defect in the property.

The seller's agent also should make clear to the buyer-customer that the licensee works on behalf of the seller on all negotiable issues. It is important to note at this point that almost every term or condition in any potential sales contract is fully negotiable between the buyer and the seller. The fact that TREC-promulgated forms for contracts may call for certain costs to be paid by the buyer and other costs to be paid by the seller in no way prohibits principals in the transaction from reallocating those costs to the other party through negotiation.

It is the licensee's legal obligation to make the contract conform to the intent of the principals. Therefore, licensees may add factual statements and business details desired by the principals and should strike from the contract only those items not desired by them (22 TAC § 537.11(f)). A fine line exists here between modifying the contract to "conform the instrument to the intent of the parties" and engaging in the unauthorized practice of law. All Texas licensees should be thoroughly familiar with the provisions and implications of TRELA § 1101.155; .252; .254; .652(a)(8); .654; and 22 TAC § 537.11 before they attempt to assist in contract negotiations.

A nonrepresented buyer should deal with the seller's agent as though dealing or negotiating directly with the seller. The buyer should be told in the initial interview not to disclose anything to the seller's agent that the buyer would not tell the seller. Additionally, the buyer should be told not to expect to receive any information from the seller's agent that the seller would not want to tell the buyer directly. The seller's agent must be careful in responding to questions such as "How low will the seller go?" "Will the seller take less?" "How can I get the seller to compromise on terms and come down in price?" Questions like these should elicit carefully rehearsed answers so that the agent appears professional and competent, replies honestly and fairly, and is not disloyal to the client or misleading to the customer.

SUMMARY

The broker who consistently acts in the sole capacity of a seller's agent has little trouble distinguishing the client from the customer. Until the early 1990s, firms with large shares of the market often chose this type of relationship to lessen the risk of conflicts of loyalty in selling their own listings. However, with the passage of laws requiring better information and disclosures to the parties, buyers and sellers are becoming more aware of agency options. As a result, many Texas firms are experimenting with a variety of agency policies. Some firms have clearly stated policies of not offering cooperation with other brokers except on an individual, case-by-case basis. Great care should be exercised, both with in-house sales and cooperative sales, to avoid conduct that might be interpreted as creating implied agencies with the buyers where none is intended. Supervising brokers can and should develop policies and procedures and competently train licensed associates to act consistently with company policy.

In the majority of residential real estate transactions, an agent other than the listing agent procures the buyer. It is important to make an early decision about whether the other agent is a subagent of the seller or an agent of the buyer. This depends on whether subagency was offered and whether it was accepted. If accepted, the subagent owes client-level services to the seller and customer-level services to the buyer.

KEY POINTS

- Expressed listing agreements can be written or oral.
- Implied listing agreements are created by words or conduct of the parties.
- Early disclosure of seller agency helps lessen the chance that the buyer will claim later that the broker also represented the buyer.
- Written disclosures and brochures help clarify that the buyer is the customer and the seller is the client. Warning: Do not substitute the word *impartially*, or *equally*, for its sometime synonym *fairly* in the context of how an agent for the seller-client will treat the buyer-customer. The customer must be treated fairly by law, but not impartially or equally, relative to the client.
- A seller's subagent owes a general duty of fairness and honesty to the buyer (customer) but owes full fiduciary duties to the seller (client).

- Under an MLS, offering of subagency is optional. As a matter of routine, the listing office should clarify subagency status of any other broker.
- Some brokers don't feel very effective as subagents, especially if they favor the buyer in a transaction.
- Some cooperating brokers prefer to treat certain buyers as customers, and thus, subagency to the seller is the appropriate relationship.
- It is easy to appear to treat buyers as clients, leading the buyers to believe they are clients, and thus create an accidental undisclosed agency relationship.

SUGGESTIONS FOR BROKERS

Review with your licensed associates the types of services they can provide to accommodate at least some of the needs of the buyer while remembering that they act as agents of the seller.

To ensure that your licensed associates do not accidentally create an implied or accidental agency with the buyer, require that the associates have the buyer acknowledge in writing that your firm and your associates act as agents of the seller, not as agents of the buyer.

Develop a company policy regarding net listing that includes the TREC requirements for disclosure.

When you act as the nonlisting or other broker, decide whether you prefer to represent the buyer or to represent the seller as a subagent. Choose what works best for you, and to be safe, get the informed written consent of all parties to act in that manner. Because principals may incur some liability by the acts of their subagents, listing brokers should tell sellers of the risks, as well as the benefits, of using subagents.

CHAPTER 5 QUIZ

1. A listing broker owes which of the following duties to the prospective buyer-customer?
   a. Loyalty
   b. Obedience
   c. Agency disclosure
   d. All of the above

2. Three different subagents show a property to the same buyer over a span of two weeks. Which subagent is entitled to a share of the commission?
   a. The subagent who procures the sale.
   b. The subagent who first showed the property to the buyer.
   c. The subagent who last showed the property to the buyer.
   d. All three subagents above receive an equal share of the commission.

3. A listing broker normally can do all of the following EXCEPT
   a. sell the listing broker's own listings.
   b. advertise listed properties.
   c. hold open houses.
   d. split fees with a buyer's broker without the seller's knowledge.

4. A buyer approaches Broker Smith, an exclusive seller's agent, and requests to be represented in the purchase of a home. Smith should
   a. explain that there are no real benefits to buyer representation.
   b. explain that while he cannot personally work with the buyer, one of his associates may do so.
   c. describe the services that the buyer may receive as a customer, but if the buyer still wants representation, refer the buyer to a buyer's broker.
   d. show the buyer only properties listed by other brokers.

5. A net listing requires that the
   a. seller accepts the net amount of money remaining after all costs of sale.
   b. seller independently determines the value of the property.
   c. agent advises the seller of the value of the property.
   d. agent limit the amount of commission charged.

6. The listing that allows the seller to list with several brokers is the
   a. exclusive right to sell.
   b. exclusive agency.
   c. open listing.
   d. net agency.

7. According to TRELA, brokers are responsible for the negligent acts of subagents
   a. under no circumstances.
   b. to the extent that they knew of the negligent acts.
   c. no matter whether they knew of the negligent acts or not.
   d. only when they encourage the subagent to commit a negligent act.

8. A subagent brings a full-priced offer to purchase to the listing broker but is later informed that the seller has elected not to sell the property. The subagent
   a. has no right to sue under the terms of the listing agreement.
   b. may file suit against the listing broker for his commission.
   c. may force the listing broker to file suit against his client.
   d. may file suit against the seller for his commission.

9. The seller says he will list with you as long as he gets enough to pay his loan balance and closing costs. Your commission will be anything above those costs. This is an example of a(n)
   a. open listing.
   b. one-time showing agreement.
   c. net listing.
   d. fixed commission listing.

10. A buyer asks a broker, who is the subagent of the listing broker, whether the seller would accept $4,000 less than the asking price. The listing broker already has told the subagent that the seller will take $5,000 less. Which is the BEST response for the subagent?
    a. "Go ahead and make the offer because the seller needs to sell before the bank forecloses."
    b. "You may make the offer, and we'll see what the seller says. But remember, you may want to make your very best offer the first time because we don't discuss the existence or nonexistence of other offers."
    c. "I can't present an offer that is less than the asking price."
    d. "If I get the seller to accept this low offer, I want a $1,000 bonus. But remember, you may want to make your very best offer the first time because we don't discuss the existence or nonexistence of other offers."

DISCUSSION QUESTIONS

1. Why can't licensed associates take listings with them when they transfer to new firms?

2. In exclusive seller agency brokerage firms, what is the best way to handle a transaction in which the seller wants help in finding a replacement property?

3. How would you offer to help a prospective buyer you meet at an open house and still remain loyal to the seller?

4. What should the associate of a listing broker say when the nonrepresented buyer asks common questions such as the following:

    - How low will the seller go?
    - Do you think the property is worth what the seller is asking?
    - Are there any other offers on the property?
    - Have you had any contracts that fell through?

5. Does a subagent owe the seller any different fiduciary duties from those owed by the listing broker?

6. Can a subagent sue the seller for a commission if the seller defaults and the listing broker elects not to sue? Why or why not?

7. What are the pros and cons of a seller offering subagency to other brokers?

8. What are some of the differences between client-level services and customer-level services?

9. Do you feel more effective as a real estate agent working with a buyer when you are a subagent or a buyer's broker?

Chapter 6

Buyer Agency

Although this chapter refers to buyer agency, it should be noted that tenants may be represented by brokers as well. By substituting tenant for buyer and landlord for seller, the licensee can apply the same principles to the leasing of real estate. Buyer agency exists when the agency relationship focuses on the person who wishes to buy or lease property.

Buyer agency is not a revolutionary business practice. For decades, brokers have been employed to represent buyers. In fact, buyer representation in commercial real estate transactions is and always has been the rule rather than the exception. Brokers also have represented themselves, their business ventures, their relatives, and undisclosed principals in the acquisition of real estate. In residential transactions, however, it was not until the late 1990s in Texas that purchasers began to routinely employ a broker under written contract in the selection, negotiation, or acquisition of real estate. Attitudes have changed due to better consumer education and higher expectations and demand for advocacy.

Residential consumers recognize that they can benefit from client-quality representation, whether they are buyers or sellers. Once residential brokers began to offer their services to buyers, buyer agency rapidly became a growing market segment. Most brokers now offer client-level service to buyers. Although many brokers prefer not to take on the risks associated with dual representation (Chapter 8), it is rare to find a brokerage office today that limits services to exclusive seller agency as discussed in Chapter 5.

Many licensees do not understand the basic differences between conduct and duties of agency when representing sellers, buyers, or both. This chapter explores the factors that affect the broker's decision to treat certain buyers as clients (rather than as customers) or as one of two clients.

Chapter 6 Buyer Agency

LEARNING OBJECTIVES *This chapter addresses the following:*

- Deciding to Represent the Buyer
  - Factors to Consider
- The Creation of Buyer Agency
  - Representation Agreements
  - Advantages and Disadvantages of Exclusive Buyer Agency
- Benefits of Buyer-Agency Relationships
  - Agency Benefits to Buyer or Tenant
  - Benefits to Buyers' Agents
- Fee Arrangements
  - Retainer Fee
  - Seller-Paid Fee
  - Commission Split
  - Buyer-Paid Fee
  - Net Purchase Price
  - Gross Price
- Written Notification of Compensation to Broker
- Procuring Cause
- Purchase Agreement
  - Earnest Money Deposit
  - Assignability
  - Seller Financing
  - Contract Acceptance
  - Extended Closing
  - Inspection
  - Property Condition
  - Pests
  - Assessments
  - Title Matters
  - Financing and Other Contingencies
  - Miscellaneous Checklist
- Buyer's Broker Disclosures
  - Disclosures to Buyer
  - Disclosures to Seller or Listing Broker
  - Buyers as Customers

■ DECIDING TO REPRESENT THE BUYER

When a prospective buyer enters a broker's office asking to see homes for sale, the broker does not necessarily have to represent the buyer in an agency capacity, even if the broker specializes in representing buyers. A seller's agent spends a considerable amount of time leading up to the listing of the seller's property. Likewise, an agent dealing with a prospective buyer, spends time discussing the buyer's preferences and qualifications.

In some cases, a licensee may not feel comfortable in a fiduciary relationship with a particular buyer. This may be because of preexisting agency relationships the company may have with sellers or because of an analysis of this particular buyer in terms of the buyer's cash, credit, or capacity to buy, seriousness in buying, or incompatible personality traits. Nevertheless, the licensee still may want to serve that same buyer as a customer. In addition, some licensees choose to spend time showing a buyer properties listed in the multiple listing service (MLS) with other brokers and choose to act as a subagent of the seller. It is not necessary that a broker create an agency relationship to help a buyer locate a property. In fact, some brokers, in order to avoid creating conflicting loyalties with their client-seller, prefer an office policy that dictates treating buyers as customers on in-house sales but as clients when working with listing brokers on cooperative sales, also known as nonexclusive single agency.

The professional licensee recognizes that adequately representing a buyer is a significant responsibility. The licensee is held to a higher standard of care in working with a client than with a customer. A buyer who feels the licensee has given poor advice may threaten to sue the agent for breach of fiduciary duty. The buyer might ask, "Who got me into this deal, anyway?" Deciding to offer client-level services, whether the client is the seller or the buyer, is a serious business decision with significant legal and economic consequences. For this reason, some brokers prefer to work with buyer prospects on a customer-level basis and with only select buyers on a client-level basis.

Factors to Consider

Unless company policy does not permit buyer representation, nothing prevents licensees from showing properties to a buyer as a client, provided the licensees clarify their role early in the transaction. When working with a buyer, licensees should decide, disclose, and obtain necessary consents to act. Licensees can act as agents of buyers, subagents of sellers (a licensee not associated with the listing broker but representing the seller through the listing broker), or perhaps agents for both parties. In deciding whether to represent the buyer, licensees should keep several points in mind:

- The broker, not the licensed associate of the broker, is the primary agent of the buyer. If the broker already represents the seller, dual representation questions will arise if the broker's associate acts in such a way as to give the impression that the broker also represents the buyer. As with seller's listings, if the associated licensee who obtained a buyer's representation agreement leaves the brokerage firm, the agreement remains with the firm. A buyer's

representation agreement cannot be transferred automatically to the new brokerage firm with which the licensee is now affiliated.
- The real estate licensee can, with proper disclosures, provide valuable services to a buyer without creating an agency relationship. This is especially true with in-house sales. Real estate firms that wish to avoid representing more than one party develop ways to accommodate some of the needs of buyers in a seller-oriented service business without crossing into agency representation of buyers.
- Few brokers are exclusively buyers' brokers. Even though some brokers start out representing buyers only, those brokers often find that satisfied buyers eventually turn into sellers and want the brokers to list their properties for sale. The practice of representing either buyers or sellers exclusively is known as exclusive single agency, and some brokers feel that this practice avoids potential conflicts that may arise when representing buyers and sellers.
- The buyer's broker can, with proper authority, appoint subagents to help in the search for the right property. This is especially useful in long-distance transactions—for example, when employees of nationwide companies are transferred and relocated.

■ THE CREATION OF BUYER AGENCY

As with seller-agency, a buyer-agency relationship can be created by verbal agreement or by implication; it may also be created by expressed agreement either orally or in writing. Texas requires only an intermediary agreement to be in writing (TRELA § 1101.559 (a)). The requirement that some note or memorandum of an agreement to pay a commission be in writing is a limiting requirement only if the Texas broker wishes to pursue legal action for the recovery of any agreed-upon commission (TRELA § 1101.806 (c)). While a written agreement is certainly preferable for any type of agency agreement, many express buyer agency and listing agreements are oral, with written confirmation noted in the sales contract.

Representation Agreements

A buyer's agent should clarify the types of services to be offered to the buyer-client (in addition to the traditional services rendered by real estate licensees to buyer-customers). These could include such tasks as

- providing data relating to market values,
- assistance in determining favorable financing,
- the structuring of the offer to purchase,
- advice during contract negotiations, and
- assistance in investment analyses.

The buyer's agent should mention the potential need for the buyer to consult with legal, tax, and other expert advisers.

Buyer-representation agreements can take many forms, depending on what the buyer and the buyer's agent want and are able to negotiate. Even if a licensee decides not to work as an agent with the buyer, the licensee and the buyer may enter into a general written understanding of their working relationship. This can be especially useful in large real estate firms that have many listings and need to avoid claims that the broker has illegally represented more than one party. Under one arrangement, the buyer agrees to work exclusively with the licensee and recognizes that the licensee renders specified customer-level services. Under this arrangement, the licensee is acting as an agent or a subagent of the seller and generally will be paid by the seller.

Buyers' brokers frequently develop their own buyer-representation agreement forms. Brokers who draft their working agreements without good legal counsel may be taking unnecessary risks, but they are not considered to be engaged in the unauthorized practice of law by so doing. In commercial transactions that involve large commissions, brokers often have their attorneys prepare comprehensive listing agreements. The Texas Real Estate Commission (TREC) has no state-approved or promulgated forms for agency agreements, listing agreements, buyer-representation agreements, or agreements for representing more than one party. However, the Texas Association of REALTORS® (TAR) and local REALTORS® associations do have such forms, for use by their members only.

In some residential real estate transactions, the form used by the buyer's broker is not comprehensive, unlike those that may be found in big commercial transactions or the more carefully crafted agreements of the exclusive buyer's broker firms. These more generalized agreements are designed to encourage trust and understanding, although they typically may not enable the real estate agent to prevail in a lawsuit. Control of the client arises from the trust relationship itself, not from a supposedly ironclad agreement. Still, the form should be specific on essential items to minimize misunderstandings and disputes.

Some of the key points to consider in any buyer's broker agreements are

- exclusivity of representation,
- termination date,
- conflicts of interest,
- role of the agent, and
- compensation and/or fees.

More comprehensive buyer-representation agreements are as protective as well-written exclusive-right-to-sell listing agreements. For example, most buyer's agent agreements have an enforceable exclusive-right-to-purchase clause that allows the broker legal recourse for compensation if the buyer purchases a property without compensating the broker during the period of the agreement, even if the broker did not show the buyer the property. The Texas Association of REALTORS® (TAR) Residential Buyer/Tenant Representation Agreement (TAR-1501) is shown as a sample buyer-representation agreement in Figure 6.1. A thorough reading of the TAR sample agreement will show that each of the following topics is addressed in detail.

Exclusive right to purchase. Novice buyers' agents are sometimes uncomfortable asking buyers to sign exclusive representation agreements. Some develop a nonexclusive agreement containing an automatic right-to-terminate provision. More experienced buyers' agents already have developed their counseling

FIGURE 6.1

Residential Buyer/Tenant Representation Agreement

RESIDENTIAL BUYER/TENANT REPRESENTATION AGREEMENT
USE OF THIS FORM BY PERSONS WHO ARE NOT MEMBERS OF THE TEXAS ASSOCIATION OF REALTORS® IS NOT AUTHORIZED.
©Texas Association of REALTORS®, Inc. 2006

1. **PARTIES:** The parties to this agreement are:

    Client: _____

    Address: _____
    City, State, Zip: _____
    Phone: _____ Fax: _____
    E-Mail: _____

    Broker: _____

    Address: _____
    City, State, Zip: _____
    Phone: _____ Fax: _____
    E-Mall: _____

2. **APPOINTMENT:** Client grants to Broker the exclusive right to act as Client's real estate agent for the purpose of acquiring property in the market area.

3. **DEFINITIONS:**
    A. *"Acquire"* means to purchase or lease.
    B. *"Closing"* in a sale transaction means the date legal title to a property is conveyed to a purchaser of property under a contract to buy. *"Closing"* in a lease transaction means the date a landlord and tenant enter into a binding lease of a property.
    C. *"Market area"* means that area in the State of Texas within the perimeter boundaries of the following areas:_____
    _____
    _____.
    D. *"Property"* means any interest in real estate including but not limited to properties listed in a multiple listing service or other listing services, properties for sale by owners, and properties for sale by builders.

4. **TERM:** This agreement commences on _____ and ends at 11:59 p.m. on _____.

5. **BROKER'S OBLIGATIONS:** Broker will: (a) use Broker's best efforts to assist Client in acquiring property in the market area; (b) assist Client in negotiating the acquisition of property in the market area; and (c) comply with other provisions of this agreement.

6. **CLIENT'S OBLIGATIONS:** Client will: (a) work exclusively through Broker in acquiring property in the market area and negotiate the acquisition of property in the market area only through Broker; (b) inform other brokers, salespersons, sellers, and landlords with whom Client may have contact that Broker exclusively represents Client for the purpose of acquiring property in the market area and refer all such persons to Broker; and (c) comply with other provisions of this agreement.

7. **REPRESENTATIONS:**
    A. Each person signing this agreement represents that the person has the legal capacity and authority to bind the respective party to this agreement.
    B. Client represents that Client is not now a party to another buyer or tenant representation agreement with another broker for the acquisition of property in the market area.

(TAR-1501) 4-14-06   Initialed for Identification by: Broker/Associate _____, and Client _____, _____   Page 1 of 4

FIGURE 6.1

Residential Buyer/Tenant Representation Agreement (continued)

Buyer/Tenant Representation Agreement between _____

    C. Client represents that all information relating to Client's ability to acquire property in the market area Client gives to Broker is true and correct.

    D. Name any employer, relocation company, or other entity that will provide benefits to Client when acquiring property in the market area: _____.

8. INTERMEDIARY: *(Check A or B only.)*

❏ A. <u>Intermediary Status</u>: Client desires to see Broker's listings. If Client wishes to acquire one of Broker's listings, Client authorizes Broker to act as an intermediary and Broker will notify Client that Broker will service the parties in accordance with one of the following alternatives.

    (1) If the owner of the property is serviced by an associate other than the associate servicing Client under this agreement, Broker may notify Client that Broker will: (a) appoint the associate then servicing the owner to communicate with, carry out instructions of, and provide opinions and advice during negotiations to the owner; and (b) appoint the associate then servicing Client to the Client for the same purpose.

    (2) If the owner of the property is serviced by the same associate who is servicing Client, Broker may notify Client that Broker will: (a) appoint another associate to communicate with, carry out instructions of, and provide opinions and advice during negotiations to Client; and (b) appoint the associate servicing the owner under the listing to the owner for the same purpose.

    (3) Broker may notify Client that Broker will make no appointments as described under this Paragraph 8A and, in such an event, the associate servicing the parties will act solely as Broker's intermediary representative, who may facilitate the transaction but will not render opinions or advice during negotiations to either party.

❏ B. <u>No Intermediary Status</u>: Client does not wish to be shown or acquire any of Broker's listings.

Notice: **If Broker acts as an intermediary under Paragraph 8A, Broker and Broker's associates:**
- may not disclose to Client that the seller or landlord will accept a price less than the asking price unless otherwise instructed in a separate writing by the seller or landlord;
- may not disclose to the seller or landlord that Client will pay a price greater than the price submitted in a written offer to the seller or landlord unless otherwise instructed in a separate writing by Client;
- may not disclose any confidential information or any information a seller or landlord or Client specifically instructs Broker in writing not to disclose unless otherwise instructed in a separate writing by the respective party or required to disclose the information by the Real Estate License Act or a court order or if the information materially relates to the condition of the property;
- shall treat all parties to the transaction honestly; and
- shall comply with the Real Estate License Act.

9. COMPETING CLIENTS: Client acknowledges that Broker may represent other prospective buyers or tenants who may seek to acquire properties that may be of interest to Client. Client agrees that Broker may, during the term of this agreement and after it ends, represent such other prospects, show the other prospects the same properties that Broker shows to Client, and act as a real estate broker for such other prospects in negotiating the acquisition of properties that Client may seek to acquire.

10. CONFIDENTIAL INFORMATION:

    A. During the term of this agreement or after its termination, Broker may not knowingly disclose information obtained in confidence from Client except as authorized by Client or required by law. Broker may not disclose to Client any information obtained in confidence regarding any other person Broker represents or may have represented except as required by law.

    B. Unless otherwise agreed or required by law, a seller or the seller's agent is not obliged to keep the existence of an offer or its terms confidential. If a listing agent receives multiple offers, the listing agent is obliged to treat the competing buyers fairly.

(TAR-1501) 4-14-06   Initialed for Identification by: Broker/Associate _____, and Client _____, _____

FIGURE 6.1

Residential Buyer/Tenant Representation Agreement (continued)

Buyer/Tenant Representation Agreement between _____

11. BROKER'S FEES:

A. Commission: The parties agree that Broker will receive a commission calculated as follows: (1) ____% of the gross sales price if Client agrees to purchase property in the market area; and (2) if Client agrees to lease property in the market a fee equal to *(check only one box)*: ❏ _____% of one month's rent or ❏ ____% of all rents to be paid over the term of the lease.

B. Source of Commission Payment: Broker will seek to obtain payment of the commission specified in Paragraph 11A first from the seller, landlord, or their agents. If such persons refuse or fail to pay Broker the amount specified, Client will pay Broker the amount specified less any amounts Broker receives from such persons.

C. Earned and Payable: A person is not obligated to pay Broker a commission until such time as Broker's commission is *earned and payable*. Broker's commission is *earned* when: (1) Client enters into a contract to buy or lease property in the market area; or (2) Client breaches this agreement. Broker's commission is *payable*, either during the term of this agreement or after it ends, upon the earlier of: (1) the closing of the transaction to acquire the property; (2) Client's breach of a contract to buy or lease a property in the market area; or (3) Client's breach of this agreement. If Client acquires more than one property under this agreement, Broker's commissions for each property acquired are earned as each property is acquired and are payable at the closing of each acquisition.

D. Additional Compensation: If a seller, landlord, or their agents offer compensation in excess of the amount stated in Paragraph 11A (including but not limited to marketing incentives or bonuses to cooperating brokers) Broker may retain the additional compensation in addition to the specified commission. Client is not obligated to pay any such additional compensation to Broker.

E. Acquisition of Broker's Listing: Notwithstanding any provision to the contrary, if Client acquires a property listed by Broker, Broker will be paid in accordance with the terms of Broker's listing agreement with the owner and Client will have no obligation to pay Broker.

F. In addition to the commission specified under Paragraph 11A, Broker is entitled to the following fees.
  (1) Construction: If Client uses Broker's services to procure or negotiate the construction of improvements to property that Client owns or may acquire, Client ensures that Broker will receive from Client or the contractor(s) at the time the construction is substantially complete a fee equal to: _____.
  (2) Service Providers: If Broker refers Client or any party to a transaction contemplated by this agreement to a service provider (for example, mover, cable company, telecommunications provider, utility, or contractor) Broker may receive a fee from the service provider for the referral.
  (3) Other: _____
  _____
  _____.

G. Protection Period: "Protection period" means that time starting the day after this agreement ends and continuing for _____ days. Not later than 10 days after this agreement ends, Broker may send Client written notice identifying the properties called to Client's attention during this agreement. If Client or a relative of Client agrees to acquire a property identified in the notice during the protection period, Client will pay Broker, upon closing, the amount Broker would have been entitled to receive if this agreement were still in effect. This Paragraph 11G survives termination of this agreement. This Paragraph 11G will not apply if Client is, during the protection period, bound under a representation agreement with another broker who is a member of the Texas Association of REALTORS® at the time the acquisition is negotiated and the other broker is paid a fee for negotiating the transaction.

H. Escrow Authorization: Client authorizes, and Broker may so instruct, any escrow or closing agent authorized to close a transaction for the acquisition of property contemplated by this agreement to collect and disburse to Broker all amounts payable to Broker.

I. County: Amounts payable to Broker are to be paid in cash in _____ County, Texas.

(TAR-1501) 4-14-06   Initialed for Identification by: Broker/Associate _____, and Client _____, _____

FIGURE 6.1

Residential Buyer/Tenant Representation Agreement (continued)

Buyer/Tenant Representation Agreement between _____

12. **MEDIATION:** The parties agree to negotiate in good faith in an effort to resolve any dispute that may arise related to this agreement or any transaction related to or contemplated by this agreement. If the dispute cannot be resolved by negotiation, the parties will submit the dispute to mediation before resorting to arbitration or litigation and will equally share the costs of a mutually acceptable mediator.

13. **DEFAULT:** If either party fails to comply with this agreement or makes a false representation in this agreement, the non-complying party is in default. If Client is in default, Client will be liable for the amount of compensation that Broker would have received under this agreement if Client was not in default. If Broker is in default, Client may exercise any remedy at law.

14. **ATTORNEY'S FEES:** If Client or Broker is a prevailing party in any legal proceeding brought as a result of a dispute under this agreement or any transaction related to this agreement, such party will be entitled to recover from the non-prevailing party all costs of such proceeding and reasonable attorney's fees.

15. **LIMITATION OF LIABILITY:** <u>Neither Broker nor any other broker, or their associates, is responsible or liable for Client's personal injuries or for any loss or damage to Client's property that is not caused by Broker. Client will hold broker, any other broker, and their associates, harmless from any such injuries or losses. Client will indemnify Broker against any claims for injury or damage that Client may cause to others or their property.</u>

16. **ADDENDA:** Addenda and other related documents which are part of this agreement are:
    - ☑ Information About Brokerage Services
    - ☐ Protecting Your Home from Mold
    - ☐ Information Concerning Property Insurance
    - ☐ General Information and Notice to a Buyer
    - ☐ Protect Your Family from Lead in Your Home
    - ☐ Information about Special Flood Hazard Areas
    - ☐ For Your Protection: Get a Home Inspection
    - ☐ _____

17. **SPECIAL PROVISIONS:**

18. **ADDITIONAL NOTICES:**

    A. Broker's fees and the sharing of fees between brokers are not fixed, controlled, recommended, suggested, or maintained by the Association of REALTORS® or any listing service.

    B. Broker's services are provided without regard to race, color, religion, national origin, sex, disability or familial status.

    C. Broker is not a property inspector, surveyor, engineer, environmental assessor, or compliance inspector. Client should seek experts to render such services in any acquisition.

    D. If Client purchases property, Client should have an abstract covering the property examined by an attorney of Client's selection, or Client should be furnished with or obtain a title policy.

    E. Buyer may purchase a residential service contract. Buyer should review such service contract for the scope of coverage, exclusions, and limitations. The purchase of a residential service contract is optional. There are several residential service companies operating in Texas.

    F. Broker cannot give legal advice. This is a legally binding agreement. READ IT CAREFULLY. If you do not understand the effect of this agreement, consult your attorney BEFORE signing.

Broker's Printed Name _____ License No. _____   Client _____ Date _____

By: _____
Broker's Associate's Signature   Date   Client _____ Date _____

(TAR-1501) 4-14-06

skills to a point where they are as comfortable in securing buyer's agent exclusive representation agreements as sellers' agents are in securing exclusive-right-to-sell listings from sellers.

Agents know that an exclusive-right-to-sell or exclusive-right-to-buy agreement means better control over the transaction and provides a better means for the buyer's agent to protect the agent's investment of time, energy, and skill. They also know that an "open" buyer-agency agreement can lead to the same type of procuring-cause disagreements between brokers and buyers as can occur in seller subagency or open-listing situations.

The buyer must make the same choice as the seller in an open listing: Does the buyer-client want more agents working on her behalf, but with less commitment, motivation, or knowledge of the buyer's needs? It is also much more important for the agent to have exclusive-agency rights when the agent is compensated by a contingent fee rather than by an hourly fee.

Termination date. Both the agent and the buyer should be clear as to when the agency relationship will terminate. A specific termination date on any buyer-representation contract is required by Texas state licensing law. The expiration period is fully negotiable and can be longer or shorter than in a listing agreement with a seller. If the agent wants to be covered for a sale that takes place on a certain property after the agreement expires, the agent should insert an extending carryover clause to specify the protection period and the procedures for registering prospects. The agreement may be terminated anytime by mutual consent of the agent and principal.

Conflicts of interest. A problem exists if the buyer wants to purchase a property already listed by the broker or another associate in the same office. If the broker has a buyer-representation agreement with the buyer, under Texas law all licensees associated with that broker also represent the buyer and must act in that buyer's best interests in any transaction. To attempt to avoid conflicts that may result when representing more than one party, the buyer-representation agreement may contain a withdrawal provision whereby the agreement becomes void in any transaction in which a conflict arises. In this case, the buyer would be free to seek outside representation or counsel in making the offer and is not obligated to pay a fee or commission. The seller then would compensate the broker.

Another method to consider is renouncing one or the other agency relationship. Some brokers use the LIFO approach (last in, first out), in which the broker represents, for a single transaction only, the buyer or the seller, depending on who signed the representation agreement first. The last one in can choose self-representation or find outside representation and is not obligated to pay the broker any fee. All of these approaches have risks in that once agency is begun, it is not simple to disengage one part of the relationship or to avoid its consequences.

Some brokerage firms have developed a practice of representing buyers in the purchase of all properties except those listed with the firms. In this fashion, in-house listings are shown first, before buyer representation begins. If no acceptable in-house listings are found, the agent then enters into a buyer-representation agreement and thereafter works solely as a buyer's agent when showing properties listed by other brokers. This practice reduces the possibility of transactions involving two represented parties while preserving the opportunity for the agent to make an in-house sale.

Of course, this leads to an obvious problem if a buyer now represented by the firm wants to reconsider a property listed by the firm that had been seen earlier or if a new listing acquired by the broker meets the buyer's needs. If the broker does not wish to represent both parties, either the buyer or the seller would have to agree to cancel the agency agreement and allow the agent to act as the sole agent of the other party.

Because some risk does arise when a party terminates agency and reverts to customer status, some agents may choose to terminate both agreements and refer the parties to other agents. From a practical perspective, few agents wish to lose business by referring their buyers and sellers to other agents. Instead, agents take measures to minimize their risk through careful practice, making sure the parties fully understand the changing roles of the agent.

Other firms that specialize in representing buyers take the position that they will not actively solicit listings to sell. They will, however, occasionally list a property for one of their satisfied buyer-clients who now want to sell a property. They also will register a seller's property with the understanding that this property will be exposed to their buyer-clients. There is a clear disclaimer of agency with the seller, and no fee is required to register the property.

Another conflict may arise if more than one buyer-client is interested in the same property. This is the reverse of the situation of a listing broker working with a customer who is interested in more than one of the broker's listings in the same location. Some buyer-representation agreements contain a disclosure that the buyer's agent may enter into agreements with other buyers to locate property, making it possible that two or more buyers will be interested in the same property. If this should occur, the buyer's agent might seek an agreement authorizing the broker to show the property to all buyer-clients, with the understanding that

- none of the buyer-clients will consider the arrangement to be a conflict of interest, and
- all such multiple interests will be strictly confidential to the agent.

Remember that in the business of real estate, no form of agency is so pure that potential conflicts of interest cannot arise. If a broker decides beforehand how to handle possible conflicts, some serious problems may be avoided.

Advantages and Disadvantages of Exclusive Buyer Agency

There is a more dramatic solution to the above-mentioned potential conflicts of interest: Some brokers have chosen to limit their practice to exclusive buyer agency. This indicates that the broker represents only buyers and will not list a seller's property for sale, whereas most brokers who offer buyer representation also will offer representation services to sellers. The brokers who practice exclusive buyer agency promote themselves to buyers both aggressively and successfully.

Some of the advantages of exclusive buyer agency are the following:

- It reduces the possibility of the unauthorized representation of more than one party because exclusive buyers' brokers do not take listings.
- Buyers have greater confidence that they will see all the properties available from every source.
- Buyers have greater confidence that they will receive 100 percent undivided loyalty and expert advice on all property negotiations.
- Buyer loyalty to the agent increases under an exclusive buyer-representation agreement.
- Exclusive buyer agency tends to prevent lapses or mistakes in negotiating objectives and styles that often occur when brokers switch back and forth from one role to the other, as do brokers who practice nonexclusive agency.
- An exclusive buyer's agent is more likely to be able to charge and collect retainer fees because buyers are sure of the 100 percent commitment they receive from the broker.

The disadvantages of exclusive buyer agency include the following:

- Buyers sometimes want to sell; however, the firms will not take the listings.
- Because the company has no listings, the possibility of earning commissions from both the listing side and the selling side of the business is eliminated.
- A potential conflict of interest arises if two buyer-clients want to make offers on the same property.
- Exclusive buyer agency raises compensation issues, such as who pays the fee and whether listing brokers will cooperate and split any fees.

Single property. A broker may wish to contract to represent a buyer with respect to a single property only. The situation could be handled in a way similar to the case of the unrepresented seller in Chapter 5 (one-time-listing agreement). Remember, in a one-time-listing agreement, the licensee becomes the agent of the seller, but only for a specifically named buyer. This secures an agency relationship with at least one of the consumers in the transaction (the seller), while securing the ability to collect a commission should the transaction close.

In the original problem, what if the buyer-customer is interested in a specific property? If the seller is not represented by another broker or the seller is unrepresented and does not wish to enter in to a one-time-listing agreement, then the agent's status in the transaction is unclear. This could be resolved by having the buyer enter in to a one-time-buyer-representation agreement, but only for the specifically named property. For example, using the TAR form, the market area indicated in paragraph 3C would be limited to the specifically named property rather than a general market area, such as Texas or Nueces County. The buyer would revert to customer status for all other properties.

The one-time-buyer-representation agreement works particularly well when dealing with investors who ask a licensee to "be on the lookout" for particular types of properties. TREC would preclude the licensee from entering into a contract that had an open-ended termination date (§ 1101.652(b)(12)). To contractually represent a buyer in this case, the broker should prepare a brief letter agreement after first determining that the buyer is unaware of any similar property in the general location. For example, the agent might ask whether the buyer has been shown any large apartment buildings in the midtown area. If not, the investor-buyer agrees to a one-time-buyer-representation agreement but only for the specifically named property. The agent does not reveal the exact location of this property until the agreement is signed. This technique has proved helpful when the seller refuses to list a particular commercial property and the buyer does not want client status in regard to any other property except the one to be shown. Remember, the licensee must make clear which party is represented in this transaction and secure a signature from the party agreeing to pay the commission (§ 1101.652(b)(7)–(8); .806(c)).

■ BENEFITS OF BUYER-AGENCY RELATIONSHIPS

Agency Benefits to Buyer or Tenant

Following are some of the benefits to the buyer (or tenant) who receives client-level services.

Tailored buyer-representation contract. In a buyer-representation (or tenant-representation) agreement with the broker, the buyer can tailor the agent's services to meet the buyer's needs and adjust the compensation accordingly. This applies not only to large national companies seeking housing for relocated employees or sites for chain stores or restaurants but also to purchasers seeking residences or investment opportunities. In some cases, the buyer has already identified the property and the financing and wants the agent to handle the negotiations. In addition, licensees should not stray outside their area of expertise. While generally familiar with local market issues and developments, a licensee may not wish to take on the responsibility of showing properties anywhere in the state of Texas! Using Figure 6.1 as an example, paragraph 3C could indicate "Nueces and San Patricio counties." The purchaser who wished to look at properties in another county would be free to enter into a buyer-representation agreement with a broker from that county, as long as the other broker insures that agreement excludes Nueces and San Patricio counties.

Access to a larger marketplace. In practice, traditional agents frequently limit their search of properties to those properties in which the broker's commission is protected. Thus, they limit their search to properties listed in-house or in the MLS. The buyer's agent whose guarantee of commission is protected, although not necessarily paid, by a buyer-client is motivated to show the buyer all available properties that meet the stated requirements, including

- open-listing properties,
- properties exclusively listed with other brokers,
- for-sale-by-owner properties,
- foreclosure and probate sales,
- sales by lenders of real estate owned properties,
- sales by trusts and pension plans,
- properties owned by a government agency, and
- properties not yet on the market.

Stronger negotiating strategy. The buyer's agent views the entire transaction from the buyer's perspective, without the divided and diminished loyalty that would be demanded of an agent representing more than one party. Therefore, the buyer is in a stronger negotiating position. Also, the buyer may want the protection of an agent in dealings with an unrepresented owner. Some buyers fear that the reason an owner does not list with a broker is because something is wrong with the property.

Fiduciary responsibility of the agent. Under Texas licensing laws and the common law, the buyer's agent is held to a higher standard of skill and care in dealing with the buyer than a subagent of the seller or the seller's listing agent, who works with the buyer on a customer basis. Buyers' agents have an affirmative duty to their clients to thoroughly investigate and completely disclose all facts that bear on a buyer's decision to buy. On the other hand, buyers' agents have a duty to be honest and deal fairly—not equally or impartially—with sellers, but they owe no duty to advise and counsel sellers.

The buyer's agent is held to the same standard of performance in dealing with the buyer that the listing broker is held to in dealing with the seller. There is nothing unique about the responsibility and duties of the buyer's agent. There is no new fiduciary duty or ethical responsibility that the buyer's agent must learn. What is different is that the agent owes conventional common, statutory, and administrative law fiduciary duties to a different group of participants, namely buyers. The quantity and quality of client-level services are at least the same as those a listing agent would give sellers. It is simply the other side of the representation coin. Buyers are, quite simply, not legally entitled to this level of service unless they retain their own real estate agents to represent them.

Confidentiality. Confidentiality can be especially important when the buyer wishes to remain anonymous. For example, Sarah, a movie star, considers purchasing a new mansion. If the seller learns the identity of the intended buyer, the seller may likely hold firm or increase the asking price. A buyer's agent acting for an undisclosed principal may be able to negotiate a better price and better terms for the anonymous buyer.

More counseling, less selling. As opposed to persuasion to buy, the buyer can expect to receive more counseling, expert opinion, advocacy, and advice regarding the acquisition decision. When an agent is hired by the seller under an exclusive-right-to-sell listing, the agent's emphasis is on selling the property. When the buyer hires an agent under an exclusive-right-to-represent agreement, the agent does not sell a house but instead assists a buyer in purchasing a house. In a very real sense, the buyer's agent is a purchasing agent, not a selling agent. This agent's emphasis is on helping the client evaluate different properties and alternative courses of action, and then getting the best deal possible once having elected to go forward with negotiations on a property.

A buyer's agent might recommend inspection of a home at random times of the day and perhaps might check with the neighbors to gain more complete information about the property or the seller. Buyers' agents do their best to find out things about a property that the seller or the listing agent might not want to disclose or might not feel obligated to disclose, such as excess noise, sewage odors, high energy costs, traffic congestion, or unauthorized seller improvements. Buyers also expect their agents to review any proposed contract to determine whether unfavorable provisions necessitate hiring a real estate attorney. To illustrate the level of service due a client, consider the following example.

■ **EXAMPLE** George refers Betty to Sally of Bay Realty. Betty is interested in looking at properties. Betty says she wants someone to represent her best interests, and if she works well with Sally, she will purchase other properties through Sally. Sally decides to work with Betty on a client basis. Betty indicates she will pay Sally for her help and advice or will see that Sally is paid by the seller as a condition of any subsequent contract. She signs an exclusive buyer-representation agreement. Sally shows Betty a country property listed in the MLS with Sam of Main Realty, and Betty decides to buy it. Sally properly notifies Sam that she disclaims any subagency to Sam and states that she and Bay Realty represent the buyer and not the seller.

■ **QUESTION** In the course of negotiations, Sally deals with a number of important items, such as (1) price and appraised value, (2) seller financing, (3) earnest money, amount, and default remedies, (4) condition of property, (5) contingencies, and (6) fixtures and inventory. How should Sally treat each item, recognizing that her primary allegiance is to Betty?

■ **DISCUSSION** Sally must be honest and make appropriate disclosure to the seller; as Betty's agent, however, she owes a greater duty of skill, care, and disclosure to protect Betty's best interests. Sally can advise Betty how she might persuade the seller to modify the terms and reduce the selling price and what alternative courses of action Betty might take. Sally should handle each item as follows:

Price and appraised value. Sally should analyze the property and the seller's position to obtain the lowest realistic price for Betty. She should do a comparative market analysis (CMA) on the property and consider getting Betty's permission to submit the CMA, along with any lower offer on the property, to the seller through Sam. Sally may ask to see any appraisals that have been made and may suggest obtaining another appraisal to support a lower-price offer. Sally, as the buyer's agent, legally negotiates with the seller through Sam for a lower price. She would not do so as a subagent. In a buyer's market, Sally might suggest that Betty prepare two offers and not reveal the higher offer unless and until the seller rejects the first offer. Subagents who did that would breach their fiduciary duties.

Seller financing. Sally need not suggest that Betty submit tax returns and a credit report unless these are requested by the seller. Sally might suggest seeking legal advice regarding favorable financing terms, such as no due-on-sale clause, no prepayment penalty, liberal grace periods and minimal late charges, default remedies limited to judicial foreclosure with no deficiency against Betty (nonrecourse), or deferred interest.

Earnest money. Sally can suggest that the earnest money be relatively modest or be reflected in an unsecured note. Conversely, she might suggest a substantial earnest money deposit to convey the buyer's serious intent to purchase the property.

Condition of property. Sally might suggest seeking the advice of an attorney regarding the use of additional clauses addressing such items as a property inspection that makes the purchase contingent on Betty's satisfaction; a requirement that the seller pay for a residential service contract; and written warranties regarding roofing, plumbing, and termites.

Contingencies. Sally can explain the meaning of standard contingency clauses as they appear in TREC-promulgated addenda. Of course, she should be very careful not to engage in the unauthorized practice of law when dealing with contingencies and should never add any language of her own.

Fixtures and inventory. Sally may advise Betty to request in her offer additional personal property for the same purchase price, such as paintings and Oriental rugs. Sally should review any written inventory list before the offer is prepared and check to see that no substitution of items occurs.

Other items. As a buyer's agent, Sally must be careful not to reveal to the seller or the listing agent facts regarding Betty's bargaining position—for example, plans to buy adjoining parcels or adjoining condominium apartment units or that a resale buyer waits in the wings. Sally has no duty to disclose the name of the buyer or that Sally might lend Betty money to make the down payment. However, in Texas, if Sally is being paid by Betty and also expects to be paid by Sam, that fact must be clearly disclosed and consented to by all parties or Sally and/or Bay Realty could face TREC disciplinary hearings and possible loss of license (TRELA § 1101.652(b)(7); (8)).

Sally must use her skill to research and investigate the contemplated acquisition. She must advise Betty of any facts relevant to the purchase decision that can be used to negotiate better terms (for example, that the seller is near foreclosure, is filing for divorce, or has already bought a new home; the property is about to be rezoned; the neighbors are unruly; or the house was burglarized four times last year).

Sally can accept an incentive fee for obtaining a reduction in the listed price. But, again, if Sally receives compensation from more than one party in the transaction, that fact must be agreed to by all parties.

Sally must do more than produce copies of relevant documents for Betty. She must be sure Betty understands the impact on her purchase decision of key provisions in the documents. If she feels it is necessary, Sally should recommend that Betty obtain legal, title, or property inspection advice from outside experts.

Sally has a duty to express any doubts she may have about the suitability of the property for Betty, especially if she feels that the property is, in Sally's opinion, overpriced.

Benefits to Buyers' Agents

The buyer's agent can expect certain benefits from an agency relationship with a buyer.

Greater client loyalty. Traditionally, real estate agents work with "wandering" buyers on the chance of earning a fee, sometimes even if the chance is remote. With an exclusive-right-to-purchase representation agreement, the agent has greater control and little fear of losing the buyer to an owner or to another brokerage. For many of the same reasons that traditional brokers seldom take open listings (oral or written) with sellers, buyers' agents may be reluctant to do so as well.

Avoid conflict of loyalty. The buyer's agent should feel no ethical discomfort or hesitancy in withholding from the seller-customer information on the buyer's future plans for the property, including immediate resale or obtaining options on adjoining properties. Nor should the buyer's agent be reluctant to disclose to the buyer the broker's opinion that the property is overpriced or that the seller's terms are unrealistic. As a matter of fact, the agent is duty-bound to express such opinions to a buyer-client.

Within the bounds of honesty and fairness to the seller-customer, the buyer's agent can develop with the buyer a negotiating strategy that promotes the buyer's best interests at all times and seeks to obtain reasonable concessions from the seller. Healthy and complete negotiations are not as likely in traditional real estate transactions where agents represent sellers' interests only. While a buyer and a seller are not hostile in the sense of a plaintiff and a defendant in a lawsuit, they do have competing interests. The buyer's agent will be able to represent the buyer's best interests in this spirit of competition while negotiating honestly to arrive at a transaction agreeable to both the buyer and the seller.

In addition to price, many other items must be negotiated in every transaction. Among these are

- initial and additional earnest money deposits;
- down payment;
- seller financing;
- interest rate;
- due date;
- sales price;
- commissions;
- terms;
- home warranty;
- termite report;
- assessments;
- appraisal;
- closing costs;
- title report;
- possession date;
- impound, reserve, or escrow account on the seller's loan (in assumption situations);
- title and escrow agent;
- personal property and inventory;
- discount points;
- repairs;
- inspection contingencies;
- hazard insurance;
- default remedies; and
- extensions.

During the offer and counteroffer stage of the transaction, any one of these items can provide an opportunity for conflict between the buyer and the seller and, thus, a deal-making compromise. The buyer's agent is able to negotiate all these items on the buyer's behalf. Neither a listing agent nor a cooperating agent acting as the seller's subagent has the legal ability to negotiate on the buyer's behalf.

No liability for acts of the listing broker. Because a buyer's agent has no agency relationship with either the seller or the listing broker, the buyer's agent is not vicariously liable for their acts (TRELA § 1101.805(d)). In addition, buyers' agents tend either to verify information about the property given by the listing broker or to require that the seller give certain warranties or representations concerning such conditions of a property as roof, plumbing, and boundary concerns. This reduces the agent's exposure to claims for misrepresentation, for concealment of material defects, or for failure to ascertain material facts. Although changes in Texas law have reduced the broker's liability for the unknown acts of other brokers, it is felt that a buyer's agent is clearly separated from the acts of the listing broker. This may have the effect of further reducing the chance of the buyer's agent being sued for things that are not the agent's fault. However, in Texas, the buyer's agent has an increased responsibility to the buyer-client to use due diligence to discover problems that may adversely affect the client.

FEE ARRANGEMENTS

An entire book could be written on all the possible methods of compensating a buyer's broker. Keep in mind that the broker's first concern is to become comfortable with the agency relationship that exists and the types of services to be provided. The mechanics of compensation seem to fall into place once the agency relationship is clearly understood. Often, the buyer's broker's fee is paid out of the sales proceeds, either through an authorized commission split or through a credit from the seller to the buyer at closing.

Seller-oriented brokers can benefit from understanding the methods by which buyers' brokers structure their compensation arrangements. Because listing brokers will receive offers from buyers represented by their own brokers, each listing broker should become acquainted with how the offers may be structured and how fees are handled. The following sections summarize the ways in which buyers' brokers can be paid for their services. The way in which fees are to be paid should be stated in writing and clearly understood well in advance to avoid conflict between the buyer and the broker.

Retainer Fee

Regardless of how a broker is compensated, some brokers feel more comfortable obtaining advance payments. This can serve as a screening device to determine whether a buyer is serious about buying. However, some states have extensive restrictions on advance fees. For example, in California the broker cannot withdraw monies from retainer trust accounts to cover hourly fees until several days after an accounting has been made to a client for services performed, and statements must be sent every calendar quarter and at termination. In Texas, however, no such requirement exists.

If a retainer fee is to be taken, some benefit or service must accrue to the person paying the fee; otherwise, it may be considered one of the two unconscionable acts under the Texas Deceptive Trade Practices and Consumer Protection Act. If no research is done for the client, no houses shown, no counseling, advising, or any other service performed and the client cancels the agreement, it may be difficult for the broker to justify keeping the retainer fee.

If the retainer fee from the buyer is retained by the broker and the transaction closes with the buyer's broker being compensated from the seller's side of the transaction, the broker technically receives compensation from both parties, a fact that must be disclosed and consented to by all parties. Some brokers choose to refund the retainer fee on closing to avoid this problem and make as much cash available for the buyer as possible. Tax counsel should be consulted regarding the deductibility of the retainer portion as a professional fee.

When deciding to require a retainer fee, the broker should establish a consistent office policy. In other words, the broker should not decide selectively that some buyers must pay a retainer fee and others will not be required to do so.

Seller-Paid Fee

No legal or ethical barriers prohibit the seller from paying the buyer's broker fee or authorizing the listing broker to share fees with the buyer's broker. Either is a matter of contract and may be handled in advance by appropriate language in both the seller's listing agreement and the buyer-representation agreement. Substantial legal authority backs up the proposition that the payment of fees does not determine whom a licensee represents. As long as the agency relationship is clear and explicit, it does not matter legally whether the buyer or the seller pays the fee. If the agency is unclear, however, a court will likely consider who paid the fee to be an important factor in determining who is the agent's principal.

Currently, in residential sales, the traditional commission-sharing arrangement between the listing broker and the other broker is the most widely accepted method of compensation for the buyer's broker. In essence, the seller is notified of the arrangement and agrees that the other broker represents the buyer and that the commission may be split between the listing broker and the buyer's broker. This tends to keep the transaction simple. However, there is some precedent to support the notion that this practice may create conflicts of interest and misunderstandings, especially regarding procuring-cause issues.

In Texas, some buyer's broker specialists are using and promoting the practice of the buyer's inserting a condition in the sales contract that requires that the seller pay the buyer's broker on behalf of the buyer or reimburse the buyer for brokerage expenses at closing so that the buyer may pay his or her broker. The broker should not draft these conditional terms.

Traditionally, the buyer's broker receives a share of the commission from the listing broker out of the sales proceeds. However, two alternative methods of providing compensation exist:

- The listing broker agrees to reduce the commission by the amount of the usual split with the cooperating broker so that the seller either can reduce the price by a like amount (the net offer approach) or can give an offsetting credit on the buyer's closing statement in the amount of the cooperating broker's share.
- The buyer's broker receives the amount of the fee negotiated with the buyer. If the amount offered by the seller to the cooperating broker exceeds the fee that the buyer is obligated to pay, any difference is credited to the buyer. If the amount is not sufficient to pay the fee, the buyer pays the difference to the broker.

When employing compensation methods that differ from the traditional splitting of the listing broker's fee, cover letters should be drafted and accompany the offer to explain this arrangement to both the listing agent and the seller. The inherent problem with this approach is a lack of sophistication on the part of sellers, buyers, and some brokers, making such agreements difficult to negotiate, particularly in residential transactions.

Commission Split

In a number of states, real estate agents do not use formal written agreements to represent buyers. Commissions are normally paid out of an authorized commission split with the listing broker or by the seller's crediting the buyer with a specified amount out of the sales proceeds. There usually is a written acknowledgment of buyer representation in the state-required agency disclosure form, with a written confirmation also included in the purchase agreement. (Note that Texas does not have such a form.) The preferred practice is to use a formal written buyer-representation agreement that addresses the issues of exclusivity, compensation, scope of services, termination, and conflicts of interest.

In Texas, no state-approved or state-promulgated form covers buyer representation, seller representation, or representation of more than one party. The Texas Association of REALTORS®, however, produces such forms for its membership (see Figures 5.2 and Figure 6.1). Some of the larger local REALTOR® associations also have developed separate forms for their own local memberships.

A buyer's broker, if planning on a traditional fee-split method, must determine from the listing broker, at initial contact, whether the listing broker is authorized and willing to split the commission with the buyer's broker (as opposed to a subagent of the seller). If the listing broker is not authorized to split the commission, the buyer's broker should advise the buyer of that fact. The buyer then may decide to reduce the offering price to a net amount that reflects that the buyer is to pay his broker's fee. The seller and the listing broker will have to reach their own agreement on whether to reduce the listing broker's commission.

Now that most MLSs accept listings in which sellers can offer cooperation regarding commissions but not subagency, there will be an increased general acceptance by sellers, buyers, and brokers of such commission-splitting arrangements. Sellers primarily are concerned with selling their property and netting a certain amount of money from the sales proceeds. Most sellers are much less concerned about whether their brokers split commissions with someone labeled as a buyer's broker or as a subagent of the seller. In fact, sellers often feel that the other broker, even if described as a subagent, actually works for the buyer. Some sellers feel that compensation for both the listing broker and the selling broker is already part of the listing and purchase price; that is, they feel there really are two fees—the listing fee and the selling fee.

■ **EXAMPLE** In *LA&N Interests, Inc. v. Fish*, a buyer's broker and his licensed associate felt that they had been unjustly deprived of a commission in a transaction and sued their client and the competing broker to recover their commission and damages for interference with their buyer's brokerage agreement. The buyer-client bought a property with the assistance of another broker, and the buyer's broker was paid nothing, even though the buyer's broker had an exclusive-agency representation agreement with the buyer. The buyer's brokerage agreement with the buyer-client clearly stated that the client "shall have no liability or obligation to pay a Professional Service Fee to [the buyer's broker]" but rather that the seller would pay the buyer's broker fee. This flaw—assuming that some party other than the client would pay the commission—led to the broker's not being able to recover from his client. Neither was he able to recover from the seller, who had never agreed to pay him in the first place.

Although listing brokers typically voluntarily reduce their share of the commission if another broker as subagent finds the buyer, a few listing brokers adamantly resist such a reduction or split if a buyer's broker is involved. In the first instance, why should a seller or a listing broker consent to a split? Simply because it is more likely to lead to a sale of the listed property. The listing broker, some sellers reason, should not be paid twice as much just because the buyer works with a buyer's broker instead of a seller's subagent.

■ **EXAMPLE** Assume that the seller signs an exclusive-right-to-sell listing agreement with a 7 percent commission. Most of the transaction participants expect that the 7 percent commission will cover all the sales commissions involved, with the listing broker and the other broker each earning 3.5 percent. Most sellers would refuse to sign if the total commissions were 10.5 percent, with the listing broker receiving 7 percent.

Why would a broker not consent to a split commission? The listing broker would not consent if there is an opportunity to obtain a full rather than a reduced commission. If the listing agreement contains a clause permitting such a split with a buyer's broker, listing brokers who are REALTORS® should reconsider this refusal in view of the ethical restrictions in the NAR Code of Ethics. These articles require that the broker cooperate with other brokers and act in the best interests of the client at all times. If the listing broker's refusal to share commissions results in too low an offer, or no offer at all, the seller may have grounds for complaint, especially if it appears that the broker's sole motivation was to receive a greater fee than usual in a cooperative sale.

In any event, an agent's fiduciary duty of full disclosure to the client under TREC rules requires that the listing broker advise the seller of the general company policy regarding cooperation and compensation of buyers' agents. In brief, listing brokers should do everything possible to make it easy for the buyer's broker to show the seller's property and make an offer.

Buyer-Paid Fee

Buyers may elect to pay the commission directly to their broker. This may avoid any implication of seller agency or conflict of interest that may be present when the seller pays the brokerage fee. An experienced buyer's broker, not wanting a nonclient to control payment, may prefer being paid directly by the buyer rather than receive a commission split from the listing broker or be paid directly by the seller at closing. Buyer-paid compensation can take several forms, such as an hourly rate, a percentage fee, or a flat fee.

■ **EXAMPLE** Sam, the listing broker, and Carol, the other broker representing the seller through the listing broker as a subagent of the seller, agree on a 50-50 commission split. The property is a commercial warehouse not listed in the MLS. The listing commission is 5 percent. The offer is submitted at $1 million on a $1.2 million listing. The seller accepts the offer, provided that Sam reduces his fee to 4 percent. Sam agrees to do so but fails to inform Carol. Carol now receives $20,000 instead of $30,000.

Hourly rate. Under this arrangement, the agent is, in essence, a consultant, charging a noncontingent hourly rate. It is payable regardless of whether a title transfer is contemplated, for example, when a consultant advises on whether to develop a shopping center or a commercial office building. A variation may be an hourly fee that is applied against an incentive fee if the agent finds the right property for the buyer. This requires that an agent keep time sheets and be diligent in record keeping and billing practices.

Percentage fee. A buyer's agent may charge a percentage fee based on the selling price of the property bought by the client, just as most listing agents do. The obvious problem the percentage fee creates is the appearance of a potential conflict of interest because the higher the purchase price, the greater the fee—making the percentage fee seem seller-oriented. The prime benefit of the percentage fee is that real estate licensees and clients are accustomed to this arrangement.

Many buyers' agents begin by charging buyers on a percentage basis and later progress into charging flat fees (discussed below). Other agents combine an hourly rate with a percentage of the purchase price. Rates may vary when the seller is not represented by a listing broker because the buyer's agent may have to do more of the background work and handle negotiations with the seller.

Flat fees (contingent or noncontingent). A buyer's agent is sometimes compensated on a flat fee, payable if a buyer purchases a property located through the agent. The amount of the flat fee is based on the estimate by the agent of the work and skills involved, the potential fee that will be paid by the seller, and the probability of success.

A contingent flat fee often is based on what the buyer will pay for the agent's services, depending on the price range of the home or an estimate of the amount of work involved.

■ **EXAMPLE** Betty is looking for a property in the $175,000 to $225,000 range. A cooperating broker might expect to receive a fee of $6,000 on a $200,000 sale.

Carol, a buyer's broker, charges the buyer a $6,000 flat contingent fee. Whether Betty selects a property for $175,000 or for $225,000, the fee to Carol remains $6,000.

Another method is the noncontingent flat fee. The agent predicts the amount of work necessary to accomplish the client's objectives and then sets a flat fee. This approach is seldom used unless the agent has gained a great deal of experience in representing buyers.

Some buyer-representation agreements provide that the buyer is obligated to pay the fee but is entitled to a credit for any amounts the seller agrees to pay. Thus, the buyer would not pay the buyer's broker fee in the usual MLS sale, although the buyer might pay the fee directly if the agent located an unlisted property, a builder-owned house, or a for-sale-by-owner property. An experienced buyer's agent might encourage the client to make such a stipulation, just as the client might base a sale on the condition that the seller fix the roof.

Disclosure of fee. A buyer's broker paid directly by the buyer might disclose the exact amount of the fee on the offer to purchase. In this way, the seller and the listing broker have a clear understanding of what fees are being paid. It is easier for the seller to see that the net proceeds will be about the same with a gross price offer. The seller could be paying both brokers or could accept a net price offer, with the buyer paying the buyer's broker's commission and the seller paying the listing broker a reduced commission.

An argument can be made for not disclosing the amount of fees on the offer to purchase based on confidentiality. If, in fact, the buyer's broker has contracted to receive less than the typical commission split, the amount of the difference could accrue to the buyer's benefit.

Net Purchase Price

The net purchase price is the sales price reduced by the buyer's brokerage fee. A theory supporting the net price method is that the buyer has only a certain amount for the down payment. A portion of that money no longer will be deducted from the seller's proceeds to pay the other broker but now will be used to pay the buyer's broker. The restructured brokerage fees will not increase the acquisition costs. The overall transaction will not change, even if a loan is involved. If accepted, a net offer may result in lower title and closing costs, which are now based on the lower purchase price.

■ **EXAMPLE** Betty makes a full-price offer to the seller on a $100,000 listing in the following way: a net purchase price of $97,300, plus Betty agrees to pay Carol, her buyer's broker, a cash fee of $2,700. The seller acknowledges that the buyer's broker represents the buyer and not the seller in this transaction. Carol inserts a provision in the sales contract that the buyer agrees to pay the sum of $97,300 to the seller and $2,700 to Carol for services rendered.

Lenders. The amount of a maximum loan is based on a percentage of the purchase price plus the buyer's broker's commission. The commission is thus paid from the loan proceeds rather than from the buyer's personal cash. A different approach is used in a net offer situation. So that a lender will add to the sales price a buyer's broker's commission as an acquisition cost, the broker might provide the lender with a copy of the purchase contract in which the buyer acknowledges the buyer's broker's commission. This makes it easier for a lender to visualize the economic adjustments made in the transaction.

Federal Housing Administration (FHA) regulations specifically authorize an add-back to the purchase price of the buyer's broker's fee under Section 532 of the National Housing Act. The notable exception is a Department of Veterans Affairs (VA) loan. The VA does not allow lenders to include buyer's broker's fees in the loans to be paid by veteran purchasers. This position is based on the belief that

- the buyer's broker's fee may increase the acquisition cost;
- buyers are adequately protected by the requirement to furnish a certificate of reasonable value and reasonable closing costs and by access to many properties through general advertising; and
- selling brokers, although representing sellers, do not ignore buyers' interests.

Note that no VA rule prohibits the buyer's broker from receiving a seller-approved commission split from the listing broker. Thus, a VA transaction can include a buyer's broker, but the broker must be compensated by or through the seller. This is similar to the seller's paying the points on the buyer's loan.

Gross Price

An alternative method of buyer's broker compensation that is gaining some acceptance in residential sales transactions is the gross-price method. The buyer pays the gross purchase price. The purchase contract provides that the seller then pays the buyer's broker's commission. The seller acknowledges and accepts that the buyer's broker solely represents the buyer and not the seller, despite the payment of the fee by the seller. To ease the listing broker's and the seller's concerns, some brokers add that this fee is the sole compensation of the buyer's broker in the transaction. Texas licensees should recall that it is grounds for loss of license to be paid by more than one party to a transaction without the full knowledge and consent of all parties.

This method satisfies all outside participants in the transaction, such as appraisers, lenders, and insurers, and it is easier to finance the contract amount. This method helps reduce the concerns over excess commission expense and double charging, and it seems easier for the seller to understand and respond to a customary sales price offer. The seller's main difficulty is psychological: The seller and the listing broker may feel that while they pay the buyer's broker's fee, the buyer receives the services. This flaw is less serious when using the gross-price method of fee payment, where a buyer's broker's commission can be built into the contract price through the terms of the buyer's offer. As a consequence, the cash required, the mortgage amount, the net proceeds to the seller, and the sales price are approximately the same as they would be in the traditional sale, in which both brokers represent the seller and both commissions are included in the contract price. To avoid loan underwriting problems, some brokers include the following language in the purchase contract: "Seller credits $ [dollar amount] toward buyer's expenses listed on the closing statement."

Some advantages of the sellers paying the commission are that it

- clears up questions of who works for whom and who pays whom;
- protects the buyer's agent from the listing agent's breaches and other chances of losing commissions because of badly crafted listing agreements;
- protects the buyer-client from having to pay the broker's commission at closing if the seller refuses to pay, but it provides the option to do so should the situation require;
- allows no reasonable basis for procuring-cause disputes;
- presents no suggestion of interfering with the listing broker's commission agreement with the seller;
- works equally well for listed, unlisted, builder, MLS, or non-MLS properties;
- places responsibility for securing the compensation of the buyer's broker directly on the shoulders of the client whose interests were served by the broker; and
- does not trigger the TRELA § 1101.652(b)(8) prohibition concerning payment from more than one party in the transaction without knowledge and consent of both, unless the buyer's broker has collected a retainer fee from the buyer in advance.

Some disadvantages are that it

- is relatively untested in the courts in Texas;
- may change expected tax advantages for the parties; and
- may cause some confusion among lenders until it is widely recognized, thus impeding some transactions.

It is important for brokers to understand compensation alternatives when they consider representing buyers. Many brokers working with buyer prospects now realize that they need not give away their time and expertise. Brokers should study the different methods of representation and develop their skills so that they can comfortably discuss with buyers and listing brokers the amounts and various methods of compensation. For assistance in this area, many buyers' broker books and seminars are helpful.

WRITTEN NOTIFICATION OF COMPENSATION TO BROKER

Regardless of who will be responsible for the payment of fees or commissions to the broker, it is strongly advised that such agreements be in writing. Although Texas law does not require that listing contracts or buyer-representation contracts be in writing, a broker will have no legal recourse against a seller or a buyer who refuses to pay a fee unless the agreement was written (TRELA § 1101.806(c)).

In addition to written buyer or seller commission agreements, brokers are also advised to have written agreements relating to fee splits between cooperating brokers. Most MLSs require that listing brokers disclose all fee arrangements to other brokers when the property is published in the MLS. In addition, the "Broker Information and Ratification of Fee" section that appears at the bottom of a standard TREC contract form spells out under what conditions and in what amounts any compensation will be paid from the listing broker to the other broker.

The following example shows the need for comprehensive commission agreements.

■ **EXAMPLE** In *Trammel Crow Company No. 60, et al. v. William Jefferson Harkinson* (40 Tex. Sup. Ct. J. 425, 1997), a broker acting as a tenant's agent located a commercial rental space for the client. Subsequently, the client went around the broker and negotiated a lease directly with the property owner, who was represented by a different broker. The owner's agent was paid according to the representation agreement between the owner and the listing broker, which did not address payment of a commission to a tenant's broker.

The tenant's broker sought payment of a commission from the owner's broker. The supreme court found that the tenant's broker was not entitled to a commission because there was no contract between the tenant's broker and the property owner.

Comment: If the tenant's broker had had a clause in the tenant's representation agreement that required payment by the tenant in the event the owners did not agree to pay, the tenant's broker may have had a legitimate claim for a commission from the tenant, unless other issues precluded payment.

■ PROCURING CAUSE

According to John Reilly's *The Language of Real Estate*, procuring cause is "that effort that brings about the desired result." Occasionally, more than one real estate licensee works with a buyer in locating a property. Without a clearly written agreement, disputes may arise over which licensee was the procuring cause of the sale and thus is entitled to a share of the commission. These disputes are sometimes resolved in arbitration using guidelines such as those developed by NAR.

In Texas, when a buyer or a tenant in a commercial or residential transaction desires representation and contracts with a buyer's broker or a tenant representative, procuring cause generally becomes a legal nonissue. This is true even if the buyer or the tenant was first shown a property by the listing or leasing agent or their subagents and even if negotiations have begun. However, creating an agency relationship will not, in itself, prevent claims filed asserting procurement by another licensee.

■ PURCHASE AGREEMENT

Attorneys representing buyers often view TREC-promulgated contract forms for residential sales as being seller-oriented or at least as containing some buyer compromises. Therefore, some buyers prefer to work with their own attorneys to develop acceptable purchase agreements. Such an agreement can be similar in format to the standard purchase contract, except that it is prepared from the buyer's perspective. Other buyers' agents prefer to use a special buyer's addendum, which can be attached to the standard form of purchase agreement.

When assisting a buyer with the preparation of an offer to purchase, the buyer's agent should keep in mind that

- the agent is not an attorney and must avoid the unauthorized practice of law;
- any complicated drafting should be left to an attorney, although it may be appropriate for the agent to suggest various negotiating strategies and certain contingencies and financing techniques that should be incorporated into the offer;
- the offer should not be so one-sided that it is unfair or unrealistic; and
- although the agent should help the buyer evaluate key contract terms, the agent should not decide what is best for the buyer.

What follows is a discussion of important items for the buyer's agent to consider before preparing an offer to purchase. Some items will influence price negotiations. Some states, including Texas, require the use of preapproved forms, and this requirement may affect the ability of a buyer's agent to use some of these suggestions.

Again, keep in mind that TREC contract forms may be adjusted to conform to the intent of the principals, not necessarily rigidly copied. It should be noted, however, that modifications to a promulgated form should be at the direction of the principal—not at the discretion of the agent. (Also remember that this chapter looks at these contract terms from the point of view of the buyer and the buyer's agent. Many of these statements would be reversed in the negotiating strategy of the seller's agent or the subagent.)

Earnest Money Deposit

In Texas, earnest money is not essential to the validity of a contract. A real estate contract in Texas is just valid with or without earnest money. Earnest money is not the consideration necessary to make the contract valid. It is money or something else of value, usually to be held in escrow by a third party, to be given to the seller in the event of the buyer's default on the contract before closing.

Earnest money is meant to provide a nonjudicial remedy for damages incurred by the seller because of the buyer's default. It is an alternative remedy to a lawsuit for damages, specific performance, injunction, or other legal action. However, its major significance is that a seller does not have to go to court to get the earnest money; that is why earnest money is referred to as a nonjudicial remedy. Traditionally, the buyer gives the earnest money check to the broker to accompany the offer and to be deposited by the broker. Currently, TREC-promulgated forms do not indicate that necessity, stating only that the buyer shall deposit the earnest money with the escrow agent named in the contract "upon execution of this contract by both parties."

Buyer's brokers should keep the following in mind when their clients agree to deposit earnest money in the course of a transaction:

- Discuss with the buyer-client the strategy of depositing a large amount of earnest money as a negotiation tool to drive down the sales price, giving an offer (in the eyes of the seller) an advantage over competing offers without such security. Remember, though, that a large deposit also increases the buyer-client's potential financial loss. If the buyer-client is risk-averse, he or she might want to keep the initial deposit low, with any additional deposit to be made 10 days to 15 days (or within some other acceptable period) after the seller accepts the offer. If a substantial deposit is made, suggest that the client consider the use of an interest-bearing account to benefit the buyer.

- Avoid giving the deposit directly to the seller. As stated earlier, TREC contract forms do not provide for sellers or sellers' agents or subagents to deposit earnest money. Nor do they provide for earnest money checks to be carried back and forth with the contract documents. They are to be deposited by buyers or designated licensees on execution of the contract by both parties unless otherwise agreed. If done differently, the contract should specify exactly how it will be handled. The selection of the escrow agent in the contract is a fully negotiable item; however, the issue must be agreed on by the parties or no enforceable contract exists.
- Where appropriate, request that the seller deposit a sufficient sum of earnest money to cover any closing and title cancellation charges, buyer's moving and storage expenses, and some money for the buyer's broker if the contract is terminated due to the seller's default. If the buyer-representation agreement calls for the broker to get half of any earnest money put up and forfeited by the seller, the amount requested must be doubled; otherwise, the buyer will not receive enough to cover reasonable potential damages.

Assignability

In Texas, most standard contracts are assignable unless otherwise stated. An assignable contract is one in which the rights to the contract can be given, or assigned, to some other party. Of course, the parties should understand this clearly before entering into any negotiations.

Seller Financing

If the buyer asks the seller to carry back a note and mortgage or a similar security instrument, such as a deed of trust or an installment sales contract, the buyer should specify in the purchase agreement the key provisions to be inserted in the financing document for the buyer's benefit. These might include

- no prepayment penalty,
- no due-on-sale clause,
- nonrecourse liability (the seller's remedy is to foreclose on the property without the buyer being personally liable for any deficiency),
- extended grace periods, and
- deferral of interest.

Depending on the terms of the seller-provided financing (maturity date, interest rate, and amount of down payment), the buyer should be flexible in selecting the offering price. These provisions are provided for in a TREC-promulgated addendum for seller financing that should be the only form used, unless the buyer's or the seller's attorney drafts another addendum. Don't try to create them in the special provisions paragraph of the contract. Such action is grounds for loss of license and a basis for lawsuit by the client if the terms are drafted incorrectly and lead to damage to the buyer. Notwithstanding this caution, the buyer-client, as a party to the purchase contract, has the right to insert any desired provision in a contract offer. The client's agent must follow the client's instructions, but when substantial modifications are made, the agent should advise the client to seek competent legal advice first.

Contract Acceptance

The seller's acceptance of the offer is effective only if delivered in writing to the buyer or the buyer's agent. This gives buyers the longest time possible in which to revoke an offer if they choose, for whatever reason.

Extended Closing

For their own protection, buyers should consider whether they want to be given the contractual right to extend closing dates beyond those in the TREC form if they have difficulty arranging financing or otherwise meeting the closing dates.

Inspection

The buyer's offer could be made contingent on one or more professional inspections. If there are problems with the condition of the property, the buyer may be justified in canceling the contract, based on the results of the inspection. The TREC-promulgated sales contracts provide for an option fee to be paid by the buyer to the seller, giving the buyer the unrestricted right to inspect and the unrestricted right to terminate the contract for some agreed-on period after the acceptance of the offer.

The contract provides boxes that may be checked indicating that if the property is purchased, the option fee will or will not be credited to the buyer. Buyers' agents or sellers' agents or subagents attempting to create their own version of this provision will be engaging in the unauthorized practice of law. Keep in mind, however, that a principal or an attorney acting for a client may use alternative inspection language in addenda. Likewise, professional organizations such as the Texas Association of Realtors® may create alternative inspection addendum forms for optional use by their members.

Property Condition

The seller should submit a property condition disclosure report for the buyer's approval. A buyer's agent may counsel the buyer-client to require that the seller agree to the following:

- No personal property items will be substituted for those at the property when it was shown and that were expected, by the buyer, to be included in the purchase price.
- The property is in the same or the required improved condition at the time of possession by the buyer, as so contracted.
- The property is clear of debris, and the appliances and the plumbing, heating, and electrical systems are in good working condition.
- All required building permits have been issued.
- All adverse environmental conditions will be removed.
- The present use is lawful.

TREC contract forms already include some of these concerns. Texas law requires that most sellers furnish buyers with a Seller's Disclosure of Property Condition in accordance with Section 5.008 of the Texas Property Code. TREC has produced an approved, but not promulgated, form that licensees may use to meet this Property Code requirement. Sellers subject to this disclosure requirement to the buyer must do so by the time specified in the Property Code or the transaction may be subject to rescission by the buyer. A licensee who fails to make the client aware of the necessity and availability of this form for use could face a lawsuit from a damaged client and loss of license under TRELA § 1101.652(b)(1).

Pests

The buyer may want to require that the seller agree to pay for a pest-clearance report from a licensed exterminator chosen by the buyer, and the seller may agree to repair all pest damage or to treat the home if necessary. The seller may be required to treat for fleas and/or termites and other wood-infesting organisms, using care not to use chemicals that may make the dwelling unsafe after use.

Assessments

The seller should agree to pay all assessments at closing, on the theory that the enhanced value of these improvements has been reflected in the sales price. Suppose that an assessment is outstanding at a low interest rate (a $20,000 sewer assessment payable in ten years at 6 percent, for example). Rather than have the seller pay off the assessment, consider having the buyer assume the assessment and lower the purchase price accordingly or credit the amount against the down payment.

Title Matters

The seller should agree to correct any title defect by a certain date; in fact, the closing can be postponed at the buyer's election to allow the defect to be cleared. The buyer may want to consider paying for the owner's title insurance policy to have the nonnegotiable right, under the Real Estate Settlement Procedures Act (RESPA), to choose the title insurer. Under RESPA, regardless of who pays for the title policy, the buyer cannot be required to use a specific title insurer as a condition of sale. By the same token, a seller cannot be forced to pay for a title policy. Thus, from a practical perspective, the party paying for the policy usually chooses the title insurer.

Financing and Other Contingencies

Financing contingencies should be structured so that the buyer has enough time to perform. It is appropriate to make the contract subject to the review and approval of the buyer's attorney or tax adviser. If the buyer cannot meet a contingency, such as obtaining loan approval, the buyer should have the choice to cancel, extend, or waive the condition and proceed to close, perhaps obtaining funds from another source.

If the property increases in value after the offer is accepted and before title transfers, the buyer who didn't qualify for financing could benefit by waiving the contingency and assigning his or her rights in the contract to another buyer for a profit. The buyer should use reasonable efforts to meet the contingency and not use the contingency clause as a bad-faith means to tie up the seller's property.

Miscellaneous Checklist

In a seller's market, the buyer may not be in a good position to demand too many concessions from the seller. The buyer's agent should consider covering some of the following items with the client for possible inclusion in a purchase contract for the buyer's benefit:

- The buyer is permitted occupancy prior to closing.
- The buyer is granted a right of first refusal to acquire any adjoining property owned by the seller.
- The buyer is given credit for any impound (escrow) accounts on assumed mortgages.
- The buyer is given the right to lock in points on a loan.
- The seller pays the appraisal fees and points on the loan.
- The buyer can extend the satisfaction date of any seller-provided financing.
- The buyer-borrower is given the right of first refusal if the seller discounts the sale of any purchase-money mortgage that the seller carried back.
- The seller agrees to allow the buyer-borrower to substitute collateral on any seller-provided financing.
- The seller provides a corporate resolution if the seller is a corporation, indicating, among other things, who is duly authorized by the corporation to sign all necessary documents on behalf of the corporation.
- The seller covers the buyer's expenses if the seller refuses to close on time.
- The seller permits the buyer to show the property to prospective tenants prior to closing.
- The seller allows the buyer reasonable access to the property to permit inspection by buyer's representatives such as interior designers and architects.

The seller's agent or subagent should urge the seller to consider resisting any or all of these concessions unless the seller-client gains some exceptional benefit in return. Sometimes an overly aggressive buyer's agent gives advice that works to the buyer's disadvantage in the negotiations. The buyer must keep in mind that each concession requested from the seller may result in refusal of an offer and the possible loss to the buyer of a desirable property. Similarly, overly aggressive listing agents may give sellers negotiating advice such as rejecting an offer or encouraging sellers to make harsh counteroffers that are unacceptable to buyers and actually harm the sellers. In both examples, the agents may have gone beyond their legitimate roles and breached fiduciary duties to their clients.

■ BUYER'S BROKER DISCLOSURES

Disclosures to Buyer

Before entering into a buyer-representation agreement, the real estate agent is required by TRELA § 1101.652(b)(7); (8); and § 1101.558(b) to make an oral or a written disclosure of any agency representation relationships the broker may have with parties whose properties the buyer may be interested in considering. TRELA requires that a real estate licensee disclose in writing the licensee's true position when offering listing properties for sale (§ 1101.652(b)(16)).

Specifically,

> *22 TAC 535.144 **When Acquiring or Disposing of Own Property or Property of Spouse, Parent or Child.***
>
> *(b) A licensee, when engaging in a real estate transaction on his or her own behalf, on behalf of a business entity in which the licensee is more than a 10% owner, or on behalf of the licensees spouse, parent, or child, is obligated to disclose in writing to any person with whom the licensee deals that he or she is a licensed real estate broker or salesperson acting on his or her own behalf or on behalf of the licensee's spouse, parent or child in any contract of sale or rental agreement or in any other writing given prior to entering into any contract of sale or rental agreement. contract of sale or rental agreement.*

In addition, TRELA § 1101.558(c) requires that the broker provide the buyer with a written statement describing seller agency, buyer agency, and intermediary brokerage (Information About Brokerage Services). Although the law no longer requires it, the broker probably should make any agency disclosures in writing and try to obtain the signature of the buyer acknowledging receipt of the disclosures and the written statement.

Disclosures to Seller or Listing Broker

TRELA § 1101.558 requires that agents disclose their representative capacities to other parties and to the agents of other parties at the time of first contact. As stated in "Disclosure to Buyer" in the previous paragraph, said notice would include the special relationship noted in 22 TAC § 535.144. When dealing with listing brokers, the buyer's broker also should be careful to reject any offer of subagency that may have been made.

The NAR Code of Ethics and Standards of Practice (*see* Chapter 11) requires that the buyer's agent disclose that relationship to the listing agent at first contact and provide written confirmation of that disclosure no later than the signing of the purchase agreement. As soon as the buyer's agent calls for an appointment, the buyer's agent should inform the listing broker that the buyer's agent represents the buyer and rejects any offer of subagency made. If the property is not listed, the buyer's agent should disclose the relationship to the seller at first contact and make any requests for compensation from the seller at that time.

Buyers as Customers

Although this chapter has focused on buyer agency, remember, not every buyer wants or needs to be represented by an agent. Some buyers appreciate the flexibility of dealing with several brokers and avoiding commitments and loyalties to any one of them. Such buyers who work with a number of brokers may acquire enough facts to enable them to make a decision, such as information about property values and seller motivation, although they may be unaware of any fiduciary duties owed to the seller or landlord by the broker. Others enjoy the "free ride" given by many brokers, hoping that the buyer will make an offer to purchase through them. Still other buyers prefer to deal directly with the listing broker because they hope to obtain some inside information that they can use to make the best deal or because they fear they may lose the opportunity to buy the home they really want if they make an offer through another agent. This fear of missed opportunity may be based on the time factor involved in presenting an offer in a seller's market. Another concern is that an unprofessional listing agent might produce an equivalent or a better offer in-house after having first seen the buyer's offer submitted by the buyer's agent.

■ SUMMARY

In the past, in most real estate transactions, the seller was represented by a real estate agent, but the buyer was not. Today, primarily owing to better disclosure and information that agents are required to provide, many buyers now seek the same level of client service that sellers typically receive from agents. The decision to represent a buyer is a serious one because the agent will be held to a high standard of care and will owe fiduciary duties to the buyer. Both the agent and the buyer must weigh the various benefits of buyer representation. It is strongly recommended that brokers use a written buyer-agency agreement and carefully discuss alternative methods of compensation. In helping the buyer or the buyer's attorney prepare the purchase agreement, the agent should consider the negotiable aspects of the transaction from the buyer's perspective.

■ KEY POINTS

- Whether to represent the buyer is an important decision because the agent then owes the full range of fiduciary responsibilities. The real estate licensee may want to be selective and not represent every buyer who walks in the front door.
- Buyer brokerage does not mean that the broker is in the business of representing buyers only. Most buyers' agents regard buyer agency as one of the options available to them in single-agency or nonexclusive-agency practices.
- Not every buyer wants or needs representation. Some prefer to represent themselves, especially those not wanting to risk a missed opportunity in a fast-moving seller's market.
- Written buyer-representation agreements are preferable to oral ones.
- In showing buyers in-house listings, brokers must take care to avoid unintentional and unauthorized representation of more than one party. If such representation is to be authorized, the broker must make full disclosure of the potential conflicts of interest to both buyer and seller.
- A buyer's agent must disclose to the listing broker at initial contact that the licensee is a buyer's agent and must clearly reject any offer of subagency. Frequently, the listing broker will be authorized to share fees with buyers' agents and allow them equal access to property for showing.
- Buyers' agents in Texas should seriously consider benefits and drawbacks of being compensated by buyers-tenants rather than by sellers-landlords, as is the most common practice in Texas today.

■ SUGGESTIONS FOR BROKERS

Establish an office policy on how to handle an offer received from a buyer's agent on one of your listings. Discuss with the seller the possibility that you will receive offers from buyers' agents and that these offers may require a commission split or an adjustment in the offering price when the buyer will pay the buyer's agent directly. Discuss the net effect these offers will have on the seller's position, and advise the seller accordingly.

CHAPTER 6 QUIZ

1. When a buyer's agent shows a property listed through an MLS, the agent is the fiduciary of which of the following?
   a. Buyer
   b. Buyer's broker
   c. Seller
   d. MLS

2. Buyer agency
   a. must be created with a written buyer-representation agreement.
   b. may be created by the actions of a licensee as well as by written agreements.
   c. while legal, is seldom practiced by brokers in Texas.
   d. excludes the possibility of a brokerage firm's obtaining listings from sellers.

3. Megan, a broker, entered into a buyer-representation agreement with Sue, a buyer, using the TAR Residential Buyer/Tenant Representation Agreement (see Figure 6.1). The commission agreement under paragraph 11A was for 2.5 percent. Sue subsequently enters into a $210,000 purchase contract with a seller. The listing office agrees to pay a buyer's broker 2 percent of the sales price. How much commission is Megan entitled to at closing?
   a. $5,250 ($4,200 from the listing broker; $1,050 from Sue)
   b. $4,200 ($4,200 from the listing broker; zero from Sue)
   c. $9,450 ($4,200 from listing broker; $5,250 from Sue)
   d. $5,250 (zero from the listing broker; $5,250 from Sue)

4. Which requires that a buyer purchase only through a particular broker?
   a. The buyer pays the broker a commission.
   b. The buyer signed an exclusive representation agreement.
   c. The buyer asked the agent to help negotiate the purchase of an already identified property.
   d. The buyer signed an open buyer-representation agreement.

5. Buyer-representation agreements
   a. are promulgated forms available from TREC.
   b. impose duties on buyers' brokers similar to those that listing agreements impose on sellers' brokers.
   c. differ from listing agreements in that listings require definite termination dates while buyer-representation agreements do not.
   d. in order to be binding, must provide that the buyer compensate the broker for the representation services.

6. The increase in buyer representation is due primarily to
   a. better disclosure and information required of brokers.
   b. the infusion of more buyers into the marketplace.
   c. brokers seeking and promoting compensation by both parties.
   d. all of these.

7. In which case must a real estate broker obtain a written agreement with a buyer?
   a. Broker to act as a buyer's agent
   b. Broker wishing to take legal action against a buyer for commission
   c. Both of these
   d. Neither of these

8. Which is a possible benefit of buyer agency?
   a. Greater client loyalty
   b. Better protection against conflicts of loyalty
   c. No liability for acts of the listing broker
   d. All of these

9. Which would be a disadvantage of exclusive buyer agency?
   a. The broker would not be able to list a property owned by the buyer-client.
   b. The broker could never earn full commission on an in-house sale.
   c. There is a potential conflict of interest if two buyer-clients wish to offer on the same property.
   d. All of these are potential disadvantages.

10. The listing broker has agreed to pay the cooperating broker a fee of 2 percent of the sales price. The buyer is represented and has agreed in writing to pay her broker a nonrefundable $2,000 flat fee. Which statement is *TRUE*?
    a. All parties must be notified of the compensation agreement between the buyer and her broker.
    b. As an agent of the buyer, the broker has no duty to disclose the dual compensation.
    c. The broker for the buyer may disclose the dual compensation only if authorized to do so by his client.
    d. The dual compensation must be disclosed only if it impacts on the ultimate tax advantage of the buyer.

DISCUSSION QUESTIONS

1. Can a buyer's broker participate in the MLS and receive a share of the listing broker's commission?

2. Why would a listing broker reduce a portion of the sales commission so the seller could credit that portion to the buyer for payment of the buyer's broker's commission?

3. How might a buyer's broker handle conflicts of interest involving in-house sales?

4. Name at least four important elements of a well-drafted buyer's broker-representation agreement.

5. Name at least five important points for a buyer's broker to cover in a purchase contract.

CHAPTER 7

Representing More Than One Party in a Transaction: Intermediary Brokerage

For many years, brokers were accustomed to representing only one principal in a transaction. Traditionally, the seller was represented by an agent and treated as a client, whereas the buyer was not represented by an agent and was treated as a customer. The growth of buyer representation, however, created new issues for brokers, who now are frequently faced with the prospect of a buyer being represented by the firm and wishing to purchase a property listed by the same firm. The specter of representing both principals in a single transaction raises many questions about potentially conflicting duties. How, for example, can a broker place the interests of a client above all others if, in fact, there are two clients, each entitled to the fiduciary duties created by agency relationships with the broker?

This chapter explores the issues of multiple representation and the status of intermediary brokerage as defined in the License Act and the duties of the intermediary broker. Students should have a clear understanding of these concepts before they become involved in a real estate transaction that involves representing more than one party.

LEARNING OBJECTIVES *This chapter addresses the following:*

- The Path from Dual Agency to Intermediary Brokerage
- Representation of More Than One Party in a Transaction
  - Conflicting Positions

- Common-Law Dual Agency (Implied and Express)
- Volatile Issues
■ Former Statutory Dual Agency Rules in Texas
  - Duties of the Statutory Dual Agent
■ Intermediary Brokerage
■ General Concepts
  - The Appointment Process
  - Appointed Licensees—Who and When?
  - Status of Intermediary Brokers and Appointed Licensees
■ Concerns Related to Intermediary Practice
■ Nonresidential Intermediary Applications
  - Exchanges
  - Syndications
  - Commercial Leasing Agent
■ Intentional versus Unintended Dual Representation
  - Prior Relationships
  - In-House Sale
  - Cooperating or Other Broker
  - Broker as Principal
  - Adopting the Buyer
  - Nonagency

■ THE PATH FROM DUAL AGENCY TO INTERMEDIARY BROKERAGE

Until 1993, Real Estate License Act (TRELA) was silent on the subject of dual agency (i.e., if, when, and how a broker could represent more than one party in a real estate transaction). Texas has, however, always recognized the concept of common-law dual agency. Unfortunately, common-law rules are complicated and often appear contradictory. As a result, this arrangement has long been discouraged by the Texas Real Estate Commission (TREC). With the growth in buyer-agency, more and more brokers attempted to profit from representing both sides in the transaction despite the lack of statutory guidelines. Legal problems materialized as brokers applied their own individual "how to" interpretation to common law cases. In 1993, the legislature, in an effort to assist brokers in dual representation, authorized a modified form of this practice—statutory dual agency. The TRELA was amended to outline the specific duties of a broker who was functioning in this new form of dual representation. Even with the statutory guidelines, many felt that this form of representation was inherently dangerous, and TREC did not recommend the practice. Even the preamble to the Code of Ethics and Standards of Practice of the National Association of REALTORS® (see Chapter 10), recognizes "that cooperation with other real estate professionals promotes the best interests of those who utilize their services. REALTORS® urge exclusive representation of clients."

Effective January 1, 1996, the language relating to statutory dual agency was removed from TRELA and replaced by a new form of relationship between the broker and two represented parties. This practice is known as intermediary brokerage.

Although the intermediary relationship was the recommended method for representing more than one party, the License Act did not prohibit a broker from acting as a common law dual agent. However, as of September 2005, TRELA no longer permits brokers to act as common law dual agents and requires brokers to act as intermediaries when representing more than one party.

To understand the intermediary duties of a broker, it is helpful to trace the evolution of this status from its beginning and to understand the pressures and concepts that caused this evolution. From this starting point, it becomes clearer why intermediary brokerage sometimes appears to have the same duties as the former statutory dual agency.

REPRESENTATION OF MORE THAN ONE PARTY IN A TRANSACTION

The broker may, by accident or design, become the agent for both buyer and seller in the same transaction. In the past, these actions were governed by common law and, for a while, by a statutory form of dual agency for real estate licensees. Common law is law that has evolved by custom or precedent set by the courts as contrasted with statutory law, which is enacted by legislatures. In either case, when licensees undertake to represent more than one principal in the same transaction, they should be fully informed of their duties and obligations and fully aware of the possible conflicts of interest.

In general, the agent representing more than one principal owes to each principal the same fiduciary duties of obedience, loyalty, disclosure, confidentiality, accounting, and reasonable care. Because full client-level service to both cannot possibly be provided, the agent must alert the clients that each will receive less than full representation. The agent cannot presume that each client will be satisfied just because the transaction closes and the agent is helpful and honest. Both clients must understand what level of service each will waive (and thus fail to receive) when they consent to multiple representation.

It is sometimes difficult to define in specific terms the responsibilities that an agent owes to a buyer and to a seller when both are being represented by the same agent. Much depends on the type of agency services that are expected by the respective principals. For example, if the parties expect the agent to act impartially, giving neither party advice or opinion, one party later might claim that the agent favored the other party during the transaction. On the other hand, the seller and the buyer who give informed consent to have a broker direct one associate in the firm to negotiate on the seller's behalf and another associate from the same firm to negotiate on the buyer's behalf have, arguably, agreed to a limited agency. Therefore, they have waived any challenge to the brokerage's dual representation. Nevertheless, brokers attempting to represent more than one principal must be careful to act in a manner consistent with the principals' instructions.

A key issue in representing more than one party in a transaction is to obtain the informed consent of both. Unfortunately, a licensee may become the agent of both parties without intending to do so, thus creating an illegal and potentially dangerous type of agency known as undisclosed dual agency. Licensees should take measures to avoid a dual representation that is unintended or created by accident.

Conflicting Positions

The positions of buyer and seller are inherently in conflict, at least on some issues. The two of them may be very friendly and share the goal of making a transaction work. In law, however, their interests are considered distinct and adverse, and each may need protection of these interests. The objectives of the buyer and the seller are seldom identical in a transaction. The agent is placed in the delicate position of using any knowledge about either side in a way to attempt to please both sides and complete the transaction. It may appear that one side does not receive full representation because the agent may find it impossible to remain totally neutral.

A disgruntled buyer or seller may decide at any time to challenge the agent's actions. In hindsight, either client may later assert that the agent violated the trust given the agent because the representation tipped in favor of the other client. The provisions in a contract that benefit one side may burden the other. If the agent wants to represent the interests of more than one party in a transaction, the agent is expected and required to maintain a delicate balance and avoid the risk of sacrificing the interests of one client for those of the other.

Conflicting expectations of two represented parties may make the agent's job difficult, especially because a real estate transaction is characterized by negotiation of price within a reasonable range. The process of negotiation is an expected and usual part of consummating a transaction. Fortunately, many transactions, particularly in residential sales, are typified by negotiations based on fair market value. Such negotiations do not necessarily create adversarial win-lose situations but, rather, set the stage for win-win transactions. While this is desirable in all transactions, it becomes a requirement in transactions in which more than one party is represented by a broker. The ultimate issue is whether the buyer and the seller can benefit best by having a single broker represent both parties. If so, multiple representation is lawful, provided both clients give their informed consent.

Common-Law Dual Agency (Implied and Express)

Chapter 4 discussed agency relationships that are created by actions or conduct in regard to a principal rather than by some express agreement. This is called implied agency, and it imposes the full burden of agency duties on the agent. Sometimes this implied agency is intentional, but more often than not, it is accidental. The classic example is that of nonrepresented buyers being led to believe that a licensee is acting as an agent for them, when in fact the licensee is an agent of the seller. When this occurs, a form of dual representation arises, known as undisclosed, nonconsensual dual agency. The effect is to create an illegal form of agency whereby the broker (through the broker's own actions or the actions of an associated licensee) unknowingly becomes an agent of both buyer and seller without their knowledge and consent. Interestingly, in most of these situations, the buyer, the seller, and the broker are unaware that dual representation is occurring. This situation exposes the broker to considerable liability from both principals and is clearly a position to be avoided by the broker, if not by the principals themselves.

Consensual dual agency, whereby the broker knowingly becomes an agent of both principals with their express knowledge and consent, has long been established as a legal (if somewhat confusing) form of agency in Texas under common law. An in-depth discussion of common law dual agency is beyond the scope of this text; the rules are complicated, ambiguous, and appear to impose conflicting duties on the agent. Although consensual dual agency is recognized under general agency law, it is no longer a permitted form of representation by real estate brokers.

Volatile Issues

As long as both buyer and seller are happy with the transaction, the question of dual agency probably will not arise. But if either party becomes unhappy, for whatever reason, even months after closing, multiple representation may provide the mechanism to undo the transaction, recover commissions from the offending broker, seek money damages, and result in revocation of broker licensure. It is no legal defense that the multiple representation was unintended or was performed with all good intentions to help both buyer and seller. Buyers and sellers generally neither know nor care about the subject of agency law until someone wants to back out of a transaction and consults an attorney. It is then that a principal often learns that the required (and appropriate) level of service was not received. Multiple representation cases have a high rate of success for plaintiffs (the person bringing the suit) and high monetary rewards.

Multiple representation, even when disclosed and intended, may be risky, despite the fact that in some cases, neither party loses and both, perhaps, gain. Mutual gain might occur, for example, if the agent discloses the seller's urgency to sell and also the buyer's recent profitable cash sale of another property. These and other confidential disclosures may actually speed up acceptance of an agreement on price and terms fully acceptable to both parties. Nevertheless, an agent takes a calculated risk whenever concealing or revealing information that potentially compromises the position of one of the principals. The principal later may argue in court that the agent's loyalty was improperly directed to the transaction itself and the compensation to be derived from it and not in the client's best interests.

■ FORMER STATUTORY DUAL AGENCY RULES IN TEXAS

In an effort to clarify the dual-agency role for both the public and licensees, the Texas legislature passed an amendment to TRELA, effective September 1, 1993, that created a modified form of dual agency. It established specific guidelines for brokers when acting as dual agents and limited the liability of common law dual-agency practice. Although the statute has been repealed and TRELA no longer addresses dual agency, it is important to look at the provisions of the statute to better understand the intermediary brokerage rules discussed in the following sections.

Duties of the Statutory Dual Agent

Specifically, the state at one time provided that a broker, when acting as an agent for more than one party, should

- not disclose to the buyer or tenant that the seller or the landlord would accept a price less than the asking price unless otherwise instructed in a separate writing by the seller or landlord;
- not disclose to the seller or the landlord that the buyer or the tenant would pay a price greater than the price submitted in the written offer to the seller or the landlord unless otherwise instructed in a separate writing by the buyer or the tenant;
- not disclose any confidential information or any information a party specifically instructs a real estate broker in writing not to disclose unless otherwise instructed in a separate writing by the respective party or required to disclose such information by law; and
- treat all parties to the transaction honestly and impartially, so as not to favor one party to the disadvantage of the other party.

Many brokers who had refused to practice dual agency under the old common law rules found some comfort in the specific language of the statute, and the practice of statutory dual agency became more common in the real estate industry in Texas. Still, this form of limited agency had its drawbacks for both brokers and principals. From the broker's perspective, it created a delicate balancing act in which the broker and all the involved sales associates were required to remain totally impartial during the transaction. As a result, the broker and the associates could offer no advice or opinions to either party during the transactions that might act to the disadvantage of the other party. The broker was exposed to liability if either party felt that the other party was given any preferential treatment during the course of the transaction.

Limitations of the broker's services. From the principals' perspective, neither the buyer nor the seller could expect the same level of service from the broker as when the broker acted as a single agent for either. The seller, when represented solely by the agent, received the full advice and opinions of the agent when negotiating offers from nonrepresented buyers. In the dual-agency transaction, however, that same seller now found that the agent could provide factual information but no preferential advice or opinions during negotiations. The buyer who had become accustomed to full representation experienced the same reduction in the services provided by the agent. Many principals found that this limited form of agency was not exactly what they thought they had bargained for and were dissatisfied with the transaction.

It was critical for the broker, when acting as a statutory dual agent, to be certain that both the associated licensees and the principals fully understood the limitations of this form of agency and that all parties agreed to the terms. Unfortunately, case law has illustrated that in some transactions, the brokers, the associates, and/or the principals had no clue.

INTERMEDIARY BROKERAGE

General Concepts

Recognizing the inherent shortcomings and the limitations created by the statutory dual agency, the Texas legislature passed Senate Bill 489, which, among other things, eliminated statutory dual agency and amended TRELA to substitute statutory intermediary brokerage. Effective January 1, 1996, TRELA authorized brokers to act on behalf of both parties to a transaction in an intermediary role as follows:

> § 1101.559. BROKER ACTING AS INTERMEDIARY.
>
> (a) A broker may act as an intermediary between parties to a real estate transaction if:
>
> (1) the broker obtains written consent from each party for the broker to act as an intermediary in the transaction; and
>
> (2) the written consent of the parties states the source of any expected compensation to the broker.
>
> (b) A written listing agreement to represent a seller or landlord or a written agreement to represent a buyer or tenant that authorizes a broker to act as an intermediary in a real estate transaction is sufficient to establish written consent of the party to the transaction if the written agreement specifies in conspicuous bold or underlined print the conduct that is prohibited under Section 1101.651(d).
>
> (c) An intermediary shall act fairly and impartially. Appointment by a broker acting as an intermediary of an associated license holder under Section 1101.560 to communicate with, carry out the instructions of, and provide opinions and advice to the parties to whom that associated license holder is appointed is a fair and impartial act.

In addition, TRELA permits the appointment of associated licensees as follows:

> § 1101.560. ASSOCIATED LICENSE HOLDER ACTING AS INTERMEDIARY.
>
> (a) A broker who complies with the written consent requirements of Section 1101.559 may appoint:
>
> (1) a license holder associated with the broker to communicate with and carry out instructions of one party to a real estate transaction; and
>
> (2) another license holder associated with the broker to communicate with and carry out instructions of any other party to the transaction.
>
> (b) A license holder may be appointed under this section only if:
>
> (1) the written consent of the parties under Section 1101.559 authorizes the broker to make the appointment; and
>
> (2) the broker provides written notice of the appointment to all parties involved in the real estate transaction.

(c) A license holder appointed under this section may provide opinions and advice during negotiations to the party to whom the license holder is appointed.

Specific prohibitions regarding the intermediary rule are addressed in TRELA § 1101.651(d) as follows:

§ 1101.651. CERTAIN PRACTICES PROHIBITED.

(d) A broker and any broker or salesperson appointed under Section 1101.560 who acts as an intermediary under Subchapter L may not:

(1) disclose to the buyer or tenant that the seller or landlord will accept a price less than the asking price, unless otherwise instructed in a separate writing by the seller or landlord;

(2) disclose to the seller or landlord that the buyer or tenant will pay a price greater than the price submitted in a written offer to the seller or landlord, unless otherwise instructed in a separate writing by the buyer or tenant;

(3) disclose any confidential information or any information a party specifically instructs the broker or salesperson in writing not to disclose, unless:

(A) the broker or salesperson is otherwise instructed in a separate writing by the respective party;

(B) the broker or salesperson is required to disclose the information by this chapter or a court order; or

(C) the information materially relates to the condition of the property;

(4) treat a party to a transaction dishonestly; or

(5) violate this chapter.

Finally, the role of intermediary prevails over common law dual agency:

§ 1101.561. DUTIES OF INTERMEDIARY PREVAIL.

(a) The duties of a license holder acting as an intermediary under this subchapter supersede the duties of a license holder established under any other law, including common law.

(b) A broker must agree to act as an intermediary under this subchapter if the broker agrees to represent in a transaction:

(1) a buyer or tenant; and

(2) a seller or landlord.

Consider how this might work in practice. The statute requires written permission from both parties before the broker may act as an intermediary, and the agreement must disclose any source of compensation expected by the broker. This may be accomplished in a listing contract with a seller (*see* Chapter 5, Figure 5.2, paragraph 9) or a written buyer-representation contract with a buyer (*see* Chapter 6, Figure 6.1, paragraph 8). The respective agreements give the seller or the buyer the option of authorizing the broker to act as an intermediary. These agreements are considered sufficient by TREC, as long as the broker's compensation is clarified.

If the intermediary situation arises, the broker cannot disclose

- the highest price a buyer might pay, until authorized to do so in writing;

- the minimum price a seller will take, unless authorized to do so and
- confidential information about either party, unless the parties auth... law requires a disclosure.

Finally, the broker must treat all parties to the transaction honestly and fairly, while complying with the act.

Sound familiar? At least to this point, the intermediary brokerage language is almost identical to the former language regarding statutory dual agency. A broker accustomed to acting as a dual agent under the old statutory provisions would see no practical difference between the two. In fact, many brokers mistakenly believe that *intermediary* is simply another term for a dual agent. However, the language in TRELA § 1101.560; .651 provides the major departure from the old dual-agency statute by providing for the appointment of licensees to assist buyers and sellers in an intermediary transaction by offering advice and opinions during negotiations.

The Appointment Process

The ability of the broker to make appointments is the *key difference* between statutory dual agency and the intermediary status. This enhances the level of service that can be given to represented buyers and sellers during in-house transactions.

As you recall, one of the major drawbacks in dual-agency arrangements is the reduction of services that can be provided to the principals. When acting as an agent for either buyer or seller, full fiduciary duties must be given to the principal the agent represents. Clients are entitled to accurate information and can look to their agents for advice and opinions during the negotiations. The advice and opinions given clients are designed to place the broker's clients in the best negotiating position and offer clients the best advantage in meeting their goals. In dual agency, with two clients, the agents were restricted from giving such advice to either client, creating a form of limited agency.

Under dual agency, buyers and sellers, accustomed to the full-service representation of single agency, saw dramatic reductions in the level of service that the broker could provide. Although information could be given to each party, no preferential advice or opinions could be given to either, and both parties had to be treated equally.

Advice and opinions from appointed licensees. In the intermediary transaction, if one or more licensees are appointed to the seller and different licensees are appointed to the buyer, the principals are able to receive services similar to those of single agency. Although other legal distinctions may exist between an intermediary broker and a dual agent, the practical difference between the former statutory dual agent and the current intermediary broker lies in the ability to expand the limited services of the former statutory dual agent through the appointment process afforded the new intermediary broker. Thus, the appointed licensee is freed from the limitations placed on the former statutory dual agent, which required an absolute balance between the parties and prohibited giving preferential negotiating advice or opinions to either. The appointed licensees (not the intermediary) may now give to their respective principals services similar to those given when acting as a single agent. In other words, an appointed licensee may give the party to whom he or she has been appointed advice and opinions that may not be in the best interest of the other party. Keep in mind, however, that the appointed licensee is still prohibited from disclosing how little a seller may accept, how much a buyer may be willing to pay, or any other confidential information about either party. In addition, appointees must treat the parties fairly and comply with TRELA.

Appointed Licensees—Who and When?

The appointment process raises several questions for brokers who wish to extend the company's services to buyer and seller clients through the appointment process. First, remember that before appointments may be made, the broker must have the written consent of both parties to act as an intermediary and their permission to make appointments. The statute provides that with this written consent the broker may appoint one or more associated licensees to work with the buyer and different licensees to work with the seller. The broker cannot self-appoint to either and must maintain the role of the intermediary. Thus a broker who works alone or a broker with only one associate cannot make appointments and must conduct the transaction as an intermediary without appointees. If no appointments are made, any involved associates are required to carry out the same duties as the intermediary broker—no preferential advice or opinions to either party are permitted.

Timing of the appointments and notification to the principals are important. Until a buyer who is represented by the firm wishes to negotiate on a property listed by the firm, no potential for an intermediary transaction exists and therefore appointments need not be made. Likewise, if the broker has chosen not to make appointments, the involved associates carry out the transaction as if they were intermediaries, offering neither advice nor opinions to buyer or seller during negotiations that might work to the disadvantage of the other party.

It is extremely important that parties clearly understand that during an intermediary transaction no preferential advice or opinions can be given by the associates working with the principals, unless appointments are made. If, however, the parties wish to have an associate appointed to each of them, thereby gaining the expanded advice and opinions of the associate, the appointment must be made before such advice or opinions are given to either party. The broker, or an authorized representative of the broker, must make the appointments, and written notification of these appointments must be given to both the buyer and the seller. Note that while the actual appointments of the licensees may be made orally, the notification to the parties announcing the appointments and identifying the appointees must be given to the buyer and the seller in writing. Neither the statute nor TREC provides specific language for the notification. Members of the Texas Association of REALTORS® may use form TAR 1409, Intermediary Relationship Notice (see Figure 7.1), to indicate that an intermediary transaction is occurring and whether appointments are to be made in order to identify the appointed licensees.

REALTORS® frequently refer to this form as the "second consent" form. Remember, if the clients agreed in the written listing or buyer-representation contracts to permit the intermediary relationship should the buyer become interested in an in-house property, then the licensee has met the requirement under TRELA to obtain written consent. Considerable time may elapse, however, between the time their respective contracts were signed and when the buyer indicates a desire to begin negotiation on an in-house listing. The form also serves to meet the statutory requirement to identify the appointed licensees by name to all parties (§ 1101.560 (b)). Licensees who are not members of TAR should develop in-house forms to give similar notice to the parties. Unless appointments are made, the broker is not required to notify the parties that an intermediary transaction is occurring as long as the written consent to act as an intermediary was previously obtained, although the prudent broker will make it clear to the parties, preferably in writing, that an intermediary transaction is taking place.

An obvious timing problem may arise if an intermediary transaction occurs during the absence of the broker and no appointments have been made. If this occurred, the licensee associate could not give advice or opinions until the appointment process had been completed. Clearly, this might be too late because the negotiations might be completed before the broker is available to make the required appointments. One solution might be for the broker to give the authority to make appointments to others in the firm. Another possibility could be to preappoint listing associates to work as appointees to sellers—and selling associates working under buyer-representation contracts to work as appointees to buyers—should an intermediary transaction arise. Keep in mind that a preappointment would have no effect until an intermediary transaction actually occurred. The parties still would have to be furnished with written notice of the appointments as soon as the intermediary transaction was undertaken.

Who is to be appointed? The appointees could be any licensees of the firm other than the broker. However, in a practical sense, it would be most common for the associate who obtained the listing to be appointed to the seller and the associate who obtained the buyer-representation contract to be appointed to the buyer. Exceptions might be where listing agents sold their own listings to buyers with whom they were working under the terms of a buyer-representation contract. For appointments to be made in these circumstances, a second licensee would be required to enter the transaction, to be appointed to either buyer or seller, because the statute requires that different licensees be appointed to buyer and seller. Would this indicate, then, that a licensee could not participate on both sides of the transaction and receive the increased commission? No, the practical solution might be for the broker to decline to make appointments and to instruct the associate to conduct the transaction as an intermediary transaction, giving no preferential advice or opinions to either party. In any event, a broker should have a well-reasoned, written office policy to avoid confusion and conflict within the office regarding these matters.

FIGURE 7.1

Example of Intermediary Relationship Notice

[Handwritten note: consent not notice / could be consent if it was disaffirmed]

TEXAS ASSOCIATION OF REALTORS®

INTERMEDIARY RELATIONSHIP NOTICE

USE OF THIS FORM BY PERSONS WHO ARE NOT MEMBERS OF THE TEXAS ASSOCIATION OF REALTORS® IS NOT AUTHORIZED.
©Texas Association of REALTORS®, Inc. 2004

To: _____ (Seller or Landlord)
and _____ (Prospect)
From: _____ (Broker's Firm)
Re: _____ (Property)
Date: _____

A. Under this notice, "owner" means the seller or landlord of the Property and "prospect" means the above-named prospective buyer or tenant for the Property.

B. Broker's firm represents the owner under a listing agreement and also represents the prospect under a buyer/tenant representation agreement.

C. In the written listing agreement and the written buyer/tenant representation agreement, both the owner and the prospect previously authorized Broker to act as an intermediary if a prospect who Broker represents desires to buy or lease a property that is listed by the Broker. When the prospect makes an offer to purchase or lease the Property, Broker will act in accordance with the authorizations granted in the listing agreement and in the buyer/tenant representation agreement.

D. Broker ☐ will ☐ will not appoint licensed associates to communicate with, carry out instructions of, and provide opinions and advice during negotiations to each party. If Broker makes such appointments, Broker appoints:

_____ to the owner; and
_____ to the prospect.

E. By acknowledging receipt of this notice, the undersigned parties reaffirm their consent for broker to act as an intermediary.

F. Additional Information: *(Disclose material information related to Broker's relationship to the parties, such as personal relationships or prior or contemplated business relationships.)*

[Handwritten note: Contract]

The undersigned acknowledge receipt of this notice

_____   _____   _____   _____
Seller or Landlord   Date   Prospect   Date

_____   _____   _____   _____
Seller or Landlord   Date   Prospect   Date

(TAR-1409) 1-7-04

The following examples and short questions and answers may help illustrate how and when an intermediary transaction may arise and when appointments may be made.

■ **EXAMPLE** Broker Able has listed seller Sharp's house. The listing agreement permits Able to act as an intermediary if the occasion arises. Customer Jones, an unrepresented buyer, asks Able to present an offer on the Sharp property.

■ **QUESTION** What kind of agency relationships will be operational?

■ **DISCUSSION** Because Jones has no representation agreement, Able simply will act as the agent for the seller, giving Sharp full representation services while treating Jones fairly and honestly. Note in Figure 7.2 that the broker can give preferential advice and opinions to the seller, thereby tipping the scale in favor of the seller.

■ **EXAMPLE** Broker Able has entered into a buyer-representation agreement with buyer Baker. The buyer-representation agreement permits Able to act as an intermediary should the occasion arise. Baker, a represented buyer, wishes to negotiate a contract on seller Sharp's house.

■ **QUESTION** What is Able's position in the transaction?

■ **DISCUSSION** Because the listing agreement with the seller and the written buyer-representation agreement authorized Able to act as an intermediary, the intermediary brokerage relationship will become operational without requiring further notice to the principals. (Although the statutes do not require notice to the principals when the intermediary transaction begins, a prudent broker will advise the principals that an intermediary agency is in place.)

Throughout the transaction, Able must carefully adhere to the requirements of intermediary brokerage. Because Able operates alone, no appointments may be made, and the principals will receive the limited services permitted by the intermediary rules. Both parties must be treated honestly and fairly, but no advice or opinions may be given to either party in the negotiations. Observers of this transaction would see no difference between this intermediary transaction and the former statutory dual-agency

FIGURE 7.2

Seller Representation Only

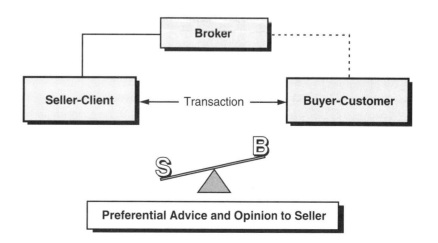

FIGURE 7.3

Broker as an Intermediary

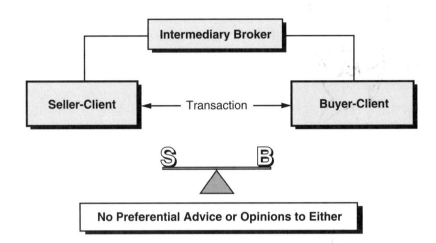

transaction if both were performed correctly. Note that in example 2, the scale must be kept in balance, as shown in Figure 7.3. No preferential advice or opinions can be given to either seller or buyer.

■ **EXAMPLE** Broker Able hires a new sales associate, Sally, who promptly engages buyer Smith in a buyer-representation agreement. The written agreement authorizes Able to act as an intermediary and to make appointments when appropriate. Smith becomes interested in and wishes to make an offer to purchase seller Sharp's house, currently listed by Able.

■ **QUESTION** What will be the roles of Able and Sally in the transaction?

■ **DISCUSSION** Able will act as an intermediary and will direct Sally to act as Able's agent and carry out the duties of an intermediary, but she will not be considered "appointed." Both Able and Sally must remain impartial. No preferential advice or opinions may be given to either Smith or Sharp. The principal's interests must be kept in strict balance.

■ **QUESTION** May Able make appointments in this transaction?

■ **DISCUSSION** No. Able has only one sales associate; therefore, the appointment process is inappropriate. A broker with more than one associate may appoint different associates to the buyer and the seller; the broker cannot be appointed to either.

■ **QUESTION** Could Able appoint Sally to Smith and simply serve Sharp as an intermediary?

■ **DISCUSSION** No. The statutes prohibit appointments to only one side of the transaction. If a licensee is appointed to the buyer, a different licensee must be appointed to the seller. For example, Figure 7.4 shows the scales being maintained in balance by both the broker and the sales licensee.

■ **EXAMPLE** Broker Able hires another associate, Jim Bob, who lists a home owned by seller Susan. The listing agreement authorizes Able to act as an intermediary and to make appointments, if appropriate. Sally, who represented buyer Smith in

FIGURE 7.4

Intermediary Broker with One Associate and without Appointments

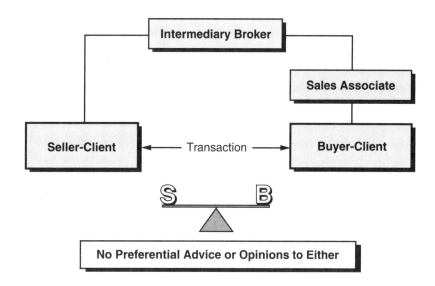

an unsuccessful attempt to purchase the Sharp property (example 3), wishes to make an offer on the Anxious property.

■ **QUESTION** What are the potential roles of Able?

■ **DISCUSSION** Able may complete the transaction as an intermediary with or without making appointments.

■ **QUESTION** If no appointments are made, what will be the roles of Sally and Jim Bob?

■ **DISCUSSION** Sally and Jim Bob will be instructed to carry out the duties of their intermediary broker. Neither associate may give advice or opinions to the principals with whom they are working. Both principals must be treated exactly the same. Figure 7.5 illustrates this option. Note that the broker and both associates are required to keep the scale in balance. No advice or opinions are given to either party.

FIGURE 7.5

Intermediary Broker with Two Sales Associates and without Appointments

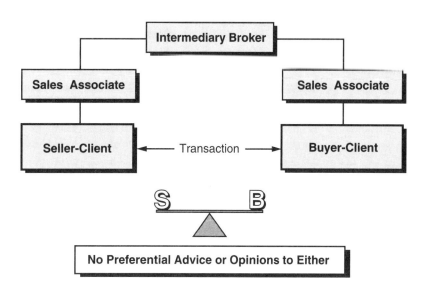

■ **QUESTION** If broker Able wishes to make appointments, how is this accomplished?

■ **DISCUSSION** Able will advise Sally that she is the appointed associate for Smith and will advise Jim Bob that he is the appointed associate for Susan. In addition, both principals must receive written notification of the appointments naming the licensee appointed to the other party. (*See* Figure 7.1, TAR Intermediary Relationship Notice) Keep in mind that the identities of the parties must be disclosed to each other.

■ **QUESTION** How will the appointments change the roles of Able and her associates, Sally and Jim Bob?

■ **DISCUSSION** Able's role will not change. She will carry out her duties as an intermediary, being careful not to take any action that would favor one party over the other. However, the roles of the appointed licensees change. Sally will now be permitted to give advice and opinions to Smith and assist in the negotiations. Jim Bob will now be able to give similar services to Susan. Figure 7.6 depicts the intermediary transaction with appointments. Note that while the broker must maintain a balanced scale, the appointed licensees will be able to give advice and opinions during the negotiations to attempt to tip their individual scales in favor of the principal to whom they have been appointed. The parties and the appointed associates must be aware that the intermediary broker is prohibited from providing preferential advice or opinion to either party.

■ **EXAMPLE** Sally, an agent of broker Able, is working with buyer Smith, a buyer represented by the company. Smith wishes to negotiate on a property owned by seller Jones. Sally is also the listing agent for the Jones property. Both representation contracts permit Able to act as an intermediary and to make appointments.

■ **QUESTION** If Able wishes to conduct an intermediary transaction, what options are available regarding appointments?

FIGURE 7.6

Intermediary Broker with Two Associates and with Appointments

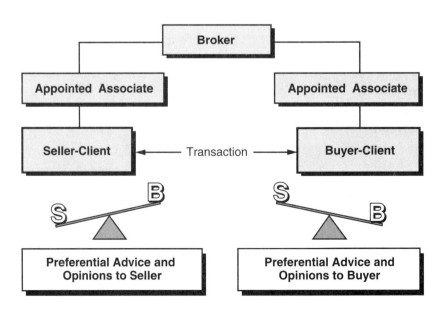

■ **DISCUSSION** If Able wished to make appointments, Sally could be appointed to either the buyer or the seller, but a different associate would have to be appointed to the other party. This would require the involvement of a new associate in the transaction, possibly causing concern for the principals. In addition, Sally might be required to share some commission with the other associate, depending on company policy. The practical solution for the broker and the associate would be not to make appointments. Although the broker is authorized to decide whether appointments are to be made or not, the broker should consider whether this solution is also in the best interests of the parties involved.

■ **QUESTION** If no appointments are made, how would this change the roles that Able and Sally could play?

■ **DISCUSSION** Able would remain as the intermediary and instruct Sally to carry out the duties of the intermediary while working with both the buyer and the seller. No new associate would be required to enter the transaction. Figure 7.7 shows the transaction without appointments. Again, the broker and the sales licensee must keep the scales in balance. It would be best for the broker to confirm this choice with the principals to ensure that they would agree with the decision not to make appointments.

Status of Intermediary Brokers and Appointed Licensees

Intermediary brokerage is a relatively new concept in Texas real estate law. Consequently, many questions remain unanswered regarding the nature of this form of brokerage. Such questions relate to the nature of the agency relationship, representation issues, and fiduciary duties, if any. The general interpretation of the TREC is as follows:

- An intermediary is an agent, but with different duties from those of a single agent.
- Subject to the limitations imposed by TRELA § 1101.651(d), an intermediary offers a limited form of representation to the parties. This representation may be broadened by the use of "appointed associates."

FIGURE 7.7

Intermediary Broker with One Sales Associate and without Appointments

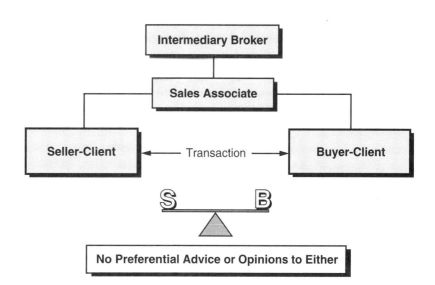

- As an intermediary, although the scope of agency is more limited, certain fiduciary duties are imposed on the agent.
- The License Act has no provision for a broker to "opt out" of an agency relationship when acting as an intermediary.

Although TRELA § 1101.559(a) states that a "broker may act as an intermediary between parties to a real estate transaction," at least for the purposes of negotiating the transaction, TREC's interpretation of the word *may* is taken to be permissive rather than conditional. That is to say, the use of *may* confirms the authority of the broker to act as an agent rather than to suggest an alternative nonagency relationship. Keep in mind that these represent only interpretations of the statute. The statutory language is not clear on these issues, and perhaps the courts will be required to ultimately determine the agency capacity and fiduciary duties—if any—that accrue to the intermediary broker.

While attorneys debate the issue of agency versus nonagency status of the intermediary, brokers must grapple with the everyday application of the statute. From a practical perspective, TREC has offered some guidelines for the licensee. Until the courts, the legislature, or TREC changes these opinions, the licensee would be well advised to follow these interpretations. The label that we attach to the broker may be less important than a clear understanding of the broker's duties when acting as an intermediary, as described in TRELA § 1101.559; 651(d), and discussed earlier in this chapter. Some direction is found in TRELA § 1101.561, which states that the duties of an intermediary, as described in § 1101.559; 651(d), "supersede the duties of a license holder established under any other law, including common law." But as we have just seen, the explicit duties described in the statute are very limited: conditional nondisclosure, honesty, and compliance with the License Act. It was initially believed that many of the questions surrounding intermediary brokerage would be resolved by the issuance of additional TREC regulations and by interpretation of this law in the courts. Yet the wording in the statute has not changed and case law remains limited. In the meantime, licensees should exercise caution when attempting to act in an intermediary role and understand the possible pitfalls, as well as the potential benefits.

Keep in mind that the intermediary provisions of TRELA will affect a minority of real estate transactions. Only during in-house transactions involving a represented buyer and a represented seller will the intermediary circumstance arise, and then only when all parties have agreed, in writing, to the arrangement. Although few of the licensee's transactions may involve the intermediary rules, if a broker attempts to undertake a single intermediary transaction, there should be a clear understanding as to how the broker should proceed. In an attempt to clarify some of the issues surrounding the intermediary law, TREC, through its legal counsel, has compiled the list of frequently asked questions from licensees that are found in Appendix B. The responses are those of the commissioners through the general counsel for TREC.

■ CONCERNS RELATED TO INTERMEDIARY PRACTICE

Even with the guidelines provided by statute and the rules of TREC, many brokers and attorneys feel that the specter of attempting to represent more than one party in a transaction presents too many legal and ethical problems to be practical. The TREC in no way recommends intermediary practice and only provides certain guidelines and suggestions for brokers who choose to offer intermediary services.

Consider, for example, that in an intermediary transaction appointments have been made to the respective parties. The appointed associates are now permitted to give advice and opinions to their party that may not be in the best interest of the other party. Still, confidential information must be kept confidential. How far may the appointed associate go as an advocate? At what point will the associate violate confidentiality? What if one party feels that the associate appointed to the other party is more experienced or competent and that they are now at a disadvantage during negotiations? These and many other issues have yet to be resolved, and understandably many brokers are very leery of this type of practice.

Certainly before attempting intermediary practice, a broker should carefully study the law and determine company policy regarding procedures. Once established, the policies and procedures should be reviewed by an attorney competent in this area of law. Finally, a company training program should be developed and delivered to ensure that the policies and procedures are properly implemented.

■ **EXAMPLE** Kelly, a first-time buyer, engaged Jackie, through her broker, to act as a buyer's agent. In the process of finding a suitable home, Kelly became interested in a property listed by Jackie. The buyer's representation agreement authorized Jackie's broker to act as an intermediary should the potential arise.

During the negotiations, Kelly complained to Jackie that it appeared that all the advice and opinions were being offered to the seller rather than to her. In fact, the only advice offered to the buyer was that she should pay the full price for the property and meet all other demands made by the seller. After the complaint from the buyer, Jackie told Kelly that if Kelly didn't like the way she was being represented that Kelly's broker would represent Kelly and Jackie would represent the seller.

Subsequently, Kelly's broker, by phone, informed Kelly that he would represent her interests rather than the seller's, again recommended that at least a full-price offer be tendered, and never spoke with Kelly again. After several negotiations through Jackie, Kelly ended up paying slightly more than full asking price. Later she complained again that all the emphasis seemed to be placed on the seller's need rather than her own, but she ultimately closed on the transaction, paying more than market value.

■ **QUESTION** 1. Is it permissible for a listing associate to negotiate the sale of her own listing to a buyer whom she also represents through her broker? 2. In the above example, how should the process of making appointments be handled? 3. What issues arose when the broker, in effect, appointed the listing agent to the seller and told the buyer that he would represent her interests rather than the seller's?

■ **DISCUSSION** This example illustrates the lack of understanding of the intermediary statutes and points to the fact that brokers who do not understand the role of an intermediary should not attempt the practice.

In reference to the first question above, nothing prevents a listing associate from negotiating a sale of that listing to a represented buyer. However, in this case, no appointments could be made and neither the seller nor the buyer should receive any advice or opinions that would act to the disadvantage of the other party.

If, in reference to the second question, appointments are to be made, one or more associates of the broker may be appointed to give advice and opinions to one party and one or more other associates of the broker could have been appointed to offer advice and opinions to the other party (TRELA § 1101.560; 651(d)). Once the appointments were made, both parties should receive written notification of the respective appointments naming the appointed associates. Under no circumstance should this broker attempt to appoint himself to either party.

A number of legal and ethical questions arise from this example and clearly point out the dangers of attempting to act as an intermediary without fully understanding the rules. In addition to demonstrating the lack of understanding of the fundamentals of intermediary brokerage, the broker, by claiming to represent the buyer rather than the seller in the transaction, violated fiduciary duties to the seller whom he had originally agreed to represent in the listing contract.

■ NONRESIDENTIAL INTERMEDIARY APPLICATIONS

The representation of more than one party is not confined to residential transactions, and brokers should be alert to the potential for undisclosed dual-representation issues arising in real estate exchanges; syndications; and farm and ranch, industrial, special-use, and commercial property transactions. Keep in mind that in any of the transactions the statutory Information About Brokerage Services notice must be given to the parties and an agency disclosure made prior to the beginning of the transaction.

Exchanges

Some brokers help owners exchange property under the Internal Revenue Code of 1986, Section 1031, "Tax-Deferred Exchange Provisions." Clear disclosure must be made when only a single broker is involved with more than one party to an exchange. An intermediary relationship would probably best serve the interests of the parties as well as those of the broker. With one agent and two commissions at stake, the nonprofessional broker has ample temptation to compromise the interests of either or both parties. Often more than one broker is involved in an exchange.

Syndications

Possible undisclosed dual-representation problems may arise in several situations in which the general partner of a limited partnership syndication is also a broker. Examples include the following:

- ■ The general partner sells or leases partnership property for a fee to be paid by the partnership.
- ■ The general partner sells her own property to the partnership for a fee.

- The general partner, on behalf of the partnership, buys property listed with another firm and seeks a commission split.
- The general partner, on behalf of the partnership, buys unlisted property and seeks compensation from the seller-owner.

The general partner has fiduciary obligations to the other general partners and limited partners. The broker should represent and be paid by the partnership only, unless full disclosure is made and written consent is obtained from all principals and brokers involved.

Commercial Leasing Agent

Brokers involved in commercial real estate leasing may find themselves in situations where both parties desire representation. Leasing agents often work under exclusive-right-to-lease listings from developers or building owners. Usually, an MLS does not require the listing of commercial leases. In commercial leasing, a great deal of negotiation regarding lease terms and concessions frequently occurs between the owner and the potential lessee. The leasing agent is usually at the center of such negotiations and should be careful to ensure that both owner and lessee understand the role of the leasing agent.

Many times, the lessee is sophisticated and is represented by an attorney or an accountant; the lessee should not look to the owner's leasing agent for advice of a legal or financial nature. Often the principals complete their own negotiations and look to the broker as an effective go-between. The lessee looks to the leasing agent more for accurate information and figures, especially about market trends and economic factors, typically not within the attorney's field of expertise.

For those cases when the lessee has no adviser and looks to the leasing agent for negotiating advice and opinions, a cautious leasing agent will have the owner and lessee consent to an intermediary agreement permitting appointments. The broker might further recommend that the lessor and lessee each obtain legal counsel.

Leasing agents may work with lessees to locate and evaluate specific sites. It is not unusual for a leasing agent to approach the owner of an unlisted building. In these no-listing transactions, there should be a clear written understanding as to whom the leasing agent represents, especially when the owner is asked to pay the commission. There is no difference between residential and commercial licensees regarding agency disclosure requirements.

■ INTENTIONAL VERSUS UNINTENDED DUAL REPRESENTATION

[handwritten note: only done through Intermediary]

In considering the representation of more than one party to a transaction, one must determine whether such representation is intentional or unintentional. An intentional representation of more than one party as an intermediary may present some serious business risks, but it does provide the broker an opportunity to discuss the pros and cons of multiple representation and obtain written consent designed to minimize risk. In addition, the specific requirements to act as an intermediary are stated in the law.

The chief concerns, however, focus on the unintended or accidental representation of more than one party. A broker who doesn't know that multiple representation is occurring has no contractual way to minimize the risks inherent in the dual representation and by default will become an undisclosed dual agent. While any form of undisclosed agency violates the statutes, undisclosed dual agency is particularly troublesome.

Most commonly, unintended dual representation occurs in one of the following contexts:

- The listing broker or licensed associate represents both the buyer and the seller.
- Separate associates from the listing office (an in-house sale) represent the buyer and the seller.
- Another broker represents the buyer and also acts as a subagent of the seller.
- The real estate licensee acts as a buyer or a seller.
- Written agreement with the seller; only verbal agreement with the buyer.

The conduct of the listing broker's licensed associate may be such that the buyer is led to believe that the associate represents the buyer. Eager to develop rapport with the buyer prospect, the salesperson sometimes gives the buyer that impression. In its handbook *Who Is My Client?*, NAR lists the following examples of statements often used by real estate brokers that can create implied agency relationships with buyers:

- "I'll take care of everything. I'll handle the sale for you."
- "I'll see if I can get the seller to come down on the price."
- "This listing has been on the market for six months. That tells me it's overpriced. Let's offer $80,000 and see what they say."
- "I'll get you the best deal I possibly can."
- "Trust me. I'm sure the seller won't counter at that price."
- "If the seller is going to insist on a full-price sale, I think you should tell him no. Then we can try an offer on that house your wife liked so much. I'm sure those sellers will be more realistic."
- "If they insist on the full $210,000, I'll remind them that the furnace is 15 years old and the carpet is fraying. That should justify at least a $7,000 reduction."

Prior Relationships

Sometimes a dual representation arises based on a prior relationship between the listing broker and the buyer.

■ **EXAMPLE** Mike of Prospect Realty lists George's house. Mike has represented Linda on several sales and purchases of property. Mike tells Linda about the house, and Linda wants Mike to prepare an offer at 10 percent below the asking price. Linda mentions she'll pay near the asking price, if necessary.

■ **QUESTION** Whom does Mike represent?

■ **DISCUSSION** As the listing salesperson, Mike owes primary allegiance to George, the seller. Based on his prior relationship with Linda, however, Mike may, under implied agency principles, also be held to represent Linda. This could put Mike's firm, Prospect Realty, into an unintended dual representation role.

Mike's options are either to disclose the prior relationship and obtain consents from Linda, George, and the broker of Prospect Realty permitting an intermediary transaction or to disclaim any agency to Linda. The second option requires clarification to Linda that Mike can work with her, but only on a customer basis, because Mike would be the agent of the seller only.

If Mike is acting through his broker in an intermediary role or as a lawful dual agent, he has a duty to Linda not to reveal her bargaining intentions. Neither can Mike tell Linda that his other principal, George, will take $10,000 less than the listed price or reveal any of George's other bargaining intentions. These usually inappropriate duties are the norm of intermediary brokerage, and mutually exclusive duties are the dilemma of the intermediary. With clear disclosure and consents, Mike, under the first option, may be authorized to keep confidential his discussions regarding price and terms. On the other hand, if Mike disclaims an agency relationship with Linda, under the second option, he would have to tell George that Linda has expressed a willingness to increase her first offer. Had Mike followed proper information and disclosure procedures, the options would have been discussed at first contact with Linda. If the second option were selected, Linda should have been advised not to disclose any bargaining information that she did not want George to know. In either event, Mike should tell George about his prior business relationship with Linda.

In-House Sale

Even though the selling salesperson working with a represented buyer in an in-house sale is someone other than the listing salesperson, a dual representation exists because the employing broker has become an intermediary or a dual agent through the conduct of the two salespersons.

■ **EXAMPLE**   Joe, a salesperson with Pacesetter Realty, lists Harry's house. Kathy, also of Pacesetter Realty, has been looking for two months to find the right house for her client, Lisa. She shows Lisa the house that Joe listed. Lisa loves it and wants Kathy to negotiate on her behalf for a lower price, a long closing period, and favorable financing terms. Lisa wants Kathy secretly to look for a resale buyer at a quick profit, ideally in a back-to-back closing.

■ **QUESTION**   Who represents whom?

■ **DISCUSSION**   Unless Pacesetter Realty has written consent to act as an intermediary, it now represents both the seller and the buyer as an undisclosed dual agent. The knowledge possessed by both Joe and Kathy will be imputed to Pacesetter Realty and to each other. Pacesetter Realty is still the broker and would, therefore, be advocating for both sides against each other. The only logical conclusion is that Pacesetter Realty has become an unlawful dual agent. The danger here is of actually trading inside information within the same office.

The best answer may lie in the intermediary transaction with appointments. Joe, the listing agent, would be appointed to give advice and opinions to seller Harry, thereby protecting Harry's interests. Kathy, working with represented buyer Lisa, would be appointed to assist Lisa with advice and opinions toward meeting her goals. Because in the intermediary agreement both parties have agreed that certain information may be kept confidential, the fact that Lisa is hoping to resell quickly at a profit is moot.

Some brokers are not aware that this two-salesperson situation in an in-house sale creates a dual-representation conflict and, therefore, will not attempt to obtain proper consents. The broker may believe that both buyer and seller will be treated fairly and that each will receive full representation from their respective associates.

The broker often becomes aware of the conflict for the first time when served with notice of a lawsuit. It is then that the listing broker discovers, for example, that the salesperson never told the seller that the real reason for extending the closing date was to close the sale of the buyer's home, which was also listed by the broker. The seller then claims a breach of fiduciary duty because the broker failed to point out the seller's options in agreeing to an extension (for example, as a condition for extending, the seller possibly could have asked for compensating concessions). Trying to reverse unintended dual agency by attempting to get an intermediary agreement at the point of a lawsuit comes too late to protect the broker.

Cooperating or Other Broker

The other broker in the transaction often acts as the agent of the buyer in negotiations to acquire a property listed in an MLS. If subagency is offered and the broker fails to disclaim the offer of subagency, the other broker may be deemed the subagent of the seller and the implied agent of the buyer.

■ **EXAMPLE** Patricia of Supreme Real Estate checks the MLS book in her search for a home for Nancy Sue. There was no expressed agreement, either written or oral, that Patricia represented Nancy Sue. Patricia sees an interesting house and calls Jeff from South Side Realty about his listing. She arranges to see the property and subsequently submits Nancy Sue's offer. The negotiations are long and hard, but after a series of four different offers and counteroffers, the seller agrees to Nancy Sue's offer. Before closing, Nancy Sue gets cold feet and asks for a return of her deposit money.

■ **QUESTION** Does Nancy Sue have a valid claim for rescission of the contract based on undisclosed dual representation?

■ **DISCUSSION** Even though it may have no relevance to the true reason why Nancy Sue wants to back out of the contract, she might assert that she relied on the fact that she believed that Patricia was her agent. Later, Nancy Sue alleges she discovered that Patricia and Supreme Real Estate were really subagents of the seller. Because Supreme Real Estate acted as an undisclosed dual representative, she argues, either the buyer or the seller can legally refuse to close, even though no damages are proven. Patricia should have clarified her agency status to both Nancy Sue and Jeff when she first contacted Jeff to view the property. Under typical MLS rules, if subagency is offered, according to current Texas common law, Patricia will probably be presumed to be the subagent of the seller unless she rejects the offer of subagency and declares that she is a buyer's agent. As a subagent, Patricia must act as a subagent, taking care to protect the interest of the seller and not act as an agent of the buyer. In this case, she negotiated hard for Nancy Sue, and it may very well be that Patricia and Supreme Real Estate were unintended agents of Nancy Sue, as well as intended agents of the seller through the subagency rules.

Real estate licensees should note that professional liability often is based on the law of agency and the failure of a licensee to live up to the duties of an agent when held to be acting as one. Subagency may complicate this problem by creating an unintended dual representation with an inherent conflict of interest.

Broker as Principal

Brokers should be especially alert to dual-representation problems when they or their associates or employees, licensed or otherwise, buy or sell property for their own accounts. This can happen in several contexts.

Buying an in-house listing. On occasion, a broker or one of the broker's associates decides to make an offer on one of the broker's own listings. As a rule, brokers should not purchase their own listings, especially if they are real bargains. The risks to the professional image of the broker are too great, not to mention the risks of loss of commission for breach of the duties of good faith and loyalty and loss of license under TRELA rules and regulations. To minimize exposure to liability, brokers desiring to purchase in-house listings should recommend that sellers obtain confirming appraisals and retain other consultants or advisers.

■ **EXAMPLE** Debra lists her home with broker Sid for $100,000. After six months of marketing, Debra has received only one offer, for $75,000. Sid offers to pay $95,000 by way of an assumption of the $80,000 first mortgage and further agrees to reduce the 7 percent listing fee to 3.5 percent. Five days before closing, Sid meets Betty, a recent arrival to town, who buys the home from Sid for $110,000 five days after closing.

■ **QUESTION** Did Sid breach a fiduciary duty to Debra?

■ **DISCUSSION** Sid probably did breach his fiduciary duty if he did not inform Debra immediately on learning of Betty's offer. Under 22 TAC § 535.156 (b) and (c), a broker "must put the interest of the licensee's principal above the licensee's own interest" and the broker has "an affirmative duty to keep the principal informed at all times of significant information applicable to the transaction." Under 22 TAC § 535.16, Sid is obligated "under a listing contract to negotiate the best possible transaction for the principal the broker has agreed to represent."

Even if, technically, Sid were found to have breached no fiduciary duty, the appearance of wrongdoing is there. Sid may have a difficult time proving to a jury that he acted in Debra's best interests, particularly if the home's appraised value exceeded the listing price.

At best, there will always be a doubt in Debra's mind as to whether Sid stole a profit opportunity from her. Even if Betty had not appeared until a few days after closing, Sid would have a tough time convincing a jury that he didn't knowingly underprice the house at the time of the listing, which would be not only an additional breach of fiduciary duty but also a deceptive trade practice.

Sid should offer to return to Debra all or a fair portion of the quick profit or allow Debra the opportunity to sell directly to Betty. Such an attitude enhances the broker's professional standing in the community. In fact, it may enhance the broker's reputation so much that it more than makes up for the temporary loss of revenue. However, whether it is more profitable is not an appropriate standard by which to measure moral conduct. It is easy for brokers to say they promote their clients' best interests above anyone else's, including their own. It is much more effective to demonstrate this. (See *Wilson v. Donze*, 692 S.W.2d 735 [Tex. App. 2 Dist. 1985].) In this case, the broker had a duty to obtain the best price possible, even above the asking price. Though the seller ultimately determines the list price, the broker's duty is still to obtain the best possible price.)

The risks of a lawsuit increase if the licensee buying an in-house listing competes against offers submitted by other licensees on behalf of buyers or by buyers' agents on behalf of their clients. The listing agent has an unfair competitive advantage over other buyers because the agent knows all the bids. TRELA § 1101.652(b)(2), which prohibits dealing in bad faith and dishonest dealings, also applies. The listing agent should reveal to other buyers the price and terms of any prior or subsequent offer made by the listing agent. Otherwise, the agent risks possible action by a buyer for breach of the general duties of fairness and honesty. Such an action could be based on failure to present the buyer's offer in a timely manner, failure to notify the buyer after the agent outbid the buyer, or failure to reveal information the buyer might have used to justify a more attractive offering price, such as a pending beneficial zoning change.

State licensing law often requires that real estate licensees disclose in writing their true position when offering to buy property listed with the broker. Although TRELA § 1101.652(b)(16) requires this disclosure, it does not require that it be in writing. Remember that although TRELA is the general law governing licensees, TREC rules may also apply. In this case, the requirement for "written" notification is addressed by TREC rule:

> *22 TAC 535.144 When Acquiring or Disposing of Own Property or Property of Spouse, Parent or Child.*
>
> *(b) A licensee, when engaging in a real estate transaction on his or her own behalf, on behalf of a business entity in which the licensee is more than a 10% owner, or on behalf of the licensees spouse, parent, or child, is obligated to disclose in writing to any person with whom the licensee deals that he or she is a licensed real estate broker or salesperson acting on his or her own behalf or on behalf of the licensee's spouse, parent or child in any contract of sale or rental agreement or in any other writing given prior to entering into any contract of sale or rental agreement.*

As the buyer, the listing agent must remember that unless the agency has been terminated, the broker is still a fiduciary of the seller. The agent must act primarily for the benefit of the seller and owes the seller the standard duties of full disclosure, skill, and care, in addition to honesty and fairness. There may a question as to whether a broker can self-represent in buying a client's property and continue to place that client's interests first. A jury might also find it difficult to accept.

Buying property listed in an MLS. A licensee may decide to purchase a property listed in an MLS by another firm either for themselves, or for a family member (i.e., spouse, parent or child) or a business entity (more than 10 percent ownership interest) previously described in 22 TAC § 535.144. The licensee should disclaim any subagency to the seller. Otherwise, the seller may claim that the licensee-buyer owed fiduciary duties to the seller under any MLS offer of subagency. Note that licensees are not normal consumers and may be required, under agency law, to disclose their opinions of value or of the likelihood of future appreciation (22 TAC § 535.16(c)).

Sellers have won cases against cooperating brokers who bought for their own accounts, or that of close relatives. The success of these suits has been based on failure by licensees to disclose the true market value (one week after purchase of a property, for example, a licensee listed it on a financial statement as having a $20,000 greater value) or to disclose that a simple subdivision of the property would increase its market value (in one case, by 25 percent). The sellers won because the other agent owed fiduciary duties to the sellers based on the rules of subagency. These cases might have turned out differently had the licensee rejected subagency from the beginning, made all proper disclosures, and documented them before proceeding.

If a commission split will occur, the listing agent should fully disclose this fact. This amount is often used as part of the down payment. The cooperating broker should disclose in the purchase contract that the receipt of such a split does not create an agency relationship between the other licensee (the buyer) and the seller. It is much safer for the licensee-buyer to disclaim subagency, deduct the fee from the offering price, and not participate in the fee paid by the seller.

Buying from the FSBO. Licensees buying FSBO (for sale by owner) properties (again, either for themselves or acting on behalf of a close relative or business entity described above) should disclaim any agency relationship with the sellers and should not approach the sellers under the guise of representing the sellers' best interests or listing the properties. Otherwise, under the law, they may be deemed agents of the sellers. If the licensees are deemed agents, they will be held to a higher standard of care with a greater duty of disclosure to sellers (22 TAC § 535.16(c)).

The FSBO seller often agrees to pay a reduced commission to the licensee-buyer as a courtesy fee. The seller may later argue that the payment of a fee to the licensee-buyer was enough to create an agency relationship. At a minimum, licensees buying for their own account should insert disclaimer language, such as the following: "Seller understands that buyer is a Texas real estate licensee buying for the licensee's own account and is not acting as an agent of the seller. Seller is not relying on the licensee for any advice or counsel regarding the sale. The licensee has advised seller that seller is free to obtain an independent consultant or agent to represent the seller's interest."

Licensed associates buying properties for their own accounts. Some realty firms prohibit or limit the right of their associates to buy properties listed with their firms. Office policies vary, however a broker may reasonably insist that a property be offered to the public for at least 45 days or more before anyone in-house can make an offer on the property. These firms believe that the risk of alienating clients and prospective buyers outweighs any benefits to the brokerage firms.

Associates who do offer to buy property listed with their broker (again, either for the licensee or assisting another buyer meeting the relationship standard defined in 22 TAC § 535.144) should have the contract clearly state that the seller understands that the buyer is associated with the listing broker.

If the associate buys property listed in the MLS (offering subagency) and receives a commission split, both the associate and the broker are considered subagents of the seller unless they clearly disclaim any agency relationship. As subagents, both would owe complete fiduciary duties to the seller. Another approach, thought by some to be somewhat safer for the associate-buyer, would be to take a buyer's agent position, offer a lower net price, and not participate in any fee paid by the seller. The associate would have to discuss compensation with the cooperating broker, who normally would expect to receive a portion of the commission split from the listing broker.

Selling licensees' own property. Licensees who sell their own properties must disclose to prospective purchasers that they are licensed brokers or salespersons. For the protection of both the brokers and the buyers, licensees also should make clear to buyers that they are not acting as agents for the buyers and that the buyers are free to seek independent representation. The full disclosure of the business and family relationships described in 22 TAC § 535.144 applies to this type of transaction as well.

Some brokers limit the number of properties owned by associates that can be sold at reduced commission rates. Brokers fear that associates will create the impression of spending valuable time competing for qualified buyers with sellers who have listed properties with the brokers. Other brokers prohibit their associates from marketing their personally owned properties to past or present clients to avoid any impression of impropriety. Associates should always inform their brokers of any intention to sell their own properties.

Adopting the Buyer

If no other broker is involved, the listing agent often spends a good deal of time with the buyer both before and after the contract is signed. A clear conflict arises in a back-to-back sale if the agent signs a listing with the buyer to resell the property before an offer has been made. More likely, however, is a situation in which an agent "adopts" a buyer during the closing process, agreeing, for example, to list other properties of the buyer, to cooperatively develop a property, or to perform any other actions that may create an implied or express conflict of interest or representation agreement with the buyer.

Suppose the listing agent is asked by a buyer prior to closing to look for a resale buyer at $10,000 more than the contract price. While it is not illegal to take a listing from a buyer after the contract is signed, the listing agent ethically and legally must disclose the dual representation to the seller. The seller might feel, in retrospect, that the agent, before the contract was signed, failed to disclose the existence of a resale buyer and possible higher selling price so that the agent could make a double commission.

Again, the intermediary role might be in the best interest of all parties, especially the broker. The principals would, by agreement, not be entitled to full disclosure. Both principals could have a licensee appointed to give advice and opinions and protect their individual interests while maintaining confidential negotiating details. It is best to discuss the possibility of future representation of a buyer before the agent begins to work with the buyer. If representation in a future transaction is contemplated, it is wise to enter into a buyer-representation contract for the first transaction. If, as in this case, the first transaction involves a property listed by the broker, the broker could, with the written consent of both buyer and seller, conduct the first transaction as an intermediary and the second resale transaction as a single agent for the buyer who has now become the seller.

A key ingredient in all the preceding scenarios is a full and complete disclosure of the role the broker is to play. When parties agree to allow a broker to act in any capacity that gives any principal less than the full fiduciary duties of an agent, the principals should be fully informed of the limitations and give their informed consent.

Nonagency

While it may be possible for a broker and principals to sign a consensual nonagency agreement, nothing in the License Act addresses a nonagency status. In fact, the Texas Real Estate Commission interprets TRELA as agency law; therefore, it is presumed that in a brokerage transaction, the licensee, while acting under the provisions of the act, is the agent of someone—the buyer, the seller, or both. Brokers attempting to operate as nonagents may find that the presumed nonagency status has actually created a "gratuitous" agency bearing all the liability of agency without the right to compensation.

Some states provide for nonagency status for real estate licensees who may provide real estate services as transactional brokers, facilitators, or middlemen. A broker in Texas attempting to maintain a nonagency status will find no comfort in TRELA if a dispute arises in the transaction. Likewise the courts have determined that brokers, while attempting to act as middlemen, may become an agent if they attempt to perform any services on behalf of a property owner. (*See West v. Touchstone*, 620 S.W.2d 687 [Tex.Civ.App., Dallas 1981].)

■ SUMMARY

Statutory changes during the 1995 legislative session made sweeping changes in the area involving representation of more than one party to a transaction. Statutory dual agency was removed and replaced with intermediary brokerage. The statutory intermediary brokerage status in Texas presented the solution to the problems inherent in trying to represent both sides in a transaction. The key distinction between the old statutory dual agent and the intermediary broker lies in the ability of the intermediary to offer a broader range of services to represented buyers and sellers during in-house transactions. These extended services are accomplished through allowing appointed licensees of the broker to give preferential advice and opinions to the party to whom the licensee has been appointed, while the intermediary broker remains neutral throughout the transaction.

Undisclosed dual representation is a clear breach of an agent's fiduciary duty of loyalty. Even when an agent intends to act as an agent of both parties, such dual representation violates TRELA if adequate disclosure is not given to both the buyer and the seller and unless an agreed intermediary relationship is established under TRELA. Many dual representations are accidental and arise because of the conduct of the licensees. Brokers need to establish internal management controls to lessen the risks of both unintended and underdisclosed dual representation.

The concepts of intermediary brokerage practice are difficult to grasp for new brokers and newly licensed salespersons. FAQ's compiled by TREC are provided for review in Appendix B.

■ KEY POINTS

- A broker must agree to act as an intermediary when representing more than one party in a transaction.
- It is possible for a company to sell its own listings without creating intermediary brokerage, provided the buyers remain as customers.
- Intermediary brokerage, with the option of appointed licensees for each party, is authorized in Texas and became effective in January 1996. Theoretically, an intermediary broker may act as an agent for both parties, but the broker's duties differ from those the broker assumes when acting as a single agent for either party. The duties and obligations of the intermediary are limited to those set out in TRELA § 1101.559; .651(d). The purpose of the statute is to extend greater services to represented buyers and sellers in in-house transactions. It also is designed to reduce the liability of brokers when they conduct transactions in which both principals are represented by the same broker. This new law has yet to be fully interpreted by TREC regulations or by decisions of the courts.
- A broker who expects to become an intermediary should lay a foundation early by discussing the possibility of an intermediary transaction with in-house sales at the initial interviews with both the potential seller and the potential buyer. The possibility of an intermediary transaction should never be sprung on a client after a relationship is established. Consent to conduct an intermediary transaction should be authorized in the listing contract or in a buyer-representation contract.
- In comparison with single agency, the intermediary brokerage practice offers reduced services to the parties in the transaction. However, this shortcoming has been reduced by the ability of the broker to appoint associates to the buyer and seller for the intermediary transaction. These appointed associates may give preferential advice and opinion to their respective parties during the transaction.
- Although the intermediary broker may be exposed to legal liability by failing to follow the intermediary guidelines carefully, the broker may benefit from this practice through in-house sales to represented buyers.

■ SUGGESTIONS FOR BROKERS

A broker who is considering offering intermediary services to buyers and sellers should fully understand the requirements of the intermediary and develop a company policy regarding such practices. In addition, the broker should address the issue of appointed associates and be prepared to train associates who may be involved in such transactions.

CHAPTER 7 QUIZ

1. An associate of a broker, while working with a nonrepresented buyer, begins to give advice and opinions to the buyer during negotiations with a seller represented by the broker. MOST likely the broker has become a(n)
   a. single agent of the buyer.
   b. intermediary.
   c. undisclosed dual agent.
   d. facilitator.

2. Currently, the form of dual representation known as dual agency is
   a. not permitted by TRELA.
   b. permitted under statutory rules.
   c. encouraged by TREC.
   d. permitted under common law rules.

3. The major difference between the former statutory dual agency and the current intermediary status is that with intermediary status,
   a. appointed licensees can give advice and opinions.
   b. agents have the same restrictions as the broker.
   c. the broker can give advice and opinions.
   d. confidential information can be relayed.

4. If an intermediary situation arises, the broker cannot disclose
   a. the highest price the buyer might pay, until authorized to do so in writing.
   b. the minimum price a seller will take, unless authorized to do so in writing.
   c. confidential information of either party, unless the parties authorize it or law requires disclosure.
   d. any of these.

5. In a transaction involving appointed associates, which of the following is TRUE?
   a. Associates may be appointed to either the buyer or the seller.
   b. The broker may be appointed to the buyer, while an associate is appointed to the seller.
   c. Written notification of the intermediary transaction and the appointed associates must be given to both parties.
   d. Written notification and identification of the appointed associates must be given to both parties.

6. Broker Able's represented buyer wishes to negotiate on a property listed by broker Smith in a different firm. During this transaction, which broker(s) may act as an intermediary?
   a. Able
   b. Smith
   c. Neither Able nor Smith
   d. Both Able and Smith

7. In an intermediary transaction, if a broker appoints an associate to the seller,
   a. an associate also must be appointed to the buyer.
   b. the broker must take an appointment to the buyer.
   c. the same associate also must be appointed to the buyer.
   d. the broker must appoint someone from another firm to the buyer.

8. Unintentional dual representation can occur when
   a. another broker acts as a subagent and represents the buyer.
   b. the listing broker represents both the buyer and seller.
   c. a licensee acts as a buyer or a seller.
   d. any of these takes place.

9. A small company consists of a broker and one associate. During an intermediary transaction, the
   a. broker may be appointed to one party and the associate may be appointed to the other party.
   b. broker is prohibited from making appointments.
   c. associate may be appointed to both parties.
   d. broker may be appointed to both parties.

10. What occurs when an associate who has listed a property shows a represented buyer that same property and an intermediary transaction develops?
    a. The associate may be appointed to both the seller and the buyer.
    b. The associate may be appointed to either the seller or the buyer.
    c. The associate may *not* be appointed to either the seller or the buyer.
    d. The associate may appoint another associate to work with the buyer.

DISCUSSION QUESTIONS

1. What are the key differences between the former statutory dual agent and the current intermediary broker?
2. Why might a broker make or not make appointments in an intermediary transaction?
3. What issues should be considered in office policy regarding appointed associates?

CHAPTER 8

Nonexclusive Single Agency

Some people in the real estate industry, modify the term *agency* with the adjectives *single, nonexclusive,* or *exclusive*. While not recognized legal terms, *single agency, exclusive,* and *nonexclusive* are terms used to describe forms of agency different from intermediary brokerage. They are descriptive business-model terms that, on the surface, appear to distinguish intermediary brokerage (dual representation) from other business models that limit the broker to representing only one side of the transaction. The broker practicing single agency or nonspecific client-based agency must understand the specific procedural and position features of both representing sellers and representing buyers.

This chapter presents an overview of the following agency practice issues applied to a broker who has decided to practice single agency without limiting the broker's client base to only one category of clients.

■ **LEARNING OBJECTIVES** *This chapter addresses the following:*

- Practicing Nonexclusive Single Agency
- Counseling Sessions Prior to Engagement
  - Conflicts of Interest
- Advantages and Disadvantages

■ PRACTICING NONEXCLUSIVE SINGLE AGENCY

While exclusively representing the seller (either as listing broker or subagent of the listing broker) was the norm until the growth of buyer agency, it is rare to find brokers today who limit the scope of their brokerage business to exclusively servicing only one side of the transaction. For example, a broker may elect a business model of only working for sellers (never buyers), while another broker elects a business model of only working for buyers (never sellers). In earlier chapters, we described this type of broker as either an exclusive seller's agent (*see* Chapter 5) or exclusive buyer's agent (*see* Chapter 6). Another descriptive term for that type of business model would be *exclusive single agency* (exclusively representing only sellers in one case and exclusively representing only buyers in the other).

Most brokers and their associates, however, have become quite comfortable with the concepts of representing buyers as well as sellers; nevertheless, there are brokers who may still hesitate to take on the added risks described in Chapter 7 of representing both parties in a single transaction (intermediary). A broker who is prepared to offer representation to either side of the transaction, but never both, could be said to offer nonexclusive single agency. These brokers and their associates represent either buyers or sellers, either tenants or landlords, or only one party to an exchange of property, but never both in the same transaction. Nonexclusive single-agency brokerage, in general, is therefore oriented more toward the person in the transaction rather than toward that person's relationship to the property. That is, the broker focuses on the person's needs, whether that person buys, sells, leases, exchanges, develops, or builds real estate.

The nonexclusive single-agency type of brokerage practice best appeals to the real estate professional interested in developing and maintaining long-term broker-client relationships in which the agent becomes part of the family advisory team, similar to the relationship with a family doctor, a lawyer, and an accountant.

In some cases, the single-agency broker is paid directly by the broker's client, be it buyer, seller, tenant, or landlord. In other cases, the single-agency broker is compensated indirectly by the other party as a condition of the contract or is paid by an authorized commission split from the broker representing the other side in the transaction.

James B. Warkentin, in *Buyer Brokering: How to Represent and Get Paid by the Buyer*, describes single agency as follows:

> *Single agency means that each principal can choose to be represented by their own broker or to represent themselves. Since all listed sellers have their own broker, this area is not a problem. It is the buyer who needs the choice of being a client of his [or her] own broker or representing himself [or herself]. Client quality services are always greater than customer quality services. This is in the nature of the relationship. For example, you are a client with your attorney, a customer with a new car salesperson.*

Some licensees confuse the concept of a single agency (either exclusive or nonexclusive) with the inability of a single-agency broker to conduct an in-house transaction. Any nonrepresented buyer might purchase any listing held by a single-agency broker without creating a conflict for the broker. The seller would be represented as the client, and the buyer would be treated as the customer. While a nonexclusive single-agency broker often works with both sides, that broker will not work for both sides. The dedicated nonexclusive single-agency broker will not, in any given transaction, act in a representative capacity for both buyer and seller or both landlord and tenant. Instead, the nonexclusive single-agency broker usually attempts to maintain an ongoing, long-term, agency relationship with a client, depending on whether the client's needs at the time are buying or selling.

■ **EXAMPLE** Broker Jim lists and sells Sara's house while representing Sara as a seller's agent. During this transaction, Jim locates a new home for Sara that is listed by another broker. As a single agent (that is, not offering intermediary services), Jim would most likely wish to continue his agency relationship with Sara during this new transaction and represent Sara as a buyer's agent. Unless Jim acts as an agent for Sara in the second transaction, he would be in the position of simultaneously treating Sara as a client in the sale of her home and as a customer in the second transaction. In the second transaction, broker Jim would be acting as a subagent of the listing broker. This is not an illegal relationship; however, many questions relating to fiduciary duties might arise.

If Jim worked only as an exclusive buyer's agent, he would not have listed Sara's house and could have served her only in the purchase of the new home, thus eliminating the possibility of earning two commissions in the transactions. Conversely, if Jim operated only as an exclusive seller's agent, he would have served Sara as her agent in the sale of her home but could not change his role to become Sara's agent when she became a purchaser of the new property. Although this would make it possible to earn a second commission, it would be contrary to the goals of a broker wishing to maintain pure exclusive single agency.

■ **EXAMPLE** Reconsider the example in Chapter 5, on page 102, "Sally as the selling associate with no prior relationship with the buyer." Sally wishes to show Bob, a potential buyer, the Main Street property, listed by a fellow associate of Bay Realty, and the King Street property, listed by Southside Realty. In this scenario, however, presume that Bay Realty offers both seller agency and buyer agency (nonexclusive representation), but does not offer services to buyers represented by the firm on properties listed by the firm. Further presume that Bob would like to be represented as a buyer-client.

■ **QUESTIONS** 1. What role can Sally play when showing Bob the Main Street property (in-house transaction)? 2. What role can Sally play when showing Bob the King Street property listed by Southside Realty? 3. At what point should Sally and Bay Realty agree to represent Bob? 4. How will circumstances change if Bob decides to reconsider the Main Street property after Bay Realty agrees to represent him?

■ **DISCUSSION** Keep in mind that Bay Realty, while offering representation to both sellers and buyers, will not act as representatives of both parties in the same transaction. Of course, Bob first must be made aware of the services that may be offered to buyers and sellers by brokers and, more specifically, the services offered by Bay Realty. Bob should understand that neither Sally nor any other associate of Bay Realty can represent him on the Main Street property or on any other property listed by Bay Realty. However, because Bay Realty does not limit representation to sellers, it could represent him as a client on either the King Street property or any other property listed by another broker who allows cooperation by brokers who represent buyers.

After a thorough discussion of these alternatives, if Bob wishes to view any property listed by Bay Realty, he should do this before he enters into a representation agreement with Bay Realty. If no suitable property is found, then Bay Realty and Bob could enter into a representation agreement for properties listed by other brokers. If Bob is not satisfied with customer status on Bay Realty's listings, he should be referred to another brokerage firm that will offer the desired representation.

The most difficult situation would occur if Bob decided to negotiate on a listing of Bay Realty after it agreed to represent him. Because Bay Realty does not offer representation to buyers and sellers in the same transaction, it could consider one of the following options:

- Rescind the representation agreement with Bob and show the properties to him as a customer, notifying the sellers that Bob is a prior client and that the seller may not receive full disclosure regarding Bob's financial status or that other matters gained in confidence;
- Rescind the listing agreement with the seller and show Bob the property as a client while serving the seller as a customer, notifying Bob that the seller is a prior client and that he may not receive full disclosure regarding the seller's matters.
- Refer Bob to another brokerage firm and represent the seller only. When addressing issues of representation, the broker should keep in mind that principals must always agree before proceeding. Sellers who enter into listing agreements with brokers must be informed as to the various roles that licensees may play. It is sellers who must decide whether to authorize brokers to represent buyers as well as themselves when showing their properties.

The advantage, then, of nonexclusive single agency for the broker in both examples is that the broker practicing nonexclusive single agency can continue to maintain a client relationship in each transaction and also earn two commissions. The advantage to the consumer being represented is true representation with undivided loyalty in both the sale and the purchase.

■ COUNSELING SESSIONS PRIOR TO ENGAGEMENT

Usually, the nonexclusive single-agency practitioner does not agree to represent a client without first conducting a counseling session. Modern real estate practice is much more than just listing and selling. Buying property differs from buying an expensive car, for which the title, specifications, and warranties are relatively consistent and clear. The real estate client's objectives, criteria, and limitations must be clearly understood. The agent's job is to help develop this information before attempting to market or locate a property for a client. Then the property must be diligently investigated and the interests of others in the property ascertained. Most important, both agent and client must be comfortable in working together to meet the client's objectives.

Nonexclusive single agency brokers represent clients, not just buyers/tenants or sellers/landlords. Some brokers specialize in representing buyers; however, they quickly realize that in certain cases, their satisfied buyer clients may someday want to employ them to sell their property. In such a case, when a seller lists property with a nonexclusive single-agency broker, the broker will make full disclosure at the outset to buyer prospects that the broker represents the seller only. If a buyer makes an informed decision to continue a transaction without representation, the broker may commence working with the buyer to provide customer service, but not client representation.

Conflicts of Interest

Because the broker practicing nonexclusive single agency never acts as an intermediary, the broker may have to withdraw from representing one or both clients if a buyer-client becomes interested in a property listed by that broker. Typically, the broker will inform the buyer of the need to terminate the agency relationship for that particular transaction. If the buyer decides to continue with the transaction without representation, the broker will work with the buyer as a customer in this purchase from the seller-client.

Caution is advised if the seller asks the agent to disclose information about the buyer that was obtained in the earlier confidential agency relationship. Confidential information remains confidential even after the agency relationship is terminated. The agent should disclose to the seller-client that the buyer was, until recently, a client of the brokerage firm, and that confidential information about the buyer that was learned in the previous relationship cannot be disclosed. Should the seller object to the disclosure limitations, the broker may need to refer the seller-client to another broker for representation. However, there is no prohibition against revealing information about the former client that has been learned since the termination of the previous agency (the former buyer-client, now a buyer-customer, should be fully informed about the implications of the changed relationship).

As discussed in Chapter 7, some nonexclusive single-agency brokers and their associates will show all of the firm's listings to a buyer-customer before agreeing to represent that buyer as a client. While this lessens the chances of a conflict of interest, it doesn't eliminate the possibility that a buyer-client may later, after confidential matters and motives have been disclosed, decide to buy an in-house listing that was shown when the buyer was a customer. Nor does it preclude the ideal home for the buyer from coming into the firm's listing inventory after the buyer-customer has been converted to a buyer-client.

ADVANTAGES AND DISADVANTAGES

Here are some advantages of nonexclusive single agency.

- For the broker, nonexclusive single agency
  — allows the agent to represent sellers and buyers, but in different transactions; therefore, the agent has a wider potential client base and can participate in more transactions with any given client, reducing the time and money required to produce new clients;
  — reduces agent liability for undisclosed dual representation or intermediary brokerage;
  — increases client loyalty for professionalism, resulting in more referrals; and
  — allows the agent to have a long-term, continuing client-level relationship with an individual, whether the individual buys or sells.
- For buyers and sellers, nonexclusive single agency
  — ensures that clients receive full representation and the undivided loyalty of their agent; and
  — allows an individual to have a long-term, continuing client-level agency relationship with a specific and trusted agent, whether the individual buys or sells or acts as a landlord or tenant.

There also are some disadvantages of nonexclusive single agency.

- For brokers and associates, nonexclusive single agency also
  — reduces the possibility of earning an undivided commission when both parties require representation in a transaction. However, when only one of the parties desires representation, a broker practicing single agency might receive an undivided commission that otherwise would have been split with a subagent or the broker representing the other party;
  — may result in loss of a buyer-client interested in a listing of the firm; and
  — produces difficulty with switching back and forth from client to customer.
- For buyers and sellers, nonexclusive single agency
  — may not allow licensees to show their company's listings to buyer-clients without creating dual representation, thereby reducing a seller-client's access to potential buyers, although, in the event of a conflict of this type, the prospect could be referred to another brokerage firm.

SUMMARY

A nonexclusive single-agency practice enables a broker to represent buyers or sellers. These brokers and their associates must be careful to avoid conflicts of interest caused by selling properties listed by the firm to buyer-clients. Because buyers in today's real estate market generally desire representation, the broker must consider the impact on their financial interests of not offering intermediary services and must develop viable alternatives for the already represented buyer who becomes interested in a property listed by the firm. The use of a clear agency disclosure statement is helpful.

KEY POINTS

- The nonexclusive single-agency broker represents either buyers or sellers, but never both in the same transaction.
- With nonexclusive single agency, clients receive full representation, but they may have to switch to customer status if a conflict arises, or the broker may have to withdraw from a transaction altogether.

SUGGESTIONS FOR BROKERS

If you choose the nonexclusive single-agency type of practice, decide how to handle the situation in which a prospective buyer wants you to locate property but does not want to sign a buyer-representation agreement. Single-agency practitioners will be limited in helping a buyer investigate properties listed by other brokers in the MLS if the buyer intends a broker to act as a subagent of the seller.

CHAPTER 8 QUIZ

1. The nonexclusive single-agency broker represents all of the following EXCEPT
   a. the tenant or landlord.
   b. the buyer or seller.
   c. the vendee or vendor.
   d. both parties to a transaction.

2. The nonexclusive single-agency broker is LEAST likely to
   a. be a seller's agent.
   b. be a buyer's agent.
   c. be a subagent of the seller.
   d. have conflicts concerning representation issues.

3. Betty wants to make an offer on a property listed by Sally, a single-agency broker. Who can help Betty submit an offer to buy?
   a. Another broker
   b. Betty herself
   c. Sally
   d. All of these

4. All of the following are advantages of nonexclusive single agency EXCEPT
   a. it reduces liability associated with intermediary practice.
   b. the broker has a wider potential client base than exclusive single agency.
   c. it reduces the possibility of undivided commissions.
   d. it allows the broker and client to have a long-term professional relationship.

5. Which BEST describes the nonexclusive single-agency broker's initial meeting with a prospective buyer or seller?
   a. The buyer or seller signs the listing agreement.
   b. The broker counsels the buyer or seller.
   c. The buyer or seller consults the broker.
   d. The broker receives an advance retainer fee.

6. If a buyer wants to be represented on a property listed by a single-agency firm, the nonexclusive single-agency firm
   a. should refer the buyer to a buyer's agent.
   b. should persuade the buyer to negotiate through the firm as a customer.
   c. should cancel the listing with the seller and represent the buyer in order to receive the greater commissions earned in an in-house sale.
   d. cannot serve the buyer in any capacity and maintain the single agency status.

7. The nonexclusive single-agency firm works
   a. always with the buyer and for the seller.
   b. always for the buyer and with the seller.
   c. for either the buyer or the seller.
   d. all of these.

8. A nonexclusive single agency firm would NOT
   a. practice intermediary brokerage.
   b. have salespersons or broker associates.
   c. represent the buyer or the seller.
   d. list properties.

9. A firm offering nonexclusive buyer agency would NOT
   a. ensure that clients receive full representation.
   b. reduce agent liability for undisclosed dual agency.
   c. represent both the buyer and the seller in the same transaction.
   d. allow the agent to have a long-term relationship with the client.

10. Nonexclusive single-agency brokers are similar to brokers offering intermediary services in all of the following ways EXCEPT
    a. Both may represent buyers and sellers within the same transaction.
    b. Both may represent buyers and sellers.
    c. Both may represent sellers.
    d. Both may represent buyers.

DISCUSSION QUESTIONS

1. How does the nonexclusive single-agency broker normally handle the situation when both the buyer and the seller want the broker to represent them?

2. Why does nonexclusive single-agency practice not result in two brokers being required for every transaction?

3. What relation does buyer brokerage have to single-agency practice?

4. What is the difference between working with a buyer and working for a buyer?

CHAPTER 9

Clarifying Agency Relationships

Most real estate licensees operate on the basis of high ethical standards that require fairness and honesty to customers and clients. Disclosure of their agency relationship to the buyer or the seller in a real estate transaction has been required for decades. No consensus exists among real estate professionals on the best way to discuss and document agency relationships. However, Texas agency disclosure laws apply to commercial licensees as well as to residential licensees and to leases as well as to sales.

In many transactions, at least one person has the wrong impression of who represents whom. While there are no easy solutions, licensees can—and must—take steps to eliminate any confusion. The purpose of this chapter is to help licensees develop workable strategies to reduce complaints and avoid possible lawsuits while at the same time enhancing their professional reputation.

■ **LEARNING OBJECTIVES**   *This chapter addresses the following:*

- Disclosure Policy
  - Decide
  - Disclose
  - Document
  - Do as You Say
- Developing a Company Policy
  - Phases 1 to 5

■ DISCLOSURE POLICY

Much of the present confusion over agency relationships would be eliminated if licensees would

- decide in each particular transaction whether to represent the buyer or the seller, and whether intermediary brokerage is anticipated;
- disclose to the buyer and the seller whom they represent as soon as there is an agreement on the representation;
- document the disclosure with an adequate and timely written confirmation; and
- do as they had declared, acting consistently with the disclosed decision.

Decide

Each transaction is different. A licensee must be prepared to decide in each transaction whom to represent and what the licensee's relationship will be to other participants. However, the licensee must take care not to proceed without consulting the parties involved. Because agency is a consensual relationship, a licensee may decide whom to represent but must get the party's informed (and preferably written) consent to that representation.

Identification of the principal-client is sometimes difficult for licensees; it probably is more so for the buyers and the sellers. Depending on the circumstance, the licensee may be representing only the seller, only the buyer, both the seller and the buyer, or possibly neither. The key for licensees is to understand fully the implications and obligations of each of the wide variety of situations that may develop. Before deciding on the appropriate working relationship, the licensee must define what role to play in each transaction. For example, a licensee may handle new property sales differently from resales, commercial property differently from residential property, and first-time buyers differently from sophisticated buyers.

In any single transaction or in any relationship with a particular individual in multiple transactions, the real estate licensee can choose from the following basic working relationships:

- Agent for either seller (or landlord) or buyer (or tenant), but not both (nonexclusive single agency)
- Intermediary broker between both buyer and seller, with the possibility of appointed licensees to each party
- Subagent for either buyer or seller (an agent who is working through another broker)
- Agent only for buyers (exclusive buyer agency)
- Agent only for sellers (exclusive seller agency)
- Agent for neither buyer or seller (nonagency)

Some relevant questions from the listing broker's perspective include the following:

- Is the listing salesperson the only licensee from the firm who is involved in the transaction, or is this an in-house sale of another salesperson's listing or one from a branch office of the firm?

- If a licensee from another firm presents an offer, is that licensee a subagent of the seller or an agent of the buyer?
- Does the listing agent have any prior or current relationship with the buyer, such as having listed the buyer's home, having acted as the property manager on one of the buyer's rental properties, or having agreed to act as the buyer's agent in future transactions?
- Is the licensee working with a buyer who is only a customer, not a client?
- Is the agent acquiring or disposing of his or her own property or the property of his or her spouse, parent, or child? A business entity in which the agent is more than a 10 percent owner?

Following are some relevant questions from the perspective of a licensee from another firm:

- Is this a multiple listing service (MLS) sale?
- Is subagency being offered to other licensees?
- Is there a prior or present business relationship with the buyer? (This would be the case if, for example, the other licensee had listed the buyer's two-bedroom home and helped the buyer submit an offer on a three-bedroom home that is contingent on the sale of the buyer's two-bedroom home.)

It is not always easy to decide whom the real estate broker and associated licensees represent. When in doubt, ask these questions:

- Who is our client, and what services must we perform?
- Who is our customer, and what services can we perform?
- If the transaction involves intermediary brokerage, are there appointed associates, and what services can and cannot be performed for each party?

Disclose

It is not enough for the broker to decide whom to represent. Real estate agents must discuss with prospective sellers and buyers (or landlords and tenants) all proposed agency relationships so that the principals can make informed choices. Agency is a consensual relationship that to expressly create requires a delegation of authority by the principal and consent by the agent. As discussed in Chapter 4, agency created ostensibly or by implication leaves one or more parties uncertain as to whether or not an agency relationship even exists. It is equally important for buyer and seller to know who will not be their agent. Buyers and sellers expressly alerted to the fact that an agent does not represent them will recognize that they must take greater responsibility throughout a transaction to protect their own interests. Timing of disclosure is therefore critical, and disclosure should occur before anyone can claim that an agency relationship already has been formed. If disclosure is delayed until closing or even until an offer is prepared, it is too late. Expectations of agency probably already have been created, and actions have been taken and confidences made in reliance on those expectations. For example, a buyer who presumes she is represented by the licensee has the expectation throughout the relationship that she is receiving advice and opinion from that licensee regarding a negotiating strategy that protects the buyer's financial interest. TRELA therefore requires the licensee to provide the written Information About Brokerage Services as early as possible to a consumer followed immediately by a clear and expressed statement of any agency relationship that may already exist:

> TRELA § 1101.558(b) outlines the specific duties of licensees to disclose their agency relationships. (See TRELA Appendix A.) TRELA also requires that certain written information be given to prospective buyers, sellers, tenants, and landlords regarding the roles that a broker may assume in a transaction. Specifically § 1101.557(a) and 1101.558(b) read as follows:

> § 1101.557(a) A broker who represents a party in a real estate transaction or who lists real estate for sale under an exclusive agreement for a party is that party's agent.

> § 1101.558(b) A license holder who represents a party in a proposed real estate transaction shall disclose, orally or in writing, that representation at the time of the license holder's first contact with:
>
> (1) another party to the transaction; or
>
> (2) another license holder who represents another party to the transaction.

In addition to the specific requirements for agency disclosure, § 1101.558(d) requires that the licensee furnish prospective parties to a transaction a written information statement regarding the roles that the broker might be taking in the transaction. This statement must be given at the first meeting at which substantive discussion occurs regarding real property.

A substantive dialogue can occur at a face-to-face meeting or by written communication (including email) that involves a discussion relating to a specific real property. If the substantive dialogue occurs at other than a face-to-face meeting, the required written statement should be sent to the party promptly. The written statement may be produced in any format desired by the broker so long as the language is unchanged and the print is no smaller than 10-point type.

The Texas Real Estate Commission (TREC) has produced Information About Brokerage Services, a form that may be used by licensees, that meets the statutory requirement, and that is shown as Figure 9.1 (Note: § 1101.558(e) allows the words *tenant* and *landlord* to be substituted for *buyer* and *seller*.) Many licensees mistakenly think the information statement is also a disclosure of their agency status. Not so! By circling "buyer," "seller," "tenant," or "landlord" and signing the form, the consumer is given notice in writing of the types of potential representation. The consumer must then make the choice as to the level of service he or she desires in the transaction. However, the statute requires both the written information statement and a disclosure of any agency relationships. The agency disclosure is a separate duty; it can be either oral or written. Clearly, the careful broker will make sure the agency disclosure is written and acknowledged by the parties involved, even though Texas law does not require that agency disclosure be in writing.

TRELA § 1101.558 (c) grants certain exceptions to providing the written information about brokerage services (*see* Figure 9.1). Exceptions occur when

- the proposed transaction is for a residential lease for not more than one year and no sale is being considered;

FIGURE 9.1

TREC Information About Brokerage Services

10-10-11

Approved by the Texas Real Estate Commission for Voluntary Use
Texas law requires all real estate licensees to give the following information about brokerage services to prospective buyers, tenants, sellers and landlords.

Information About Brokerage Services

Before working with a real estate broker, you should know that the duties of a broker depend on whom the broker represents. If you are a prospective seller or landlord (owner) or a prospective buyer or tenant (buyer), you should know that the broker who lists the property for sale or lease is the owner's agent. A broker who acts as a subagent represents the owner in cooperation with the listing broker. A broker who acts as a buyer's agent represents the buyer. A broker may act as an intermediary between the parties if the parties consent in writing. A broker can assist you in locating a property, preparing a contract or lease, or obtaining financing without representing you. A broker is obligated by law to treat you honestly.

IF THE BROKER REPRESENTS THE OWNER:
The broker becomes the owner's agent by entering into an agreement with the owner, usually through a written - listing agreement, or by agreeing to act as a subagent by accepting an offer of subagency from the listing broker. A subagent may work in a different real estate office. A listing broker or subagent can assist the buyer but does not represent the buyer and must place the interests of the owner first. The buyer should not tell the owner's agent anything the buyer would not want the owner to know because an owner's agent must disclose to the owner any material information known to the agent.

IF THE BROKER REPRESENTS THE BUYER:
The broker becomes the buyer's agent by entering into an agreement to represent the buyer, usually through a written buyer representation agreement. A buyer's agent can assist the owner but does not represent the owner and must place the interests of the buyer first. The owner should not tell a buyer's agent anything the owner would not want the buyer to know because a buyer's agent must disclose to the buyer any material information known to the agent.

IF THE BROKER ACTS AS AN INTERMEDIARY:
A broker may act as an intermediary between the parties if the broker complies with The Texas Real Estate License Act. The broker must obtain the written consent of each party to the transaction to act as an intermediary. The written consent must state who will pay the broker and, in conspicuous bold or underlined print, set forth the broker's obligations as an intermediary. The broker is required to treat each party honestly and fairly and to comply with The Texas Real Estate License Act. A broker who acts as an intermediary in a transaction:

(1) shall treat all parties honestly;

(2) may not disclose that the owner will accept a price less that the asking price unless authorized in writing to do so by the owner;

(3) may not disclose that the buyer will pay a price greater than the price submitted in a written offer unless authorized in writing to do so by the buyer; and

(4) may not disclose any confidential information or any information that a party specifically instructs the broker in writing not to disclose unless authorized in writing to disclose the information or required to do so by The Texas Real Estate License Act or a court order or if the information materially relates to the condition of the property.

With the parties' consent, a broker acting as an intermediary between the parties may appoint a person who is licensed under The Texas Real Estate License Act and associated with the broker to communicate with and carry out instructions of one party and another person who is licensed under that Act and associated with the broker to communicate with and carry out instructions of the other party.

If you choose to have a broker represent you, you should enter into a written agreement with the broker that clearly establishes the broker's obligations and your obligations. The agreement should state how and by whom the broker will be paid. You have the right to choose the type of representation, if any, you wish to receive. Your payment of a fee to a broker does not necessarily establish that the broker represents you. If you have any questions regarding the duties and responsibilities of the broker, you should resolve those questions before proceeding.

Real estate licensee asks that you acknowledge receipt of this information about brokerage services for the licensee's records.

Buyer, Seller, Landlord or Tenant   Date

Texas Real Estate Brokers and Salespersons are licensed and regulated by the Texas Real Estate Commission (TREC). If you have a question or complaint regarding a real estate licensee, you should contact TREC at P.O. Box 12188, Austin, Texas 78711-2188 , 512-936-3000 (http://www.trec.texas.gov)

TREC No. OP-K

- the licensee meets with a party who is represented by another licensee (for example, a seller who has listed his/her property with another firm, but happens to be home when the buyer's agent arrives to show the listing);
- there is no substantive discussion regarding a specific property (for example, a consumer is simply inquiring about market conditions);
- the meeting occurs at an open house; or
- the meeting occurs after the parties have entered into a contract to sell, buy, or lease (for example, the seller has contracted to sell the property and happens to be home when the buyer's agent arrives to open the house for the inspector.)

Although these are the guidelines provided by TRELA, licensees may be wise to present the form early in the meeting. For example, a buyer who comes into the office to inquire about market conditions is most probably considering a future purchase. Although the conversation does not immediately turn to specific properties, the wise policy would be to present the TREC Information About Brokerage Services form (*see* Figure 9.1) as early as possible in the discussion. It is sometimes difficult to determine just when a conversation turns to more substantive matters that require the presentation of the written disclosure. Disclosure of information about agency relationships in general and whom the licensee currently represents, if anyone, relative to the contemplated transaction must also take place according to Texas law as described. In addition, when attempting to secure a listing, the seller and the licensee should discuss

- whether the property is to be listed in the MLS;
- whether the prospective listing broker intends to operate as an intermediary, with buyers produced from the broker's client pool;
- who will have access to listing information;
- whether other licensees will be authorized to cooperate in the search for buyers;
- whether other licensees will be subagents of the seller's or buyers' agents; and
- whether the listing broker intends to share fees with subagents or with buyers' agents.

These matters should be clearly stated in a written listing contract between the broker and the seller.

Timing of agency disclosure. When working with buyers or tenants, the timing of the agency disclosure is frequently a problem. Disclosure is especially difficult with respect to a first-time buyer, who has no clue as to the distinction between client–level and customer-level services. They may have walked into the broker's office in response to a general advertisement or may have met the listing licensee at an open house where the Information About Brokerages Services was not provided. No one seriously contends that the listing licensee should stop buyers after a friendly handshake and immediately present them with the written statutory information statement or make an agency disclosure. Normally the prospect has a decision to make: do they or do they not desire representation? The written statutory disclosure helps the consumer make that decision. A suggestion to help that decision process would be to develop a personalized disclosure brochure that includes the statutory language required by TRELA § 1101.558 and outlines the types of working relationships your firm offers to buyers and sellers. The broker could also outline some of the customer-level services the brokerage can provide to one person while remaining the exclusive agent of the other person (*see* Figure 9.2).

FIGURE 9.2

Comparison of Consumer Services

With Representation (Client)	Consumer Services	Without Representation (Customer)
☑	Accountability	☑
☑	Disclose Material Facts	☑
☑	Fairness	☑
☑	Honesty	☑
☑	Act Under **YOUR** Instructions	
☑	Confidentiality	
☑	Full Disclosure	
☑	Help Negotiate	
☑	Objective Evaluation	
☑	Opinions and Advice	
☑	Price Counseling	

Texas law, however, is quite specific and requires that a licensee who already represents a party in a proposed real estate transaction must disclose that representation at the time of the licensee's first contact with (1) another party to the transaction or (2) another licensee who represents another party to the transaction. The penalty for failure to expressly (oral or written) disclose the already established agency role under TRELA § 1101.652(b)(7) and (8) is that

> *(b) The commission may suspend or revoke a license issued under this chapter or take other disciplinary action authorized by this chapter if the license holder, while acting as a broker or salesperson: . . .*
>
> > *(7) fails to make clear to all parties to a real estate transaction the party for whom the license holder is acting;*
> >
> > *(8) receives compensation from more than one party to a real estate transaction without the full knowledge and consent of all parties to the transaction;*

Again, the disclosures of agency status required here may be made orally or in writing. Licensees should be cautioned that they must comply with both provisions. While § 1101.558 requires only that a licensee who already represents a party in a proposed transaction disclose that fact, § 1101.652(b)(7) requires a licensee "to make clear to all parties to a real estate transaction the party for whom the license holder is acting." The clear implication that can be drawn from that wording is that a licensee who does not represent any party in a transaction should disclose that fact as well (e.g., licensees buying or selling a property for their own account and representing only themselves; or licensees simply referring a consumer to another office but anticipating a referral fee). Otherwise, it could easily be assumed by one of the parties that the licensee represents that party or, conversely, represents the other party.

The licensee must be sensitive to the problems created if the buyer is led to reveal confidential bargaining and financial information to the licensee, who, it turns out, actually represents the seller. Because the licensee is then obligated to relay such information to the seller, the seller receives an unfair advantage over the buyer. The uninformed buyer could, for example, suddenly shift a conversation from a general advertisement or market conditions to inquiries about a specific property the office has already listed, all in the same sentence as indicating they have limited funds, will need serious assistance from the seller on closing costs, are desperate to close in 30 days, and, by the way, they have just been released from prison after serving a sentence for embezzlement! This is a buyer who seriously needs the fiduciary duty of confidentiality a buyer's agent can, and must, offer.

In practice, the real estate licensee may not, at first meeting, know whether to work with the buyer on a client or a customer basis. The first meeting might cover only general business practices, commission structures, and market area specialty, and might be designed to convince the buyer to work with the licensee. Nevertheless, proper disclosure must be made and the licensee is well advised to make the disclosures early in the conversation. If, in fact, the broker is going to represent the buyer, they should enter into a written agreement that specifies the details of the relationship.

Ambiguous situations. There will, of course, be situations that are somewhat ambiguous, in which licensees may be unsure whether to discuss representation.

Take the case of a real estate licensee who views a number of new listings of other brokers while on a company caravan tour. The licensee may not yet know whether revisiting such properties will be on behalf of a client or a customer. However, if meeting the seller face to face, the licensee must disclose agency status, particularly if the licensee is previewing the property for a prospective buyer-client. If meeting only with the seller's agent, the licensee minimally must discuss status and future possibilities if, for example, that licensee has prospective clients who might be interested in purchasing that property.

A licensee must be especially careful to address squarely such undecided status in any discussions with the buyer, the seller, the tenant, the landlord, and other licensees. Agency and other working relationships should be firmed up as soon as possible in dealing with the buyer, but definitely before preparation of the buyer's offer.

Open houses have also created situations in which licensees may be unsure of disclosure policies. TREC, in an effort to clarify this circumstance, has stated that there is no requirement to give an open-house visitor the Information About Brokerage Services notice unless the party begins to ask in-depth questions or indicates an interest in making an offer on the property (§ 1101.558(a)(1)). Nevertheless, this does not relieve licensees of the duty to disclose to prospective buyers that they represent the seller—this can be done either orally or in writing.

What some listing agents do at an open house, for example, is show the property and answer general questions of a factual nature on such topics as available financing, municipal services, and estimated closing costs. Questions concerning the seller's marketing position are addressed by the seller's agent and subagents in ways designed to encourage prospective buyers to make their best offer. If the conversation begins to move into any substantive discussion regarding a transaction, the licensee should immediately provide the prospect with the Information About Brokerage Services notice and take time to discuss and identify what the working relationship will be. At this point, an agency disclosure statement should be made before going further.

Intermediary. Another disclosure issue will arise if the transaction involves intermediary brokerage. Recall that before entering into an intermediary transaction, written consent must be obtained from both parties (§ 1101.1101.559(a)). Typically this consent will be given in the listing agreement with the seller and in the buyer-representation contract with the buyer. Once consent has been obtained, the statute does not require any further notification when an intermediary transaction begins unless the broker appoints associates to the seller and the buyer. Remember that if the broker makes appointments, the parties must be informed in writing that appointments have been made, and such written notice must give the names of the appointees and identify the parties to whom they have been appointed (§ 1101.560(b)). Even if no appointments have been made, the prudent broker should ensure that the parties are clear that an intermediary transaction is occurring. The Texas Association of REALTORS® Intermediary Relationship Notice is an example of a form (*see* Figure 7.1) that accomplishes both notification objectives.

Document

To establish that the required disclosures have been given, the licensee should make the disclosures in writing and keep a copy of the disclosure forms signed by the buyer or the seller. This documentation will be especially important if any legal action results from the transaction. In addition, licensees should obtain written confirmation on the final contract that they have disclosed whom they represented and that the status of that representation has not changed. It is important that licensees obtain such written proof because the oral declaration of licensees in a lawsuit is given little weight in proving whom a licensee represented. It is sometimes equally important for licensees to prove that they were not agents of the buyer or the seller.

Do as You Say

If the buyer and licensee decide that the broker will not represent the buyer but instead will show properties to the buyer as a subagent of sellers who have their properties listed in the MLS, the licensee should act as a subagent. A subagent of the seller, for example, would not suggest that the buyer start by testing the seller with a nothing-down offer and a requirement that the seller carryback a note with interest deferred until the final balloon payment. Nor would a subagent of the seller suggest any negotiating strategies contrary to the best interests of the seller. However, the experienced buyer-customer could initiate any or all of these terms in submitting an offer to purchase the seller's property.

DEVELOPING A COMPANY POLICY

TRELA § 1101.803 states that the broker "is liable to the commission, the public, and the broker's clients for any conduct engaged in . . . by the broker or by a salesperson associated with or acting for the broker." With the variety of possible agency relationships available for a broker to chose from, TREC rule 22 TAC 535.2(i) states that a broker must actually maintain current written policies and procedures to ensure that "each sponsored salesperson is advised of the scope of the salesperson's authorized activities subject to the Act and is competent to conduct such activities." It therefore is essential that every brokerage firm develop its own written policy manual; one segment of that manual clearly must be the written company policy regarding the types of agency representation practiced within that firm. The most effective way to establish a company policy on agency practice is to follow a simple but organized approach. Here's a suggested method.

Phase 1

Review the various agency options. Some options include

- exclusive seller agency,
- exclusive buyer agency,
- nonexclusive single agency, and
- seller-buyer agency with consensual intermediary brokerage for in-company transactions.

Phase 2

Review the advantages and disadvantages of each option as outlined previously.

Phase 3

Consider the size and experience of the office staff, the type of specialization (residential, commercial, farm and ranch, property management, apartment locating, etc.), local market opportunities, and financial expectations of the brokerage. For example, if most of the brokerage income comes from the sale of other brokers' listings, exclusive seller agency is probably not the best option.

Phase 4

Write a company policy on agency. Start with a preliminary plan (*see* Figure 9.3), but make sure to submit the plan to key members of the brokerage staff and business and legal advisers for additional input.

A comprehensive plan should include a basic statement of policy. The plan should describe the procedures for handling common situations from the perspectives of both the listing office and the selling office. The plan should discuss the use of agency disclosure forms, especially the timing of oral or written agency disclosures and the furnishing of a mandatory written statement regarding representation alternatives. Above all, the plan should comply with all state laws. Company plans that are developed using textbook models or borrowed from out-of-state brokers should be carefully modified to conform to the Texas environment. Policies and procedures are generally written to protect the broker and associated licensees; however, they should clearly focus on serving both clients and customers while maintaining the highest ethical standards.

FIGURE 9.3

Sample Ingredients of a Company's Agency Policies and Procedures Manual

Basic Agency Philosophy
  Strict adherence to state disclosure laws
  Company disclosure guidelines
  Summary of company policy

Handling Common Situations
  Listing presentations
  Buyer representation presentations
  Intermediary representation without appointments
  Intermediary representation with appointments
  In-house sales without intermediary status
  Subagency representation
  Buying property for own account
  Open houses

Dealing with Outside Companies
  Cooperation regarding fee splitting, showing, presenting offers
  Offer of subagency
  Interacting with buyer's agents

Guidelines for the Use of Company Agency Forms
  When
  Why
  How
  Benefits

Common Agency Questions

For example, a policy manual may include the following section on dealing with buyers at an open house:

- ***Open House.*** *Meeting potential buyers at an open house offers arguably one of the most complex agency situations in real estate. When a prospect comes into your open house, our duty is to the seller and we must use our efforts to sell the house to the prospect. This means that you cannot suggest other competing properties or offer to represent buyers until they have communicated to you that they are not interested in the property. If the buyers show interest in the property or indicate that they might like to purchase the property, you must treat them as customers and make immediate disclosures concerning agency options and positions, as required by state law and this policy manual, as follows:*
  - *Confirm in writing or orally that the buyers understand that you represent the seller, and answer any questions that they might have.*
  - *Determine that the prospects are interested in the property.*
  - *Before substantive discussions concerning the buyers' qualifications for buying or points of negotiation in any subsequent offer, provide the buyers with the company brochure, which contains the written statement required by TRELA § 1101.558 and Our Valued Customer letter (or other company-specific material).*

Document in your file that you have delivered and discussed the written statement required by TRELA § 1101.558. Request that the buyers sign the written statement, give them the original, and retain copies for the company file on this property and a separate file on these customers. Should the buyers refuse to sign the notice, make a notation on the notice to that effect and retain copies as defined above.

Phase 5

The broker should commence in-company training sessions and monitor the effectiveness of the policy. By using role-play and sample dialogue in training sessions, the sales staff can become more comfortable and competent in discussing agency in a way that showcases their professionalism. Rather than isolate discussions of agency, salespersons should be taught to integrate agency into their regular presentations. Finally, once you are certain your sales staff understands the policy, make sure they follow it. Be prepared to make exceptions in justified cases and to make changes to existing policy if exceptions begin to be the rule. (*See* Figure 9.4.)

■ SUMMARY

Much of the confusion about agency relationships can be eliminated as brokers become more comfortable and competent in discussing their roles in real estate transactions. Brokers should develop a company disclosure policy so they can control agency relationships and avoid unintended and illegal agencies. A basic policy consists of these four steps: (1) decide, (2) disclose, (3) document, and (4) do. Without a doubt, timely and proper disclosure is the key ingredient to a successful and effective agency program.

FIGURE 9.4

Agency Office Policy

Agency Office Policy—Points to Ponder

Probably the best defense a company has today regarding problems in the area of agency is a well reasoned, written policy regarding agency relationships authorized and practiced by the company. Although the specific policy will be tailored to individual companies, an agency policy might include the issues on the following list.

How does your company address the following agency issues?

- A definition and explanation of duties of a seller's representative
- A definition and explanation of duties of a buyer's representative
- A definition and explanation of duties of an intermediary
- Statement regarding written listing agreements
- Instructions regarding procedures and paperwork (including brokerage services, notices, and disclosures)
- Listing fees or commissions
- Policy regarding intermediary authorization in the listing agreement
- Statement regarding cooperation nd compensation with other brokers (subagents and buyer agents)
- Procedures with first meeting with prospective buyers
- Policy regarding buyer representation
- Requirements for written buyer representation agreements
- Policy regarding intermediary authorization in the buyer representation agreements
- Commission or fee statements in buyer representation
- Policy relating to working with nonrepresented (customer) buyers, including written Information About Brokerage Services and agency disclosure statments
- Policy statement relating to selling other firms listings as subagents or buyer's agent
- Policy relating to the sale of a FSBO to a buyer client or customer
- Policy relating to the in-house sale to a customer
- Policy relating to the intermediary transaction
- Policy relating to appointed associates (who and when)
- Disclosure of previous agency relationships and working with close friends and relatives
- Working with seller clients in purchasing a subsequent property
- Policy regarding working with competing buyers as customers or clients
- Policy relating to associates purchasing of the company's listings or listings of other companies
- Associates selling their own properties or the property owned by another associate of the company

Source: From *2000 and Beyond: An MCE Update.* Used with permission.

KEY POINTS

- Because real estate transactions vary widely, a brokerage firm must decide what role the firm and its associates will play.
- Once agency roles in a specific transaction have been decided, the licensee must give full disclosure to all participants in that transaction.
- Throughout the transaction, the licensee should take great care to properly document all aspects of the transaction.

- Once committed to a course of action, licensees must follow through and perform as agreed.
- The firm must develop a written company policy outlining the basic agency philosophy, how to handle common real estate situations, dealing with other firms, and use of agency forms.

SUGGESTIONS FOR BROKERS

Develop a personalized disclosure brochure that includes the written statement required by TRELA § 1101.558 and outlines the types of working relationships your firm offers to buyers and to sellers.

Outline some of the customer-level services you can provide to one person while remaining the exclusive agent of the other person.

Be careful not to use confusing language that might weaken the impact of meaningful agency disclosure and duties. A broker who attempts to cloud the issues may find such a brochure being used in a lawsuit. Use of the § 1101.558 written statement should help set the stage for meaningful discussions of your professional relationship and the needs of the prospect.

Although it is not required by law, attempt to get the prospective buyer or seller to sign an acknowledgment of receipt of the company form or letter, which discloses whom your brokerage represented, if anyone, at the time of first contact. If your company represents no one relative to the particular consumer being interviewed, say so in the form or letter. Also get an acknowledgment of receipt of the written information statement required by § 1101.558. Then, if a relationship with the party appears imminent, carefully discuss the anticipated type of client or customer or other relationship before reaching a written agreement or obtaining consents and beginning a working relationship.

CHAPTER 9 QUIZ

1. When should a licensee disclose to the buyer the agency status of the listing broker?
   a. On recordation of the deed
   b. At the first contact with the buyer
   c. When the purchase contract is signed
   d. When the buyer telephones the broker to arrange an introductory meeting

2. Which is the BEST stage of the transaction to present the required TRELA § 1101.558(d) written statement to the seller regarding agency options?
   a. Just prior to submission of a first offer to the seller
   b. Immediately after listing the seller's property
   c. Immediately prior to signing the listing agreement
   d. At the time of the first substantive dialogue with the seller

3. The other broker working with a buyer might represent
   a. the buyer.
   b. the seller.
   c. the listing broker.
   d. all of these.

4. The listing broker should discuss all of the following with the seller at the time of the listing EXCEPT
   a. offer of subagency.
   b. sharing of the listing fee.
   c. listing in the MLS.
   d. buyer's motivation.

5. If a buyer-customer tells the listing broker that the buyer will pay up to the listed price but first wants to submit an offer 10 percent below that price, what should the broker tell the seller?
   a. The buyer is qualified.
   b. The buyer has made a good offer.
   c. Don't risk losing the buyer by making a counteroffer.
   d. The buyer is willing to pay up to the listed price.

6. When buyers attending open houses are "merely lookers," there is
   a. no need for licensees to disclose their relationship with the seller.
   b. still a need for licensees to disclose their relationship with the seller in writing.
   c. still a need for licensees to disclose their relationship with the seller, at least orally.
   d. no need for licensees to disclose their relationship with the seller, unless a buyer asks.

7. The buyer is considered to have received the required agency disclosure when the licensee
   a. delivers the TREC Information About Brokerage Services notice to the buyer and has the buyer sign the form.
   b. delivers the TREC Information About Brokerage Services notice to the buyer.
   c. discloses the agency relationship, either verbally or in writing, to the buyer.
   d. completes a purchase contract for the buyer.

8. There is no requirement for a licensee to deliver information regarding brokerage services to a buyer who is
   a. seeking to be represented by the firm.
   b. represented by another agent.
   c. referred by a former client.
   d. a friend.

9. When buyers' agents show a property listed by another firm, those buyers' agents must
   a. deliver the Information About Brokerage Services notice and disclose their representation of the buyer to the seller.
   b. verbally disclose their representation of the buyer to the seller.
   c. deliver the Information About Buyers' Services notice to the seller.
   d. assume that the seller has been informed of the representation.

10. A broker should develop company policies that outline
    a. how to handle common real estate situations.
    b. how to deal with other firms.
    c. use of agency forms.
    d. all of these.

DISCUSSION QUESTIONS

1. What are the four steps a broker should take to clarify agency relationships?

2. In deciding whether to act as an agent of a buyer, what are some relevant questions for a listing broker to ask?

3. In deciding whether to act as a subagent of a listing broker while working with a buyer, what are some relevant questions for another broker to ask?

4. What are some key areas of the prospective agency relationship that the listing broker should discuss with the seller during the listing appointment?

5. When is the best time to make the disclosure of seller agency to the buyer?

CHAPTER 10

Employment Issues

The extent of legal responsibility of those persons who hire someone else to act for them depends on the relationship. As a rule, the more extensively the person who contracts for a service controls the manner in which the service is performed, the greater that person's responsibility. For example, an employer has appreciable control over how an employee works. When employees act within the scope of their employment, the employer is responsible for any harm those employees cause. In real estate brokerage, the licensee's classification either as an independent contractor or as an employee is important for several reasons, including the establishment of agency relationships through employment contracts and listing agreements. Chapter 5 discussed, in detail, the listing agreement as the primary employment agreement between brokers and sellers. Likewise, Chapter 6 took an in-depth look at the buyer-representation agreement as the primary employment agreement between brokers and buyers. This chapter explores some general employment issues and agreements as they affect brokers and licensed associates in their roles as principals and agents.

LEARNING OBJECTIVES

This chapter addresses the following:

- Employment Relationships between Brokers and Principals
- Employment Relationships between Brokers and Associates
    - Employee versus Independent Contractor
    - Sales Associate and Broker Associate Compensation
- Employment and Compensation of Personal Assistants
- Employment Relationships between Brokers and Subagents

- MLS Subagency Agreements
- Non-MLS Subagency Agreements
- Agreements between Brokers
■ Other Compensation Issues
  - Nonlicensee Compensation
  - Foreign Brokers or Brokers Licensed in Other States

■ EMPLOYMENT RELATIONSHIPS BETWEEN BROKERS AND PRINCIPALS

Brokers generally enter into employment contracts with property owners through listing agreements and property management agreements. Likewise, brokers enter into employment agreements with buyers and tenants through buyer-tenant-representation agreements. As discussed in previous chapters, these agreements set out the terms of employment and address issues of compensation.

Under the terms of most employment contracts with principals, brokers are responsible for the payment of brokerage expenses associated with the agreement. In addition, the broker pays any income tax due because of any compensation received during the course of the employment.

Although brokerage fees are generally paid at the time of closing and funding of the transaction, many courts have ruled that the broker's fees are considered "earned and payable" when the broker produces a "ready, willing, and able" buyer under the terms of a listing agreement. This concept is addressed in the TAR Residential Real Estate Listing Agreement (see Figure 5.2, paragraph 5B). The basic theory is that the broker was hired to find a suitable buyer for the seller's property, and when that has been accomplished, the broker should be entitled to a commission even if the seller decides not to sell. Under TAR's Residential Buyer/Tenant Representation Agreement (see Figure 6.1 paragraph 11C), the buyer-agent fee is "earned and payable" as soon as the buyer enters into a contract to buy or lease a property and is payable even if the buyer later breaches the sales contract with the seller. It is not illegal in Texas for a broker to represent a seller or a buyer on the basis of a verbal agreement. However, the broker will find little recourse against the principal who refuses to pay the broker on the strength of a verbal agreement. In order to recover compensation from the seller, the broker will be required to bring suit against the seller (there are exceptions for commercial brokers who may obtain a contractual voluntary lien for commission). For a broker to bring suit for a commission, TRELA § 1101.806 requires

- the broker prove that he/she was duly licensed at the time the brokerage services began;
- that the agreement for compensation be in writing and signed at least by the party to be charged the commission; and
- that at the time of signing the contract to purchase, the buyer was advised in writing that they should have an abstract of title examined by an attorney, or to secure a policy of title insurance.

The following case illustrates the importance of obtaining a clear and concise written agreement of commission prior to proceeding with brokerage activities.

■ **EXAMPLE** In *Neary v. Mikob Properties, Inc.*, 340 S.W. 316 (Tex. App. Dallas 2011), Neary and his company, St. John Holdings (SJH), filed suit to recover a brokerage fee associated with the sale of eight apartment complexes. Neary held a valid broker license at the time; however, SJH was not licensed as a business entity by TREC at the time of the transaction. The brokerage fee was not addressed in the actual purchase agreement. Instead, Neary claimed that a November 17, 2003, document titled "Term Sheet," combined with a series of e-mails before and after the "Term Sheet," established a contract for a brokerage fee of 2 percent of the sales price and that SJH was Neary's "agent for receipt of his commission." The seller claimed that the "Term Sheet" did not meet the written requirement of TRELA § 1101.806 and that since SJH was not licensed as a broker, SJH could not file suit for recovery of a commission. Although the "Term Sheet" was signed, written in above the signatures was the sentence, "This term sheet is a guideline only, and is not binding." Furthermore, the "Term Sheet" identified the purchaser as a Texas limited liability company "to be formed"; the term "seller" was used, but no seller was identified; and the property was identified as eight complexes but with no addresses or legal descriptions. The e-mails were between the brokers, and although several proposals were set forth, the e-mails did not settle on an amount the brokers were to be paid. Nowhere in the "Term Sheet" was there any indication of the relationship between Mikob Properties, Inc., and the broker allegedly signing on the company's behalf, a man named Kobernick.

■ **DISCUSSION** The court ruled that TRELA § 1101.806 (c) clearly provides that a broker cannot maintain a suit for a commission unless it is based on an agreement that has been rendered in written form and signed by the person against whom the broker seeks to enforce the commission. So the issue before the court was whether or not the combination of emails and the "Term Sheet" met the requirement for a written commission agreement. The court noted that to comply an agreement must

- be in writing and signed by the person to be charged the commission;
- promise that a definite commission will be paid or must refer to a written commission schedule;
- state the name of the broker to whom the commission is to be paid; and
- either itself or by reference to some other existing writing, identify with reasonable certainty the property to be conveyed (i.e., a legal description).

The court ruled that the sellers had signed no written agreement to pay a commission and that the "Term Sheet" and e-mails did not constitute a written agreement. Furthermore, the "Term Sheet" identified SJH as the broker, not Neary, and SJH was not a business entity holding a broker license in Texas at the time of the transaction.

Employment Relationships between Brokers and Associates

In Texas, about two-thirds of all brokers work for the remaining one-third. The broker is held responsible to the state and the public for the conduct of licensees who are either licensed under the broker or working as independent contractors or employees. The responsible broker is frequently referred to as a sponsoring broker, principal broker, or designated broker. The employed, associated, or sponsored licensee is then licensed either as a salesperson or as a broker. An associate who is a broker generally is called a broker associate. Texas offers no broker associate license.

An active salesperson licensee is required to work under the sponsorship of an actively licensed broker. The broker may either be an individual or a business entity. 22 TAC § 535.1(2) defines the term *business entity* as "a corporation, limited liability, partnership or other entity authorized under the Texas Business Organizations Code." Under certain circumstances, the broker might even be a business entity from another state qualified to do business in Texas (22 TAC 535.53(b)). If the broker is a business entity, however, then one of its managing officers must be licensed as an individual broker in Texas who then acts as the designated broker for the business entity. Unlike a salesperson licensee, a person licensed as a broker may work independently or may enter into an agency relationship with another broker (broker associate) to represent that broker in dealings with the public.

Based on the TRELA and the doctrine of respondeat superior ("let the master answer"), the broker is liable to the commission, the public, and the broker's clients for any conduct engaged in under TRELA by the broker or by a licensee associated with the broker during the ordinary course of employment (§ 1101.803; 22 TAC § 535.2(a); 22 TAC § 535.141(c)). In the case of a business entity, the designated broker of the business entity is the person held liable (22 TAC 535.2(l)). Under general agency concepts, each of these licensed associates is the agent of the broker and represents the broker in a fiduciary capacity. Listings are made in the name of the broker, not the salesperson or the broker associate. The broker is the party responsible to the public and to clients, whether acting directly or indirectly through the broker's agents. If a broker has a listing (open or exclusive), that broker and all the licensed associates of that firm represent the seller in a fiduciary capacity. This is true of all licensed associates working in each of the listing broker's offices. (This rule, however, does not apply to franchise organizations in which each franchised brokerage firm is independently owned.)

It is important to understand that licensed salespersons cannot lawfully sell their services directly to the public. Salespersons must perform all tasks under the direct supervision of a broker. This is true even if the salesperson is, for tax purposes, an independent contractor. Under agency and licensing law and for purposes of supervision, salespersons who are licensed with a broker are agents and employees of the broker and act for the broker. The phrase *acts for*, as used in the TREC rules cited here, is equivalent to the description of an agency relationship (TRELA § 1101.351; .557; .803).

Licensed salespersons cannot legally

- list property in their own names (22 TAC § 535.154(d)(4); § 535.2(f));
- enter into buyer agency or intermediary agreements in their own names, either orally or in writing;
- sue directly sellers, buyers, landlords, or tenants for unpaid commissions (generally);
- open their own offices without hiring a broker to be responsible for all those licensees in the offices;
- work independently without having a licensed sponsoring broker to shelter or hold each salesperson's license;

- hold a license under more than one broker at the same time;
- take listings or buyer-tenant-representation agreements when they move to a new brokerage office with or without the current broker's consent (although the broker may release represented owners or buyers from their agreements and allow a salesperson's new broker to attempt to contract with the owners, buyers, or tenants);
- advertise in their own names unless the broker's name also appears, and it is clear to the public which one is the broker (TRELA § 1101.652(b)(23); 22 TAC § 535.154(d)(g));
- open their own client trust accounts for sales or rentals (22 TAC § 535.159(f));
- accept compensation directly from clients or other brokers for real estate sales and transactions without the broker's consent (TRELA § 1101.651(b); 22 TAC § 535.3); or
- pay a commission to any person except through the broker under whom they are licensed or with that broker's knowledge and consent (TRELA § 1101.651(c); 22 TAC § 535.3).

Broker associates, on the other hand, because they have the same state license as the principal broker, may be allowed to do virtually any of these things if the broker they work for does not prohibit the broker associate from running another brokerage operation. This practice is not the norm, however, and any broker associate attempting any of the above-listed actions without the principal broker's knowledge and consent would likely be at risk.

TREC does not regulate the broker's contractual arrangements with other brokers. The principal broker of a broker associated with the company should keep in mind—and make the associate aware—that the License Act holds the principal broker responsible for the acts of associated broker licensees (TRELA § 1101.803). In addition, in any lawsuit against the associate broker, if the plaintiff (the person bringing the suit) believes the associate acted in the name of the principal broker, the broker will most likely be named in the lawsuit and may be held liable for the damages caused by an associated broker. It is important to understand that when an associate of the broker secures a listing or buyer-representation agreement, it is the principal broker who is employed by the buyer or the seller.

In Texas, it is not legally possible to construct a figurative internal wall within a brokerage firm and argue that because different licensed associates act for the buyer and the seller, no dual representation exists. In Texas, such an attempt likely would not hold up in court or at a TREC disciplinary hearing. By analogy, a large law firm could not have one of its associates on the tenth floor represent the seller of a commercial warehouse and another associate on the eleventh floor represent the buyer without first obtaining from the buyer and the seller very complete and detailed consent to such dual representation and agreement to receive a very limited form of fiduciary representation.

Some brokerage firms advertise that they have salespersons who represent buyers and other salespersons who represent sellers. For example, Tom from Executive Realty, as the listing agent, innocently might tell an interested buyer who has expressed a desire to obtain her own agent, "I can't be your agent, but Dorothy in our branch office is very knowledgeable, loves to represent buyers, and can give you the type of representation you want."

Tom's firm must be careful to develop its company policies within the bounds of agency law. It is the firm, not the associates, that—by law—represents the buyer or the seller. Listing brokers should set up internal management controls to ensure that their associates understand these basic agency principles.

Employee versus Independent Contractor

Brokers engage salespersons as either employees or independent contractors. Any agreements between brokers and their associates should be in the form of written contracts that define the obligations and responsibilities of the relationships. Whether an associate operates under the broker as an employee (compensation based on time) or as an independent contractor (compensation based on results) will affect the relationship between them. (*See* Figure 10.1.)

At minimum, TREC rule 22 TAC § 535.2(i), requires the broker to maintain written policies and procedures to ensure the following:

1. *Each sponsored salesperson is advised of the scope of the salesperson's authorized activities subject to the Act and is competent to conduct such activities.*
2. *Each sponsored salesperson maintains their license in active status at all times while they are engaging in activities subject to the Act.*
3. *Any and all compensation paid to the sponsored salesperson for acts or services subject to the Act is paid by, through, or with the written consent of the sponsoring broker.*
4. *Each sponsored salesperson is provided on a timely basis, prior to the effective date of the change, notice of any change to the Act, Rules, or commission promulgated contract forms.*
5. *In addition to completing statutory minimum continuing education requirements, each sponsored salesperson receives such additional educational instruction the broker may deem necessary to obtain and maintain on a current basis competency in the scope of the sponsored salesperson's practice.*
6. *Each sponsored salesperson complies with the commission's advertising rules.*

FIGURE 10.1

Independent Contractor versus Employee

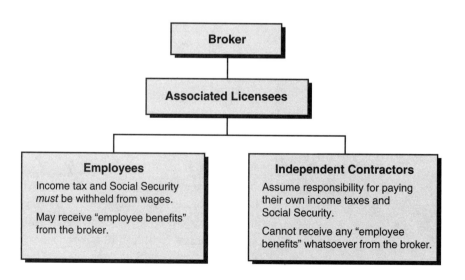

7. *All trust accounts . . . are handled by the broker with appropriate controls.*
8. *Records are properly maintained.*

The nature of the employer-employee relationship allows a broker to exercise certain controls over associates who are employees. The broker may require that an employee adhere to regulations concerning such matters as working hours, office routine, dress, or conduct. As an employer, a broker is required by the federal government to withhold Social Security and income taxes from wages paid to employees. The broker also is required to pay unemployment compensation taxes, as required by state and federal laws. In addition, a broker may be required to provide employees with such benefits as health insurance and profit-sharing plans.

Independent contractors operate more freely than employees, and the broker may not control their activities in the same way. Crucial elements of preserving independent contractor status are that the

- independent contractor's services must be performed under the terms of a written contract between the broker and the associate;
- broker may control what the independent contractor does, but not how it is done; and
- contract must state that the independent contractor assumes responsibility for paying any required income and Social Security taxes and receives nothing from the broker that could be construed as an employee benefit.

Fearful that the strictly mandated written policies and controls noted above might jeopardize the independent contractor relationship where Internal Revenue Service (IRS) was concerned, the rule states that the section was not meant to create or require an employer/employee relationship between a broker and a sponsored salesperson (22 TAC § 535.2(m)).

In Texas, brokers are not required to carry worker's compensation coverage for independent contractors.

To ensure that all licensed associates are treated by the IRS and the Texas Employment Commission as independent contractors, brokers are urged to maintain close contact with competent tax counsel and have their policies and procedures reviewed frequently for compliance. The broker should exercise great care to ensure that independent contractors understand their personal obligations under law.

Some people believe that the difference between an independent contractor and an employee is that the former works on a commission-only basis and the employee is salaried. That may be relevant, but it is not conclusive. Many salespersons are paid on commission but are considered employees because of other features of their employment situations.

Sales Associate and Broker Associate Compensation

An associate's compensation is set by mutual agreement between the broker and the associate. A broker may agree to pay a salary or a share of the commissions from transactions originated by an associate. Associates may have a drawing account against their individual earned share of commissions. In such a case, the associate should sign a note for each draw to preserve the independent contractor status, if such status is desired.

A departure from traditional compensation plans is the 100 percent commission plan. Generally, in a brokerage firm that has adopted this system, associates pay a monthly service charge to the broker (to cover the costs of office space, telephone service, supervision, and administration) and receive 100 percent of the commissions from the sales they negotiate.

■ EMPLOYMENT AND COMPENSATION OF PERSONAL ASSISTANTS

Many busy brokers and associates have found that employing personal assistants allows them to become more productive. Assistants are generally given responsibilities that do not require licensure, such as holding open houses, maintaining records, scheduling, and placing signs and lockboxes on properties. Some licensees employ assistants who are licensed so that more extensive duties can be assigned.

Employment agreements must be carefully considered. It may be difficult to employ a personal assistant as an independent contractor because the essence of the relationship is that the employer carefully directs and controls the actions of the assistant. Because an independent contractor must be able to perform duties independent of employer control or direction, it may be difficult, if not impossible, to convince the IRS that such a relationship exists with an assistant. Before entering into such an agreement, it would be wise to consult an attorney or CPA who is familiar with all aspects of employment law.

■ EMPLOYMENT RELATIONSHIPS BETWEEN BROKERS AND SUBAGENTS

Listing agreements and buyer representation agreements may, with the agreement of the principal, include a clause that allows the broker to appoint subagents. A buyer's broker, if given such permission, may appoint subagents as readily as a seller's broker.

MLS Subagency Agreements

Under most pre-1993 multiple listing service (MLS) rules, all listings submitted to an MLS were required to contain mandatory offers of subagency to all other members. After discovering numerous potential legal problems with such a practice, and the growth of buyer-agency, most MLS systems now offer participants optional subagency; that is, the systems allow their participants to place listings that offer cooperation and compensation to either buyer-agents or subagents of the listing broker.

Non-MLS Subagency Agreements

Any brokers, even if they are not members of a multiple listing service (MLS) system, can voluntarily contract with each other to create their own broker-to-broker cooperative agreements, to cover either one property at a time or all properties in their respective inventories for any agreed period of time. Remember, a licensee cannot pursue litigation for recovery of a commission unless the agreement to compensate was in writing. It is generally accepted that compensation indicated in the MLS would constitute such an agreement between brokers. If the cooperating broker is not a member of the MLS, however, then the cooperating broker would be well advised to obtain something in writing from the listing broker designating the cooperative fee.

Agreements between Brokers

The special block titled "Broker Information" that appears on the last page of the TREC residential sales contract has a blank where listing brokers indicate what they have agreed to pay the "other broker." It is merely a confirmation that the listing broker will compensate the other broker in a transaction by an amount specified in this abbreviated agreement, when and if the listing broker is compensated by the seller-principal.

If the buyer's broker is not protected by a buyer-representation agreement, and if at the closing, the seller refuses to compensate the listing broker because of an alleged breach of fiduciary duty by the listing broker, the buyer's broker has no way to secure compensation from anyone in the transaction. Although buyer's brokers may not be fully protected by this TREC-developed compensation agreement, it can serve as a useful memorandum of the initial intent of the parties to the agreement.

Compensation to a broker operating under the terms of a buyer-tenant representation agreement is dictated by the terms of the agreement. The Texas Association of REALTORS® agreement (see Figure 6.1) permits payment to be made directly by the buyer-client to the broker or permits the broker to be compensated through funds provided by the seller. In addition, the agreement may provide that the broker receive a flat fee, hourly compensation, and/or a retainer fee. Most often, the buyer's broker will be paid through funds paid by the seller in the same way that a subagent is usually compensated. Remember that, as in listing agreements, the compensation to a buyer's broker is fully negotiable between the buyer and the broker. The fact that a listing office may be offering a cooperating fee that is less than the buyer agreed the agent would receive, is strictly a compensation issue that must be resolved between the buyer and the buyer's agent.

OTHER COMPENSATION ISSUES

Nonlicensee Compensation

In Texas, licensees are not permitted to share commissions with unlicensed parties, other than a principal in the transaction, or those parties exempt from licensure pursuant to § 1101.005. This has been construed to include cash payments of money in any amount, or any gifts exceeding $50 in value (22 TAC § 535.20(a)). Additionally, a 1990 Texas law prohibits a broker from sharing a sales commission with an attorney unless the attorney is also licensed as a broker (22 TAC § 535.31). However, an attorney may conduct real estate transactions for compensation as long as the attorney is paid directly by the principal.

Unlicensed brokerage owners. The issue of an unlicensed person who owns all or part of a real estate company sharing in the income earned by the company is clarified in 22 TAC § 535.147(b) as follows:

> *An unlicensed person may share in the income earned by a business entity licensed as a broker or exempted from the licensing requirements under the Act if the person engages in no acts for which a license is required and does not lead the public to believe that the person is in the real estate brokerage business.*

Foreign Brokers or Brokers Licensed in Other States

An exception to the prohibition for compensation to individuals not licensed in Texas states that a licensed broker may pay a commission to a licensed broker of another state. This exemption is valid only if the out-of-state broker does not attempt to physically conduct in Texas any of the negotiations for which commission or other compensation is paid (TRELA § 1101.651(a)).

A second exception relates to brokers who are residents of a foreign state that does not require a person to be licensed to act as real estate broker. This addresses real estate practitioners outside the United States. The rules permit compensation to real estate professionals in other countries, even though that country may not require licensure of those persons engaged in the practice of real estate in that country (22 TAC § 535.131(b)).

■ SUMMARY

Although brokerage firms vary widely in size, few brokers perform their agency duties without the assistance of associated licensees. Consequently, much of a firm's success hinges on the broker-associate relationship. An agreement between a broker and an associate should be set in a written contract that establishes the obligations and responsibilities of each party. The salesperson may work on the broker's behalf as either an employee or an independent contractor.

A broker's compensation generally takes the form of a commission, paid either by the seller, under the terms of a listing agreement, or a buyer, under the terms of a buyer-representation agreement. Generally, the broker receiving compensation may share the commissions with other brokers who are acting as subagents of the seller or as buyers' agents.

■ KEY POINTS

- Brokers enter into employment agreements with property owners, buyers, and tenants through listing and representation agreements.
- Sponsoring brokers and associated broker and salesperson licensees enter into employment agreements and conduct brokerage activities as employees of the firm or as independent contractors.
- Salesperson licensees cannot perform brokerage activities independently. All activities must be under the direction of the sponsoring broker.

- Independent contractors must (1) have a written contract with the broker, (2) be allowed to determine how they carry out brokerage functions, and (3) pay their own income and Social Security taxes.
- Brokers may contract with other brokerage firms to represent their clients in a subagency capacity. Subagency can be achieved through an MLS or directly with selected brokers for a particular property or for an agreed-on period of time.
- Brokers may not share compensations with unlicensed persons, other than the principals in a transaction, except as provided in TRELA.
- Brokers licensed in other states may share in a broker's compensation, however all negotiations physically conducted with Texas must be handled by Texas licensees. (TRELA § 1101.651; 22 TAC 535.131 (a)–(b))

■ SUGGESTIONS FOR BROKERS

Brokers should carefully document relationships with associates by entering into a written employment agreement with each associate. In addition, because most associates are not considered employees, the broker should understand and adhere to the strict guidelines regarding independent contract status—most importantly, the requirements relating to directing how independent contractor duties are to be performed.

CHAPTER 10 QUIZ

1. While employed by a real estate broker, a salesperson has the authority to
   a. act as an agent for the seller.
   b. assume responsibilities assigned by the broker.
   c. accept a commission from another broker.
   d. advertise the property on the salesperson's own behalf.

2. Agreements that set the employment terms of an associated licensee include
   a. listing agreements.
   b. buyer-representation agreements.
   c. independent contractor agreements.
   d. property management agreements.

3. A broker has the right to dictate which of the following to an independent contractor?
   a. Number of hours worked
   b. Work schedule
   c. How duties are performed
   d. Duties

4. When a broker engages other brokers as associates of the company,
   a. the broker associate generally works under the guidance of the sponsoring broker.
   b. TREC will issue an associate broker license to the associated broker.
   c. the sponsoring broker will not incur any liability for the broker associate.
   d. broker associates will take listings in their own names.

5. Even though the broker and the associate have a written independent contractor agreement,
   a. if the broker's conduct is that of an employer, the IRS will probably not consider that an employer-employee relationship exists.
   b. if the broker's conduct is that of an employer, the IRS will probably determine that an employer-employee relationship exists.
   c. the broker associate can conduct business activities free of any guidance.
   d. the broker will reimburse associates for all expenses.

6. An associate's compensation is set by
   a. mutual agreement between the broker and the associate.
   b. the local Board of REALTORS®.
   c. TRELA.
   d. TREC.

7. Unlicensed personal assistants hired by licensees
   a. can work for broker licensees only.
   b. must be taking real estate courses.
   c. are allowed to carry out all of the licensees' real estate duties.
   d. carry out limited functions that do not require a real estate license.

8. Multiple listing service (MLS) listings
   a. require that compensation be paid by the seller.
   b. all carry a mandatory offer of subagency.
   c. do not cooperate with buyers' agents.
   d. offer optional subagency.

9. Brokers who do NOT belong to an MLS can
   a. elect to reject offers of subagency.
   b. have individual agreements with other brokers.
   c. have individual agreements with other brokers for limited periods of time.
   d. do all of these.

10. The term *foreign broker* relates to a broker
    a. licensed in another state or country.
    b. licensed in another country.
    c. of foreign descent.
    d. of a different firm.

DISCUSSION QUESTIONS

1. Explain why classifying a real estate salesperson as an independent contractor does not relieve the broker of responsibility for the salesperson's actions.

2. Discuss the differences between how a broker and a salesperson are compensated.

3. Discuss the exceptions to TRELA concerning payment of fees to individuals unlicensed in Texas.

CHAPTER 11

Agency, Ethics, and the Law

The expectation of legal and ethical conduct by an agent (and the principal) is fundamental to the concepts of agency law. This basic principle is at once extraordinarily simple and vexingly complex. Simple in the sense that most licensees—both brokers and sales associates—recognize the need to "do the right thing," yet it's often complex to determine exactly what the right thing is and how to communicate the individual agent's and the brokerage company's policies to the various stakeholders. Perhaps more important is the need to ensure that the plans and policies are actually implemented. Chapter 12 addresses the Texas Deceptive Practices Act covering general consumer protection law. This chapter will discuss other Texas laws, regulations, and ethical duties more specific to the real estate licensee.

■ **LEARNING OBJECTIVES** *This chapter addresses the following:*

- Current Environment
- Distinctions between Law, Ethics, and Morals
    - Law Defined
    - Ethics Defined
    - Morals Defined
- Legal and Ethical Guidelines for Licensees
- Federal and State Law Relating to Conduct
    - Federal and State Law Relating to Conduct
    - Federal Law

- Texas State Law
  - Local Municipal Codes and Ordinances
- TRELA and Rules of the Commission
  - The Real Estate License Act
  - The Texas Real Estate Commission (TREC)
- Professional Codes of Ethics
  - TREC Canons of Professional Ethics and Conduct
  - National Association of Realtors® Code of Ethics and Professional Standards
  - Individual Company Policy, Procedure, and Codes of Ethics and Conduct
  - Personal Beliefs and Individual Ethics
  - Law and Ethics in Practice
- A Practical Guide for Everyday Practice
  - An Alternate Solution
- When Enough Is Not Enough: Minimum Ethical Standards
- The Bottom Line on Ethics

CURRENT ENVIRONMENT

Perhaps never in history have the business and political communities faced the level of public scrutiny that they do today. In a decade that witnessed highly publicized scandals centered on the unethical conduct leading to the collapse of major companies such as the Houston-based energy company Enron and the accounting firm Arthur Anderson, the public has been further outraged by acts committed by those who have at times brought the American financial system to the brink of disaster. Individual unethical and criminal acts by those, such as Bernie Madoff and his bogus investment company may have caused financial ruin to thousands of individual investors, pale in comparison to the colossal mortgage-backed securities debacle created in the financial institutions of this country. In essence, millions of real estate mortgages were bundled, promoted, and sold by Wall Street investment bankers as highly rated securities. In fact, large percentages of the underlying mortgage loans were made to poorly qualified borrowers. Predictably, as the borrowers were unable to meet their payment obligations, massive numbers of properties went into foreclosure and the underlying properties lacked sufficient market value to satisfy the outstanding loans. The fallout impacted millions of investors and rocked global financial markets. Ostensibly, only a U.S. federal bailout of high-profile companies such as Goldman Sachs, J.P Morgan Chase, Bank of America, AIG, Citigroup, Wells Fargo, and many others averted a potential collapse of the U.S. financial system.

Although the press and public sentiment fell squarely against these high-profile companies, one might ask where the ethical breaches actually originated. Clearly, these firms were major players, but in a larger sense many others contributed to the problems. Where did the real problem and breach of ethics begin? Was it the Wall Street banker overselling the end product, the mortgage insurers, the rating companies, or much further down the chain? Is the blame more rightly placed on the secondary market purchasers, the primary lenders and their underwriters, or perhaps the real estate broker or salesperson who may have knowingly sold properties to buyers clearly beyond their means in the long term? What about the buyer who falsified documents with the knowledge that the no-documentation or asset-based loan policies of certain lenders would probably not discover the falsification. If blame is to be placed, obviously there are plenty to share in this complex problem. On the other hand, many of those involved may argue that the role that they played was not only legal, but met the ethical standards of their industry or company.

In any event, each unfolding new event lends more credence to the popular view that general moral decay and public abuse is on the rise. Support for this view may be evidenced by the more complex societal and business structures leading into uncharted ethical waters. Indeed, an ever-growing number of real estate business models and resulting menu of services are confusing to those within the industry—much less buyers and sellers on the outside. Even today with the increased governmental scrutiny and required disclosure, the typical (or sophisticated) principal has little chance of understanding the duties and obligations of the agent. Thus, a brokerage company or individual licensee willing to risk unethical behavior for bottom-line gain may still go undetected, and the public is left with only the trust that the precepts of moral behavior and ethical conduct will prevail.

Individuals, businesses, and society in general are continually faced with questions relating to conduct that may not be clearly governed by law, and certainly the practice of real estate is no different. This chapter attempts to distinguish differences between legal versus ethical conduct and introduce the student to some of the ethical/legal decisions they may face in their real estate practices.

■ DISTINCTIONS BETWEEN LAW, ETHICS, AND MORALS

Law Defined

The following definition of the term *law* is excerpted from *Black's Law Dictionary*, Eighth Edition (2006, p. 200):

> *The aggregate of legislation, judicial precedence, and accepted legal principles; the body of authoritative grounds of judicial and administrative action; esp., the body of rules, standards, and principles that the courts of a particular jurisdiction apply in deciding controversies brought before them (the law of the land).*

Ethics Defined

Although there are many attempts to define ethics, few find much comfort in a single all-comprehensive definition because ethics involve a multitude of factors or circumstances that, when viewed by different parties, result in dramatically different opinions regarding whether the actions were ethical. As a result, many organizations have created standards of ethical conduct for their members. Again, we draw on *Black's Law Dictionary* (2006, p. 912) for the following definition of the term *legal ethics*:

> *The minimum standards of appropriate conduct within the legal profession, involving the duties that its members owe one another, their clients, and the courts. Also termed etiquette of the profession.*

A broader definition of the term *ethics* is found in *Webster's Unabridged Dictionary*, Second Edition (2001):

> *The rules of conduct recognized in respect to a particular class of human actions or a particular group, culture, etc.; medical ethics; Christian ethics.*

Morals Defined

While the terms *ethical* and *moral* are often taken to be synonymous, there are subtle distinctions between the two. Once more, *Black's Law Dictionary* provides a definition (2006, p. 1030):

- Private Morality: "A person's ideals, character, and private conduct which are not valid governmental concerns..."
- Public Morality: "The ideals or actions of an individual to the extent they affect others."

In a sense, the law represents what we are required to do and is enforceable by governmental entities. Ethics refers to commonly accepted standards of conduct or actions and are frequently refined and tailored to specific industries or companies, and may be enforced against their members or employees. Morals deal with an individual's personal beliefs or actions and can be enforced only by conscience unless those actions violate the legal rights of others (e.g., people can think, or believe, or feel as they wish as long as they do not act on those beliefs in such a way as to violate the rights of others).

It should be evident then that at times an individual may be faced with the dilemma of choosing a course of action when personal morals, professional ethics, and the law are in conflict. The final course chosen will be dictated by which of the three has the greater influence on the individual. As a result, two individuals may consider the same set of facts and respond in totally different ways. By the same token, an individual faced with two similar sets of facts may take different actions based on the particular circumstances surrounding those facts.

A great deal has been written on the subject of ethical and moral behavior, including application models for ethical decision making; however, our discussions will be limited to real estate practice with a focus on the ethical duties imposed on Texas real estate licensees acting under agency agreements.

Legal and Ethical Guidelines for Licensees

While practicing real estate, licensees in Texas may be guided by the following:

- Federal law
- Texas general civil and criminal statutes
- Local municipal codes and ordinances

- The Real Estate License Act (TRELA)
- Rules of the Texas Real Estate Commission
- Private professional codes of ethics, (e.g. the National Association of REALTORS® Code of Ethics)
- A real estate company's Code of Ethics or Policies
- Individual ethics and moral principles

FEDERAL AND STATE LAW RELATING TO CONDUCT

Federal Law

Although much real estate law is governed by individual states, federal legislation plays an important role in real estate practice. These address overriding national concerns that would apply in any state. Examples of such federal regulation are as follows:

- The Sherman Antitrust Act
- Federal Truth in Lending Law
- Federal Fair Housing Law
- Environmental laws (Environmental Protection Agency)
- Americans with Disabilities Act
- Equal Credit Opportunity Act
- Community Reinvestment Act
- Home Mortgage Disclosure Act

Clearly, a licensee must be familiar with a number of federal rules and regulations in order to avoid practices resulting in federal litigation. These laws provide the overarching framework for real estate licensees in all states.

Texas State Law

While the federal government has a number of laws affecting real estate practitioners, state laws can vary and create the need for individual state real estate licenses. Several key Texas laws affecting licensees include the Texas Deceptive Trade Practices Act (*see* Chapter 12), the Texas Fair Housing Act, and The Real Estate License Act (*see* Appendix A).

Local Municipal Codes and Ordinances

Municipalities are authorized to enact local ordinances and codes, many of which have a direct impact on real estate. Specifically, city building codes, habitability and occupancy codes, as well as fair housing ordinances, have major implications for the licensee, and a thorough knowledge of these codes and ordinances is essential to the practitioner.

TRELA AND RULES OF THE COMMISSION

The Real Estate License Act

As described in Chapter 12, the Texas Deceptive Trade Practices Act (DTPA) illustrates how providers of goods and services (including real estate licensees) are subject to powerful consumer laws. Other laws and regulations are specific to real estate brokers and salespersons.

The Texas state legislature first began regulating practitioners in 1939 with the passage of the Real Estate Dealer's Act. This was followed in 1949 with the passage of The Real Estate License Act (TRELA), the creation of the Texas Real estate Commission (TREC), and a requirement for licensure. Like the federal government, Texas legislators have since passed a number of laws relating to the practice of real estate within the state as well as modifying and substantially expanding TRELA.

TRELA establishes a baseline for actions by Texas licensees and members of the Texas Real Estate Commission. Subsection N, § 1101.651–§ 1101.655, provides a "laundry list" of specific violations that can result in revocation or suspension of the licensee, placing the licensee on probation and/or assessing administrative penalties (fines) against the licensee. Licensees should keep in mind that a legal action against a licensee through the courts is an action separate and distinct from a complaint filed through the TREC. Texas courts cannot suspend or revoke a real estate license; however, the grounds for the suit may be the basis of a complaint filed against the licensee through TREC resulting in loss of licensure. A complete copy of TRELA is included in Appendix A.

The Texas Real Estate Commission (TREC)

Subchapter B of TRELA defines the membership of the Commission as consisting of nine members appointed by the governor with the advice and consent of the senate. Six of these members must be licensed as real estate brokers and three must be from the general public. Subchapter D of TRELA establishes the powers and duties of the Commission. TREC is empowered under TRELA to enact rules and regulations, including the regulation of individual licensees.

PROFESSIONAL CODES OF ETHICS

Almost without exception, businesses and professions have adopted voluntary codes of ethics for their employees or members. These codes of ethics represent the rules of professional conduct expected of their members. Typically, these codes or rules are helpful in guiding decision making and actions with the intricacies of a specific business, profession, or industry. Although these codes do not carry the weight of law, they may be enforced against association members who agree to such enforcement power as a condition of membership. Even courts of law will use industry codes in interpreting and applying legal actions against professionals.

TREC Canons of Professional Ethics and Conduct

TRELA § 1101.151(b) grants TREC the authority to establish standards of conduct and ethics for persons licensed under the act. Thus by rule, 22 TAC § 531 (*see* Figure 11.1) includes the five very basic canons of professional ethics and conduct that apply to all real estate licensees. Notice the canons also support the federal Fair Housing Act by prohibiting discriminatory practices against protected classes. The canons are similar in content to voluntary general business ethics and common law agency principles from a variety of sources, including case law, statutory law, and codes of ethics of many professional and trade associations.

National Association of REALTORS® Code of Ethics and Professional Standards

Perhaps the oldest and most recognized code within the real estate industry is the National Association of REALTORS® (NAR) Code of Ethics (COE). Established in 1908, NAR adopted the original COE in 1913 as a required code of conduct for the membership. Today, NAR represents one of the largest professional organizations in the country and has powerful political influence through political action committees and professional lobbyists.

In addition to NAR, Texas practitioners may be members of the Texas Association of REALTORS® (TAR) and local associations of REALTORS®—all affiliate organizations of NAR. Approximately 50 percent of all Texas licensees are members of these organizations and are authorized to use the professional term REALTOR®. Although often used generically, the word REALTOR® is a trademarked term and should not be used by non-members. Although only REALTORS® are required to adopt and subscribe the NAR Code of Ethics, the code offers excellent guidelines for all licensees, REALTOR® or otherwise. The NAR Code of Ethics and Standards of Practice are shown in Figure 11.2. A thorough reading of this material is strongly encouraged. The code is not discussed in detail in this text because only members of the NAR trade association are bound by the articles and standards.

Individual Company Policy, Procedure, and Codes of Ethics and Conduct

TREC now requires brokers to develop written policy and procedure manuals for their own companies (22 TAC § 535.2(i)). Many individual brokers include specific sections relating to codes of conduct and ethics expected of their employees and associate licensees. These serve as the guiding principles for the company and employees, and agents are often required to sign statements indicating that they agree to abide by the policies established by the company. In many cases, the company conducts training classes for new associates to ensure that the licensee understands and is willing to meet the company's standards of practice.

Personal Beliefs and Individual Ethics

Earlier in this chapter, we described ethics as those things that we think or believe to be the right course of action in a given circumstance after processing the legal and moral implications. These personal or core beliefs have been inculcated into the young by parents, schools, churches, communities, states and countries. These core beliefs typically include respect for others, being truthful and honest, fulfilling

FIGURE 11.1

Canons of Professional Ethics and Conduct

RULES OF THE TEXAS REAL ESTATE COMMISSION
CHAPTER 531 CANONS OF PROFESSIONAL ETHICS AND CONDUCT FOR REAL ESTATE LICENSEES

§531

§531.1. Fidelity. *[Adopted January 1, 1976; amended February 23, 1998]* A real estate broker or salesperson, while acting as an agent for another, is a fiduciary. Special obligations are imposed when such fiduciary relationships are created. They demand:

(1) that the primary duty of the real estate agent is to represent the interests of the agent's client, and the agent's position, in this respect, should be clear to all parties concerned in a real estate transaction; that, however, the agent, in performing duties to the client, shall treat other parties to a transaction fairly;

(2) that the real estate agent be faithful and observant to trust placed in the agent, and be scrupulous and meticulous in performing the agent's functions;

(3) that the real estate agent place no personal interest above that of the agent's client.

§531.2. Integrity. *[Adopted January 1, 1976; amended February 23, 1998]* A real estate broker or salesperson has a special obligation to exercise integrity in the discharge of the licensee's responsibilities, including employment of prudence and caution so as to avoid misrepresentation, in any wise, by acts of commission or omission.

§531.3. Competency. *[Adopted January 1, 1976; amended February 23, 1998]* It is the obligation of a real estate agent to be knowledgeable as a real estate brokerage practitioner. The agent should:

(1) be informed on market conditions affecting the real estate business and pledged to continuing education in the intricacies involved in marketing real estate for others;

(2) be informed on national, state and local issues and developments in the real estate industry; and

(3) exercise judgment and skill in the performance of the work.

§§531.10-531.17. Minimum Appraisal Standards. *[Repealed March 1, 1991]*

§531.18. Consumer Information Form 1-1. *[Adopted February 1, 1990; amended November 1, 1991; Ref: §1101.202(a)(2)]*

(a) The Texas Real Estate Commission adopts by reference Consumer Information Form 1-1 approved by the Texas Real Estate Commission in 1991. This document is published by and available from the Texas Real Estate Commission, P.O. Box 12188, Austin, Texas 78711-2188.

(b) Each real estate inspector or active real estate broker licensed by the Texas Real Estate Commission shall display Consumer Information Form 1-1 in a prominent location in each place of business the broker or inspector maintains.

§531.19. Discriminatory Practices. *[Adopted February 19, 1990; Ref: AG OP.JM-1093]* No real estate licensee shall inquire about, respond to or facilitate inquiries about, or make a disclosure which indicates or is intended to indicate any preference, limitation or discrimination based on the following: race, color, religion, sex, national origin, ancestry, familial status, or handicap of an owner, previous or current occupant, potential purchaser, lessor, or potential lessee of real property. For the purpose of this section, handicap includes a person who had, may have had, has, or may have AIDS, HIV-related illnesses, or HIV infection as defined by the Centers for Disease Control of the United States Public Health Service.

FIGURE 11.2

REALTOR® Code of Ethics

Code of Ethics and Standards of Practice of the NATIONAL ASSOCIATION OF REALTORS®
Effective January 1, 2012

Where the word REALTORS® is used in this Code and Preamble, it shall be deemed to include REALTOR-ASSOCIATE®s.

While the Code of Ethics establishes obligations that may be higher than those mandated by law, in any instance where the Code of Ethics and the law conflict, the obligations of the law must take precedence.

Preamble

Under all is the land. Upon its wise utilization and widely allocated ownership depend the survival and growth of free institutions and of our civilization. REALTORS® should recognize that the interests of the nation and its citizens require the highest and best use of the land and the widest distribution of land ownership. They require the creation of adequate housing, the building of functioning cities, the development of productive industries and farms, and the preservation of a healthful environment.

Such interests impose obligations beyond those of ordinary commerce. They impose grave social responsibility and a patriotic duty to which REALTORS® should dedicate themselves, and for which they should be diligent in preparing themselves. REALTORS®, therefore, are zealous to maintain and improve the standards of their calling and share with their fellow REALTORS® a common responsibility for its integrity and honor.

In recognition and appreciation of their obligations to clients, customers, the public, and each other, REALTORS® continuously strive to become and remain informed on issues affecting real estate and, as knowledgeable professionals, they willingly share the fruit of their experience and study with others. They identify and take steps, through enforcement of this Code of Ethics and by assisting appropriate regulatory bodies, to eliminate practices which may damage the public or which might discredit or bring dishonor to the real estate profession. REALTORS® having direct personal knowledge of conduct that may violate the Code of Ethics involving misappropriation of client or customer funds or property, willful discrimination, or fraud resulting in substantial economic harm, bring such matters to the attention of the appropriate Board or Association of REALTORS®. *(Amended 1/00)*

Realizing that cooperation with other real estate professionals promotes the best interests of those who utilize their services, REALTORS® urge exclusive representation of clients; do not attempt to gain any unfair advantage over their competitors; and they refrain from making unsolicited comments about other practitioners. In instances where their opinion is sought, or where REALTORS® believe that comment is necessary, their opinion is offered in an objective, professional manner, uninfluenced by any personal motivation or potential advantage or gain.

The term REALTOR® has come to connote competency, fairness, and high integrity resulting from adherence to a lofty ideal of moral conduct in business relations. No inducement of profit and no instruction from clients ever can justify departure from this ideal.

In the interpretation of this obligation, REALTORS® can take no safer guide than that which has been handed down through the centuries, embodied in the Golden Rule, "Whatsoever ye would that others should do to you, do ye even so to them."

Accepting this standard as their own, REALTORS® pledge to observe its spirit in all of their activities whether conducted personally, through associates or others, or via technological means, and to conduct their business in accordance with the tenets set forth below. *(Amended 1/07)*

Duties to Clients and Customers

Article 1

When representing a buyer, seller, landlord, tenant, or other client as an agent, REALTORS® pledge themselves to protect and promote the interests of their client. This obligation to the client is primary, but it does not relieve REALTORS® of their obligation to treat all parties honestly. When serving a buyer, seller, landlord, tenant or other party in a non-agency capacity, REALTORS® remain obligated to treat all parties honestly. *(Amended 1/01)*

- **Standard of Practice 1-1**

  REALTORS®, when acting as principals in a real estate transaction, remain obligated by the duties imposed by the Code of Ethics. *(Amended 1/93)*

- **Standard of Practice 1-2**

  The duties imposed by the Code of Ethics encompass all real estate-related activities and transactions whether conducted in person, electronically, or through any other means.

  The duties the Code of Ethics imposes are applicable whether REALTORS® are acting as agents or in legally recognized non-agency capacities except that any duty imposed exclusively on agents by law or regulation shall not be imposed by this Code of Ethics on REALTORS® acting in non-agency capacities.

  As used in this Code of Ethics, "client" means the person(s) or entity(ies) with whom a REALTOR® or a REALTOR®'s firm has an agency or legally recognized non-agency relationship; "customer" means a party to a real estate transaction who receives information, services, or benefits but has no contractual relationship with the REALTOR® or the REALTOR®'s firm; "prospect" means a purchaser, seller, tenant, or landlord who is not subject to a representation relationship with the REALTOR® or REALTOR®'s firm; "agent" means a real estate licensee (including brokers and sales associates) acting in an agency relationship as defined by state law or regulation; and "broker" means a real estate licensee (including brokers and sales associates) acting as an agent or in a legally recognized non-agency capacity. *(Adopted 1/95, Amended 1/07)*

- **Standard of Practice 1-3**

  REALTORS®, in attempting to secure a listing, shall not deliberately mislead the owner as to market value.

- **Standard of Practice 1-4**

  REALTORS®, when seeking to become a buyer/tenant representative, shall not mislead buyers or tenants as to savings or other benefits that might be realized through use of the REALTOR®'s services. *(Amended 1/93)*

FIGURE 11.2

REALTOR® Code of Ethics (continued)

- **Standard of Practice 1-5**
  REALTORS® may represent the seller/landlord and buyer/tenant in the same transaction only after full disclosure to and with informed consent of both parties. *(Adopted 1/93)*

- **Standard of Practice 1-6**
  REALTORS® shall submit offers and counter-offers objectively and as quickly as possible. *(Adopted 1/93, Amended 1/95)*

- **Standard of Practice 1-7**
  When acting as listing brokers, REALTORS® shall continue to submit to the seller/landlord all offers and counter-offers until closing or execution of a lease unless the seller/landlord has waived this obligation in writing. REALTORS® shall not be obligated to continue to market the property after an offer has been accepted by the seller/landlord. REALTORS® shall recommend that sellers/landlords obtain the advice of legal counsel prior to acceptance of a subsequent offer except where the acceptance is contingent on the termination of the pre-existing purchase contract or lease. *(Amended 1/93)*

- **Standard of Practice 1-8**
  REALTORS®, acting as agents or brokers of buyers/tenants, shall submit to buyers/tenants all offers and counter-offers until acceptance but have no obligation to continue to show properties to their clients after an offer has been accepted unless otherwise agreed in writing. REALTORS®, acting as agents or brokers of buyers/tenants, shall recommend that buyers/tenants obtain the advice of legal counsel if there is a question as to whether a pre-existing contract has been terminated. *(Adopted 1/93, Amended 1/99)*

- **Standard of Practice 1-9**
  The obligation of REALTORS® to preserve confidential information (as defined by state law) provided by their clients in the course of any agency relationship or non-agency relationship recognized by law continues after termination of agency relationships or any non-agency relationships recognized by law. REALTORS® shall not knowingly, during or following the termination of professional relationships with their clients:
  1) reveal confidential information of clients; or
  2) use confidential information of clients to the disadvantage of clients; or
  3) use confidential information of clients for the REALTOR®'s advantage or the advantage of third parties unless:
     a) clients consent after full disclosure; or
     b) REALTORS® are required by court order; or
     c) it is the intention of a client to commit a crime and the information is necessary to prevent the crime; or
     d) it is necessary to defend a REALTOR® or the REALTOR®'s employees or associates against an accusation of wrongful conduct.
  Information concerning latent material defects is not considered confidential information under this Code of Ethics. *(Adopted 1/93, Amended 1/01)*

- **Standard of Practice 1-10**
  REALTORS® shall, consistent with the terms and conditions of their real estate licensure and their property management agreement, competently manage the property of clients with due regard for the rights, safety and health of tenants and others lawfully on the premises. *(Adopted 1/95, Amended 1/00)*

- **Standard of Practice 1-11**
  REALTORS® who are employed to maintain or manage a client's property shall exercise due diligence and make reasonable efforts to protect it against reasonably foreseeable contingencies and losses. *(Adopted 1/95)*

- **Standard of Practice 1-12**
  When entering into listing contracts, REALTORS® must advise sellers/landlords of:
  1) the REALTOR®'s company policies regarding cooperation and the amount(s) of any compensation that will be offered to subagents, buyer/tenant agents, and/or brokers acting in legally recognized non-agency capacities;
  2) the fact that buyer/tenant agents or brokers, even if compensated by listing brokers, or by sellers/landlords may represent the interests of buyers/tenants; and
  3) any potential for listing brokers to act as disclosed dual agents, e.g., buyer/tenant agents. *(Adopted 1/93, Renumbered 1/98, Amended 1/03)*

- **Standard of Practice 1-13**
  When entering into buyer/tenant agreements, REALTORS® must advise potential clients of:
  1) the REALTOR®'s company policies regarding cooperation;
  2) the amount of compensation to be paid by the client;
  3) the potential for additional or offsetting compensation from other brokers, from the seller or landlord, or from other parties;
  4) any potential for the buyer/tenant representative to act as a disclosed dual agent, e.g., listing broker, subagent, landlord's agent, etc., and
  5) the possibility that sellers or sellers' representatives may not treat the existence, terms, or conditions of offers as confidential unless confidentiality is required by law, regulation, or by any confidentiality agreement between the parties. *(Adopted 1/93, Renumbered 1/98, Amended 1/06)*

- **Standard of Practice 1-14**
  Fees for preparing appraisals or other valuations shall not be contingent upon the amount of the appraisal or valuation. *(Adopted 1/02)*

- **Standard of Practice 1-15**
  REALTORS®, in response to inquiries from buyers or cooperating brokers shall, with the sellers' approval, disclose the existence of offers on the property. Where disclosure is authorized, REALTORS® shall also disclose, if asked, whether offers were obtained by the listing licensee, another licensee in the listing firm, or by a cooperating broker. *(Adopted 1/03, Amended 1/09)*

- **Standard of Practice 1-16**
  REALTORS® shall not access or use, or permit or enable others to access or use, listed or managed property on terms or conditions other than those authorized by the owner or seller. *(Adopted 1/12)*

Article 2
REALTORS® shall avoid exaggeration, misrepresentation, or concealment of pertinent facts relating to the property or the transaction. REALTORS® shall not, however, be obligated to discover latent defects in the property, to advise on matters outside the scope of their real estate license, or to disclose facts which are confidential under the scope of agency or non-agency relationships as defined by state law. *(Amended 1/00)*

- **Standard of Practice 2-1**
  REALTORS® shall only be obligated to discover and disclose adverse factors reasonably apparent to someone with expertise in those areas required by their real estate licensing authority. Article 2 does not impose upon the REALTOR® the obligation of expertise in other professional or technical disciplines. *(Amended 1/96)*

- **Standard of Practice 2-2**
  (Renumbered as Standard of Practice 1-12 1/98)

- **Standard of Practice 2-3**
  (Renumbered as Standard of Practice 1-13 1/98)

FIGURE 11.2

REALTOR® Code of Ethics (continued)

- **Standard of Practice 2-4**
  REALTORS® shall not be parties to the naming of a false consideration in any document, unless it be the naming of an obviously nominal consideration.

- **Standard of Practice 2-5**
  Factors defined as "non-material" by law or regulation or which are expressly referenced in law or regulation as not being subject to disclosure are considered not "pertinent" for purposes of Article 2. *(Adopted 1/93)*

Article 3
REALTORS® shall cooperate with other brokers except when cooperation is not in the client's best interest. The obligation to cooperate does not include the obligation to share commissions, fees, or to otherwise compensate another broker. *(Amended 1/95)*

- **Standard of Practice 3-1**
  REALTORS®, acting as exclusive agents or brokers of sellers/landlords, establish the terms and conditions of offers to cooperate. Unless expressly indicated in offers to cooperate, cooperating brokers may not assume that the offer of cooperation includes an offer of compensation. Terms of compensation, if any, shall be ascertained by cooperating brokers before beginning efforts to accept the offer of cooperation. *(Amended 1/99)*

- **Standard of Practice 3-2**
  To be effective, any change in compensation offered for cooperative services must be communicated to the other REALTOR® prior to the time that REALTOR® submits an offer to purchase/lease the property. *(Amended 1/10)*

- **Standard of Practice 3-3**
  Standard of Practice 3-2 does not preclude the listing broker and cooperating broker from entering into an agreement to change cooperative compensation. *(Adopted 1/94)*

- **Standard of Practice 3-4**
  REALTORS®, acting as listing brokers, have an affirmative obligation to disclose the existence of dual or variable rate commission arrangements (i.e., listings where one amount of commission is payable if the listing broker's firm is the procuring cause of sale/lease and a different amount of commission is payable if the sale/lease results through the efforts of the seller/landlord or a cooperating broker). The listing broker shall, as soon as practical, disclose the existence of such arrangements to potential cooperating brokers and shall, in response to inquiries from cooperating brokers, disclose the differential that would result in a cooperative transaction or in a sale/lease that results through the efforts of the seller/landlord. If the cooperating broker is a buyer/tenant representative, the buyer/tenant representative must disclose such information to their client before the client makes an offer to purchase or lease. *(Amended 1/02)*

- **Standard of Practice 3-5**
  It is the obligation of subagents to promptly disclose all pertinent facts to the principal's agent prior to as well as after a purchase or lease agreement is executed. *(Amended 1/93)*

- **Standard of Practice 3-6**
  REALTORS® shall disclose the existence of accepted offers, including offers with unresolved contingencies, to any broker seeking cooperation. *(Adopted 5/86, Amended 1/04)*

- **Standard of Practice 3-7**
  When seeking information from another REALTOR® concerning property under a management or listing agreement, REALTORS® shall disclose their REALTOR® status and whether their interest is personal or on behalf of a client and, if on behalf of a client, their relationship with the client. *(Amended 1/11)*

- **Standard of Practice 3-8**
  REALTORS® shall not misrepresent the availability of access to show or inspect a listed property. *(Amended 11/87)*

- **Standard of Practice 3-9**
  REALTORS® shall not provide access to listed property on terms other than those established by the owner or the listing broker. *(Adopted 1/10)*

- **Standard of Practice 3-10**
  The duty to cooperate established in Article 3 relates to the obligation to share information on listed property, and to make property available to other brokers for showing to prospective purchasers/tenants when it is in the best interests of sellers/landlords. *(Adopted 1/11)*

Article 4
REALTORS® shall not acquire an interest in or buy or present offers from themselves, any member of their immediate families, their firms or any member thereof, or any entities in which they have any ownership interest, any real property without making their true position known to the owner or the owner's agent or broker. In selling property they own, or in which they have any interest, REALTORS® shall reveal their ownership or interest in writing to the purchaser or the purchaser's representative. *(Amended 1/00)*

- **Standard of Practice 4-1**
  For the protection of all parties, the disclosures required by Article 4 shall be in writing and provided by REALTORS® prior to the signing of any contract. *(Adopted 2/86)*

Article 5
REALTORS® shall not undertake to provide professional services concerning a property or its value where they have a present or contemplated interest unless such interest is specifically disclosed to all affected parties.

Article 6
REALTORS® shall not accept any commission, rebate, or profit on expenditures made for their client, without the client's knowledge and consent.

When recommending real estate products or services (e.g., homeowner's insurance, warranty programs, mortgage financing, title insurance, etc.), REALTORS® shall disclose to the client or customer to whom the recommendation is made any financial benefits or fees, other than real estate referral fees, the REALTOR® or REALTOR®'s firm may receive as a direct result of such recommendation. *(Amended 1/99)*

- **Standard of Practice 6-1**
  REALTORS® shall not recommend or suggest to a client or a customer the use of services of another organization or business entity in which they have a direct interest without disclosing such interest at the time of the recommendation or suggestion. *(Amended 5/88)*

Article 7
In a transaction, REALTORS® shall not accept compensation from more than one party, even if permitted by law, without disclosure to all parties and the informed consent of the REALTOR®'s client or clients. *(Amended 1/93)*

Article 8
REALTORS® shall keep in a special account in an appropriate financial institution, separated from their own funds, monies coming into their possession in trust for other persons, such as escrows, trust funds, clients' monies, and other like items.

FIGURE 11.2

Realtor® Code of Ethics (continued)

Article 9
REALTORS®, for the protection of all parties, shall assure whenever possible that all agreements related to real estate transactions including, but not limited to, listing and representation agreements, purchase contracts, and leases are in writing in clear and understandable language expressing the specific terms, conditions, obligations and commitments of the parties. A copy of each agreement shall be furnished to each party to such agreements upon their signing or initialing. *(Amended 1/04)*

- **Standard of Practice 9-1**
  For the protection of all parties, REALTORS® shall use reasonable care to ensure that documents pertaining to the purchase, sale, or lease of real estate are kept current through the use of written extensions or amendments. *(Amended 1/93)*

- **Standard of Practice 9-2**
  When assisting or enabling a client or customer in establishing a contractual relationship (e.g., listing and representation agreements, purchase agreements, leases, etc.) electronically, REALTORS® shall make reasonable efforts to explain the nature and disclose the specific terms of the contractual relationship being established prior to it being agreed to by a contracting party. *(Adopted 1/07)*

Duties to the Public

Article 10
REALTORS® shall not deny equal professional services to any person for reasons of race, color, religion, sex, handicap, familial status, national origin, or sexual orientation. REALTORS® shall not be parties to any plan or agreement to discriminate against a person or persons on the basis of race, color, religion, sex, handicap, familial status, national origin, or sexual orientation. *(Amended 1/11)*

REALTORS®, in their real estate employment practices, shall not discriminate against any person or persons on the basis of race, color, religion, sex, handicap, familial status, national origin, or sexual orientation. *(Amended 1/11)*

- **Standard of Practice 10-1**
  When involved in the sale or lease of a residence, REALTORS® shall not volunteer information regarding the racial, religious or ethnic composition of any neighborhood nor shall they engage in any activity which may result in panic selling, however, REALTORS® may provide other demographic information. *(Adopted 1/94, Amended 1/06)*

- **Standard of Practice 10-2**
  When not involved in the sale or lease of a residence, REALTORS® may provide demographic information related to a property, transaction or professional assignment to a party if such demographic information is (a) deemed by the REALTOR® to be needed to assist with or complete, in a manner consistent with Article 10, a real estate transaction or professional assignment and (b) is obtained or derived from a recognized, reliable, independent, and impartial source. The source of such information and any additions, deletions, modifications, interpretations, or other changes shall be disclosed in reasonable detail. *(Adopted 1/05, Renumbered 1/06)*

- **Standard of Practice 10-3**
  REALTORS® shall not print, display or circulate any statement or advertisement with respect to selling or renting of a property that indicates any preference, limitations or discrimination based on race, color, religion, sex, handicap, familial status, national origin, or sexual orientation. *(Adopted 1/94, Renumbered 1/05 and 1/06, Amended 1/11)*

- **Standard of Practice 10-4**
  As used in Article 10 "real estate employment practices" relates to employees and independent contractors providing real estate-related services and the administrative and clerical staff directly supporting those individuals. *(Adopted 1/00, Renumbered 1/05 and 1/06)*

Article 11
The services which REALTORS® provide to their clients and customers shall conform to the standards of practice and competence which are reasonably expected in the specific real estate disciplines in which they engage; specifically, residential real estate brokerage, real property management, commercial and industrial real estate brokerage, land brokerage, real estate appraisal, real estate counseling, real estate syndication, real estate auction, and international real estate.

REALTORS® shall not undertake to provide specialized professional services concerning a type of property or service that is outside their field of competence unless they engage the assistance of one who is competent on such types of property or service, or unless the facts are fully disclosed to the client. Any persons engaged to provide such assistance shall be so identified to the client and their contribution to the assignment should be set forth. *(Amended 1/10)*

- **Standard of Practice 11-1**
  When REALTORS® prepare opinions of real property value or price, other than in pursuit of a listing or to assist a potential purchaser in formulating a purchase offer, such opinions shall include the following unless the party requesting the opinion requires a specific type of report or different data set:
  1) identification of the subject property
  2) date prepared
  3) defined value or price
  4) limiting conditions, including statements of purpose(s) and intended user(s)
  5) any present or contemplated interest, including the possibility of representing the seller/landlord or buyers/tenants
  6) basis for the opinion, including applicable market data
  7) if the opinion is not an appraisal, a statement to that effect
  (Amended 1/10)

- **Standard of Practice 11-2**
  The obligations of the Code of Ethics in respect of real estate disciplines other than appraisal shall be interpreted and applied in accordance with the standards of competence and practice which clients and the public reasonably require to protect their rights and interests considering the complexity of the transaction, the availability of expert assistance, and, where the REALTOR® is an agent or subagent, the obligations of a fiduciary. *(Adopted 1/95)*

- **Standard of Practice 11-3**
  When REALTORS® provide consultive services to clients which involve advice or counsel for a fee (not a commission), such advice shall be rendered in an objective manner and the fee shall not be contingent on the substance of the advice or counsel given. If brokerage or transaction services are to be provided in addition to consultive services, a separate compensation may be paid with prior agreement between the client and REALTOR®. *(Adopted 1/96)*

- **Standard of Practice 11-4**
  The competency required by Article 11 relates to services contracted for between REALTORS® and their clients or customers; the duties expressly imposed by the Code of Ethics; and the duties imposed by law or regulation. *(Adopted 1/02)*

FIGURE 11.2

REALTOR® Code of Ethics (continued)

Article 12

REALTORS® shall be honest and truthful in their real estate communications and shall present a true picture in their advertising, marketing, and other representations. REALTORS® shall ensure that their status as real estate professionals is readily apparent in their advertising, marketing, and other representations, and that the recipients of all real estate communications are, or have been, notified that those communications are from a real estate professional. *(Amended 1/08)*

- **Standard of Practice 12-1**

  REALTORS® may use the term "free" and similar terms in their advertising and in other representations provided that all terms governing availability of the offered product or service are clearly disclosed at the same time. *(Amended 1/97)*

- **Standard of Practice 12-2**

  REALTORS® may represent their services as "free" or without cost even if they expect to receive compensation from a source other than their client provided that the potential for the REALTOR® to obtain a benefit from a third party is clearly disclosed at the same time. *(Amended 1/97)*

- **Standard of Practice 12-3**

  The offering of premiums, prizes, merchandise discounts or other inducements to list, sell, purchase, or lease is not, in itself, unethical even if receipt of the benefit is contingent on listing, selling, purchasing, or leasing through the REALTOR® making the offer. However, REALTORS® must exercise care and candor in any such advertising or other public or private representations so that any party interested in receiving or otherwise benefiting from the REALTOR®'s offer will have clear, thorough, advance understanding of all the terms and conditions of the offer. The offering of any inducements to do business is subject to the limitations and restrictions of state law and the ethical obligations established by any applicable Standard of Practice. *(Amended 1/95)*

- **Standard of Practice 12-4**

  REALTORS® shall not offer for sale/lease or advertise property without authority. When acting as listing brokers or as subagents, REALTORS® shall not quote a price different from that agreed upon with the seller/landlord. *(Amended 1/93)*

- **Standard of Practice 12-5**

  REALTORS® shall not advertise nor permit any person employed by or affiliated with them to advertise real estate services or listed property in any medium (e.g., electronically, print, radio, television, etc.) without disclosing the name of that REALTOR®'s firm in a reasonable and readily apparent manner. This Standard of Practice acknowledges that disclosing the name of the firm may not be practical in electronic displays of limited information (e.g., "thumbnails", text messages, "tweets", etc.). Such displays are exempt from the disclosure requirement established in this Standard of Practice, but only when linked to a display that includes all required disclosures. *(Adopted 11/86, Amended 1/11)*

- **Standard of Practice 12-6**

  REALTORS®, when advertising unlisted real property for sale/lease in which they have an ownership interest, shall disclose their status as both owners/landlords and as REALTORS® or real estate licensees. *(Amended 1/93)*

- **Standard of Practice 12-7**

  Only REALTORS® who participated in the transaction as the listing broker or cooperating broker (selling broker) may claim to have "sold" the property. Prior to closing, a cooperating broker may post a "sold" sign only with the consent of the listing broker. *(Amended 1/96)*

- **Standard of Practice 12-8**

  The obligation to present a true picture in representations to the public includes information presented, provided, or displayed on REALTORS®' websites. REALTORS® shall use reasonable efforts to ensure that information on their websites is current. When it becomes apparent that information on a REALTOR®'s website is no longer current or accurate, REALTORS® shall promptly take corrective action. *(Adopted 1/07)*

- **Standard of Practice 12-9**

  REALTOR® firm websites shall disclose the firm's name and state(s) of licensure in a reasonable and readily apparent manner.

  Websites of REALTORS® and non-member licensees affiliated with a REALTOR® firm shall disclose the firm's name and that REALTOR®'s or non-member licensee's state(s) of licensure in a reasonable and readily apparent manner. *(Adopted 1/07)*

- **Standard of Practice 12-10**

  REALTORS®' obligation to present a true picture in their advertising and representations to the public includes the URLs and domain names they use, and prohibits REALTORS® from:

  1) engaging in deceptive or unauthorized framing of real estate brokerage websites;
  2) manipulating (e.g., presenting content developed by others) listing content in any way that produces a deceptive or misleading result; or
  3) deceptively using metatags, keywords or other devices/methods to direct, drive, or divert Internet traffic, or to otherwise mislead consumers. *(Adopted 1/07)*

- **Standard of Practice 12-11**

  REALTORS® intending to share or sell consumer information gathered via the Internet shall disclose that possibility in a reasonable and readily apparent manner. *(Adopted 1/07)*

- **Standard of Practice 12-12**

  REALTORS® shall not:
  1) use URLs or domain names that present less than a true picture, or
  2) register URLs or domain names which, if used, would present less than a true picture. *(Adopted 1/08)*

- **Standard of Practice 12-13**

  The obligation to present a true picture in advertising, marketing, and representations allows REALTORS® to use and display only professional designations, certifications, and other credentials to which they are legitimately entitled. *(Adopted 1/08)*

Article 13

REALTORS® shall not engage in activities that constitute the unauthorized practice of law and shall recommend that legal counsel be obtained when the interest of any party to the transaction requires it.

Article 14

If charged with unethical practice or asked to present evidence or to cooperate in any other way, in any professional standards proceeding or investigation, REALTORS® shall place all pertinent facts before the proper tribunals of the Member Board or affiliated institute, society, or council in which membership is held and shall take no action to disrupt or obstruct such processes. *(Amended 1/99)*

- **Standard of Practice 14-1**

  REALTORS® shall not be subject to disciplinary proceedings in more than one Board of REALTORS® or affiliated institute, society, or council in which they hold membership with respect to alleged violations of the Code of Ethics relating to the same transaction or event. *(Amended 1/95)*

FIGURE 11.2

REALTOR® Code of Ethics (continued)

- **Standard of Practice 14-2**
  REALTORS® shall not make any unauthorized disclosure or dissemination of the allegations, findings, or decision developed in connection with an ethics hearing or appeal or in connection with an arbitration hearing or procedural review. *(Amended 1/92)*

- **Standard of Practice 14-3**
  REALTORS® shall not obstruct the Board's investigative or professional standards proceedings by instituting or threatening to institute actions for libel, slander, or defamation against any party to a professional standards proceeding or their witnesses based on the filing of an arbitration request, an ethics complaint, or testimony given before any tribunal. *(Adopted 11/87, Amended 1/99)*

- **Standard of Practice 14-4**
  REALTORS® shall not intentionally impede the Board's investigative or disciplinary proceedings by filing multiple ethics complaints based on the same event or transaction. *(Adopted 11/88)*

Duties to REALTORS®

Article 15
REALTORS® shall not knowingly or recklessly make false or misleading statements about other real estate professionals, their businesses, or their business practices. *(Amended 1/12)*

- **Standard of Practice 15-1**
  REALTORS® shall not knowingly or recklessly file false or unfounded ethics complaints. *(Adopted 1/00)*

- **Standard of Practice 15-2**
  The obligation to refrain from making false or misleading statements about other real estate professionals, their businesses, and their business practices includes the duty to not knowingly or recklessly publish, repeat, retransmit, or republish false or misleading statements made by others. This duty applies whether false or misleading statements are repeated in person, in writing, by technological means (e.g., the Internet), or by any other means. *(Adopted 1/07, Amended 1/12)*

- **Standard of Practice 15-3**
  The obligation to refrain from making false or misleading statements about other real estate professionals, their businesses, and their business practices includes the duty to publish a clarification about or to remove statements made by others on electronic media the REALTOR® controls once the REALTOR® knows the statement is false or misleading. *(Adopted 1/10, Amended 1/12)*

Article 16
REALTORS® shall not engage in any practice or take any action inconsistent with exclusive representation or exclusive brokerage relationship agreements that other REALTORS® have with clients. *(Amended 1/04)*

- **Standard of Practice 16-1**
  Article 16 is not intended to prohibit aggressive or innovative business practices which are otherwise ethical and does not prohibit disagreements with other REALTORS® involving commission, fees, compensation or other forms of payment or expenses. *(Adopted 1/93, Amended 1/95)*

- **Standard of Practice 16-2**
  Article 16 does not preclude REALTORS® from making general announcements to prospects describing their services and the terms of their availability even though some recipients may have entered into agency agreements or other exclusive relationships with another REALTOR®. A general telephone canvass, general mailing or distribution addressed to all prospects in a given geographical area or in a given profession, business, club, or organization, or other classification or group is deemed "general" for purposes of this standard. *(Amended 1/04)*

  Article 16 is intended to recognize as unethical two basic types of solicitations:

  First, telephone or personal solicitations of property owners who have been identified by a real estate sign, multiple listing compilation, or other information service as having exclusively listed their property with another REALTOR® and

  Second, mail or other forms of written solicitations of prospects whose properties are exclusively listed with another REALTOR® when such solicitations are not part of a general mailing but are directed specifically to property owners identified through compilations of current listings, "for sale" or "for rent" signs, or other sources of information required by Article 3 and Multiple Listing Service rules to be made available to other REALTORS® under offers of subagency or cooperation. *(Amended 1/04)*

- **Standard of Practice 16-3**
  Article 16 does not preclude REALTORS® from contacting the client of another broker for the purpose of offering to provide, or entering into a contract to provide, a different type of real estate service unrelated to the type of service currently being provided (e.g., property management as opposed to brokerage) or from offering the same type of service for property not subject to other brokers' exclusive agreements. However, information received through a Multiple Listing Service or any other offer of cooperation may not be used to target clients of other REALTORS® to whom such offers to provide services may be made. *(Amended 1/04)*

- **Standard of Practice 16-4**
  REALTORS® shall not solicit a listing which is currently listed exclusively with another broker. However, if the listing broker, when asked by the REALTOR®, refuses to disclose the expiration date and nature of such listing, i.e., an exclusive right to sell, an exclusive agency, open listing, or other form of contractual agreement between the listing broker and the client, the REALTOR® may contact the owner to secure such information and may discuss the terms upon which the REALTOR® might take a future listing or, alternatively, may take a listing to become effective upon expiration of any existing exclusive listing. *(Amended 1/94)*

- **Standard of Practice 16-5**
  REALTORS® shall not solicit buyer/tenant agreements from buyers/tenants who are subject to exclusive buyer/tenant agreements. However, if asked by a REALTOR®, the broker refuses to disclose the expiration date of the exclusive buyer/tenant agreement, the REALTOR® may contact the buyer/tenant to secure such information and may discuss the terms upon which the REALTOR® might enter into a future buyer/tenant agreement or, alternatively, may enter into a buyer/tenant agreement to become effective upon the expiration of any existing exclusive buyer/tenant agreement. *(Adopted 1/94, Amended 1/98)*

- **Standard of Practice 16-6**
  When REALTORS® are contacted by the client of another REALTOR® regarding the creation of an exclusive relationship to provide the same type of service, and REALTORS® have not directly or indirectly initiated such discussions, they may discuss the terms upon which they might enter into a future

FIGURE 11.2

REALTOR® Code of Ethics (continued)

agreement or, alternatively, may enter into an agreement which becomes effective upon expiration of any existing exclusive agreement. *(Amended 1/98)*

- **Standard of Practice 16-7**
  The fact that a prospect has retained a REALTOR® as an exclusive representative or exclusive broker in one or more past transactions does not preclude other REALTORS® from seeking such prospect's future business. *(Amended 1/04)*

- **Standard of Practice 16-8**
  The fact that an exclusive agreement has been entered into with a REALTOR® shall not preclude or inhibit any other REALTOR® from entering into a similar agreement after the expiration of the prior agreement. *(Amended 1/98)*

- **Standard of Practice 16-9**
  REALTORS®, prior to entering into a representation agreement, have an affirmative obligation to make reasonable efforts to determine whether the prospect is subject to a current, valid exclusive agreement to provide the same type of real estate service. *(Amended 1/04)*

- **Standard of Practice 16-10**
  REALTORS®, acting as buyer or tenant representatives or brokers, shall disclose that relationship to the seller/landlord's representative or broker at first contact and shall provide written confirmation of that disclosure to the seller/landlord's representative or broker not later than execution of a purchase agreement or lease. *(Amended 1/04)*

- **Standard of Practice 16-11**
  On unlisted property, REALTORS® acting as buyer/tenant representatives or brokers shall disclose that relationship to the seller/landlord at first contact for that buyer/tenant and shall provide written confirmation of such disclosure to the seller/landlord not later than execution of any purchase or lease agreement. *(Amended 1/04)*

  REALTORS® shall make any request for anticipated compensation from the seller/landlord at first contact. *(Amended 1/98)*

- **Standard of Practice 16-12**
  REALTORS®, acting as representatives or brokers of sellers/landlords or as subagents of listing brokers, shall disclose that relationship to buyers/tenants as soon as practicable and shall provide written confirmation of such disclosure to buyers/tenants not later than execution of any purchase or lease agreement. *(Amended 1/04)*

- **Standard of Practice 16-13**
  All dealings concerning property exclusively listed, or with buyer/tenants who are subject to an exclusive agreement shall be carried on with the client's representative or broker, and not with the client, except with the consent of the client's representative or broker or except where such dealings are initiated by the client.

  Before providing substantive services (such as writing a purchase offer or presenting a CMA) to prospects, REALTORS® shall ask prospects whether they are a party to any exclusive representation agreement. REALTORS® shall not knowingly provide substantive services concerning a prospective transaction to prospects who are parties to exclusive representation agreements, except with the consent of the prospects' exclusive representatives or at the direction of prospects. *(Adopted 1/93, Amended 1/04)*

- **Standard of Practice 16-14**
  REALTORS® are free to enter into contractual relationships or to negotiate with sellers/landlords, buyers/tenants or others who are not subject to an exclusive agreement but shall not knowingly obligate them to pay more than one commission except with their informed consent. *(Amended 1/98)*

- **Standard of Practice 16-15**
  In cooperative transactions REALTORS® shall compensate cooperating REALTORS® (principal brokers) and shall not compensate nor offer to compensate, directly or indirectly, any of the sales licensees employed by or affiliated with other REALTORS® without the prior express knowledge and consent of the cooperating broker.

- **Standard of Practice 16-16**
  REALTORS®, acting as subagents or buyer/tenant representatives or brokers, shall not use the terms of an offer to purchase/lease to attempt to modify the listing broker's offer of compensation to subagents or buyer/tenant representatives or brokers nor make the submission of an executed offer to purchase/lease contingent on the listing broker's agreement to modify the offer of compensation. *(Amended 1/04)*

- **Standard of Practice 16-17**
  REALTORS®, acting as subagents or as buyer/tenant representatives or brokers, shall not attempt to extend a listing broker's offer of cooperation and/or compensation to other brokers without the consent of the listing broker. *(Amended 1/04)*

- **Standard of Practice 16-18**
  REALTORS® shall not use information obtained from listing brokers through offers to cooperate made through multiple listing services or through other offers of cooperation to refer listing brokers' clients to other brokers or to create buyer/tenant relationships with listing brokers' clients, unless such use is authorized by listing brokers. *(Amended 1/02)*

- **Standard of Practice 16-19**
  Signs giving notice of property for sale, rent, lease, or exchange shall not be placed on property without consent of the seller/landlord. *(Amended 1/93)*

- **Standard of Practice 16-20**
  REALTORS®, prior to or after their relationship with their current firm is terminated, shall not induce clients of their current firm to cancel exclusive contractual agreements between the client and that firm. This does not preclude REALTORS® (principals) from establishing agreements with their associated licensees governing assignability of exclusive agreements. *(Adopted 1/98, Amended 1/10)*

Article 17

In the event of contractual disputes or specific non-contractual disputes as defined in Standard of Practice 17-4 between REALTORS® (principals) associated with different firms, arising out of their relationship as REALTORS®, the REALTORS® shall mediate the dispute if the Board requires its members to mediate. If the dispute is not resolved through mediation, or if mediation is not required, REALTORS® shall submit the dispute to arbitration in accordance with the policies of the Board rather than litigate the matter.

In the event clients of REALTORS® wish to mediate or arbitrate contractual disputes arising out of real estate transactions, REALTORS® shall mediate or arbitrate those disputes in accordance with the policies of the Board, provided the clients agree to be bound by any resulting agreement or award.

The obligation to participate in mediation and arbitration contemplated by this Article includes the obligation of REALTORS® (principals) to cause their firms to mediate and arbitrate and be bound by any resulting agreement or award. *(Amended 1/12)*

- **Standard of Practice 17-1**
  The filing of litigation and refusal to withdraw from it by REALTORS® in an arbitrable matter constitutes a refusal to arbitrate. *(Adopted 2/86)*

FIGURE 11.2

REALTOR® Code of Ethics (continued)

- **Standard of Practice 17-2**

  Article 17 does not require REALTORS® to mediate in those circumstances when all parties to the dispute advise the Board in writing that they choose not to mediate through the Board's facilities. The fact that all parties decline to participate in mediation does not relieve REALTORS® of the duty to arbitrate.

  Article 17 does not require REALTORS® to arbitrate in those circumstances when all parties to the dispute advise the Board in writing that they choose not to arbitrate before the board. *(Amended 1/12)*

- **Standard of Practice 17-3**

  REALTORS®, when acting solely as principals in a real estate transaction, are not obligated to arbitrate disputes with other REALTORS® absent a specific written agreement to the contrary. *(Adopted 1/96)*

- **Standard of Practice 17-4**

  Specific non-contractual disputes that are subject to arbitration pursuant to Article 17 are:

  1) Where a listing broker has compensated a cooperating broker and another cooperating broker subsequently claims to be the procuring cause of the sale or lease. In such cases the complainant may name the first cooperating broker as respondent and arbitration may proceed without the listing broker being named as a respondent. When arbitration occurs between two (or more) cooperating brokers and where the listing broker is not a party, the amount in dispute and the amount of any potential resulting award is limited to the amount paid to the respondent by the listing broker and any amount credited or paid to a party to the transaction at the direction of the respondent. Alternatively, if the complaint is brought against the listing broker, the listing broker may name the first cooperating broker as a third-party respondent. In either instance the decision of the hearing panel as to procuring cause shall be conclusive with respect to all current or subsequent claims of the parties for compensation arising out of the underlying cooperative transaction. *(Adopted 1/97, Amended 1/07)*

  2) Where a buyer or tenant representative is compensated by the seller or landlord, and not by the listing broker, and the listing broker, as a result, reduces the commission owed by the seller or landlord and, subsequent to such actions, another cooperating broker claims to be the procuring cause of sale or lease. In such cases the complainant may name the first cooperating broker as respondent and arbitration may proceed without the listing broker being named as a respondent. When arbitration occurs between two (or more) cooperating brokers and where the listing broker is not a party, the amount in dispute and the amount of any potential resulting award is limited to the amount paid to the respondent by the seller or landlord and any amount credited or paid to a party to the transaction at the direction of the respondent. Alternatively, if the complaint is brought against the listing broker, the listing broker may name the first cooperating broker as a third-party respondent. In either instance the decision of the hearing panel as to procuring cause shall be conclusive with respect to all current or subsequent claims of the parties for compensation arising out of the underlying cooperative transaction. *(Adopted 1/97, Amended 1/07)*

  3) Where a buyer or tenant representative is compensated by the buyer or tenant and, as a result, the listing broker reduces the commission owed by the seller or landlord and, subsequent to such actions, another cooperating broker claims to be the procuring cause of sale or lease. In such cases the complainant may name the first cooperating broker as respondent and arbitration may proceed without the listing broker being named as a respondent. Alternatively, if the complaint is brought against the listing broker, the listing broker may name the first cooperating broker as a third-party respondent. In either instance the decision of the hearing panel as to procuring cause shall be conclusive with respect to all current or subsequent claims of the parties for compensation arising out of the underlying cooperative transaction. *(Adopted 1/97)*

  4) Where two or more listing brokers claim entitlement to compensation pursuant to open listings with a seller or landlord who agrees to participate in arbitration (or who requests arbitration) and who agrees to be bound by the decision. In cases where one of the listing brokers has been compensated by the seller or landlord, the other listing broker, as complainant, may name the first listing broker as respondent and arbitration may proceed between the brokers. *(Adopted 1/97)*

  5) Where a buyer or tenant representative is compensated by the seller or landlord, and not by the listing broker, and the listing broker, as a result, reduces the commission owed by the seller or landlord and, subsequent to such actions, claims to be the procuring cause of sale or lease. In such cases arbitration shall be between the listing broker and the buyer or tenant representative and the amount in dispute is limited to the amount of the reduction of commission to which the listing broker agreed. *(Adopted 1/05)*

- **Standard of Practice 17-5**

  The obligation to arbitrate established in Article 17 includes disputes between REALTORS® (principals) in different states in instances where, absent an established inter-association arbitration agreement, the REALTOR® (principal) requesting arbitration agrees to submit to the jurisdiction of, travel to, participate in, and be bound by any resulting award rendered in arbitration conducted by the respondent(s) REALTOR®'s association, in instances where the respondent(s) REALTOR®'s association determines that an arbitrable issue exists. *(Adopted 1/07)*

The Code of Ethics *was adopted in 1913. Amended at the Annual Convention in 1924, 1928, 1950, 1951, 1952, 1955, 1956, 1961, 1962, 1974, 1982, 1986, 1987, 1989, 1990, 1991, 1992, 1993, 1994, 1995, 1996, 1997, 1998, 1999, 2000, 2001, 2002, 2003, 2004, 2005, 2006, 2007, 2008, 2009, 2010 and 2011.*

Explanatory Notes

The reader should be aware of the following policies which have been approved by the Board of Directors of the National Association:

In filing a charge of an alleged violation of the Code of Ethics by a REALTOR®, the charge must read as an alleged violation of one or more Articles of the Code. Standards of Practice may be cited in support of the charge.

The Standards of Practice serve to clarify the ethical obligations imposed by the various Articles and supplement, and do not substitute for, the Case Interpretations in *Interpretations of the Code of Ethics*.

Modifications to existing Standards of Practice and additional new Standards of Practice are approved from time to time. Readers are cautioned to ensure that the most recent publications are utilized.

©Copyright 2012 NATIONAL ASSOCIATION OF REALTORS®

166-288 (1/12 JBK)

430 North Michigan Avenue • Chicago, IL 60611-4087
800.874.6500 • www.REALTOR.org

NATIONAL ASSOCIATION *of* REALTORS®

promises, and honoring commitments. If, in fact, all people agreed to and adhered to the same core beliefs or a common morality, there would be no need for codes of conduct, rules and regulations, or even laws. Obviously, this is not the case and the farther one is removed from immediate family, community, or country, the more diverse will be the notion of what is moral or ethical.

On occasion, individuals may find their personal ethics in conflict with those professional codes and even the laws mentioned above. In the final analysis, the individual's actions will illustrate which of the above have the greatest influence on that individual.

Laws and Ethics in Practice

So, how do the above laws, legal ethics, rules and regulations, codes of ethics, and personal beliefs interact in the real world? The following questions and examples illustrate the relationships and potential conflicts.

Agent Sally, a REALTOR®, is attempting to list a single-family home for lease through the company's property management division. The property is a large four-bedroom home with unfenced frontage on a deepwater river. The owner has indicated that they do not want to rent to a family with young children due to the unprotected waterfront posing a serious danger to small children. As a mother herself, Sally shares the concern for safety and takes the listing, agreeing to work with the owner to try and find the right tenant, even though she knows that adults with children are considered protected under the familial status provisions of fair housing laws.

Over the next few weeks, several potential tenants inquire about the property, but using various excuses as to why the subject property could not be shown, the prospects were directed to other properties meeting the prospects' needs. Within a month, Sally produced a retired couple with no children living at home and secured a lease for the owner of the waterfront property.

In evaluating Sally's actions, let's look first at the laws, rules and regulations, codes, and ethics that would apply in this case:

- Federal Fair Housing Act (FFHA)
- Texas antidiscrimination law
- Municipal antidiscrimination ordinances
- TRELA
- TREC Rules and Regulations
- NAR COE
- Company policy
- Sally's personal beliefs

Federal law. The basis for antidiscrimination law is rooted in the 1866 Civil Rights Act and, more specifically, in civil rights movements of the 1950s and 1960s. The resultant Fair Housing Act and subsequent amendments make it illegal to discriminate in the sale or leasing of residential properties based on race, color, religion, sex, national origin, familial status, or handicap. These are called protected classes.

Texas state law. Individual states such as Texas have been authorized to enact and enforce state fair housing laws so long as the federally protected classes are also included in the state law. States are, however, authorized to include additional categories of protected classes, if they so choose. As a result, many states (though not Texas) have added sexual orientation, marital status, and other identifiers as additional protected classes. Thus, in Texas, compliance with the federal law conforms to compliance with Texas antidiscrimination laws.

Municipal ordinances. Cities, like states, may also have ordinances prohibiting discrimination in housing so long as the protected classes, at minimum, include the federally protected classes, as well as any additional state protected classes. Municipalities may add protected classes to either the federal or the state categories. The city in which Sally resides has adopted a city fair housing ordinance that mirrors the federal law.

TRELA. TRELA 1101.652(b)(32) specifically creates grounds for suspension or revocation of a license if the license holder

> *discriminates against an owner, potential buyer, landlord, or potential tenant on the basis of race, color, religion, sex, disability, familial status, national origin, or ancestry, including directing a prospective buyer or tenant interested in equivalent properties to a different area based on the race color, religion, sex, disability, familial status, national origin or ancestry of the potential owner, or tenant.*

TREC Rules. TREC Rule § 531.19 states that

> *no real estate licensee shall inquire about, respond to or facilitate inquires about, or make a disclosure which indicates or is intended to indicate any preference, limitation or discrimination based on the following: race, color, religion, sex, national origin, ancestry, familial status, or handicap or an owner, previous or current occupant, potential purchaser, lessor, or potential lessee of real property. For the purpose of this section, handicap includes a person who had, may have had, has, or may have AIDS, HIV-related illnesses, or HIV infection as defined by the Centers for Disease Control [CDC] of the United States Public Health Service.*

Notice that the TREC rule goes further in describing the specific activities that would be considered discriminatory and potentially actionable under TRELA as grounds for suspension or revocation of a licensee by refining the definition of handicap to include AIDS or HIV-related illnesses identified by the CDC.

Up to this point, the licensee would be relying on and subject to either legal or administrative actions by the courts or by TREC. The following guidelines would be afforded by professional or private organizations.

NAR Code of Ethics. Presuming Sally is a REALTOR® member, the following excerpts from the NAR Code of Ethics would apply to that case study:

> *Article 10*
>
> *REALTORS® shall not deny equal professional services to any person for reasons of race, color, religion, sex, handicap, familial status, national origin or sexual orientation. REALTORS® shall not be party to any plan or agreement to discriminate against a*

person or persons on the basis of race, color, religion, sex, handicap, familial status, national origin, or sexual orientation.

REALTORS®, in their real estate employment practices shall not discriminate against a person or persons on the basis of race, color, religion, sex, handicap, familial status, national origin, or sexual orientation.

Standards of Practice 10-1

When involved in the sale or lease of a residence, REALTORS® shall not volunteer information regarding the racial, religious or ethnic composition of any neighborhood nor shall they engage in any activity which may result in panic selling, however, REALTORS® may provide other demographic information.

Standards of Practice 10-2

When not engaged in the sale or lease of a residence, REALTORS® may provide demographic information related to a property, transaction or professional assignment to a party if such demographic information is (a) deemed by the REALTORS® to be needed to assist with or complete, in a manner consistent with Article 10, a real estate transaction or professional assignment and (b) is obtained or derived from a recognized, reliable, independent, and impartial source. The source of such information and additions, deletions, modification, interpretations, or other changes shall be disclosed in reasonable detail.

Standards of Practice 10-3

REALTORS® shall not print, display or circulate any statement or advertisement with respect to selling or renting of a property that indicates any preference, limitations or discrimination based on race, color, religion, sex, handicap, familial status, national origin, or sexual orientation.

Standards of Practice 10-4

As used in Article 10 "real estate employment practices" relates to employees and independent contractors providing real estate-related services and the administrative and clerical staff directly supporting those individuals.

Company policy. Individual company policy may include all the protected classes noted, as well as others, and may be more directed, if desired. Sally's company policy states the following:

No employee, or associated sales or broker licensee shall deny professional services based on race, color, religion, sex, handicap, familial status, national origin, sexual orientation, or marital status. No employee, or associated sales or broker licensee shall inquire about, respond to or facilitate inquiries about or make a disclosure which indicates or is intended to indicate any preference, limitation or discrimination based on the following: race, color, religion, sex, handicap, familial status, national origin, sexual orientation, or marital status." Sally like other sales associates was required to read and accept the company policy.

Sally's personal beliefs and ethics. Agent Sally also has personal beliefs that guide her actions as a real estate professional. They are as follows:

- Be honest, practice with integrity, and be trustworthy in all circumstances.
- Give the best professional service to all clients and customers.

- Select the best properties for each individual buyer or tenant without regard to personal commission or gain.
- Never put a child in a position of potential danger or harm.
- Never compromise your personal ethics.

Considering all the stakeholders—Sally, the client, the customer, Sally's company, and the public in general—did Sally do the right thing?

Now let's consider another case.

Pam, a single mother, has fallen on relatively hard times. Sales have been slow in her market and most of her backup funds have been used up, and unless things improve soon Pam worries that she may have to consider leaving the business—a business that she truly loves and she believes that she has a great deal to offer buyers and sellers. This weekend, Pam is holding an open house on one of her better listings, a large five-bedroom home in one of the nicer subdivisions, listed at $450,000.

After a fairly slow day, a couple entered the property, and after greeting the prospects, Pam disclosed that she was the seller's agent and invited them to view the property. During the showing, the prospects began to exhibit a definite interest in the property and began questioning Pam about possible financing alternatives and procedures for making an offer. Pam produced the Information About Brokerage Service form and began to explain the agency options. At that point, the prospects interrupted, telling Pam that they had already seen and signed such a form with another agent from a competing company. In fact, they had been shown this house and a number of other properties last week by the other agent. After careful consideration, they had decided to make an offer on this house; however, the other agent was on vacation this week and, upon seeing the open house advertised and fearing that the property might be sold, came directly to Pam to make an offer. Upon further questioning, Pam discovers that the prospects status with the other company is that of customer and that they have not entered into a buyer-representation contract. They would like to make an offer through Pam today. Pam produces the necessary paperwork, completes the offer, which was later delivered to and accepted by the seller.

The following week, the other agent, upon learning of the transaction, threatens legal action, a formal complaint to TREC, and a procuring cause complaint through the local association of REALTORS®.

Consider the levels of guidelines described in the preceding case:

- Federal law
- State law
- Local ordinances
- TRELA
- TREC
- NAR Code of Ethics
- Company code of ethics
- Pam's personal code of ethics

Were the other agent's threats justified? Did Pam do the right thing?

The examples cited in this chapter illustrate the everyday dilemmas faced by real estate licensees across the state and country. Unfortunately, there is not always a clear answer as to what is the legal and/or ethical thing to do in a given set of circumstances. Frequently, actions are justified due to the unique circumstances and conditions under which the decision to act was made. Although sometimes justified, circumstantial ethics (sometimes called relativistic ethics) can be a dangerous road to travel. That is to say, given enough time and thought, we usually can find a way to justify our actions.

Although ethical dilemmas occur in virtually every aspect of real estate practice, those specifically relating to the agency relationship can be the most difficult to sort out. Normally, when we think of agency, we think of the various relationships the licensee broker may have with the public. Seller agency, buyer agency, and intermediary agency relationships were discussed in earlier chapters, along with the duties that accrue to each. However, the other agency relationships also exist—those relating to the relationship between sales licensees and their broker, subagency, and general duties to other cooperating brokers and sales associates in a transaction. Consider some of the following examples.

■ **EXAMPLE** Tom has been an associate with Eager Realty for the past five years. His broker, Helen, recruited Tom into the business, trained him, and helped him out considerably during his trying first year. Tom recently passed his broker's test and is thinking of opening his own office. Knowing the importance of having good agents, Tom has approached several of his co-workers with his plan, and by offering generous commission splits, Tom has received commitments from two of the highest producers to move with him when he opens his own shop. They believe that they can persuade several others to move as well. Tom had made Helen aware of his ambitions to acquire a broker's license, and Helen encouraged and supported his efforts. Tom has not spoken to Helen of his plan to leave the office and open a competing firm.

What, if any, legal or ethical duties does Tom owe to Helen? To the agents he is attempting to recruit? How would you suggest he proceed?

■ **EXAMPLE** Judy, a sales associate, is discontented with her current brokerage company and has decided to transfer her license to a competing brokerage firm. Two of her very expensive listings are going to expire within two weeks. Judy has spoken with both sellers and convinced them not to renew with her current broker when they expire and to list them with her once she moves to her new brokerage firm. In addition, Judy is working with a represented buyer and two nonrepresented buyers and all three have agreed to stick with her when she moves.

What are the legal or ethical issues involved? Is Judy doing the right thing? If not how should this be handled?

■ A PRACTICAL GUIDE FOR EVERYDAY PRACTICE

Earlier in this chapter, reference was made to well-developed models for ethical behavior. Today, many companies invest substantial amounts of money in the formal training of their employees in ethical conduct. From some companies' perspective, such training is an attempt to truly establish an ethical company and help their employees to understand and abide by the company's code of conduct. In others, it may simply be an attempt to cover potential liability if the principals are challenged in court of legal-ethical violations.

Although many programs offer excellent decision-making models, some are quite involved and complex and may require considerable investments of time to reach a conclusion as to the proper actions to follow. Such models are often more practical and appropriate for the major decisions made by large companies that may have major implications for the long term. On the other hand, many times the real estate licensee is faced with making on-the-spot decisions without the luxury of time or input from others. Therefore, a more simple practical guide is needed for day-to-day decisions that take into consideration the following fundamental issues relating to the brokerage company and the individual licensee.

The proposed guide is centered on ten fundamental screening questions relating to the ethical implications of the decision that is to be made. While not a guarantee of ethical behavior, this practical framework should at least help well-meaning managers do the right thing while furthering their organizational goals.

The following discussion and the "Practitioner's Quick Guide" in Figure 11.3 has been adapted for real estate licensees from "Guiding Business Decisions in Today's Organizations."[1] The list that follows itemizes the ten fundamental areas that should be considered by a licensee or a real estate organization when viewing a decision in the context of ethical behavior. It establishes the foundation for the more detailed "Practitioner's Quick Guide" that follows. While the list may not be exhaustive, it addresses certain key elements of the process. The user may wish to add more specifics to the guide in order to customize it to a particular industry or company.

1. **Long-term goals.** How will this action or decision affect the long-term goals of the company and/or licensee?
2. **Short-term benefits**. Are the short-term benefits (quick closing, large commission) outweighed by the effect on the long-term goals?
3. **Interests of immediate stakeholders.** How does this decision impact the interests of the immediate stakeholders (buyers, sellers, selling and cooperating brokers, and sales associates)?
4. **Consumer expectations.** What are the buyer's and the seller's expectations, and how does this decision/action meet those expectations?
5. **Organizational commitment (long and short term).** Are the company and the licensee committed to follow through with the decision (promises of intense advertising or discounted services on future transactions)?
6. **Consequences of decision/policy reversal.** How will all parties be affected if the decision must be reversed?
7. **Regulators and outside stakeholder groups.** What impact will the policy or decision have on outside stakeholder groups (TREC, lenders, appraisers, title companies, etc.)?

---

[1] D. Peeples, P. Stokes, and M. Peeples, "Guiding Business Decisions in Today's Organizations," *Management in Practice*, Vol. 12, No. 2, Spring 2008.

8. **Legality and spirit of the law.** Is the decision/action not only legal but also does it meet the spirit of the law, or does it attempt to circumvent such spirit by seeking loopholes?
9. **Existing contractual and promissory obligations.** Does this decision/action conflict with existing contractual or promissory obligations.
10. **Public scrutiny.** Will this decision/action survive the "daylight test"? How would you feel if it was published in tomorrow's edition of the local newspaper?

Each of the fundamental issues listed is addressed in the Figure 11.3 questionnaire-type "Practitioner's Quick Guide" centered on key questions. The practical outcome is a practitioner's quick and simple guide for brokers, sales associates, and other decision makers within an organization for framing ethical decisions regarding strategy, policies, and/or codes. The guide may be used for a wide variety of decision-making scenarios and throughout the chain of management down to the agent in the field. The format is streamlined so that it may be used easily and quickly and can be adapted to a wide range of business models. It should be noted that not every item will necessarily be addressed with every decision-making process. For example, a major decision such as a broker adding a full-service property management division to the broker's residential real estate company may require an exhaustive application of the entire checklist list, while a comparatively smaller decision, perhaps relating to a possible change in the company's internal bonus structure, may involve only a portion of the checklist. The guide could also be used by agents in the field in a number of ethics-related decisions, such as trying to decide whether to take a listing where there exists the potential for a personal conflict of interest involving a relative or close friend who may be interested in the property. Or perhaps the issue is how to deal with a property listed by the agent's company and which the agent wishes to purchase for personal use. A key value of the checklist is the flexibility and adaptability to a wide variety of ethical decision-making scenarios.

Obviously the guide in Figure 11.3 will not resolve all the issues relating to ethical decision making in all circumstances, but it is offered as a tool to help the decision maker through a logical set of screens to better decision making. If nothing else, the guide can be used as a final check before actually implementing a decision.

An Alternate Solution

Another practical answer for ethical dilemmas lies in perhaps the oldest and most widely accepted code of conduct known as the golden rule: Do unto others as you would want done unto you. Although it may sound simplistic and dismissed by many as naïve or idealistic, the principle of the golden rule is found in almost all world religions and incorporated into almost all codes of ethics established by professional organizations or corporations. It will answer most ethical questions raised in the licensee's interactions with buyers, sellers, other licensees, business entities, and other participants related to the transaction, and the public in general. In addition, it also addresses the ethical issues of an individual's private life as well. As John C. Maxwell states in the title of his book, *There's No Such Thing as Business Ethics: There's Only One Rule for Making Decisions*, business or otherwise—the golden rule. The rule, of course, is the principal of treating others exactly as you would wish to be treated in the same circumstance. The power of the rule lies in

FIGURE 11.3

Practitioner's Quick Guide

A Practitioner's Quick-Guide for Framing Ethical Decisions Regarding Strategy, Policies, and/or Codes

____ 1. Does the decision contribute to the long-term goals and mission of the company and the licensee?

____ 2. Does the decision provide short-term benefits to the company and licensee?

____ 3. Are the interests of the following stakeholders enhanced and/or protected?

    ____ A. Stockholders/Owners   ____ D. Sales associates

    ____ B. Consumers/clients   ____ E. The community

    ____ C. Management   ____ F. Employees

____ 4. Does this decision satisfy the following consumer/stakeholder expectations?

    ____ A. Quality of service

    ____ B. Pricing

    ____ C. Appropriateness to the competency levels of the consumer/user and the licensee?

    ____ D. Risk

____ 5. Are the company and licensee willing and able to support the decision for the long term as well as the short term?

____ 6. How will a subsequent withdrawal or reversal of the decision affect stakeholder interests (buyers, sellers, the company, and sales associates?

____ 7. Does the decision meet the expectations and/or regulations of other stakeholder groups?

    ____ A. Government agencies (regulatory; IRS)?

    ____ B. Independent organizations (local association of REALTORS®, TAR, NAR, etc.)?

    ____ C. General public regarding social concerns for morality, decency, and public acceptability

____ 8. Is the decision legal–and does it also meet the intent of the law?

____ 9. Does the decision fulfill the company's contractual and promissory obligations?

____ 10. Will this decision withstand public scrutiny?

Source: Adapted from D. Peeples, P. Stokes, and M. Peeples, "A Practitioner's Quick-Guide for Guiding Ethical Decisions Regarding Strategy, Policies, and/or Codes" in "Guiding Business Decisions in Today's Organizations," *Management In Practice*, Vol. 12, No. 2, Spring 2008.

its simplicity and broad application. A reflection on the issues of conduct covered in the earlier parts of this chapter reveals that in almost every case, the law or code of proscribed conduct is consistent with the golden rule.

■ WHEN ENOUGH IS NOT ENOUGH—MINIMUM ETHICAL STANDARDS

Even when armed with a basic moral and ethical foundation and solid organizational codes and guidelines to follow, individuals are still put through difficult tests of their ethical mettle. In some cases, following company guidelines for reporting illegal or ethical conduct still does not pass the test of individual responsibility to act. For example, by company policy an employee may meet the company's requirement by reporting violations to an immediate supervisor whose responsibility may be to take either disciplinary action or to report the violation to executives higher in the company hierarchy authorized to take disciplinary action. Once reported, does the employee then have an obligation to follow up to see that appropriate action was taken?

■ **EXAMPLE** Jennifer, a new sales associate with Action Realty, overhears Andy, a senior associate with the firm, offering a cash referral fee to a nonlicensed friend for any business she or any of her friends sends to Andy. Jennifer, knowing that this violates TRELA provisions, follows company policy and reports the violation to her broker who states that she will take care of it. A few weeks later, Jennifer becomes aware that Andy is still making the offer of referral fees and has in fact paid for several referrals from his friends. Jennifer, not wanting to become further involved in the issue, takes no further action deciding that she had done her duty by reporting Andy's conduct to her broker.

Is Jennifer's position justified, or does she have a duty to report the violation to the Real Estate Commission if the broker takes no action?

Suppose Jennifer had observed Andy stealing money from another associate's unguarded purse and became aware that, despite reporting the incident to her broker, no action was taken. Would Jennifer have an obligation to warn other associates or perhaps report the theft to law enforcement? She had, after all, reported the incident to her broker as required by company policy.

It is clear that in certain circumstances, situations may arise in which agents will be able to defend certain actions by showing that they have met all legal requirements and have complied with industry rules and company policy. However, the agents are conflicted because their actions are not compatible with their personal morality.

For example, in Texas, neither an owner nor an agent is required to disclose the location of a registered sex offender living in close proximity to a listed property. Likewise, company policy might not require such disclosure; however, the agent's personal beliefs may dictate that such disclosure should be made to a potential buyer.

In the final analysis, after a potential action has been filtered through the lenses of the law, industry, professional ethical standards, and company policy, the end decision still lies with the individual's personal morality where conscience is the final arbiter.

THE BOTTOM LINE ON ETHICS

In general, most people will never be exposed to formal ethics training. Fortunately, in most cases, certain core beliefs have been inculcated into the young by parents, schools, churches, communities, municipalities, states, and nations. As stated earlier, these core beliefs include respect of others, being truthful and honest, fulfilling promises, and honoring commitments. Most people know the right thing to do. The problem lies in the application of that knowledge. It appears that misconduct is not generally the result of not knowing what is right, but rather in choosing not to do the right thing. Certainly every business has technical and procedural information that must be learned by the new licensee. But, once those matters are mastered, the golden rule applies in almost every case. Test it against virtually every ethical dilemma that you have faced and you will probably agree.

SUMMARY

Public awareness, media coverage, and governmental agencies are focused on the ethical conduct of all businesses today—not just real estate. However, the duties imposed by the law of agency in Texas go beyond the typical business/consumer transaction. Brokers and associates must be cognizant of the rules imposed by federal and state law and the rules and regulations of the TRELA and TREC. Each transaction will be unique and the licensees must consider the impact of their decisions and actions on all the relative stakeholders—buyers, sellers, their own company, as well as the cooperating brokers and related service organizations such as lenders, inspectors, appraisers, and title companies.

The "Practical Guide for Ethical Decision Making" represents one relatively simple and straightforward checklist for the practitioner in the field and could be applied to almost any kind of business. In addition, reliance on the golden rule still offers a firm foundation for business ethics.

KEY POINTS

- The current real estate and general business environment places almost all business practitioners in the public spotlight in relation to ethical conduct.
- Ethical obligations are distinguished from legal obligations as those duties that go beyond the law and focus on not just the legal thing to do, but also the right thing to do.
- Real estate licensees are governed by numerous federal, state, and local laws, the Real Estate License Act and the Rules of the Texas Real Estate Commission. The licensee should be familiar with current law and rules.
- In addition to the above-mentioned laws and regulations, licensees have a duty of ethical conduct that in some cases has been formalized by professional organizations such as NAR, TAR, local REALTOR® associations, and other professional groups.
- Decisions and actions by licensees should be reviewed in the light of long- and short-term goals of the company and the individual licensee. Consideration should be given to the impact on all relative stakeholders, the ability

to follow through, as well as the negative implications should the decision be reversed in the future. All decisions and actions should be able to stand-up to the light-of-day test.
- While ethics models and practical guides such as the one presented in this chapter may be found useful for licensees in deciding ethical points of decisions and actions, the golden rule is still considered a baseline in the these matters.

■ SUGGESTIONS FOR BROKERS

Even though sponsored licensees may have agreed to an industry code of ethics such as the NAR COE, brokers would be well advised today to adopt and implement a written company code of conduct for sponsored licensees within the company framework. Further, all employees and associates would be required to sign statements indicating that they have read, understand, and agree to abide by the code. Such codes provide an excellent vehicle for training new agents, as well as evidence that the company is committed to good service and ethical conduct. Many companies have found these documents extremely useful during court proceedings.

CHAPTER 11 QUIZ

1. Which of the following is enforceable only by conscience?
   a. Laws
   b. Morals
   c. Ethics
   d. Rules

2. The Rules of the Texas Real Estate Commission are created by
   a. statutory law.
   b. civil law.
   c. administrative law.
   d. criminal law.

3. Disputes relating to commissions between REALTOR® are settled by
   a. an arbitration committee.
   b. civil courts.
   c. justice courts.
   d. court-appointed arbitrators.

4. Failing, within a reasonable time, to respond to inquiries from a seller regarding marketing activities or efforts on the part of the listing broker would violate
   a. legal obligations.
   b. moral obligations.
   c. ethical obligations.
   d. no obligations.

5. Broker Beta invested considerable time and effort in showing properties to a nonrepresented buyer. The buyer subsequently purchased a home Beta had been shown him previously, but he purchased directly through the listing company—excluding Beta. Beta believes he is entitled to share in the commission; the listing broker disagrees. This is an example of
   a. discrimination.
   b. contractual dispute.
   c. regulatory dispute.
   d. procuring cause dispute.

6. The quick Guide for ethical decision making presented in this chapter does not consider which of the following?
   a. Existing contractual and promissory obligations
   b. Public scrutiny
   c. Commission rates
   d. Consumer expectations

7. Which statements is *TRUE*?
   a. An action may be legal but unethical.
   b. An action may be ethical but illegal.
   c. An action may be immoral but legal.
   d. All these are true.

8. Almost all codes of ethics include reference to which of the following?
   a. The preamble
   b. The golden rule
   c. Religious doctrine
   d. Legal doctrine

9. Given the current business environment, from a legal perspective, real estate practitioners should be keenly aware of
   a. consumer trends.
   b. housing availability.
   c. public scrutiny.
   d. alternate financing methods.

10. A sales licensee who receives an undisclosed direct bonus payment from a customer buyer would violate which of the following?
    a. Ethical behavior
    b. TRELA
    c. TREC rules
    d. All of these

DISCUSSION QUESTIONS

1. Sales associate James with Alpha Realty observed that a competitor's listing had been on the market for several months without selling. James contacted the property owners, discovered that the existing exclusive-right-to-sell listing with the other broker would expire in ten days, and secured an appointment with the sellers that evening. James convinced the seller to sign an exclusive-right-to-sell listing with his company that would begin immediately upon expiration of the existing listing. What are the legal and/or ethical considerations of James' actions, if any?

2. Sheila, a listing agent, had prepared an offer from her own represented buyer to present to her seller client acting under a duly authorized intermediary agreement. Subsequent to presenting the offer to the seller, a competing offer was presented to her from another brokerage company. The offers were essentially the same; however, the competing offer was for $500 more than the offer from Sheila's client. That evening Sheila presented both offers to the sellers but offered to reduce her commission by $750 in order to have her buyer's contract accepted, although no pre-existing variable-rate commission agreement was in place. The sellers accepted Sheila's offer. What are the legal and/or ethical considerations created by Sheila's actions?

3. Jim Bob, an agent with Right On Realty, decided to move his license to a competing firm. Before leaving his current company, Jim Bob contacted the sellers of his current listings, as well as all his current prospective buyers. He informed them of his upcoming move and encouraged them to contact the broker for Right On Realty and request that the broker terminate their existing contracts so that they could enter into new contracts with Jim Bob's new broker. What are the legal and/or ethical ramifications of Jim Bob's actions?

4. Broker Alex, a buyer's representative, makes an appointment through broker Betsy to show a property listed by Betsy's company. Alex discloses to Betsy that he is representing the buyer. During the conversation, Betsy tells Alex that the sellers are in the middle of a very messy divorce and are getting desperate to sell. Betsy relates this information to his buyer. The buyer as a result makes a very low offer which is subsequently accepted by the sellers. What are the legal and/or ethical ramifications of the actions of Alex and Betsy?

5. Give an example of your opinion of the following:
   a. An act that is legal but unethical
   b. An act that is ethical but illegal
   c. An act that is legal but immoral

CHAPTER 12

Deceptive Trade Practices and Consumer Protection Act

The previous chapter focused on the ethical responsibilities of licensees and pointed out that if certain basic ethical principles were adhered to, perhaps there would be no need for regulatory agencies or the courts for that matter. Unfortunately, in this less than perfect world, these principles sometimes breakdown and matters must be resolved through the formal processes of the law.

No evidence exists that misrepresentation and fraud are more prevalent in the real estate industry than in other sectors of the economy. If, however, deceptive acts occur in a real estate transaction, they may have a greater impact than in other areas for several reasons.

First, most real estate transactions involve large sums of money; as a result, people who feel deceived are more apt to take action to assert their rights. Second, licensing laws have placed substantial supervisory responsibility on brokers for the conduct of associated licensees. Deception or fraud committed by associated licensees can subject brokers to liability, including loss of license. Finally, in many transactions, little direct contact takes place between buyer and seller. Because information is often transmitted through a third party, misunderstanding and error can result in the buyer, the seller, or both feeling that they have been deceived. In fact, Texas holds through common law that the consumer is "ignorant, unthinking, and credulous" (*Spradling v. Williams*, 566 S.W.2d 561 [Tex. 1978]). Being naïve and unknowledgeable, consumers therefore have the right to believe and to rely on information regarding a property furnished to them by sellers—or in some cases information given by sellers' agents.

LEARNING OBJECTIVES

This chapter addresses the following:

- Applicability: Real Estate Broker and Salesperson Exemption from the DPTA: SB 1353
- Fraud versus Misrepresentation
- Deceptive Trade Practices and Consumer Protection Act
  - Definitions of Terms
  - Deceptive Acts
  - Verbal and Nonverbal Communications
  - Waivers of Rights under the DTPA
  - Notice and Inspection
  - Exemptions
  - Unconscionable Action
  - Producing Cause
- Damages
- Defenses
  - Unsuccessful Defenses
  - Groundless Lawsuits
- Ethical and Legal Concerns

APPLICABILITY: REAL ESTATE BROKER AND SALESPERSON EXEMPTION FROM THE DPTA: SB 1353

The Deceptive Trade Practices and Consumer Protection Act (DTPA) was passed by the Texas legislature in 1973. As the act was originally drafted, real estate transactions were excluded from coverage. In 1975, the act was amended to include transactions involving real property purchased or leased for use. As a result of allowing the DTPA to be directly applied to the professional services of brokers and salespeople, a large number of lawsuits were generated based on "acts of omission or the advice or opinion" of real estate practitioners that the consumer later believed to be in error. Although many suits were justified, many brokers and salespersons found themselves faced with lawsuits concerning circumstances over which they had no control or knowledge. Even when successful in their defenses, the economic and emotional costs could be overwhelming.

In 2011, the Texas legislature passed SB 1353 which amended the DTPA to once again exempt real estate brokers and salespersons as follows:

S.B. No. 1353

AN ACT

BE IT ENACTED BY THE LEGISLATURE OF THE STATE OF TEXAS:

SECTION 1. Section 17.49, Business & Commerce Code, is amended by adding Subsection (i) to read as follows:

(i) Nothing in this subchapter shall apply to a claim against a person licensed as a broker or salesperson under Chapter 1101, Occupations Code, arising from an act or omission by the person while acting as a broker or salesperson. This exemption does not apply to: (1) an express misrepresentation of a material fact that cannot be characterized as advice, judgment, or opinion; (2) a failure to disclose information in violation of Section 17.46(b)(24); or (3) an unconscionable action or course of action that cannot be characterized as advice, judgment, or opinion.

SECTION 2. Subsection (i), Section 17.49, Business & Commerce Code, as added by this Act, applies only to a claim arising from an act or omission that occurs on or after the effective date of this Act. A claim arising from an act or omission that occurred before the effective date of this Act is governed by the law in effect on the date the act or omission occurred, and the former law is continued in effect for that purpose.

Not surprisingly, the amendment has been met with enthusiastic approval and a sense of relief by Texas practitioners. However, licensees should pay close attention to the actions to which the exemption does not apply. In essence, licensees will not be held liable for innocent acts of omission, or advice or opinion given without an attempt to defraud or deceive. It is hoped that this exemption will place a greater burden of proof of intended deception or fraud on plaintiffs in order for the DTPA to be used in a legal action against the licensee. It should be kept firmly in mind that only future case law will actually determine how helpful the exemption will prove to be. It should also be understood that purposeful acts of fraud or deception will be subject to the full force and effect of the DTPA. For these reasons, the DTPA should be studied and understood by Texas real estate licensees.

FRAUD VERSUS MISREPRESENTATION

Fraud is a deceptive act practiced deliberately by one person in an attempt to gain an unfair advantage over another. There is always the intention to deceive. The elements of a cause of action for fraud are

- an intentional false representation of material facts, either past or present;
- reliance on the false representation by the person taking action; and
- damage as a result of the action taken based on the false representation.

Because of the very strict requirements to prove fraud, it is not as frequently pursued in court actions involving real estate transactions.

Misrepresentation, on the other hand, is a false statement made negligently or innocently that is a material factor in another's decision to contract. There does not have to be an intention to deceive. As will be shown later in this chapter, many real estate cases involved property owners and/or licensees unintentionally making false statements regarding material facts. Showing proof of misrepresentation is considerably easier than proving fraud; thus, court actions involving real estate frequently pursue this course. *See* Figure 12.1 for a comparison of fraud and misrepresentation.

FIGURE 12.1

Comparison of Actions for Fraud and Misrepresentation

Cause of Action	Factors to Be Proven	Remedies
Common-Law Fraud (From decisions in court cases)	Was a false statement made?	Rescission
	Was it made intentionally or negligently?	Actual damages
	Was the misstatement a material fact?	Actual damages and rescission
	Was the misstatement relied on?	Exemplary damages (to punish)
	Was anyone injured?	
Statutory Fraud (From laws enacted by the legislature)	Same factors as for common-law fraud	Same remedies as for common-law fraud
	Was the false promise made with intent not to perform?	Attorney fees, court costs, and expert witness fees
	Did the person who benefited from the misrepresentation know that it had been made and fail to disclose the truth?	
Deceptive Trade Practices and Consumer Protection Act	Were any specifically listed acts committed?	Economic damages
	Were any deceptive acts committed?	Damages for mental anguish
	Were any misleading statements made?	Up to 3 × economic and mental anguish damages
	Were any false statements made, including innocent misstatements?	Attorney fees and court costs
	Was an unconscionable act or course of action practiced against the victim?	
	Were any of the acts listed above the producing cause of harm to the victim?	

■ DECEPTIVE TRADE PRACTICES AND CONSUMER PROTECTION ACT

Adopted in 1973, the Deceptive Trade Practices Consumer Protection Act (DTPA) is a state law that is "intended to be liberally construed and applied to promote its underlying purposes," which are to protect Texas consumers against

- false, misleading, and deceptive business practices;
- unconscionable actions; and
- breaches of warranty.

This law creates a powerful weapon for consumers. It is effective for two reasons. First, proving that a deceptive act has occurred is easier under this law than under previous real estate statutes and even common law. Second, the law provides that consumers may recover more than their actual losses. Although an injured party can recover punitive (punishing) damages for fraud, the DTPA does not require proof that the defendant intended to deceive or mislead. The mere occurrence of a deceptive act or omission, even if done without the intent to deceive, can result in damages in excess of the actual economic loss. Ostensibly, the exemption described will protect licensees from this provision of the DTPA. Or, more specifically, the DTPA will apparently not apply unless there was an attempt to deceive by the licensee and simple acts of omission or misrepresentation would not be actionable.

From a historical perspective, the first use of the DTPA in the real estate area involved cases concerning breach of warranty in the sale of new residential properties. The initial draft of the law allowed a consumer to recover three times the amount of actual damages suffered because of defective or unworkmanlike construction in a new home purchase. This generous remedy prompted consumers to bring all breach of warranty cases under the DTPA. In recent years, the law has been used by consumers against sellers of existing homes, brokers, and lenders. The law no longer provides for the automatic trebling of damages (triple the amount of damages); however, it still allows for a recovery of damages in excess of actual economic loss.

Definitions of Terms

The DTPA includes specific definitions of 13 words or phrases that are used in the act. As you read the following sections you should keep in mind that if a DTPA lawsuit goes to court, the attorneys will be using these definitions in attempting to prove or disprove their cases, and the judge and/or jury will use these definitions in their conclusions. The following 13 definitions are found in Section 17.45 of the act:

1. *"Goods" means tangible chattels or real property purchased or leased for use.*

2. *"Services" means work, labor, or service purchased or leased for use, including services furnished in connection with the sale or repair of goods.*

3. *"Person" means an individual, partnership, corporation, association, or other group, however organized.*

4. *"Consumer" means an individual, partnership, corporation, this state, or a subdivision or agency of this state who seeks or acquires by purchase or lease, any goods or services, except that the term does not include a business consumer that has assets of $25 million or more, or that is owned or controlled by a corporation or entity with assets of $25 million or more.*

5. *"Unconscionable action or course of action" means an act or practice that, to a consumer's detriment, takes advantage of the lack of knowledge, ability, experience, or capacity of the consumer to a grossly unfair degree.*

6. *"Trade" and "commerce" mean the advertising, offering for sale, sale, lease, or distribution of any good or service, of any property, tangible or intangible, real, personal, or mixed, and any other article, commodity, or thing of value, wherever situated, and shall include any trade or commerce directly or indirectly affecting the people of this state.*

7. *"Documentary material" includes the original or a copy of any book, record, report, memorandum, paper, communication, tabulation, map, chart, photograph, mechanical transcription, or other tangible document or recording, wherever situated.*

8. *"Consumer protection division" means the antitrust and consumer protection division of the attorney general's office.*

9. *"Knowingly" means actual awareness, at the time of the act or practice complained of, of the falsity, deception, or unfairness of the act or practice giving rise to the consumer's claim or, in an action brought under Subdivision (2) of*

Subsection (a) of Section 17.50, actual awareness of the act, practice, condition, defect, or failure constituting the breach of warranty, but actual awareness may be inferred where objective manifestations indicate that a person acted with actual awareness.

10. *"Business consumer" means an individual, partnership, or corporation who seeks or acquires by purchase or lease any goods or services for commercial or business use. The term does not include this state or a subdivision or agency of this state.*

11. *"Economic damages" means compensatory damages for pecuniary loss, including costs of repair and replacement. The term does not include exemplary damages or damages for physical pain and mental anguish, loss of consortium, disfigurement, physical impairment, or loss of companionship and society.*

12. *"Residence" means a building: (A) that is a single-family house, duplex, triplex, quadruplex, or a unit in a multiunit residential structure in which title to the individual units is transferred to the owners under a condominium or cooperative system; and (B) that is occupied or to be occupied as the consumer's residence.*

13. *"Intentionally" means actual awareness of the falsity, deception, or unfairness of the act or practice, or the condition, defect, or failure constituting a breach of warranty giving rise to the consumer's claim, coupled with the specific intent that the consumer act in detrimental reliance on the falsity or deception or in detrimental ignorance of the unfairness. Intention may be inferred from objective manifestations that indicate that the person acted intentionally or from facts showing that a defendant acted with flagrant disregard of prudent and fair business practices to the extent that the defendant should be treated as having acted intentionally.*

Deceptive Acts

The act prohibits all false, misleading, and deceptive acts in the conduct of business. The law lists a number of specific activities that violate the act. Although an awareness of the enumerated prohibited acts is important, a violation of the act is not limited to those listed and could include any type of deceptive act committed in a consumer transaction. The enumerated acts in Section 17.46—commonly called the laundry list—include, among others, the

(1) *passing off goods or services as those of another;*

(2) *causing confusion or misunderstanding as to the source, sponsorship, approval, or certification of goods or services;*

(3) *causing confusion or misunderstanding as to affiliation, connection or association with, or certification by another;*

(4) *using deceptive representations or designations of geographic origin in connection with goods or services;*

(5) *representing that goods or services have sponsorship, approval, characteristics, ingredients, uses, benefits, or quantities that they do not have or that a person has a sponsorship, approval, status, affiliation, or connection that he does not;*

(6) representing that goods are original or new if they are deteriorated, reconditioned, reclaimed, used, or secondhand;

(7) representing that goods or services are of a particular standard, quality, or grade, or that goods are of a particular style or model, if they are of another;

(8) disparaging the goods, services, or business of another by false or misleading representation of facts;

(9) advertising goods or services with intent not to sell them as advertised;

(10) making false or misleading statements of fact concerning the reasons for, existence of, or amount of price reductions;

(11) representing that an agreement confers or involves rights, remedies, or obligations that it does not have or involve or that are prohibited by law;

(12) knowingly making false or misleading statements of fact concerning the need for parts, replacement, or repair service;

(13) misrepresenting the authority of a salesperson, representative, or agent to negotiate the final terms of a consumer transaction; . . .

(22) representing that work or services have been performed on, or parts replaced in, goods when the work or services were not performed or the parts replaced;
. . .

(24) failing to disclose information concerning goods or services which was known at the time of the transaction if such failure to disclose such information was intended to induce the consumer into a transaction into which the consumer would not have entered had the information been disclosed;

(25) using the term "corporation," "incorporated," or an abbreviation of either of those terms in the name of a business entity that is not incorporated under the laws of this state or another jurisdiction; . . .

(27) taking advantage of a disaster declared by the governor under Chapter 418, Government Code, by:

(A) selling or leasing fuel, food, medicine, or another necessity at an exorbitant or excessive price; or

(B) demanding an exorbitant or excessive price in connection with the sale or lease of fuel, food, medicine, or another necessity.

At first glance, many of the prohibited acts listed here appear to not be applicable to real estate transactions—for instance, those sections pertaining to repairs. Real estate licensees often find that the parties require that repairs be completed before the closing of a sale or in conjunction with property management contracts. Licensees must exercise care when involved in these aspects of transactions.

Two aspects of the enumerated acts are important to remember. First, in general application, the DTPA does not require that the consumer prove the offending party intended to deceive or misrepresent the facts. In most cases, an innocent misrepresentation is as much a violation of the act as a fraudulent misrepresentation; it is not a defense to a lawsuit brought under this act that the defendant did not know that the action was illegal. Second, the act prohibits not only misrepresentations but also misleading statements, statements that lead the consumer in the wrong direction or create a misconception of the facts. Now, because of the 2011 exemption, it is presumed that the DTPA will not apply to licensees unless it can be shown that there was an actual attempt to defraud the consumer.

Applying the laundry list of acts statutorily defined as deceptive, the following acts by licensees could still make the licensee liable for a cause of action lawsuit under the DTPA:

- Placing a listing on a Web page that is actually a listing of another firm, thus diverting a buyer's call to the licensee's office rather than directly to the listing office
- Telling a buyer that the recently installed counter is granite when in fact it is "faux" granite
- Telling the buyer that the tub in the master bath is a Jacuzzi when it is actually a generic spa
- Advertising that a property will come with a general warranty deed when in fact the seller will only convey title with a special warranty
- Telling a buyer that the seller cut the tree down because it was rubbing against the roof when in fact the tree was causing major foundation problems
- Telling the buyer that the sellers had replaced the fan on the inside air-conditioning unit when in fact they had not
- Guaranteeing an investor that a property will appreciate 20 percent over the next two years
- Sponsoring a lottery drawing promising the house will go to the purchaser of the winning ticket
- Failing to self-identify as acting as a subagent while showing a property to a prospective buyer, thus leading the buyer to believe that the licensee was the buyer's agent
- As a property manager, suddenly doubling the rent on apartments rented to families displaced by a recent tornado
- Telling a buyer that the new air conditioner meets the new 13 SEER requirement when it does not
- Telling the buyer that the house was built by XYZ Builder when in fact it was ABC Builders

If a licensee has been found liable in a DTPA lawsuit, the court cannot suspend or revoke a real estate license; however, TRELA contains provisions for suspending or revoking a license for similar violations. Some of the provisions of TRELA § 1101.652 that address actions corresponding with the DTPA are

- conduct that constitutes dishonest dealings, bad faith, or untrustworthiness (1101.652(b)(2));
- making a material misrepresentation or failing to disclose to a potential purchaser any latent structural defect or any other defect known to the broker or salesperson. Latent structural defects and other defects do not refer to trivial or insignificant defects but refer to those defects that would be a significant factor to a reasonable and prudent purchaser in making a decision to purchase (§ 1101.652(b)(3);(4));
- pursuing a continued and flagrant course of misrepresentation or making of false promises through agents, salespersons, advertising, or otherwise (§ 1101.652(b)(6));

- failing to make clear to all parties in a transaction which party he is acting for, or receiving compensation from more than one party except with the full knowledge and consent of all parties (§ 1101.652(b)(7);(8));
- accepting, receiving, or charging an undisclosed commission, rebate, or direct profit on expenditures made for a principal (§ 1101.652(b)(13));
- soliciting, selling, or offering for sale real property under a scheme or program that constitutes a lottery or deceptive practice (§ 1101.652(b)(14); (15));
- guaranteeing, authorizing, or permitting a person to guarantee that future profits will result from a resale of real property (§ 1101.652(b)(17)); and
- inducing or attempting to induce a party to a contract of sale or lease to break the contract for the purpose of substituting in lieu thereof a new contract (§ 1101.652(b)(21)).

Verbal and Nonverbal Communications

Licensees must be aware of both verbal and nonverbal communications with customers and clients. TRELA follows and expands on many of the prohibitions of the DTPA, and licensees can assume that a customer or client who files a DTPA suit also will file a complaint with the Texas Real Estate Commission. The following case demonstrates how liability can occur, even though no verbal representation had been made to the party that claimed there had been a violation of the DTPA.

- **EXAMPLE** In *Orkin Exterminating Co., Inc. v. LeSassier*, 688 S.W.2d 651 (Tex. Civ. App. 9 Dist. 1985), Ms. LeSassier contracted with Orkin Exterminating Co., Inc., for termite extermination services. On the date the serviceperson came to Ms. LeSassier's home, she let him in and then returned to her employment. Almost a year later, she noticed evidence of termite activity. An Orkin employee returned and treated her home. When she continued to have problems, she hired another firm of exterminators. She had the damage to her home repaired and sued Orkin, alleging violation of the DTPA in that Orkin had "represented that work or services had been performed when such work or services had not been performed." Orkin's defense was that the DTPA did not apply because Orkin made no verbal assertion that it had performed the termite treatment. The court held that the serviceperson's coming to Ms. LeSassier's home, beginning treatments, and then leaving, never to return, was a representation that all the treatments called for in the contract had been performed.

While licensees are not responsible for performing repairs, they could be named in a DTPA suit as a result of recommending a particular serviceperson or company to a client or customer who subsequently believes that the DTPA has been violated.

Waivers of Rights under the DTPA

Under certain circumstances, consumers may wish to waive their rights under the DTPA. For example, a buyer may wish to purchase a property in obviously poor condition. The seller, however, fearful of a lawsuit related to the condition of the property after the sale, may refuse to sell the property to the buyer unless the buyer agrees to waive the right to sue the seller under the DTPA.

In this case, the buyer may be willing to waive the right in order to acquire the property. In general, however, a waiver of the right to bring action is considered to be "contrary to public policy and is unenforceable and void" (§ 17.42(a)). This prohibition of waiver of rights had been virtually absolute until 1995, when the act was amended to allow consumers to waive their rights under certain *very* strict guidelines. A written waiver is valid and enforceable if

- it is in writing and signed by the consumer;
- the consumer is represented by an attorney, in purchasing the goods or services, who is not directly or indirectly involved in or suggested by, or identified by the defendant or the defendant's agent; and
- the consumer is not in a significantly disparate bargaining position.

The waiver is required to be in conspicuous, boldface type that is at least 10-point in size, and must be titled "Waiver of Consumer Rights" or words of similar meaning. The body of the waiver must have wording similar to the following:

> *I waive my right under the Deceptive Trade Practice Consumer Protection Act, Section 17.41 et seq., Business & Commerce Code, a law that gives consumers special rights and protections. After consultation with an attorney of my own selection, I voluntarily consent to this waiver (Sec. 17.42(c)(3)).*

One of the greatest concerns in real estate contracts has been whether a property that is purchased in "as is" condition is subject to DTPA. The following case is clear as to commercial buyers.

■ **EXAMPLE** In *The Prudential Insurance Company v. Jefferson Associates, Ltd.*, 896 S.W.2d. 156 (Texas 1995), F. B. Goldman purchased a four-story office building from Prudential Insurance in 1984 on an "as is" basis. The purchaser was allowed full access to the property to conduct inspections, which he did. In fact, Mr. Goldman had an independent engineering firm, his maintenance supervisor, and his property manager inspect the property. The inspections showed no evidence that the building contained asbestos. After the sale, Goldman conveyed the property to the limited partnership, Jefferson Associates, Ltd., of which he was a partner. Several years after the sale, it was discovered that the building had a fireproofing material that contained asbestos. Goldman sued under DTPA.

The Supreme Court of Texas concluded that there was no evidence that Prudential had knowledge of the asbestos and therefore could not disclose its existence. They also noted that the purchase price reflected the "as is" terms, and that the purchaser was responsible for accepting the risk involved in such a transaction. The court ruling stated, "A buyer who agrees, freely and without fraudulent inducement, to purchase commercial real estate 'as is' cannot recover damages from the seller when the property is later discovered not to be in as good a condition as the buyer believed it was when he inspected it before the sale." The sales contract was clear regarding the buyer's duty to satisfy himself as to condition and that he was waiving his rights to action under the DTPA.

The courts are very careful to consider all the facts in each case. It appears that courts place more responsibility on the buyer in a commercial transaction than in a residential transaction. This may be due to the assumption that commercial buyers are generally more knowledgeable, may be more likely to seek advice and opinions from experts, and may be better able to assess their risks than average residential buyers.

However, in *Prudential v. Jefferson*, the Texas Supreme Court noted that for an "as is" agreement to be effective, it must stand up to the following tests:

1. All known defects must be disclosed by the seller.
2. The seller must not obstruct the buyer's attempts to inspect the property.
3. The "as is" clause must be an important element of the contract, not an incidental or boilerplate provision.
4. The buyer and the seller must not be in disparate (relatively unequal) bargaining positions.

Subsequently, an appellate court used the *Prudential v. Jefferson* case in deciding the following "as is" residential property case, even though the purchaser was never required to sign a waiver of his rights under DTPA.

■ **EXAMPLE** In *Erwin v. Smiley*, 975 S.W.2d 335 (Tex. App. 1998), Archie and Maxine Erwin sold their property to David Smiley in "as is" condition. On several occasions prior to entering in the purchase agreement, Smiley inspected the property. On one occasion Smiley asked Mr. Erwin whether there had been termite problems. Mr. Erwin said that there had been termites and that they had remedied the problem. The purchase contract was drawn on a preprinted form showing in the "Property Condition" section that the "Buyer accepts the Property in its present condition, subject only to any lender required repairs and as is." "As is" was typed into the blank supplied on the contract.

Approximately six months after Mr. Smiley bought the house, he noticed termite trails. He had the house inspected by a termite contractor who found live termite infestation and said that he saw no evidence that the house had ever been treated for termites. The contractor also gave the opinion that the house had been infested for five to ten years. Smiley sued.

The jury in the lower court found that Archie Erwin committed false, misleading, or deceptive acts or practices and awarded Smiley $15,000 to treat and/or repair the termite damage, and $30,000 in attorney's fees. The Erwins appealed.

The appellate court observed, "The validity of the 'as is' agreement is determined in light of the sophistication of the parties, the terms of the 'as is' agreement, whether the 'as is' clause was freely negotiated, whether it was an arm's length transaction, and whether there was a knowing misrepresentation or concealment of a known fact." The court went on to say, "The evidence shows that the Erwins and Smiley were similarly situated parties and that the sale was an arm's-length transaction. This transaction involved the sale of a residence. . . . Further, both parties were represented by counsel, and there was no evidence of a special relationship between the parties which would keep it from being an arm's length transaction. The evidence also shows that the 'as is' provision was freely negotiated, not merely 'boilerplate' language in the preprinted earnest money contract form; it was specifically added. There was evidence that, during the negotiations, Archie made Smiley aware that the sale was on an 'as is' basis. Smiley consulted his attorney before signing the earnest money contract. Furthermore, Smiley testified that he did not rely on any statement that Archie Erwin made regarding the meaning of the 'as is' term." The appellate court reversed the decision of the lower court in favor of the Erwins.

This case shows that the courts are beginning to use the same standard for residential transactions as for commercial transactions. This could be due to the greater sophistication of many sellers and purchasers in today's real estate market, and the greater number of principals who are seeking legal advice during the negotiating process.

The "as is" clause is now expressly stated in the TREC-promulgated contracts (paragraph 7D) and meets the requirement of the DTPA of not being "boiler plate." In fact, it requires the parties to negotiate the scope of the "as-is" provision. Pursuant to this clause, buyers accept the property "in its present condition; provided Seller, at Seller's expense, shall" complete whatever repairs or treatments the buyers specifies. Absent fraudulent inducement, a purchaser should therefore not be able to sue the seller or the broker because a property turns out not be as they expected. The burden is on the plaintiff to prove the seller or the broker had actual knowledge of a defect, as reinforced in the following recent case.

■ **EXAMPLE** In *Boehl v. Boley*, 2011 WL 238348 (Tex. App., Amarillo, 2011), the Boehls made an offer to purchase a property owned by Boley using he TREC-promulgated One-to-Four Family Residential (Resale) Contract. Before entering into the contract, Boley indicated on the seller's disclosure that the water well had 280 feet of water in it and that he had never had any problems with the well. In paragraph 7D, the Boehls negotiated several specific repairs not related to the water well. Shortly after closing, the Boehls began experiencing problems and an inspection revealed the well was going dry and would require extensive repairs. They then sued for DTPA violations, fraud, negligent and fraudulent representations, and breach of contract.

■ **DISCUSSION** The court ruled in favor of the Boleys, finding that Boehls specifically negotiated the scope of the "as is" provision by specifying what repairs had to be made before they would accept the property "in its current condition." The Boehls provided no evidence that they were fraudulently induced into the contract; no evidence that they were hindered in their inspections (in fact, they did not have the well inspected, even though they paid extra for an option to withdraw); and no evidence that the Boleys or their broker knew of the actual condition of the well. Before the change to the DTPA in 2011, the Boehls might have pursued litigation against the broker for even the innocent misrepresentation regarding the water well and thus recovered at least actual damages plus court costs and legal fees. Now the plaintiff must prove actual knowledge and intent to deceive, charges much more difficult to prove.

Notice and Inspection

Before filing a lawsuit under DTPA, a consumer must give the would-be defendant a 60-day notice of intent to bring suit and must provide "reasonable detail of the consumer's specific complaint and the amount of economic damages, damages for mental anguish, and expenses, including attorneys' fees" (§ 17.505(a)). The defendant then may inspect the goods that are the basis of the intended action and attempt to settle the matter with the consumer.

The defendant can make an offer to settle the matter with the consumer. The law states that an offer to settle is not admission of guilt or wrongdoing. Often a defendant wants to settle just to avoid the cost and aggravation of a lawsuit.

If the defendant makes an offer to settle the matter and the consumer rejects the settlement, the defendant may file the offer with the court. If the court finds that the offer was "the same as, substantially the same as, or more than the damage found by the trier of fact (judge or jury], the consumer may not recover as damages any amount in excess of the *lesser* of

1. the amount of damages tendered in the settlement offer; or
2. the amount of damages found by the trier of fact" (§ 17.5052(g)).

If the court finds that the settlement offer was fair, it will determine what reasonable attorneys' fees would have been before the offer was rejected and use that amount in calculating the total settlement. The consumer could not recover the attorneys' fees incurred for representation in court.

Exemptions

In the past, most transactions could fall under the guidelines of the DTPA. The 1995 amendment provided for some exemptions important to real estate. The following exemption from prohibition against waiver under Section 17.49(f) may apply if the transaction is the result of a written contract and meets the following criteria:

- The contract relates to a transaction, a project, or a set of transactions related to the same project involving total consideration by the consumer of more than $100,000.
- In negotiating the contract, the consumer is represented by legal counsel who is not directly or indirectly identified, suggested, or selected by the defendant or an agent of the defendant.
- The contract does not involve the consumer's residence.
- All transactions, whether written or not, that have consideration that exceeds $500,000. This exemption does not include a consumer's residence (§ 17.49(g)).

There was another general DTPA exemption under Section 17.49(c) passed in 1995 that exempted conduct based on "opinion, advice, judgment, or professional skill" that led many to believe that brokers would fall under this exemption and that therefore the DTPA would not apply. Subsequent case law, however, generally disproved that theory. The loophole in the exemption was based on conduct that would constitute misrepresentation, misconduct, or negligence on the part of the agent. Virtually all consumer suits brought against brokers were DTPA suits in which the plaintiff attempted not only to prove misrepresentation or misconduct, but further, that the broker "willfully and knowingly" committed such acts.

This general exemption regarding professional services, however, has now been made specific to real estate transaction under the 2011 amendment to the DTPA noted earlier in this chapter. While the general exemption in 1995 did not prove very effective in insulating real estate licensees, it is hoped that this new specific language will be more helpful. Only after the provision is tested in the courts will the true impact be determined.

The problem is the ambiguity inherent to the phrase "professional service," which is defined under DTPA as a service that provides "advice, judgment, opinion, or similar professional skill."

■ **EXAMPLE** Mary, designated broker for Lake Country Realty, Inc., is asked to provide a competitive market analysis (CMA) for a property owned by Dr. Lang in a large subdivision. Most properties in the subdivision are of similar construction and size with three bedrooms and two baths. Over the years, Dr. Lang, however, has added a small office and a half-bath to his home. So Mary obtains data on nine comparable properties in the subdivision and then makes upward adjustments to her recommended listing price based on the addition of the half-bath and office. Ultimately, the property sells for slightly more than the other properties with no half-bath or office, but considerably less than Mary had projected. Based on this scenario, Mary's services would probably not serve as the basis for a cause of action under the DTPA.

■ **EXAMPLE** Gerald, a sales associate for Coastal Realty, is contacted by his friend Harry. Harry is in a hurry to sell but says he will list the property with Gerald if Gerald will market it for $318,000. Without conducting a CMA, Gerald takes the listing at $318,000 and does nothing more than put the listing in the MLS and place a For Sale sign on the property. Nine months later the property goes into foreclosure when Harry is unable to keep up with the mortgage payments. This service could probably serve as the basis for DTPA claim because it does not involve matters of advice, judgment, or professional opinion.

Even if services provided by the broker fall within the DTPA definition of professional services, the exemption from liability under DTPA do not apply to the following:

- An express misrepresentation of a material fact that cannot be characterized as advice, judgment or opinion
- An unconscionable action or course of action that cannot be characterized as advice, judgment, or opinion
- Breach of an express warranty that cannot be characterized as advice, judgment, or opinion

Unconscionable Action

The DTPA also provides that a consumer can sue if the consumer has suffered economic damages produced by unconscionable action by another. Unconscionable action is a form of deception. Equitable relief can be afforded to a person who has been tricked or swindled to such an extent that it would be unfair to allow the transaction to stand. "Unconscionable" is a difficult legal concept to grasp because it is intentionally vague. In the case that follows, the Texas Supreme Court provides some guidance in understanding the type of action prohibited.

■ **EXAMPLE** In *Smith v. Levine*, 911 S.W.2d 427 (Tex. App. 1995), the Smiths decided to sell a property they had previously leased. The tenant was interested in purchasing the house and had a structural inspection performed. The written report stated that the foundation "has deflected to the extent that it has damaged the superstructure and therefore the foundation is defective." The tenant decided against purchasing the property; however, he offered to give the seller a copy of the report if he would reimburse him for one-half of the cost. The sellers declined and subsequently marketed the property themselves. They prepared newspaper ads and brochures claiming the property was in "excellent condition."

The Levines became interested in the home. They noticed minor cracks and a slight slope to the floor in one area; however, Mr. Smith assured them that the cracks were only superficial. They had the structure inspected; their inspector reported minor and superficial cracks in the foundation. The Levines closed the transaction, giving the Smiths full price with $25,000 at closing and a promissory note for the balance. They lived in the home for three years, until they had financial difficulties and decided to sell. They listed the home with a real estate firm, disclosing their inspection reports, and subsequently accepted an offer from David Holmes to buy the home. By coincidence, Holmes employed the same structural inspector as the former tenant; the findings were the same. Holmes demanded the return of his earnest money and termination of the contract; the Levines immediately complied.

The Levines sued under DTPA. The Smiths then decided to call the promissory due and started foreclosure proceedings. Only a restraining order, issued three days before the foreclosure sale date, halted the foreclosure.

In the lower court, the jury found that the Smiths "knowingly engaged in a false, misleading or deceptive act or practice, as well as an unconscionable action or course of action, and both were a producing cause of damages to the Levines." They also found that the Smiths had knowingly or intentionally committed fraud. The jury's award was the difference in value of the house of $33,800, $14,400 each for the Levines' mental anguish, and punitive damages in the amount of $65,000 against Mr. Smith and $32,750 against Mrs. Smith. The Smiths appealed; the appellate court affirmed the lower court's decision.

Producing Cause

Under the DTPA, the consumer must prove that a misleading, deceptive, or fraudulent act was a producing cause of loss. A producing cause is a contributing factor that, in the ordinary sequence, produces injury or damage. In common-law and statutory fraud causes of action, the injured party is required to prove that the misrepresentation was of a relevant (material) fact and that this misrepresentation directly caused economic loss. Under the DTPA, the consumer is not required to prove that the deceptive act related to material fact or that the consumer relied on that misrepresentation. Furthermore, consumers are not required to prove that the misleading or deceptive act directly caused their injury, only that they were a contributing factor.

■ **EXAMPLE** In *Cameron v. Terrell and Garrett, Inc.*, 618 S.W.2d 535 (Tex. 1981), Jerry and JoAnn Cameron purchased a house. The house had been listed for sale by the sellers with their real estate agent, Terrell and Garrett, Inc. Terrell and Garrett had listed the house in the multiple listing service (MLS) and, in doing so, included a statement that the house contained 2,400 square feet. The Camerons were shown this information about the house by their real estate agent. Subsequently, the Camerons closed the sale and moved in. The Camerons then had the house measured and discovered that it contained 2,245 square feet of heated and air-conditioned space. However, if the garage, porch, and wall space were included, there was a total of 2,400 square feet. The Camerons sued Terrell and Garrett, Inc., under the Texas Deceptive Trade Practices Act, alleging misrepresentation. They claimed that Terrell and Garrett had falsely represented the number of square feet in the house. They sought actual damages of $3,419.30.

After a trial and two appeals, judgment was rendered for the Camerons. The court stated that Terrell and Garrett had misrepresented the number of square feet through the MLS and that the Camerons were consumers under the law, even though they had no contact with Terrell and Garrett. The Camerons were required to prove that they had been adversely affected by the misrepresentation.

■ **EXAMPLE** In *Weitzel v. Barnes*, 691 S.W.2d 598 (Tex. 1985), Barnes/Segraves Development Company, seller, and the Weitzels, buyers, signed a contract to purchase a remodeled home. The written contract gave the Weitzels the right to inspect, among other things, the plumbing and air-conditioning systems in the house. The contract provided that if the Weitzels were dissatisfied with the systems, they could reject the contract. A contract addendum further provided that failure of the buyers to inspect and give written notice of repairs to the seller constituted a waiver of the buyers' inspection rights and amounted to the buyers' consent to purchase the property "as is." The Weitzels did not inspect the house. Prior to and after signing the contract, the seller had told the Weitzels that the plumbing and air-conditioning systems complied with the Fort Worth building code specifications.

After moving into the house, the Weitzels found that the equipment did not function properly and was not in compliance with the city code. The Weitzels claimed that the oral representations were deceptive acts under the DTPA. Barnes/Segraves asserted as its defense the written contract provision regarding inspections, repairs, and waiver. The seller also argued that the buyers did not rely on the representations and, in fact, had notice prior to consummation of the sale that the city had posted a condemned notice on the house.

The court held for the Weitzels, reasoning that the buyers were not seeking to contradict the terms of the written agreement, nor were they claiming a breach of contract. Therefore, the verbal misrepresentations were admissible to prove a violation of the DTPA. Next, the court stated that the act does not require proof that the Weitzels relied on the oral misrepresentations. Reliance is not an element of producing cause. The court did point out that had the seller remained silent and not spoken to the quality or characteristics of the plumbing and air-conditioning systems, the seller would not have been liable. The contract provision regarding inspection, repairs, and waiver would have been controlling.

■ DAMAGES

The DTPA provides that a prevailing consumer can recover economic damages, attorney fees, and court costs. In addition, the judge or jury can award the consumer a sum of money in excess of the economic losses for mental anguish if the conduct has been committed knowingly or intentionally.

The consumer may receive no more than three times the economic damages for mental anguish if the act is committed knowingly. If the act is committed intentionally, the consumer may receive no more than three times the amount for economic damages and mental anguish.

DEFENSES

How can a person limit liability for a deceptive or misleading act or practice? The DTPA specifically limits the enforceability of any waiver (written or oral) by the consumer to sue under the act. The act, however, does establish a procedure for limiting liability and for recovering damages from a consumer if the suit is filed in bad faith and if notice and settlement provisions have been satisfied. As mentioned earlier, some defense can be mounted during the required 60-day notice period if the defendant makes a reasonable offer of settlement. In addition, a second defense is the giving of timely written notice to the consumer of the broker's reliance on some other written information. This can greatly assist brokers and salespersons because they frequently rely on information provided by others, such as sellers, property inspectors, appraisers, engineers, and perhaps even government agents. The key to the success of this defense depends on the following:

- The licensee must have received the information in writing.
- The licensee must have given written notice to the consumer prior to consummation of the sale that the licensee was relying on this written information.
- The licensee must establish that the licensee did not know and could not have known that the information was false or inaccurate.

It is important for a licensee to remember that reliance on the written information must be reasonable considering the licensee's expertise in the area. However, a licensee who can prove that this defense has been met will not be liable for the consumer's damages.

In addition to protection for licensees, the following case illustrates how giving full and complete disclosure, unlimited access for the purpose of inspections, and clearly wording the terms of a purchase contract can be a defense for sellers against an unwarranted DTPA suit.

EXAMPLE In *Zak v. Parks*, 729 S.W. 2d. 875 (Tex. App. 1987), the Zaks purchased a home with known and disclosed foundation problems from the Parks. Mr. Zak was an engineer and a licensed real estate agent and received a real estate commission from the Parks when he and his wife purchased the home. The Zaks were allowed to inspect the home and, in fact, did so four times before contracting to buy. In addition, the Zaks hired a structural expert who discovered a fracture in the foundation of the master bedroom and estimated necessary repairs to be approximately $2,000. After the inspection, an earnest money contract was drafted by Mr. Zak and signed by both Mr. and Mrs. Zak and Mr. and Mrs. Parks. It provided that the Parks would escrow funds in the amount of $2,300 "to correct structural defect of slab fracture." Any funds remaining in the escrow account after payment for repairs were to be returned to the Parks. Subsequently, the Parks placed $2,300 in an escrow account. Six weeks after closing, Mr. Zak claimed that the slab problems were greater than he had anticipated and demanded that the Parks pay $17,300 for foundation repair, $15,000 to level the house with 50 piers, and pay for numerous other unrelated repairs.

At trial, brought under the DTPA, Mr. Zak admitted that he had not used the escrowed funds to repair the foundation nor had he refunded the unused funds to the Parks. Mr. Barron, a foundation repair expert, testified that the foundation could have been repaired for less than $2,000.

The appellate court found as follows: "The written agreement limiting the Parks' liability for foundation repair, coupled with Mr. Barron's testimony, is sufficient factual evidence for the jury to decide that the lawsuit demanding that the Parks assume additional liability for foundation repair was brought in bad faith or to harass the Parks. . . . From the terms of the earnest money contract, it is clearly evident that the Zaks expressly agreed to a limit of $2,300 on the liability of the Parks for all expenses involved in repairing the slab. A lawsuit brought to recover an additional amount for repair of the slab defect is groundless as a matter of law." The court considered the case frivolous and unwarranted and entered a take-nothing judgment against Zak. In addition, Zak was ordered to pay the Parks' attorneys' fees in the amount of $42,500.

Unsuccessful Defenses

The previous case illustrated a successful defense against a DTPA claim. The following cases illustrate the powerful protection the DTPA offers to consumers and that many defenses that might have been possible under common law or statutory fraud are not available under DTPA.

■ **EXAMPLE** In *Kennemore v. Bennett*, 755 S.W.2d 89 (Tex. 1988), Thomas and Charles Kennemore contracted with builder Bill Bennett for the construction of a home. When the Kennemores refused to pay Bennett the balance due on the contract and $4,542.55 for extras, he placed a mechanic's and a materialman's lien against the property. Bennett then sued to foreclose his liens. The Kennemores defended against Bennett's suit and counterclaimed that Bennett had failed to construct the house in a good and workmanlike manner. The Kennemores asserted this breach of warranty action under the Texas Deceptive Trade Practices Act. Prior to trial, the Kennemores paid Bennett in full, but proceeded to trial on their DTPA claim against Bennett. Bennett argued that the Kennemores had waived their DTPA action by moving into the house and paying Bennett the money demanded in Bennett's lawsuit. The Texas Supreme Court held that the DTPA claim was not waived by the consumers simply because they accepted the allegedly defective home.

■ **EXAMPLE** In *Ojeda de Toca v. Wise*, 748 S.W.2d 449 (Tex. 1988), Rocio Ojeda de Toca purchased a house from Wise Developments, Inc. Approximately 11 months before the purchase, the City of Houston had recorded a document ordering that the house be demolished and placed a lien against the property for the demolition costs. Although Wise was aware of the demolition order, it did not notify Toca. While Toca was out of the country, the city demolished the house pursuant to the demolition order. Toca sued Wise for misrepresentation, fraud, and violation of the Texas Deceptive Trade Practices Act. Wise asserted in its defense that Toca had constructive notice of the demolition order under the recording statute. The court held that the legislature, in passing the DTPA, did not intend to bar a consumer's DTPA or fraud claim because an examination of the county records could have disclosed the seller's deception. The court also held that the recording statute is not to protect perpetrators of fraud. Therefore, Toca was allowed to recover from Wise for its failure to disclose the existence of the demolition order.

■ **EXAMPLE** In *Alvarado v. Bolton*, 749 S.W.2d 47 (Tex. 1988). The Alvarados purchased 50 acres of land in Fort Bend County, Texas, from Bolton. The sales contract did not reserve any mineral rights for the seller (Bolton), but at the closing the deed specifically reserved for Bolton one-half of the mineral rights. After oil was discovered on the land, the Alvarados learned of Bolton's mineral reservations and sued to reform the deed and to receive damages under the DTPA. Bolton asserted that under the doctrine of merger, once a deed is delivered and accepted, the sales contract becomes merged into the deed and only those terms in the deed can be used to resolve disputes. Therefore, because the deed specifically reserved the mineral rights and the Alvarados accepted the deed, the Alvarados were not entitled to the mineral rights.

The court held that the doctrine of merger cannot be used to defeat a DTPA claim for breach of an express warranty made in a sales contract. Therefore, the Alvarados can prevail against Bolton if they can prove that Bolton had breached the sales contract.

Groundless Lawsuits

Brokers may be faced with groundless lawsuits that rob them of time, energy, and productive activities. The law provides that if a suit is groundless, brought in bad faith, or brought for the purpose of harassment, the defendant will be compensated for reasonable attorney fees and court costs. While this does not give compensation for lost time and energy, it can have the effect of discouraging frivolous lawsuits. One of the primary objectives of the legislature in creating the 2011 exemption was to help prevent these types of lawsuits in the future.

ETHICAL AND LEGAL CONCERNS

Although this chapter has concentrated on the Texas Deceptive Trade Practices Act, a multitude of additional legal and ethical issues faced by real estate practitioners could be the subject of an entire text. For example, many state licensing laws address specific violations that might result in revocation or suspension of the agent's license (see TRELA § 1101.652). In addition, TREC rules include Chapter 531—Canons of Professional Conduct for Real Estate Licensees, which address topics such as fidelity, integrity, and competency.

Along with these state mandated laws and rules, many licensees have joined professional organizations such as the National Association of REALTORS® (NAR) and voluntarily subscribe to the NAR Code of Ethics. An in-depth discussion of other legal issues and ethical issues is contained in this text in Appendix D, "Ethical and Legal Responsibilities," and the reader is encouraged to engage in a careful study of this additional material.

SUMMARY

In 2011, the Texas legislature passed SB 1353 which amended the DTPA to once again exempt real estate brokers and salespersons unless evidence shows an attempt on part of the licensee to purposely mislead or defraud the public. Although this change to the DTPA may help brokers and salespersons, the full impact of the exemption is not yet clear and licensees are advised to become familiar with the provisions of the DTPA in order to avoid conduct that may still subject them to liability under the act.

Fraud is a deceptive act practiced deliberately by one person in an attempt to gain an unfair advantage over another. Misrepresentation is a false statement, made negligently or innocently, that is a material factor in another's decision to contract. In Texas, one of the methods for holding a person liable for fraud or misrepresentation is the DTPA, which prohibits not only false statements but also misleading statements or acts. In general, a consumer who can prove that a misleading act was the producing cause of an injury can recover economic damages, attorney fees, court costs, and additional compensation up to three times the amount of the actual losses. One defense that can be particularly useful to brokers is giving timely written notice to a buyer or a seller that the broker is relying on written information supplied by someone else. If this notice is given in a timely and proper manner, the broker may be relieved from liability for false or misleading statements contained in such written reports.

KEY POINTS

- The purpose of the DTPA is to protect consumers against false, misleading, and deceptive business practices, unconscionable action, and breaches of warranty.
- Under the DTPA, a consumer may not have to provide proof of an intention to deceive or mislead, only that the result of the action or inaction did deceive or mislead. Before filing a lawsuit, the consumer must give a 60-day notice, following which the would-be defendant may inspect the "goods" that are the subject of the complaint and attempt to settle the matter with the consumer.
- The consumer may recover economic damages, attorney fees, and court costs. If the act was done knowingly or intentionally, the consumer could receive up to three times the amount of the economic damages.
- The best defense is to encourage the use of information from reliable sources other than the broker, such as appraisers, engineers, property inspectors, and government sources.
- In 2011, the Texas legislature created a specific exemption for real estate brokers and salespersons from liability under the DTPA for innocent misrepresentations, omissions, or advice or opinions as long as there was no intent to deceive or mislead the consumer.

SUGGESTIONS FOR BROKERS

Brokers should be particularly careful to instruct all associated licensees adequately about the proper means of obtaining information and subsequently relaying that information to clients and customers. A written policy of documenting all contacts and all sources of information could be helpful in the event of a lawsuit by a client or customer.

CHAPTER 12 QUIZ

1. The DTPA prohibits as unlawful all of the following EXCEPT
   a. false acts.
   b. misleading acts.
   c. deceptive acts.
   d. moral acts.

2. Which statement is NOT true with respect to the Texas DTPA?
   a. A licensee can safely rely on a written and signed waiver.
   b. There is no requirement that the offending party intended to deceive.
   c. To prevail, the injured party must be a consumer as defined in the act.
   d. A written offer of settlement is some defense.

3. Which is NOT an example of damages available under the Texas DTPA?
   a. Economic damages
   b. Mandatory four times the actual damages
   c. Court costs and attorney fees
   d. Three times the economic damages

4. In defending against a DTPA case, licensees using the timely written notice defense must include all of the following EXCEPT
   a. that they must have given written notice to the consumer prior to consummation of the sale that the broker was relying on this written notice.
   b. that they must have received the information in writing.
   c. that they must establish that they did not and could not know that the information was false or inaccurate.
   d. that they must produce evidence that three independent sources were consulted before the written notice was submitted to the consumer.

5. Which of the following is provided by the Texas Deceptive Trade Practices and Consumer Protection Act?
   a. A reasonable offer of settlement made within specified time limits is some defense.
   b. Transmittal of written information prepared by others along with a written statement of reliance on such information is a defense.
   c. Recovery of court costs and attorney fees is possible if the lawsuit is frivolous or harassing.
   d. All of the above

6. All of the following are included in the DTPA definition of the term *consumer* EXCEPT
   a. individuals.
   b. partnerships and corporations.
   c. business consumers with assets of $25 million or more.
   d. the State of Texas.

7. To be considered a violation of the DTPA, it is
   a. not necessary for a consumer to prove that the licensee intended to deceive or misrepresent the facts.
   b. necessary for a consumer to prove that the licensee intended to deceive or misrepresent the facts.
   c. not necessary for the court to prove that the licensee intended to deceive or misrepresent the facts.
   d. necessary for the court to prove that the licensee intended to deceive or misrepresent the facts.

8. When a real estate salesperson licensee has been found guilty of a DTPA violation, the court
   a. can suspend or revoke the license of the salesperson.
   b. cannot suspend or revoke the license of the salesperson.
   c. can suspend or revoke the license of the sponsoring broker.
   d. can suspend or revoke the licenses of both the salesperson and the sponsoring broker.

9. *Unconscionable actions* in the DTPA is a vague term that allows the courts to
   a. use their discretion in deciding cases where persons have been tricked or swindled.
   b. use whatever measure they deem appropriate when deciding all DTPA cases.
   c. ignore other DTPA cases in their decisions.
   d. apply strict guidelines to DTPA cases.

10. All waivers of rights under the DTPA are
    a. automatically unenforceable by the court.
    b. automatically enforceable by the court.
    c. legal and cannot be interpreted by the court.
    d. subject to the consideration of the court.

DISCUSSION QUESTIONS

1. What types of statements might a broker make that would lead to possible innocent misrepresentations under the DTPA (e.g., saying "this is a well maintained home" when it would be better to say "this house appears to be well maintained")?

CHAPTER 13

Putting It All Together

In earlier chapters, we saw licensees facing situations involving possible lawsuits in which agency status was the main issue. If the licensees had practiced preventive brokerage, they might have lessened their risk.

LEARNING OBJECTIVES *This chapter addresses the following:*

- Preventive Brokerage
- First Contact: The Broker Working for/with the Seller
    - Listing Broker or Associate Working with Seller
    - Listing Broker or Associate Working with Buyer-Customer
    - Listing Broker and Buyer's Broker
    - Other Broker as Subagent of Seller
    - Intermediary
- First Contact: The Broker Working for/with the Buyer
    - Other Broker as Buyer's Broker
- Other Considerations
    - Presentation of Offers by the Listing Broker
    - Retained Earnest Money in the Event of a Default
    - Commissions
    - Written Agreements

- Using Rehearsed Dialogue
  - Dialogues for Brokerage Situations
- Risk Management

PREVENTIVE BROKERAGE

Whether representing the seller or the buyer, brokers should do three things:

- Use written disclosures.
- Clarify their role in the transaction.
- Use the help of others when needed.

Brokers should recognize that the most frequent basis for complaints against real estate licensees is their failure to disclose material facts. Remember, the exemption granted to licensees under the Deceptive Trade Practices Act (Chapter 12) does not apply in the case of an expressed misrepresentation of a material fact. The broker must therefore be prepared to prove in a legal dispute with a consumer that important information was, in fact, provided or, on the other hand, that such disclosure was prohibited by law. The Texas Property Code (TPC) dictates that certain sellers (not all) must provide the disclosure in written form (§ 5.008) The wise broker, however, would assure that any disclosures provided to consumers be in written form along with a request for the consumer's signature signifying receipt of the information.

Brokers also can help protect themselves by clarifying their roles in the transaction to the buyer and the seller. Before even offering to assist consumers in a transaction, licensees should discuss openly what they can and cannot do. For example, if the licensee has never handled a tax-deferred exchange or the sale of a business opportunity, the client (or customer) should be made aware of that fact and the licensee should then suggest the possible use of other experts. Article 11 of the REALTOR® Code of Ethics and Standards of Practice (*see* Chapter 11, Figure 11.2) states:

> "REALTORS® *shall not undertake to provide specialized professional services concerning a type of property or service that is outside their field of competence unless they engage the assistance of one who is competent on such types of property or service. . . ."*

To present oneself as an expert not only is grounds for loss of license but also could form the basis of a lawsuit under the Deceptive Trade Practices and Consumer Act (DTPA) (TRELA § 1101.652(b)(1)). Licensees should discuss their duties and responsibilities and those of other licensees, as well as the use of subagents and the multiple listing service (MLS).

Licensees who work with the buyer should clarify to all concerned whether the buyer is the licensee's client or customer. Regardless of the relationship, however, the licensee should make sure that the buyer in the transaction understands that the licensee does not warrant the condition of the property. Notice that this fact is expressly stated in the first paragraph of the Seller's Disclosure of Property Condition (*see* Figure 3.1) when it says "THIS NOTICE IS . . . NOT A

WARRANTY OF ANY KIND BY SELLER OR SELLERS' AGENTS." The following list describes just some of the distinctions between duties that a broker, acting as an agent for only one party in a transaction, has to a client versus the broker's duties to a customer.

- To a customer, the seller's agent points out remedies available to the seller in the event of a buyer's default on the purchase contract. To a client, the buyer's agent might discuss the meaning of liquidated damages in this context, making sure the buyer knows that the earnest money may be forfeited. (Naturally, an agent must be very careful to avoid giving legal advice [§ 1101.654]. If buyers or sellers have any questions about the standard default provisions found in the TREC- promulgated sales contract forms, they should be advised to consult an attorney.) However, if it is evident that nonjudicial alternatives would save them both money and reduce both their risks, it would be appropriate, in fact, mandatory, that the licensee make the parties aware of such alternatives.
- When the seller carries back financing, the seller's agent could negotiate or attempt to negotiate into the original offer many contract provisions that are different from those the buyer's agent might propose. Such provisions might include prepayment, due on sale, right to make improvements, nonrecourse (no personal liability), reinstatement prior to foreclosure sale, grace periods, late charges, and so on.
- To a customer, the seller's agent discloses the existence of an underground water easement. To a client, the buyer's agent goes an extra step and reviews a copy of the grant of easement, just in case any restrictions affect the buyer's expected use of the property, such as a prohibition against constructing any improvement within a certain distance of the easement.
- To a customer, the agent emphasizes the attractive features of the seller's property. To a client, the agent points out the negative features.

■ FIRST CONTACT: THE BROKER WORKING FOR/WITH THE SELLER

Particularly for newly licensed or inexperienced salespersons, the broker should consider developing a standard list of topics that should be addressed by the agent when first meeting a seller or buyer prospect. Some brokers have even developed a check-off form for use by associates to assure that all topics are consistently and thoroughly covered with each prospect. The sheet can actually form the basis of documentation regarding mandatory disclosures that may be needed should questions later arise as to whether or not the topic was covered with the consumer. The following discussion should serve as a summary of the types of topics an office acting as the seller's agent (either listing office or subagent of the listing office) might wish to cover with prospects, depending on whether the associate is making first contact with a prospective seller, a prospective buyer, a buyer's broker, or a subagent bringing a buyer customer to preview the property.

Listing Broker or Associate Working with Seller

The listing broker or associate, in working for the seller, should perform the following actions:

- At the beginning of the listing appointment, but before an agency relationship is established or the listing agreement is discussed, explain and discuss in detail the brokerage company's agency disclosure form and the broker's agency position at that time, as well as the Texas Real Estate Commission's (TREC) Information About Brokerage Services notice or the equivalent, as required by the Real Estate License Act (TRELA) § 1101.558(c), regarding the written statement concerning agency options.
- So the seller-prospect has a ready reference, provide a copy of a sample listing contract the brokerage uses such as the Residential Real Estate Listing Agreement Exclusive Right to Sell (*see* Chapter 5, Figure 5.2)
- Explain what subagency means and the optional use of subagents in an MLS and obtain the seller's authorization to use subagents.
- Explain how commission fees may be split and obtain the sellers' approval or disapproval to split fees with sellers' subagents or buyers' brokers.
- If the listing broker or associate is a member of the MLS, verify that the listing agreement contains a provision granting the seller's permission to use the MLS and to release marketing and sales data to the MLS. If the seller elects not to have the listing broker offer subagency or elects to offer it on a selective basis, a decision must be made regarding the use of an MLS.
- On the subject of compensation, explain to the seller how commissions may be split with other brokers. Because there is a big difference between authorizing the listing broker to split commissions with a buyer's broker and authorizing the broker to split with a subagent of the seller, the seller's attention should be clearly directed to this provision before signing the listing. If the listing broker decides to offer other brokers a less-than-attractive commission split, the seller should be notified because it may mean that other brokers will be less motivated to show the seller's property.
- Explain to the seller that it is customary to work with other real estate brokers or their associates to increase the likelihood of finding a suitable buyer for the seller's property.
- Explain that the listing broker's commission fee is normally a reflection of the presumption that the listing broker will be sharing the compensation with the cooperating broker in exchange for assistance in finding a buyer for the property, but that all fees or the sharing of fees between brokers are negotiable. Explain how the seller may permit the listing broker to offer a commission split to other brokers but not to offer subagency (subagency optional).
- Explain the brokerage's policies on intermediary brokerage.

Listing Broker or Associate Working with Buyer-Customer

At first contact concerning a specific property, the listing broker or associate should present and explain to a buyer-customer

- the TREC Information About Brokerage Services form, or equivalent;
- the difference between a client and a customer in terms of services, duties, and appropriate expectations;

- that the broker is employed by the seller to sell the seller's property;
- that the buyer is free to seek and retain technical advisers;
- that if the buyer decides not to buy the listed property, the buyer may wish to use the services of the listing broker to search for another appropriate property; if so, the agency relationship and whether the buyer is a customer or a client must be clarified;
- the in-house sales practices of the listing broker; and
- that it is customary for a broker to show other listed properties to prospective buyers.

In addition, listing brokers may

- provide ready access to inventory, including the MLS;
- collect pertinent data on property taxes, utility costs, and general real estate values;
- provide information on municipal services and amenities;
- discuss financing alternatives;
- discuss loan qualification and processing;
- show properties;
- make appointments and schedule conferences;
- suggest ways to improve the suitability of the home;
- clarify the buyer's needs versus wants and affordability;
- evaluate the need for property management;
- arrange for and review fire or liability insurance;
- check inventory of personal property;
- check applicable zoning and building permits;
- estimate closing costs and monthly payments;
- explain standard forms;
- explain escrow or settlement procedures;
- transmit an offer and act as liaison between the buyer and seller (though negotiating at all times on behalf of the seller's interests);
- monitor closing and time deadlines; and
- recognize the buyer's need for expert advice and suggest possible advisers.

Properties the buyer should see. The seller's agent or subagent can make appointments, show properties meeting the buyer's stated criteria, describe general features and conditions, direct the buyer to needed sources of information, complete standard forms, and transmit offers to the seller.

If the buyer decides that neither the seller's property nor any other properties listed with the broker are suitable, the agent can then discuss what further services might be provided to help the buyer locate the right property. Before beginning a search through the MLS system for suitable properties, however, a decision must be made as to whether the broker will proceed showing additional properties to the buyer while acting in a subagent capacity or in a buyer's agent capacity. Although not required, a written agreement to represent a buyer is advisable.

Listing Broker and Buyer's Broker

If the listing broker receives an offer through a buyer's broker, the listing broker should

- be cooperative, while respecting the agency relationships between the broker and the seller and between the buyer's broker and the buyer;
- agree on how best to handle payment of commissions consistent with the authorization of both the seller and the buyer;
- communicate to the seller the buyer's intention for payment of fees relative to the buyer's broker;
- be prepared for healthy and open negotiations; and
- evaluate all terms of the buyer's offer, recognizing that they were prepared with the buyer's best interests in mind.

Listing brokers should be prepared for the likelihood that they will receive offers from other brokers submitted on behalf of buyer-clients and should welcome these offers, working with the buyers' brokers in a spirit of cooperation and goodwill. At the same time, the listing broker should respect the fact that these brokers owe undivided loyalty to their respective principal. Listing brokers generally recognize that it is in the best interests of the seller to cooperate with all brokers, one of whom may have the ultimate buyer for the seller's property. The key question regarding any offer, whether from a buyer or a buyer's broker, is: What is the net effect to the seller?

Other Broker as Subagent of Seller

In those cases in which the other broker is a subagent of the seller, the other broker must

- disclose to the buyer, either orally or in writing, that the broker is an agent of the seller;
- provide the written statement required by TRELA § 1101.558, unless the buyer or the tenant is represented by an agent or the statement is not required for some other legitimate reason;
- discuss with the buyer or the tenant what type of services the subagent can and cannot give;
- notify the listing broker that the other broker is a subagent of the seller;
- verify each proposed commission-split arrangement;
- inquire whether there are any special instructions or new information or whether the home is already under contract;
- inquire about the listing broker's policies regarding handling earnest money deposits, using a lockbox, drafting offers, choosing an escrow company, and placing a loan; and
- act as a subagent of the seller, at all times in the best interests of the seller.

In deciding whether to represent the seller, the other broker should understand that as a subagent of the seller, the other broker may not be privy to the same information as the listing broker. Many sellers are reluctant to pass on confidential information to the other broker for fear the other broker will divulge this information to the buyer. Other brokers cooperating with the seller through the listing broker are normally viewed by sellers as conduits for the flow of facts and figures between buyers and sellers.

Intermediary

If the listing office offers representation to both buyers and sellers in the same transaction, the initial contact with either the buyer or the seller should address the possibility and the consequences of that situation arising. Remember, the basic requirements to establish an intermediary relationship under TRELA § 1101.559; .560 are to

- obtain the written consent of all parties in a form that meets the specific requirements set forth in TRELA § 1101.559;
- treat all parties fairly and honestly and avoid disclosure of any information that is confidential or that a party has requested not to be disclosed;
- determine whether appointments will be made and, if so, disclose in writing to all parties that such has been done; and
- comply with the provisions of TRELA.

■ FIRST CONTACT: THE BROKER WORKING FOR/WITH THE BUYER

A broker or associate engaged in initial contact with a buyer prospect might wish to have a checklist of topics similar to the list noted for sellers' agents. The first step, of course, is to determine which level of service (client or customer) the broker and the broker's associates will be offering to the buyer prospect.

For example, the buyer's broker or associate's dialogue with a prospective buyer should

- explain to the buyer the services to be rendered by first presenting and discussing the TREC Information About Brokerage Services form, or an equivalent written statement, and then explain that the broker is not the buyer's agent unless and until a consensual agreement has been reached;
- after consultation regarding the role of a buyer's broker and consent of the buyer or tenant, obtain from the buyer or tenant a written buyer-representation agreement;
- determine how fees are to be paid;
- disclose to all listing brokers and sellers of properties at the time of initial contact, before showing any properties, that the broker is a buyer's broker and reject any offer of agency or subagency from the seller, builder, or listing broker; and
- discuss with the listing broker either the possibility of a fee-splitting arrangement or how the buyer's broker's fee might affect the offering price.

Other Broker as Buyer's Broker

If the other broker decides to act as a buyer's broker, then, at initial contact when discussing the property and the seller, the other broker should

- disclose to all listing brokers of properties shown or to all owners selling their own properties the broker's status as buyer's broker, and
- disclaim any agency or subagency relationship with the seller or the listing agent.

Immediate disclosure will enable the listing broker to take appropriate action to represent the seller's best interests in any showing of the property to a prospective buyer.

As a practical matter, a broker may not have any particular customer or client in mind at the time of initial contact—for instance, on an MLS tour of homes. A broker who sometimes represents buyers should, however, inform the listing broker or the seller that the other broker may later return either with a client or with a customer. Therefore, the listing broker should keep this in mind when discussing any information concerning the seller's marketing position.

OTHER CONSIDERATIONS

Presentation of Offers by the Listing Broker

One of the important issues discussed frequently in earlier chapters is the duty of an agent to disclose information to clients. Under the minimum service due a client from the agent is the duty to inform the client if the broker receives any material information related to the transaction, including the receipt of an offer by the broker (*see* § 1101.557). A listing broker (or associate of the listing broker) will therefore be obligated to present all offers directly to the seller (or the buyer, in the case of a buyer's agent). It is not the prerogative of a broker to decide whether an offer will or will not be presented to the client, even if the broker knows (or believes) that the offer will be unacceptable to the client. Only the client has the right to accept, reject, or counter an offer. If sellers, for example, insist on considering only those offers that meet or exceed a certain price and/or terms criteria, then the licensee should obtain written instructions from the sellers stating their wishes (this should be done only after a lengthy discussion about why this is unadvisable).

It is the duty of licensee to explain an offer to the client and to give the client an accurate estimate of the costs and net proceeds. All offers should be presented as soon as possible—once the offer is available to the agent. The offer is privileged information and should be kept confidential, and the terms of the offer should not be made available to other licensees or potential buyers. Many ethics hearings have centered on the mishandling of offers by brokers.

■ **EXAMPLE** Martinez listed Roose's property for $175,000. Reese stated that he would only accept a full-price cash offer, and that he would not consider paying any closing costs. Several offers were submitted that did not meet Rowan's terms, and he immediately rejected them.

Carter viewed the property and thought it would be a nice investment. She asked her agent, Smith, to prepare an offer for $150,000 with the seller paying all closing costs. After Carter signed the offer, Smith presented it to Martinez. Martinez refused to present the offer, saying that he was sure Reese would not accept it, as he had turned down similar offers in the past.

■ **QUESTION**   1. Using only the facts in the example, was Martinez right to refuse to present the offer? 2. Would it be advisable for Smith to contact the local Board of Realtors® and file an ethics complaint?

■ **DISCUSSION**   It is very tempting to refuse to present an offer when you are "sure" that a seller will reject the offer and send you on your merry way. What many licensees do not recognize, however, is that circumstances can change at any time, and those changes might make the seller more receptive to price and/or terms that were previously unacceptable.

From an ethical standpoint, it is unfair to the seller to refuse to present an offer. Every offer gives the seller an opportunity to try to negotiate. Many sales that began with outrageous prices and terms have been negotiated to the satisfaction of both parties. We as licensees do not have the crystal ball that tells us which offer will result in acceptance and which will not.

Presentation of multiple offers.   On occasion, a listing broker may have more than one offer to present to a seller. This can occur (1) when a second offer is given to the listing broker before the first offer has been presented or (2) when a seller has received an offer, but has not yet accepted it, and another offer is made by a second buyer.

In the first case, where the broker actually has two offers to present, the broker should prepare presentations of both offers with the appropriate net proceed statements for the seller. In addition, the broker should collect as much information about the prospective buyers as possible to enable the seller to make an informed decision. For example, while one offer may net a greater net dollar amount for the seller, the financial strength of the buyer, type of financing, and other terms may make the offer less desirable than another offer that provides fewer dollars to the seller but under much more favorable terms. Remember that typical residential sellers are not very sophisticated about these issues and therefore have employed brokers to represent them in these negotiations. It is the agent's duty to give the client the best advice and opinions available.

The agent should give no preference to one offer simply because it was received before another, although in some cases the seller may wish to know and consider the information in the decision-making process. The primary duty of the agent is to give the seller as much information as possible and help the seller make the best possible decision.

The second situation occurs when the agent receives a second offer while the seller is deliberating a first offer. In this instance, the agent should immediately notify the seller of a second offer and advise the seller not to accept the first offer without first also considering the second. Consider the following situation.

■ **EXAMPLE**   Sue, a broker-associate of REI Realty, has secured a listing for the sale of the Edwards' condominium for a price of $200,000. At 10 AM on Tuesday, Bob, the owner of Maxheimer Realty, brings an offer for $185,000 to Sue. Sue knows that the seller will not be available until 8 PM that evening. At 2 PM the same day, Brenda, Sue's best friend, who is also an associate of REI Realty, rushes into the office, finds Sue, and exclaims, "Guess what—I have an offer on the Edwards' condo—overpriced though it is!" Brenda's customers have offered $192,000. Late in the afternoon, while preparing the offer presentations for the Edwards, Sue receives a call from Mr. Koepke, a prospect to whom Sue had shown the Edwards' property during an open house the previous Sunday. Koepke wishes to come into the office and make a written offer on the property.

Presuming that the three offers are comparable in terms and that the buyers are equally qualified, consider the questions that follow.

■ **QUESTIONS** 1. Should Sue disclose to Brenda the existence of the offer from Maxheimer Realty? 2. If so, how much information should be given to Brenda regarding the offer? 3. Should Maxheimer be made aware of the second offer? 4. If so, how much information should be given to Maxheimer regarding the offer? 5. Should Sue's customer be made aware of the other offers? 6. If so, how much information should be given to Sue's customer regarding the offers? 7. How should Sue handle securing the offer from Koepke, considering the fact that she already knows the details of the previous offers?

■ **DISCUSSION** In general, any information that is available to one party should be available to the other parties concerned. While the details of the other offer(s) should not be disclosed, the fact that other offers exist may be disclosed. In a sense of fairness to all participants, if one agent is made aware of an existing offer, all agents involved should be made aware. In the example above, if Brenda, in Sue's office, was told of Maxheimer's offer, Maxheimer should have been contacted and made aware that Sue now has another offer.

From the seller's perspective, it is beneficial for all parties to know that multiple offers have arrived. Buyers who are truly interested in winning the bid will often want to increase the price offered or make the terms more favorable to the seller, thus giving the seller a more profitable sale.

From the buyer's perspective, if the property is one that has high personal value, this information gives the buyer the opportunity to assess the original offer, determine whether it could be made more appealing to the seller, and determine whether the buyer's financial means will allow an adjustment that would have a better chance at a successful bid. This could be a win-win situation for all parties.

Sue is in a position of a potential conflict of interest if she writes a contract for Koepke. She knows too much about the offers that have already been submitted. It would be wise to bring the sponsoring broker (or a person of the broker's choice) into the transaction. This person could write the contract for Koepke and negotiate the details, if necessary. Sue would then be able to present all offers to the seller knowing that she did not have undue influence on the construction of Koepke's offer and unethically slant the outcome in her favor.

Presentation of subsequent or backup offers. On occasion, a buyer wishes to make an offer to a seller, even though the seller is already under contract with another buyer. The second offer is usually called a backup offer and would become effective only if the first offer did not proceed to closing.

This can create difficult situations for both the parties and the broker, particularly if the backup offer is more desirable to the seller than the first accepted offer. The parties should proceed carefully because contract law provides that the first buyer may have legal recourse if a second contract interferes with the first buyer's contract rights (called tortious interference with a contract). The seller should not entertain backup offers without permission of the first buyer because the buyer is said to have equitable title to the property. Equitable title is the buyer's right to have the property transferred once all conditions of the contract are fulfilled.

The first step in handling these issues is for the listing agent to determine whether the seller wishes to consider backup offers. The TREC one-to-four-family promulgated sales contracts provide that the seller may continue to offer the property for sale and negotiate and accept backup offers. If a buyer does not wish the seller to continue to solicit backup offers, special provisions must be added to the TREC contract offer that prohibit the seller from doing so.

Retained Earnest Money in the Event of a Default

TREC-promulgated sales contract forms do not contain a standard provision that permits the listing broker to share in a portion of the earnest money deposit retained by the seller as liquidated damages in the event the buyer defaults. However, most listing agreements (*see* Chapter 5, Figure 5.1, paragraph 5D(1)) do contain such a protection for the listing broker.

Few agreements permit the other broker, as a subagent of the seller, to share in the portion allocated to the listing broker in the event of default. The "Broker Information" section of the TREC sales contract form is silent as to a subagent broker's right to share in earnest money distributions in the event of default.

Commissions

One of the most important considerations is how to handle commissions. All commissions are negotiable. For example, TREC-promulgated sales contract forms routinely indicate that "all obligations of the parties for payment of brokers' fees are contained in separate written agreements." TAR listing and buyer-representation agreements, in turn, will usually give notice to the client that brokers' fees and the sharing of fees between brokers "are not fixed, controlled, recommended, suggested, or maintained by the Association of REALTORS® or any listing service." Who pays the commission does not determine who represents whom. The listing and the selling commissions normally are paid out of the sales proceeds at closing, but they do not have to be. In residential sales, brokerage commissions are usually paid from the seller's proceeds, but they do not have to be; the buyer or the tenant may pay the broker by agreement as well.

A broker has a duty to cooperate with other brokers on behalf of their client, but only when cooperation is within their client's best interest. For example, by advertising a property in the MLS, the listing broker encourages other brokers and their associates to review the property pricing and characteristics and to then bring qualified buyers to view the property. The offer to cooperate, however, does not include the obligation to compensate another broker. The duty to cooperate relates instead to the obligation to share information on the listed property. As discussed in Chapter 5, a growing number of listing brokers prefer to reduce their level of risk by not allowing other brokers to represent their client (i.e., they do not offer subagency). They accomplish their objective simply by withholding any offer of compensation to subagents within the MLS.

Written Agreements

Prudent brokers should attempt to enter into written agency agreements with clients. While it is sometimes legal, it is nonetheless unwise to proceed on oral agreements. Brokers must recognize that some buyers are reluctant to sign a buyer-representation agreement, even though they will be loyal customers, because

- such an arrangement has not been customary in the past,
- they fear the closing costs will increase by an additional broker fee,
- they do not want to be tied to an exclusive contract, or
- they do not understand the benefits of representation.

USING REHEARSED DIALOGUE

The broker's newly licensed or inexperienced real estate associates are usually uncomfortable discussing what frequently amounts to highly sensitive personal and financial information with people they do not know. Through sales and counseling training sessions that use role playing and sample dialogue, associates often overcome their initial uneasiness. In fact, many associates are able to use these acquired presentation and counseling skills to help distinguish them from their competitors.

Many of the top programs that deal with real estate counseling and buyer's brokerage stress learning the practical skills of how to ask more effective questions of prospects and client applicants and how to listen actively. The goal is to select from a group of prospects those who may be clients and those who may be customers.

The following section, containing possible questions to use and dialogue to develop in discussing the agency relationship issue, introduces the kinds of role-playing situations designed to reduce the anxiety level of real estate agents when discussing agency. Brokers should develop their own role-playing situations for use in training sessions and expand on the brief dialogue included here. Some licensees may prefer to write out these dialogues and practice them with a tape recorder. Often, it is not what is said, but how it is said, that makes the difference in explaining an important issue, such as what role licensees will play in a transaction and whom they will represent.

Dialogues for Brokerage Situations

The best way to become comfortable and competent in discussing agency alternatives is to role-play common situations. The following short scenarios indicate how some brokers handle such discussions of agency in a way that actually enhances the professional image of the real estate licensee. Using them as guidelines, write the dialogues in your own language and style. After completing your own versions of possible dialogues for the situations below, develop dialogues for other common situations. Try them out, critique them, and refine them, based on the concepts of agency you have learned in this text and developed through your own research.

■ **SCENE 1:** Natalie is a customer; Andrea is an associate of a firm that practices exclusive seller agency. Natalie walks into an open house where Andrea of Henderson Realty is on duty for the broker. Andrea hands Natalie a fact sheet, shows her around, and asks Natalie general questions concerning Natalie's wants and needs in housing, the general price range Natalie is considering, and square-footage requirements. Andrea senses that Natalie is not the typical looker but is serious about purchasing a property and seems very interested in this house. Andrea decides to turn the discussion to the subject of agency before the conversation gets too specific and before Natalie begins to reveal confidences or begins to develop unwarranted expectations of services and information.

Andrea: Has anyone explained to you, Natalie, how real estate licensees work and the agency relationships licensees are allowed to develop with clients?

Natalie: No.

Andrea: Regarding this house you're looking at, I am the agent for the seller. The reason I'm holding this open house is to expose the seller's property to the market in the hope that a buyer such as you will decide to purchase the property. As the seller's agent, I can point out the many features of the property; answer many of your questions about financing, ownership, and closing; help you prepare an offer the way you want it; and promptly present your offer to the seller. By law, I am obligated to treat you, as a customer for my seller's property, honestly and fairly in the transaction. There are, however, other services that I cannot perform for you as an agent of the seller. Before we proceed, I would like you to consider the information about brokerage services contained in our company's agency disclosure brochure. As a licensee, I am required to make clear whom I will represent in any given transaction.

After developing this dialogue as if Andrea were an exclusive seller's agent, assume that she and her broker practice nonexclusive single agency and see where the dialogue takes you. Critique your results in class. Then attempt the same process, assuming Andrea and her brokerage offer intermediary brokerage services. Have several classmates or family members play the part of the open-house owner who accidentally overhears the entire series of dialogues, then ask what the owner would think about the agent's conduct.

■ **SCENE 2:** A buyer's broker has an advantage over other brokers in contacting a FSBO. The buyer's broker does not look to the seller either for a listing or in an attempt to bargain a commission from the seller. The following dialogue might be used in a face-to-face meeting with a FSBO.

Kim: Good morning, Mr. Owner, I am Kim of Gold Coast Realty. I am a real estate licensee, but I am not here to ask for a listing on your home. The reason for my visit is to see if your property might fit the needs of my client. I saw your For Sale sign [ad]. Do you have a few minutes to see if you can be of help to my buyer and me?

Owner: Yes, but not a whole lot more than a few minutes. And I don't want to list my property.

Kim: I can see [understand] you're busy. I'll be very brief. My buyer, through his buyer-representation agreement with me, has agreed to include enough money in any offer he might make for your property to cover any concessions he might ask you to make, including such things as roof repairs, discount points, and my fee for services to him. Therefore, I will not personally attempt to negotiate a fee for myself from you. I am the agent for the buyer, and I will not be your agent. You will not have to list your property or publicly advertise it for sale. My buyer is ready, willing, and able to pay a fair price should you and he be able to come to a mutually acceptable agreement. If you are willing to sell for an acceptable price and terms, I would appreciate the opportunity to preview your house, with or without my client, and develop a report to my client regarding your property's suitability for his needs. Then we could prepare an offer for your consideration. Could I make an appointment with you to come back and preview your property sometime today or early tomorrow?

Owner: I'm telling you right now, I'm not listing with you and I'm not paying any commissions for anybody.

Kim: I understand, Mr. Owner, and I hear your frustration. As far as the real estate fees are concerned, my agreement with my buyer-client is an enforceable written contract in which my client has agreed to pay my fee for services to him in one of two ways. He might include enough in the offer to the owner so that the owner can pay my fee and net just as much money. Or, should my client not be able to negotiate that point with the owner but still desires the property, he has agreed to compensate me in addition to whatever the final purchase price is. Let me leave with you my company's agency disclosure form, which includes information about brokerage services. This form will confirm in writing what I've just told you. Again, I would very much like to return at a time that is more convenient to you. I'll also bring a state-required seller's disclosure of property condition form, discuss both forms with you for 10 to 15 minutes, and then preview your house for my client.

Kim, in the above scenario, practices exclusive buyer agency. If she practiced nonexclusive single agency or intermediary brokerage, would her conversation with the owner be different? Could she start talking with the owner about becoming his agent for the purchase of his next home? What conflicts of interest could develop? What would happen if her brokerage practiced the hybrid form of agency, where the client is required to consent to intermediary brokerage, in advance, should the situation require it? Develop dialogue and disclosures for these scenarios.

■ RISK MANAGEMENT

Although this chapter has covered many key elements of risk management under the general heading of preventive brokerage, many brokers today spend considerable time and effort to minimize legal exposure with buyers and sellers. One of the most effective ways to reduce risk in the specific area of agency risk is a well-defined and carefully implemented office policy manual that addresses the agency procedures of the company (*see* Chapter 10). Remember, however, that TRELA holds the broker responsible for any conduct engaged in by the broker or by a salesperson associated with or acting for the broker (§ 1101.803). The broker or office manager may not be immediately available should an associate need guidance on how to proceed with a dilemma which has arisen. Whether a large or a small office, to ensure consistent compliance with office policy, the broker should therefore assure that associates have access to a readily available set of written guidelines outlining even the most routine of office policies and procedures.

The important thing is for the broker to assure that the policy and procedures manual is a dynamic document that can be easily changed when impacted by changes in TRELA, TREC rule, local Realtor® board policy, or even technology. After all, the only constant in the real estate business is change!

The following list of topics is not all inclusive but can serve as a starting point for a broker wishing to begin developing a basic policies and procedures manual. Consider including the following outline of contents for a manual:

- Agency (*see* Chapter 10 outline of topics)
- Dealing with buyers
    — The contract—getting/servicing it
    — Length of the agreement
    — Rescission/revocation/renunciation policy
    — Commission fees
    — Dealing with the buyer as a subagent
- Dealing with sellers
    — The contract—getting/servicing it
    — Types of listings permitted
    — Rescission/revocation/renunciation policy
    — Conducting open houses and property tours
    — Company signs (standardization? content? riders?)
    — Cooperative listings between associates
- Showings
    — Company listings versus co-op listings
- The purchase agreement
    — Disclosure of relationships
    — Earnest money
    — Making appointments to present
    — Presenting the offer/counteroffer/multiple offers
    — How to handle rejection of offer
- Office policy regarding commission
    — What is the scale? fixed? sliding?
    — Referral fees
    — Bonuses
    — When and where is it payable to the associate?
    — What to do in case of a dispute with another brokerage office
    — Antitrust policy
- Closing the deal
    — What level of service/information is provided?
        - Net to consumer? Estimate of closing costs/monthly payment?
        - Review of final closing documents
        - Presence at scheduled inspections/appraisals/contractors
    — Attendance at closing
- Internal office administrative issues
    — Independent contract agreement versus employee
    — Phone/copier/conference room use
    — Additional liability insurance
    — Vacation time
    — Associate expenses versus broker expenses
    — Office conduct and dress code

- Internet policy
- Protecting privacy information
- Buying/selling for your own account
- Handling relocations and referrals
- Do-not-call policy
■ Advertising (*see* 22 § 535.154 for TREC rules)
■ Personal assistants
■ Arbitration and mediation policy
■ Sexual harassment
■ Equal housing opportunity/discrimination

Again, this list of policy and procedures manual topics should serve only as a starting list. A broker starting from scratch might wish to seek further guidance at the TAR or NAR Web sites. While it may be difficult to totally avoid risk in the real estate business, many brokers and sales licensees attempt to minimize the potential of financial loss by purchasing errors and omissions (E&O) insurance and suggesting that purchasers obtain home warranties. Still others attempt to shift risk by suggesting that the principals rely on other experts such as attorneys, title companies, lenders, appraisers, licensed property inspectors, and surveyors, to name a few. The area of risk management is a growing concern, and several texts have been devoted to this topic in detail.

■ SUMMARY

When you become comfortable handling your relationship with both customers and clients, you will experience enhanced professional stature and esteem. You will discover a sense of freedom in being able to more actively represent the best interests of your clients, whether buyers or sellers, when you negotiate against the other side, whether represented or unrepresented.

Part of that feeling of security can also come from knowing that the broker has provided an easy reference and how-to-guide regarding matters that routinely arise during the day-to-conduct of business.

■ KEY POINTS

- In practicing preventive brokerage, brokers should use written disclosures, clarify the roles of associated licensees, develop a written set of office policy and procedures, and when needed, use the services of others in their real estate transactions.
- Licensees should carefully prepare their clients and customers for the real estate transaction by explaining the process and providing disclosures.
- Offers to purchase should be presented in a timely manner. Multiple offers should be presented together, thereby giving the seller opportunity to accept the offer that best meets the selling goals. The seller should be able to choose whether or not to accept backup offers.
- There should be an understanding of how retained earnest money will be divided in case of a buyer's default.

- Commissions are negotiable and may be paid by either a client or a customer.
- Agency agreements should be in writing; however, oral agreements can create an agency relationship.
- Using rehearsed dialogue will help licensees overcome uneasiness with situations that are difficult for them.

SUGGESTIONS FOR BROKERS

Practice real-life situations in your training classes and learn the most effective ways to discuss agency relationships to prepare yourself for future discussions. Then put your practice sessions to work in the field. Allow newly licensed or inexperienced associates to accompany you or an experienced associate to view a listing presentation or an interview with a buyer prospect.

CHAPTER 13 QUIZ

1. Brokers should do all of the following EXCEPT
   a. use written disclosures.
   b. clarify their roles in the transaction.
   c. use the help of others when needed.
   d. warrant the condition of a property.

2. Listing brokers
   a. always offer subagency to other brokers.
   b. should explain brokerage policies regarding representation of clients.
   c. are not required to use disclosures other than those in the listing contract.
   d. may assume that sellers are aware of how commissions are split with other brokers.

3. When selecting properties to show a buyer-customer, the licensee
   a. should select those properties that best match the buyer's desires.
   b. should show only the company's listings because of fiduciary duties to their sellers.
   c. should match available properties with the buyer's needs, desires, and ability to pay.
   d. always should show properties somewhat above the buyer's desired price range, because buyers typically "buy up" from their initial requested price range.

4. Which term BEST describes a real estate licensee, working through a listing broker, who is paid a fee for working with a buyer but is not an agent of the buyer?
   a. Listing broker
   b. Subagent
   c. Finder
   d. Buyer's broker

5. A broker wishing to act as an intermediary in a transaction may do so only if
   a. all parties give written approval.
   b. the buyers give written approval.
   c. the sellers give written approval.
   d. the parties give written or verbal approval.

6. If a second offer is received by the listing broker while a seller is deliberating an offer, the broker
   a. must not present the second offer until the seller has made a decision on the first offer.
   b. must present the offer but explain to the seller that the second offer can be considered only as a backup offer and cannot be acted on until the first offer is negotiated.
   c. must present the second offer and explain that the seller is free to consider the second offer without regard to the first offer.
   d. should advise the licensee bringing the second offer that the seller is deliberating a first offer and to delay bringing a second offer until negotiations on the first offer are completed.

7. If earnest money is used to liquidate damages in a transaction, the listing broker is
   a. not entitled to share in the earnest money.
   b. entitled to share in the earnest money.
   c. entitled to share in the earnest money only if the listing agreement or purchase agreement contains such a provision.
   d. not entitled to share in the earnest money because listing agreements and purchase agreements never contain such a provision.

8. Who can pay the buyer's broker's fee?
   a. Seller
   b. Buyer
   c. Both seller and buyer
   d. Neither seller nor buyer

9. If a listing broker receives an offer from a buyer's broker in which the buyer's broker's fee is to be paid by the seller, the listing broker should
   a. reject the offer.
   b. renegotiate the offering.
   c. increase the listing fee.
   d. present the offer to the seller.

10. Rehearsed dialogue should
    a. never be used in presentations to buyers or sellers because it sounds like a "canned sales pitch."
    b. be used in presentations because it helps licensees become more comfortable in handling common situations.
    c. not be used in presentations because it makes licensees look insincere.
    d. be used in presentations because it guarantees that licensees will avoid lawsuits.

DISCUSSION QUESTIONS

1. You are the listing agent. A buyer wants to submit an offer to buy through you. The buyer hands you three envelopes with instructions to present a certain one first. Only if the seller rejects the offer found in the first envelope are you to present the others. What should you advise your seller? Would you do anything differently if you were the other broker acting as a subagent on an MLS listing? If you were a buyer's broker?

2. A buyer asks you how much her monthly payment will be for her mortgage loan. You explain that the monthly payment is $1,400, which will be used to pay principal, interest, taxes, and insurance. The buyer neglects to obtain fire insurance because she thinks it is included in the monthly payment when, actually, the monthly payment includes only the mortgage insurance premium. The house burns down. Are you liable? Are you more likely to be liable if you are the buyer's agent than if you are the listing agent?

3. As the other broker acting in a subagency capacity with the seller, you find a buyer who purchases a home for cash at $20,000 in excess of the true market value. Nine months later, the buyer comes to you and asks you to list the property for sale. What listing price do you suggest? How do you explain that you helped the buyer acquire the property, which was clearly overpriced?

4. Sally of Bay Realty signs a listing with George on a penthouse apartment. George asks Sally to find him a bigger penthouse. Whom does Sally represent on the current penthouse? Whom does Sally represent if she shows George a Bay Realty listing that was obtained by another agent? Whom does Sally represent if she shows George a property listed with another brokerage through the MLS? How does Sally explain to George the various working relationships open to them?

5. Review and expand on the suggested list of topics that should be covered in a well-written, detailed office policy and procedures manual.

APPENDIX A

Texas Occupations Code

FIGURE A.1

Texas Occupations Code

TEXAS OCCUPATIONS CODE

TITLE 7. PRACTICES AND PROFESSIONS
RELATED TO REAL PROPERTY AND HOUSING

SUBTITLE A.
PROFESSIONS RELATED TO REAL ESTATE

CHAPTER 1101.
REAL ESTATE BROKERS AND SALESPERSONS

As Revised and in Effect on

September 1, 2011, December 1, 2011,
January 1, 2012 and September 1, 2012

Texas Real Estate Commission
P.O. Box 12188, Austin, Texas 78711-2188
(512) 936-3000
www.trec.texas.gov

FIGURE A.1

Texas Occupations Code (continued)

CHAPTER 1101. REAL ESTATE BROKERS AND SALESPERSONS

SUBCHAPTER A. GENERAL PROVISIONS

Sec. 1101.001. SHORT TITLE. This chapter may be cited as The Real Estate License Act.

Sec. 1101.002. DEFINITIONS. In this chapter:

(1) "Broker":

(A) means a person who, in exchange for a commission or other valuable consideration or with the expectation of receiving a commission or other valuable consideration, performs for another person one of the following acts:

(i) sells, exchanges, purchases, or leases real estate;

(ii) offers to sell, exchange, purchase, or lease real estate;

(iii) negotiates or attempts to negotiate the listing, sale, exchange, purchase, or lease of real estate;

(iv) lists or offers, attempts, or agrees to list real estate for sale, lease, or exchange;

(v) auctions or offers, attempts, or agrees to auction real estate;

(vi) deals in options on real estate, including buying, selling, or offering to buy or sell options on real estate;

(vii) aids or offers or attempts to aid in locating or obtaining real estate for purchase or lease;

(viii) procures or assists in procuring a prospect to effect the sale, exchange, or lease of real estate;

(ix) procures or assists in procuring property to effect the sale, exchange, or lease of real estate;

(x) controls the acceptance or deposit of rent from a resident of a single-family residential real property unit; or

(xi) provides a written analysis, opinion, or conclusion relating to the estimated price of real property if the analysis, opinion, or conclusion:

(a) is not referred to as an appraisal;

(b) is provided in the ordinary course of the person's business; and

(c) is related to the actual or potential management, acquisition, disposition, or encumbrance of an interest in real property; and

(B) includes a person who:

(i) is employed by or for an owner of real estate to sell any portion of the real estate; or

(ii) engages in the business of charging an advance fee or contracting to collect a fee under a contract that requires the person primarily to promote the sale of real estate by:

(a) listing the real estate in a publication primarily used for listing real estate; or

(b) referring information about the real estate to brokers.

(2) "Certificate holder" means a person registered under Subchapter K.

(3) "Commission" means the Texas Real Estate Commission.

(4) "License holder" means a broker or salesperson licensed under this chapter.

(5) "Real estate" means any interest in real property, including a leasehold, located in or outside this state. The term does not include an interest given as security for the performance of an obligation.

(6) "Residential rental locator" means a person who offers for consideration to locate a unit in an apartment complex for lease to a prospective tenant. The term does not include an owner who offers to locate a unit in the owner's complex.

(7) "Salesperson" means a person who is associated with a licensed broker for the purpose of performing an act described by Subdivision (1).

(8) "Subagent" means a license holder who:

FIGURE A.1

Texas Occupations Code (continued)

(A) represents a principal through cooperation with and the consent of a broker representing the principal; and

(B) is not sponsored by or associated with the principal's broker.

(1-a) "Business entity" means a "domestic entity" or "foreign entity" as those terms are defined by Section 1.002, Business Organizations Code.

Sec. 1101.003. CORE REAL ESTATE COURSES. (a) For purposes of this chapter, "core real estate courses" include:

(1) agency law, which includes the following topics:

(A) the relationship between a principal and an agent;

(B) an agent's authority;

(C) the termination of an agent's authority;

(D) an agent's duties, including fiduciary duties;

(E) employment law;

(F) deceptive trade practices;

(G) listing or buying representation procedures; and

(H) the disclosure of agency;

(2) contract law, which includes the following topics:

(A) elements of a contract;

(B) offer and acceptance;

(C) statute of frauds;

(D) remedies for breach, including specific performance;

(E) unauthorized practice of law;

(F) commission rules relating to use of adopted forms; and

(G) owner disclosure requirements;

(3) principles of real estate, which includes:

(A) an overview of:

(i) licensing as a broker or salesperson;

(ii) ethics of practice as a license holder;

(iii) titles to and conveyance of real estate;

(iv) legal descriptions;

(v) deeds, encumbrances, and liens;

(vi) distinctions between personal and real property;

(vii) appraisal;

(viii) finance and regulations;

(ix) closing procedures; and

(x) real estate mathematics; and

(B) at least three hours of classroom instruction on federal, state, and local laws relating to housing discrimination, housing credit discrimination, and community reinvestment;

(4) property management, which includes the following topics:

(A) the role of a property manager;

(B) landlord policies;

(C) operational guidelines;

(D) leases;

(E) lease negotiations;

(F) tenant relations;

(G) maintenance;

(H) reports;

(I) habitability laws; and

(J) the Fair Housing Act (42 U.S.C. Section 3601 et seq.);

(5) real estate appraisal, which includes the following topics:

(A) the central purposes and functions of an appraisal;

(B) social and economic determinants of the value of real estate;

(C) appraisal case studies;

(D) cost, market data, and income approaches to value estimates of real estate;

(E) final correlations; and

(F) reporting;

(6) real estate brokerage, which includes the following topics:

(A) agency law;

(B) planning and organization;

FIGURE A.1

Texas Occupations Code (continued)

(C) operational policies and procedures;

(D) recruitment, selection, and training of personnel;

(E) records and control; and

(F) real estate firm analysis and expansion criteria;

(7) real estate finance, which includes the following topics:

(A) monetary systems;

(B) primary and secondary money markets;

(C) sources of mortgage loans;

(D) federal government programs;

(E) loan applications, processes, and procedures;

(F) closing costs;

(G) alternative financial instruments;

(H) equal credit opportunity laws;

(I) community reinvestment laws, including the Community Reinvestment Act of 1977 (12 U.S.C. Section 2901 et seq.); and

(J) state housing agencies, including the Texas Department of Housing and Community Affairs;

(8) real estate investment, which includes the following topics:

(A) real estate investment characteristics;

(B) techniques of investment analysis;

(C) the time value of money;

(D) discounted and nondiscounted investment criteria;

(E) leverage;

(F) tax shelters depreciation; and

(G) applications to property tax;

(9) real estate law, which includes the following topics:

(A) legal concepts of real estate;

(B) land description;

(C) real property rights and estates in land;

(D) contracts;

(E) conveyances;

(F) encumbrances;

(G) foreclosures;

(H) recording procedures; and

(I) evidence of titles;

(10) real estate marketing, which includes the following topics:

(A) real estate professionalism and ethics;

(B) characteristics of successful salespersons;

(C) time management;

(D) psychology of marketing;

(E) listing procedures;

(F) advertising;

(G) negotiating and closing;

(H) financing; and

(I) Subchapter E, Chapter 17, Business & Commerce Code; and

(11) real estate mathematics, which includes the following topics:

(A) basic arithmetic skills and review of mathematical logic;

(B) percentages;

(C) interest;

(D) the time value of money;

(E) depreciation;

(F) amortization;

(G) proration; and

(H) estimation of closing statements.

(b) The commission may designate a course as an equivalent of a course listed in Subsection (a).

(c) The commission by rule may prescribe:

(1) The content of the core real estate courses listed in Subsection (a); and

(2) the title and content of additional core real estate courses.

Sec. 1101.004. ACTING AS BROKER OR SALESPERSON. A person acts as a broker or salesperson under this chapter if the person, with the expectation of receiving valuable consideration, directly or indirectly performs or offers, attempts, or agrees to perform for

FIGURE A.1

Texas Occupations Code (continued)

another person any act described by Section 1101.002(1), as a part of a transaction or as an entire transaction.

Sec. 1101.005. APPLICABILITY OF CHAPTER. This chapter does not apply to:

(1) an attorney licensed in this state;

(2) an attorney-in-fact authorized under a power of attorney to conduct a real estate transaction;

(3) a public official while engaged in official duties;

(4) an auctioneer licensed under Chapter 1802 while conducting the sale of real estate by auction if the auctioneer does not perform another act of a broker or salesperson;

(5) a person conduction a real estate transaction under a court order or the authority of a will or written trust instrument;

(6) a person employed by an owner in the sale of structures and land on which structures are located if the structures are erected by the owner in the course of the owner's business;

(7) an on-site manager of an apartment complex;

(8) an owner or the owner's employee who leases the owner's improved or unimproved real estate;

(9) a transaction involving:

(A) the sale, lease, or transfer of a mineral or mining interest in real property;

(B) the sale, lease, or transfer of a cemetery lot;

(C) the lease or management of a hotel or motel; or

(D) the sale of real property under a power of sale conferred by a deed of trust or other contract lien.

Sec. 1101.0055. NONAPPLICABILITY OF LAW GOVERNING CANCELLATION OF CERTAIN TRANSACTIONS. A service contract that a license holder enters into for services governed by this chapter is not a good or service governed by Chapter 39, Business & Commerce Code.

Sec. 1101.006. APPLICATION OF SUNSET ACT. The Texas Real Estate Commission is subject to Chapter 325, Government Code (Texas Sunset Act). Unless continued in existence as provided by that chapter, the commission is abolished and this chapter, Chapter 1102 and Chapter 1303 of this code and Chapter 221, Property Code, expire September 1, 2019.

SUBCHAPTER B.
TEXAS REAL ESTATE COMMISSION

Sec. 1101.051. COMMISSION MEMBERSHIP. (a) The Texas Real Estate Commission consists of nine members appointed by the governor with the advice and consent of the senate as follows:

(1) six members who have been engaged in the brokerage business as licensed brokers as their major occupation for the five years preceding appointment; and

(2) three members who represent the public.

(b) Each member of the commission must be a qualified voter.

(c) Appointments to the commission shall be made without regard to the race, color, disability, sex, religion, age, or national origin of the appointee.

Sec. 1101.052. PUBLIC MEMBER ELIGIBILITY. A person is not eligible for appointment as a public member of the commission if the person or the person's spouse:

(1) is registered, certified, or licensed by an occupational regulatory agency in the real estate industry;

(2) is employed by or participates in the management of a business entity or other organization regulated by the commission or receiving funds from the commission;

(3) owns or controls, directly or indirectly, more than a 10 percent interest in a business entity or other organization regulated by the commission or receiving funds from the commission; or

(4) uses or receives a substantial amount of tangible goods, services, or funds from the commission, other than compensation or

FIGURE A.1

Texas Occupations Code (continued)

reimbursement authorized by law for commission membership, attendance, or expenses.

Sec. 1101.053. MEMBERSHIP AND EMPLOYEE RESTRICTIONS. (a) In this section, "Texas trade association" means a cooperative, and voluntarily joined statewide association of business or professional competitors in this state designed to assist its members and its industry or profession in dealing with mutual business or professional problems and in promoting their common interest.

(b) A person may not be a member of the commission and may not be a commission employee employed in a "bona fide executive, administrative, or professional capacity," as that phrase is used for purposes of establishing an exemption to the overtime provisions of the federal Fair Labor Standards Act of 1938 (29 U.S.C. Section 201 et seq.) if:

(1) the person is an officer, employee, or paid consultant of a Texas trade association in the real estate industry; or

(2) the person's spouse is an officer, manager, or paid consultant of a Texas trade association in the real estate industry.

(c) A person may not serve as a commission member or act as the general counsel to the commission if the person is required to register as a lobbyist under Chapter 305, Government Code, because of the person's activities for compensation on behalf of a profession related to the operation of the commission.

Sec. 1101.054. OFFICIAL OATH; BOND. Not later than the 15th day after the date of appointment, each appointee must take the constitutional oath of office.

Sec. 1101.055. TERMS; VACANCY. (a) Commission members serve staggered six-year terms, with the terms of three members expiring January 31 of each odd-numbered year.

(b) If a vacancy occurs during a member's term, the governor shall appoint a person to fill the unexpired term.

Sec. 1101.056. OFFICERS. (a) The governor shall designate a commission member who is a licensed broker as presiding officer. The presiding officer serves in that capacity at the pleasure of the governor.

(b) At a regular meeting in February of each year, the commission shall elect an assistant presiding officer and secretary from its membership.

Sec. 1101.057. GROUNDS FOR REMOVAL. (a) It is a ground for removal from the commission that a member:

(1) does not have at the time of appointment the qualifications required by Section 1101.051(a) or (b) or 1101.052;

(2) does not maintain during service on the commission the qualifications required by Section 1101.051(a) or (b) or 1101.052;

(3) is ineligible for membership under Section 1101.053;

(4) cannot discharge the member's duties for a substantial part of the member's term; or

(5) is absent from more than half of the regularly scheduled commission meetings that the member is eligible to attend during each calendar year, unless the absence is excused by majority vote of the commission.

(b) The validity of an action of the commission is not affected by the fact that it is taken when a ground for removal of a commission member exists.

(c) If the administrator has knowledge that a potential ground for removal exists, the administrator shall notify the presiding officer of the commission of the potential ground. The presiding officer shall then notify the governor and the attorney general that a potential ground for removal exists. If the potential ground for removal involves the presiding officer, the administrator shall notify the next highest ranking officer of the commission, who shall then notify the governor and the attorney general that a potential ground for removal exists.

Sec. 1101.058. PER DIEM; REIMBURSEMENT. A commission member is entitled to receive:

(1) $75 for each day the member performs the member's official duties; and

(2) reimbursement for actual and necessary

FIGURE A.1

Texas Occupations Code (continued)

expenses incurred in performing the member's official duties.

Sec. 1101.059. TRAINING. (a) A person who is appointed to and qualifies for office as a member of the commission may not vote, deliberate, or be counted as a member in attendance at a meeting of the commission until the person completes a training program that complies with this section.

(b) The training program must provide the person with information regarding:

(1) this chapter and other laws regulated by the commission;

(2) the programs, functions, rules, and budget of the commission;

(3) the results of the most recent formal audit of the commission;

(4) the requirements of laws relating to open meetings, public information, administrative procedure, and conflicts of interest; and

(5) any applicable ethics policies adopted by the commission or the Texas Ethics Commission.

(c) A person appointed to the commission is entitled to reimbursement for the travel expenses incurred in attending the training program regardless of whether the attendance at the program occurs before or after the person qualifies for office.

SUBCHAPTER C.
ADMINISTRATOR AND OTHER COMMISSION PERSONNEL

Sec. 1101.101. ADMINISTRATOR AND OTHER PERSONNEL. (a) The commission shall appoint an administrator.

(b) The commission may designate a subordinate officer as assistant administrator to act for the administrator in the administrator's absence.

(c) The commission may employ other subordinate officers and employees necessary to administer and enforce this chapter and Chapter 1102, including a general counsel, attorneys, investigators, and support staff.

(d) The commission shall determine the salaries of the administrator, officers, and employees of the commission.

Sec. 1101.102. DIVISION OF RESPONSIBILITIES. The commission shall develop and implement policies that clearly separate the policymaking responsibilities of the commission and the management responsibilities of the administrator and the staff of the commission.

Sec. 1101.103. CODE OF ETHICS; STANDARDS OF CONDUCT. Each member, officer, employee, and agent of the commission is subject to the code of ethics and standards of conduct imposed by Chapter 572, Government Code.

Sec. 1101.104. QUALIFICATIONS AND STANDARDS OF CONDUCT INFORMATION. The commission shall provide, as often as necessary, to its members and employees information regarding their:

(1) qualifications for office or employment under this chapter and Chapter 1102; and

(2) responsibilities under applicable laws relating to standards of conduct for state officers or employees.

Sec. 1101.105. CAREER LADDER PROGRAM; PERFORMANCE EVALUATIONS. (a) The administrator or the administrator's designee shall develop an intra-agency career ladder program. The program must require intra-agency postings of all nonentry level positions concurrently with any public posting.

(b) The administrator or the administrator's designee shall develop a system of annual performance evaluations. All merit pay for commission employees must be based on the system established under this subsection.

Sec. 1101.106. EQUAL EMPLOYMENT OPPORTUNITY POLICY; REPORT. (a) The administrator or the administrator's designee shall prepare and maintain a written policy statement to ensure implementation of an equal employment opportunity program under which all personnel transactions are made without regard to race, color, disability, sex, religion, age,

FIGURE A.1

Texas Occupations Code (continued)

or national origin. The policy statement must include:

(1) personnel policies, including policies relating to recruitment, evaluation, selection, appointment, training, and promotion of personnel;

(2) a comprehensive analysis of the commission workforce that meets federal and state guidelines;

(3) procedures by which a determination can be made of significant underuse in the commission workforce of all persons for whom federal or state guidelines encourage a more equitable balance; and

(4) reasonable methods to appropriately address those areas of underuse.

(b) A policy statement prepared under Subsection (a) must:

(1) cover an annual period;

(2) be updated at least annually; and

(3) be filed with the governor.

(c) The governor shall deliver a biennial report to the legislature based on the information received under Subsection (b). The report may be made separately or as a part of other biennial reports made to the legislature.

SUBCHAPTER D.
COMMISSION POWERS AND DUTIES

Sec. 1101.151. GENERAL POWERS AND DUTIES OF COMMISSION. (a) The commission shall:

(1) administer this chapter and Chapter 1102;

(2) adopt rules and establish standards relating to permissible forms of advertising by a license holder acting as a residential rental locator;

(3) maintain a registry of certificate holders; and

(4) design and adopt a seal.

(b) The commission may:

(1) adopt and enforce rules necessary to administer this chapter and Chapter 1102; and

(2) establish standards of conduct and ethics for persons licensed under this chapter and Chapter 1102 to:

(A) fulfill the purposes of this chapter and Chapter 1102; and

(B) ensure compliance with this chapter and Chapter 1102.

Sec. 1101.152. FEES. (a) The commission shall adopt rules to charge and collect fees in amounts reasonable and necessary to cover the costs of administering this chapter, including a fee for:

(1) filing an original application for a broker license;

(2) annual renewal of a broker license;

(3) filing an original application for a salesperson license;

(4) annual renewal of a salesperson license;

(5) annual registration;

(6) filing an application for a license examination;

(7) filing a request for a branch office license;

(8) filing a request for a change of place of business, change of name, return to active status, or change of sponsoring broker;

(9) filing a request to replace a lost or destroyed license or certificate of registration;

(10) filing an application for approval of an education program under Subchapter G;

(11) annual operation of an education program under Subchapter G;

(12) filing an application for approval of an instructor of core real estate courses;

(13) transcript evaluation;

(14) preparing a license or registration history;

(15) filing an application for a moral character determination; and

(16) conducting a criminal history check for issuing or renewing a license.

(16) conducting a criminal background check in connection with the annual renewal of

FIGURE A.1

Texas Occupations Code (continued)

a license under this chapter.

(b) The commission shall adopt rules to set and collect fees in amounts reasonable and necessary to cover the costs of implementing the continuing education requirements for license holders, including a fee for:

(1) an application for approval of a continuing education provider;

(2) an application for approval of a continuing education course of study;

(3) an application for approval of an instructor of continuing education courses; and

(4) attendance at a program to train instructors of a continuing education course prescribed under Section 1101.455.

(c) Notwithstanding Subsection (a), if the commission issues an original inactive salesperson license under Section 1101.363(b) to a salesperson who is not sponsored by a licensed broker and the salesperson is subsequently sponsored by a licensed broker, the commission may not charge:

(1) the salesperson a fee for filing a request to place the salesperson license on active status; or

(2) the broker a fee for filing a request to sponsor the salesperson.

Sec. 1101.153. FEE INCREASE. (a) The fee for filing an original application for an individual broker license and the fee for annual renewal of an individual broker license is the amount of the fee set by the commission under Section 1101.152 and a fee increase of $200.

(b) Of each fee increase collected under Subsection (a):

(1) $50 shall be transmitted to Texas A&M University for deposit in a separate banking account that may be appropriated only to support, maintain, and carry out the purposes, objectives, and duties of the Texas Real Estate Research Center;

(2) $50 shall be deposited to the credit of the foundation school fund; and

(3) $100 shall be deposited to the credit of the general revenue fund.

Sec. 1101.154. ADDITIONAL FEE: TEXAS REAL ESTATE RESEARCH CENTER. (a) The fee for the issuance or renewal of a:

(1) broker license is the amount of the fee set under Sections 1101.152 and 1101.153 and an additional $20 fee;

(2) salesperson license is the amount of the fee set under Section 1101.152 and an additional $20 fee; and

(3) certificate of registration is the amount of the fee set under Section 1101.152 and an additional $20 fee.

(b) The commission shall transmit quarterly the additional fees collected under Subsection (a) to Texas A&M University for deposit in a separate banking account that may be appropriated only to support, maintain, and carry out the purposes, objectives, and duties of the Texas Real Estate Research Center.

Sec. 1101.155. RULES RELATING TO CONTRACT FORMS. (a) The commission may adopt rules in the public's best interest that require license holders to use contract forms prepared by the Texas Real Estate Broker-Lawyer Committee and adopted by the commission.

(b) The commission may not prohibit a license holder from using for the sale, exchange, option, or lease of an interest in real property a contract form that is:

(1) prepared by the property owner; or

(2) prepared by an attorney and required by the property owner.

(c) A listing contract form adopted by the commission that relates to the contractual obligations between a seller of real estate and a license holder acting as an agent for the seller must include:

(1) a provision informing the parties to the contract that real estate commissions are negotiable; and

(2) a provision explaining the availability of Texas coastal natural hazards information important to coastal residents, if that information is appropriate.

Sec. 1101.156. RULES RESTRICTING ADVERTISING OR COMPETITIVE BIDDING. (a) The commission may not adopt

FIGURE A.1

Texas Occupations Code (continued)

a rule restricting advertising or competitive bidding by a person regulated by the commission except to prohibit a false, misleading, or deceptive practice by the person.

(b) The commission may not include in rules to prohibit false, misleading, or deceptive practices by a person regulated by the commission a rule that:

(1) restricts the use of any advertising medium;

(2) restricts the person's personal appearance or use of the person's voice in an advertisement;

(3) relates to the size or duration of an advertisement used by the person; or

(4) restricts the person's advertisement under a trade name.

Sec. 1101.157. SUBPOENA AUTHORITY. (a) The commission may request and, if necessary, compel by subpoena:

(1) the attendance of witnesses for examination under oath; and

(2) the production for inspection and copying of records, documents, and other evidence relevant to the investigation of an alleged violation of this chapter.

(b) A subpoena may be issued throughout the state and may be served by any person designated by the commission.

(c) If a person fails to comply with a subpoena issued under this section, the commission, acting through the attorney general, may file suit to enforce the subpoena in a district court in Travis County or in the county in which a hearing conducted by the commission may be held.

(d) The court shall order compliance with the subpoena if the court finds that good cause exists to issue the subpoena.

Sec. 1101.158. ADVISORY COMMITTEES. (a) The commission may appoint advisory committees to perform the advisory functions assigned to the committees by the commission. An advisory committee under this section is subject to Section 2110, Government Code.

(b) A member of an advisory committee who is not a member of the commission may not receive compensation for service on the committee. The member may receive reimbursement for actual and necessary expenses incurred in performing committee functions as provided by Section 2110.004, Government Code.

(c) A member of an advisory committee serves at the will of the commission.

(d) An advisory committee may hold a meeting by telephone conference call or other video or broadcast technology.

(e) Advisory committee meetings are subject to Chapter 551, Government Code.

Sec. 1101.159. USE OF TECHNOLOGY. The commission shall implement a policy requiring the commission to use appropriate technological solutions to improve the commission's ability to perform its functions. The policy must ensure that the public is able to interact with the commission on the Internet.

Sec. 1101.160. NEGOTIATED RULE-MAKING AND ALTERNATIVE DISPUTE RESOLUTION PROCEDURES. (a) The commission shall develop and implement a policy to encourage the use of:

(1) negotiated rulemaking procedures under Chapter 2008, Government Code, for the adoption of commission rules; and

(2) appropriate alternative dispute resolution procedures under Chapter 2009, Government Code, to assist in the resolution of internal and external disputes under the commission's jurisdiction.

(b) The commission's procedures relating to alternative dispute resolution must conform, to the extent possible, to any model guidelines issued by the State Office of Administrative Hearings for the use of alternative dispute resolution by state agencies.

(c) The commission shall designate a trained person to:

(1) coordinate the implementation of the policy adopted under Subsection (a);

(2) serve as a resource for any training needed to implement the procedures for negotiated rulemaking or alternative dispute resolution; and

(3) collect data concerning the effectiveness of those procedures, as implemented by the commission.

FIGURE A.1

Texas Occupations Code (continued)

Sec. 1101.161. GIFTS, GRANTS, AND DONATIONS. The commission may solicit and accept a gift, grant, donation, or other item of value from any source to pay for any activity under this chapter or Chapter 1102 or 1103.

SUBCHAPTER E.
PUBLIC INTEREST INFORMATION AND COMPLAINT PROCEDURES

Sec.1101.201. PUBLIC INTEREST INFORMATION. (a) The commission shall prepare information of public interest describing the functions of the commission.

(b) The commission shall make the information available to the public and appropriate state agencies.

Sec.1101.202. COMPLAINTS. (a) The commission by rule shall establish methods by which consumers and service recipients are notified of the name, mailing address, and telephone number of the commission for the purpose of directing a complaint to the commission. The commission may provide for that notice:

(1) on each application for a license or certificate of registration or written contract for services of a person regulated under this chapter or Chapter 1102;

(2) on a sign prominently displayed in the place of business of each person regulated under this chapter or Chapter 1102;

(b) The commission shall provide to a person who files a complaint with the commission relating to a license holder and to the license holder against whom the complaint is filed:

(1) an explanation of the remedies that are available to the person under this chapter; and

(2) information about appropriate state or local agencies or officials with whom the person may file a complaint.

(3) in a bill for services provided by a person regulated under this chapter or Chapter 1102; or

(4) in conjunction with the notice required by Section 1101.615; or

(5) to be prominently displayed on the Internet website of a person regulated under this chapter or Chapter 1102.

Sec.1101.203. COMPLAINT INFORMATION. (a) The commission shall maintain a system to promptly and efficiently act on complaints filed with the commission. The commission shall maintain a file on each complaint. The file must include:

(1) information relating to the parties to the complaint;

(2) the subject matter of the complaint;

(3) a summary of the results of the review or investigation of the complaint; and

(4) the disposition of the complaint.

(b) The commission shall make information available describing its procedures for complaint investigation and resolution.

(c) The commission, shall periodically notify the parties to the complaint of the status of the complaint until final disposition, unless the notice would jeopardize an undercover investigation authorized under Section 1101.204.

Sec.1101.204. COMPLAINT INVESTIGATION AND DISPOSITION. (a) The commission or commission staff may file a complaint and conduct an investigation as necessary to enforce this chapter, Chapter 1102, or a rule adopted under those chapters.

(b) The commission shall investigate the actions and records of a license holder if:

(1) a person submits a signed, written complaint; and

(2) the complaint and any evidence presented with the complaint provide reasonable cause for an investigation.

(c) The commission may not conduct an investigation of a person licensed under this chapter or Chapter 1102 in connection with a complaint submitted later than the fourth anniversary of the date of the incident that is the subject of the complaint.

(d) The commission shall promptly provide a written notice to a person licensed under this

FIGURE A.1

Texas Occupations Code (continued)

chapter or Chapter 1102 who is the subject of an investigation unless after deliberation the commission decides against notification.

(e) Notwithstanding any other provision of this chapter, an undercover or covert investigation may not be conducted unless the commission expressly authorizes the investigation after considering the circumstances and determining that the investigation is necessary to implement this chapter.

(f) An investigation or other action against a person licensed under this chapter or Chapter 1102 may not be initiated on the basis of an anonymous complaint.

(g) Repealed by Acts 2007, 80th Leg., R.S., Ch. 1411, Sec. 59(1), eff. September 1, 2007.

(h) The commission shall ensure that the commission gives priority to the investigation of a complaint filed by a consumer and an enforcement case resulting from the consumer complaint. The commission shall assign priorities and investigate complaints using a risk-based approach based on the:

(1) degree of potential harm to a consumer;

(2) potential for immediate harm to a consumer;

(3) overall severity of the allegations in the complaint;

(4) number of license holders potentially involved in the complaint;

(5) previous complaint history of the license holder; and

(6) number of potential violations in the complaint.

Sec. 1101.205. COMPLAINT INVESTIGATION OF CERTIFICATE HOLDER. The commission shall investigate a signed complaint received by the commission that relates to an act of a certificate holder or a person required to hold a certificate under Subchapter K.

Sec. 1101.206. PUBLIC PARTICIPATION. (a) The commission shall develop and implement policies that provide the public with a reasonable opportunity to appear before the commission and to speak on any issue under the commission's jurisdiction.

(b) The commission shall prepare and maintain a written plan that describes how a person who does not speak English or who has a physical, mental, or developmental disability may be provided reasonable access to the commission's programs.

SUBCHAPTER F.
TEXAS REAL ESTATE BROKER-LAWYER COMMITTEE

Sec. 1101.251. DEFINITION OF COMMITTEE. In this subchapter, "committee" means the Texas Real Estate Broker-Lawyer Committee.

Sec. 1101.252. COMMITTEE MEMBERSHIP. (a) The Texas Real Estate Broker-Lawyer Committee consists of 13 members appointed as follows:

(1) six members appointed by the commission; and

(2) six members of the State Bar of Texas appointed by the president of the state bar; and

(3) one public member appointed by the governor.

(b) Appointments to the committee shall be made without regard to the race, creed, sex, religion, or national origin of the appointee.

Sec. 1101.253. TERMS; VACANCIES. (a) Committee members serve staggered six-year terms, with the terms of two commission appointees and two State Bar of Texas appointees expiring every two years and the term of the public member expiring every six years.

(b) A committee member shall hold office until the member's successor is appointed.

(c) If a vacancy occurs during a member's term, the entity making the original appointment shall appoint a person to fill the unexpired term.

Sec. 1101.254. POWERS AND DUTIES. (a) In addition to other delegated powers and duties, the committee shall draft and revise contract forms that are capable of being

FIGURE A.1

Texas Occupations Code (continued)

standardized to expedite real estate transactions and minimize controversy.

(b) The contract forms must contain safeguards adequate to protect the principals in the transaction.

SUBCHAPTER G.
ACCREDITATION AND APPROVAL OF REAL ESTATE EDUCATIONAL PROGRAMS AND COURSES OF STUDY

Sec. 1101.301. ACCREDITATION OF PROGRAMS AND COURSES OF STUDY. (a) The commission, as necessary for the administration of this chapter and Chapter 1102, may:

(1) establish standards for the accreditation of educational programs or courses of study in real estate and real estate inspection conducted in this state, excluding programs and courses offered by accredited colleges and universities;

(2) establish by rule reasonable criteria for the approval of real estate and real estate inspection courses; and

(3) inspect and accredit real estate and real estate inspection educational programs or courses of study.

(b) The commission shall determine whether a real estate or real estate inspection course satisfies the requirements of this chapter and Chapter 1102.

(c) In establishing accreditation standards for an educational program under Subsection (a), the commission shall adopt rules setting an examination passage rate benchmark for each category of license issued by the commission under this chapter or Chapter 1102. The benchmark must be based on the average percentage of examinees that pass the licensing exam on the first attempt. A program must meet or exceed the benchmark for each license category before the commission may renew the program's accreditation for the license category before the commission may renew the program's accreditation for the license category.

(d) The commission may deny an application for accreditation if the applicant owns or controls, or has previously owned or controlled, an educational program or course of study for which accreditation was revoked.

Sec. 1101.302. BOND REQUIRED. (a) In this section, "educational institution" means a school, excluding an accredited college or university, authorized by the commission under this chapter to offer a real estate or real estate inspection educational program or course of study.

(b) An educational institution shall maintain a corporate surety bond or other security acceptable to the commission that is:

(1) in the amount of $20,000;

(2) payable to the commission; and

(3) for the benefit of a party who suffers damages caused by the failure of the institution to fulfill obligations related to the commission's approval.

Sec. 1101.303. APPROVAL OF CONTINUING EDUCATION PROVIDER OR COURSE OF STUDY. (a) If the commission determines that an applicant for approval as a continuing education provider satisfies the requirements of this subchapter or Section 1102.205 and any rule adopted under this subchapter or Section 1102.205, the commission may authorize the applicant to offer continuing education for a two-year period.

(b) If the commission determines that an applicant for approval of a continuing education course of study satisfies the requirements of this subchapter or Section 1102.205 and any rule adopted under this subchapter or Section 1102.205, the commission may authorize the applicant to offer the course of study for a two-year period.

Sec. 1101.304. EXAMINATION PASSAGE RATE DATA. (a) The commission shall adopt rules regarding the collection and publication of data relating to examination passage rates for graduates of accredited educational programs.

(b) Rules adopted under this section must provide for a method to:

(1) calculate the examination passage rate;

(2) collect the relevant data from the examination administrator or the accredited program; and

(3) post the examination passage rate data on the commission's Internet website, in a

FIGURE A.1

Texas Occupations Code (continued)

manner aggregated by educational program and by license group.

(c) In determining the educational program a graduate is affiliated with for purposes of this section, the educational program is the program the graduate last attended.

Sec. 1101.305. REVIEW COMMITTEE. (a) The commission may appoint a committee to review the performance of an educational program performing below the standards set by the commission under Section 1101.301. The committee shall consist of:

(1) at least one commission member;

(2) at least one member of the commission staff;

(3) individuals licensed under this chapter or Chapter 1102; and

(4) a representative from the Texas Real Estate Research Center.

(b) A committee formed under this section shall review and evaluate any factor causing an educational program's poor performance and report findings and recommendations to improve performance to the program and to the commission.

(c) A committee formed under this section may not revoke the accreditation of an educational program. The commission may temporarily suspend a program in the same manner as a license under Subchapter N.

SUBCHAPTER H.
LICENSE REQUIREMENTS

Sec. 1101.351. LICENSE REQUIRED. (a) Unless a person holds a license issued under this chapter, the person may not:

(1) act as or represent that the person is a broker or salesperson; or

(2) act as a residential rental locator.

(b) An applicant for a broker or salesperson license may not act as a broker or salesperson until the person receives the license evidencing that authority.

(c) A licensed salesperson may not act or attempt to act as a broker or salesperson unless the salesperson is associated with a licensed broker and is acting for that broker.

(a-1) Unless a business entity holds a license issued under this chapter, the business entity may not act as a broker.

Sec. 1101.352. LICENSE APPLICATION. (a) Each applicant for a broker or salesperson license must submit an application on a form prescribed by the commission.

(b) Each applicant for a broker or salesperson license must disclose in the license application whether the applicant has:

(1) entered a plea of guilty or nolo contendere to a felony; or

(2) been convicted of a felony and the time for appeal has elapsed or the judgment or conviction has been affirmed on appeal.

(c) The disclosure under Subsection (b) must be provided even if an order has granted community supervision suspending the imposition of the sentence.

(d) At the time an application is submitted under Subsection (a), each applicant shall provide the commission with the applicant's current mailing address and telephone number, and e-mail address if available. The applicant shall notify the commission of any change in the applicant's mailing or e-mail address or telephone number during the time the application is pending.

Sec. 1101.3521. CRIMINAL HISTORY RECORD INFORMATION REQUIREMENT FOR LICENSE. (a) The commission shall require that an applicant for a license or renewal of an unexpired license submit a complete and legible set of fingerprints, on a form prescribed by the commission, to the commission or to the Department of Public Safety for the purpose of obtaining criminal history record information from the Department of Public Safety and the Federal Bureau of Investigation.

(b) The commission shall refuse to issue a license to or renew the license of a person who does not comply with the requirement of Subsection (a).

(c) The commission shall conduct a criminal

FIGURE A.1

Texas Occupations Code (continued)

history check of each applicant for a license or renewal of a license using information:

(1) provided by the individual under this section; and

(2) made available to the commission by the Department of Public Safety, the Federal Bureau of Investigation, and any other criminal justice agency under Chapter 411, Government Code.

(d) The commission may:

(1) enter into an agreement with the Department of Public Safety to administer a criminal history check required under this section; and

(2) authorize the Department of Public Safety to collect from each applicant the costs incurred by the department in conducting the criminal history check.

Sec. 1101.353. MORAL CHARACTER DETERMINATION. (a) If before applying for a license under this chapter a person requests that the commission determine whether the person's moral character complies with the commission's moral character requirements for licensing under this chapter and pays the fee prescribed by Section 1101.152, the commission shall make its determination of the person's moral character.

(b) Not later than the 30th day after the date the commission makes its determination, the commission shall notify the person of the determination.

(c) If a person applies for a license after receiving notice of a determination, the commission may conduct a supplemental moral character determination of the person. The supplemental determination may cover only the period after the date the person requests a moral character determination under this section.

(d) The commission may issue a provisional moral character determination. The commission by rule shall adopt reasonable terms for issuing a provisional moral character determination.

Sec. 1101.354. GENERAL ELIGIBILITY REQUIREMENTS. To be eligible to receive a license under this chapter, a person must:

(1) at the time of application:

(A) be at least 18 years of age;

(B) be a citizen of the United States or a lawfully admitted alien; and

(C) be a resident of this state;

(2) satisfy the commission as to the applicant's honesty, trustworthiness, and integrity;

(3) demonstrate competence based on an examination under Subchapter I;

(4) complete the required courses of study, including any required core real estate courses prescribed under this chapter; and

(5) complete at least:

(A) three classroom hours of course work on federal, state, and local laws governing housing discrimination, housing credit discrimination, and community reinvestment; or

(B) three semester hours of course work on constitutional law.

Sec. 1101.355. ADDITIONAL GENERAL ELIGIBILITY REQUIREMENTS FOR BUSINESS ENTITIES. (a) To be eligible for a license under this chapter, a business entity must:

(1) designate one of its managing officers as its agent for purposes of this chapter; and

(2) provide proof that the entity maintains errors and omissions insurance with a minimum annual limit of $1 million for each occurrence if the designated agent owns less than 10 percent of the business entity.

(b) A business entity may not act as a broker unless the entity's designated agent is a licensed broker in active status and good standing according to the commission's records.

(c) A business entity that receives compensation on behalf of a license holder must be licensed as a broker under this chapter.

Sec. 1101.356. BROKER LICENSE EXPERIENCE AND EDUCATION REQUIREMENTS. (a) An applicant for a broker license must provide to the commission satisfactory evidence that the applicant:

(1) has had at least two years of active experience in this state as a license holder during the 36 months preceding the date the

FIGURE A.1

Texas Occupations Code (continued)

application is filed; and

(2) has successfully completed at least 60 semester hours, or equivalent classroom hours, of postsecondary education, including:

(A) at least 18 semester hours or equivalent classroom hours of core real estate courses, two semester hours of which must be real estate brokerage; and

(B) at least 42 hours of core real estate courses or related courses accepted by the commission.

(b) Subsection (a) does not apply to an applicant who, at the time of application, is licensed as a real estate broker by another state that has license requirements comparable to the requirements of this state.

(c) An applicant for a broker license who is licensed as a salesperson and is subject to the annual education requirements prescribed by Section 1101.454 must provide to the commission satisfactory evidence that the applicant has satisfied the requirements of that section. The hours completed under Section 1101.454 shall be applied to the number of hours required of the applicant under Subsection (a)(2) of this section.

Sec. 1101.356. BROKER LICENSE: EXPERIENCE AND EDUCATION REQUIREMENTS. (a) An applicant for a broker license must provide to the commission satisfactory evidence that the applicant:

(1) has had at least four years of active experience in this state as a license holder during the 60 months preceding the date the application is filed; and

(2) has successfully completed at least 60 semester hours, or equivalent classroom hours, of postsecondary education, including:

(A) at least 18 semester hours or equivalent classroom hours of core real estate courses, two semester hours of which must be real estate brokerage; and

(B) at least 42 hours of core real estate courses or related courses accepted by the commission.

(b-1) The commission by rule shall establish what constitutes active experience for purposes of this section and Section 1101.357.

(b) Subsection (a) does not apply to an applicant who, at the time of application, is licensed as a real estate broker by another state that has license requirements comparable to the requirements of this state.

Effective January 1, 2012.

Sec. 1101.357. BROKER LICENSE: ALTERNATE EXPERIENCE REQUIREMENTS FOR CERTAIN APPLICANTS. An applicant for a broker license who does not satisfy the experience requirements of Section 1101.356 must provide to the commission satisfactory evidence that:

(1) the applicant:

(A) is a licensed real estate broker in another state;

(B) has had at least two years of active experience in that state as a licensed real estate broker or salesperson during the 36 months preceding the date the application is filed; and

(C) has satisfied the educational requirements prescribed by Section 1101.356; or

(2) the applicant was licensed in this state as a broker in the year preceding the date the application is filed.

Sec. 1101.357. BROKER LICENSE: ALTERNATE EXPERIENCE REQUIREMENTS FOR CERTAIN APPLICANTS. An applicant for a broker license who does not satisfy the experience requirements of Section 1101.356 must provide to the commission satisfactory evidence that:

(1)the applicant:

(A) is a licensed real estate broker in another state;

(B) has had at least four years of active experience in that state as a licensed real estate broker or salesperson during the 60 months preceding the date the application is filed; and

(C) has satisfied the educational requirements prescribed by Section 1101.356; or

(2)the applicant was licensed in this state

FIGURE A.1

Texas Occupations Code (continued)

as a broker in the year preceding the date the application is filed.

Effective January 1, 2012

Sec. 1101.358. SALESPERSON LICENSE: EDUCATION REQUIREMENTS. (a) An applicant for a salesperson license must provide to the commission satisfactory evidence that the applicant has completed at least 14 semester hours, or equivalent classroom hours, of postsecondary education including:

(1) at least four semester hours of core real estate courses on principles of real estate;

(2) at least two semester hours of each of the following core real estate courses:

(A) agency law;

(B) contract law; and

(C) one additional core real estate course; and

(3) at least four semester hours of core real estate courses or related courses.

(b) The commission shall waive the education requirements of Subsection (a) if the applicant has been licensed in this state as a broker or salesperson within the year preceding the date the application is filed.

(c) If an applicant for a salesperson license was licensed as a salesperson within the year preceding the date the application is filed and the license was issued under the conditions prescribed by Section 1101.454, the commission shall require the applicant to provide the evidence of successful completion of education requirements that would have been required if the license had been maintained without interruption during the preceding year.

Sec. 1101.358. SALESPERSON LICENSE: EDUCATION REQUIREMENTS. (a) An applicant for a salesperson license must provide to the commission satisfactory evidence that the applicant has completed at least 12 semester hours, or equivalent classroom hours, of postsecondary education consisting of:

(1) at least four semester hours of core real estate courses on principles of real estate;

(2) at least two semester hours of each of the following core real estate courses:

(A) agency law;

(B) contract law;

(C) contract forms and addendums, and

(D) real estate finance.

(b) The commission shall waive the education requirements of Subsection (a) if the applicant has been licensed in this state as a broker or salesperson within the six months preceding the date the application is filed.

(c) If an applicant for a salesperson license was licensed as a salesperson within the six months preceding the date the application is filed and the license was issued under the conditions prescribed by Section 1101.454, the commission shall require the applicant to provide the evidence of successful completion of education requirements that would have been required if the license had been maintained without interruption during the preceding six months.

Effective September 1, 2012.

Sec. 1101.359. ALTERNATE EDUCATION REQUIREMENTS FOR CERTAIN LICENSE HOLDERS. An applicant for a broker license who is not subject to the education requirements of Section 1101.356(a)(2) and an applicant for a salesperson license who is not subject to the education requirements of Section 1101.358 or 1101.454 must provide to the commission satisfactory evidence that the applicant has completed the number of classroom hours of continuing education that would have been required for a timely renewal under Section 1101.455 during the two years preceding the date the application is filed.

Sec. 1101.360. ELIGIBILITY REQUIREMENTS FOR CERTAIN NONRESIDENT APPLICANTS. (a) A resident of another state who is not a licensed real estate broker and who was formerly licensed in this state as a broker or salesperson may apply for a license under this chapter not later than the first anniversary of the date of the expiration of the former

FIGURE A.1

Texas Occupations Code (continued)

license.

(b) A nonresident applicant is subject to the same license requirements as a resident. The commission may refuse to issue a license to a nonresident applicant for the same reasons that it may refuse to issue a license to a resident applicant.

(c) A nonresident applicant must submit with the application an irrevocable consent to a legal action against the applicant in the court of any county in this state in which a cause of action may arise or in which the plaintiff may reside. The action may be commenced by service of process or pleading authorized by the laws of this state or by delivery of process on the administrator or assistant administrator of the commission. The consent must:

(1) stipulate that the service of process or pleading is valid and binding in all courts as if personal service had been made on the nonresident in this state;

(2) be acknowledged; and

(3) if made by a corporation, be authenticated by its seal.

(d) A service of process or pleading served on the commission under this section shall be by duplicate copies. One copy shall be filed in the commission's office, and the other copy shall be forwarded by registered mail to the last known principal address recorded in the commission's records for the nonresident against whom the process or pleading is directed.

(e) A default judgment in an action commenced as provided by this section may not be granted:

(1) unless the commission certifies that a copy of the process or pleading was mailed to the defendant as provided by Subsection (d); and

(2) until the 21st day after the date the process or pleading is mailed to the defendant.

Sec. 1101.361. ADDITIONAL ELIGIBILITY REQUIREMENTS FOR CERTAIN NONRESIDENT APPLICANTS. (a) Notwithstanding Section 1101.360, a nonresident applicant for a license who resides in a municipality whose boundary is contiguous at any point with the boundary of a municipality in this state is eligible to be licensed under this chapter in the same manner as a resident of this state if the nonresident has been a resident of that municipality for at least the 60 days preceding the date the application is filed.

(b) A person licensed under this section shall maintain at all times a place of business in the municipality in which the person resides or in the municipality in this state that is contiguous to the municipality in which the person resides. The place of business must meet all the requirements of Section 1101.552. A place of business located in the municipality in which the person resides is considered to be in this state.

(c) A person licensed under this section may not maintain a place of business at another location in this state unless the person complies with Section 1101.356 or 1101.357.

Sec. 1101.362. WAIVER OF LICENSE REQUIREMENTS: PREVIOUS LICENSE HOLDERS. The commission by rule may waive some or all of the requirements for a license under this chapter for an applicant who was licensed under this chapter within the six years preceding the date the application is filed.

Sec. 1101.363. ISSUANCE OF LICENSE. (a) The commission shall issue an appropriate license to an applicant who meets the requirements for a license.

(b) The commission may issue an inactive salesperson license to a person who applies for a salesperson license and satisfies all requirements for the license. The person may not act as a salesperson unless the person is sponsored by a licensed broker who has notified the commission as required by Section 1101.367(b). Notwithstanding Section 1101.367(b), the licensed broker is not required to pay the fee required by that subsection.

(c) A license remains in effect for the period prescribed by the commission if the license holder complies with this chapter and pays the appropriate renewal fees.

Sec. 1101.364. DENIAL OF LICENSE. (a) The commission shall immediately give written notice to the applicant of the commission's denial of a license.

FIGURE A.1

Texas Occupations Code (continued)

(b) A person whose license application is denied under this section is entitled to a hearing under Section 1101.657.

Sec. 1101.365. PROBATIONARY LICENSE. (a) The commission may issue a probationary license.

(b) The commission by rule shall adopt reasonable terms for issuing a probationary license.

Sec. 1101.366. INACTIVE LICENSE: BROKER. (a) The commission may place on inactive status the license of a broker if the broker:

(1) is not acting as a broker;

(2) is not sponsoring a salesperson; and

(3) submits a written application to the commission before the expiration date of the broker's license.

(b) The commission may place on inactive status the license of a broker whose license has expired if the broker applies for inactive status on a form prescribed by the commission not later than the first anniversary of the expiration date of the broker's license.

(c) A broker applying for inactive status shall terminate the broker's association with each salesperson sponsored by the broker by giving written notice to each salesperson before the 30th day preceding the date the broker applies for inactive status.

(d) A broker on inactive status:

(1) may not perform any activity regulated under this chapter; and

(2) must pay annual renewal fees.

(e) The commission shall maintain a list of each broker whose license is on inactive status.

(f) The commission shall remove a broker's license from inactive status if the broker:

(1) submits an application to the commission;

(2) pays the required fee; and

(3) submits proof of attending at least 15 classroom hours of continuing education as specified by Section 1101.455 during the two years preceding the date the application under Subdivision (1) is filed.

Sec. 1101.367. INACTIVE LICENSE: SALESPERSON. (a) When the association of a salesperson with the salesperson's sponsoring broker terminates, the broker shall immediately return the salesperson license to the commission. A salesperson license returned under this subsection is inactive.

(b) The commission may remove a salesperson license from inactive status under Subsection (a) if, before the expiration date of the salesperson license, a licensed broker files a request with the commission advising the commission that the broker assumes sponsorship of the salesperson, accompanied by the appropriate fee.

(c) As a condition of returning to active status, an inactive salesperson whose license is not subject to the education requirements of Section 1101.454 must provide to the commission proof of attending at least 15 hours of continuing education as specified by Section 1101.455 during the two years preceding the date the application to return to active status is filed.

SUBCHAPTER I.
EXAMINATIONS

Sec. 1101.401. EXAMINATION REQUIRED. (a) The competency requirement prescribed under Section 1101.354(3) shall be established by an examination prepared or contracted for by the commission.

(b) The commission shall determine the time and place in the state for offering the examination.

(c) The examination must be of sufficient scope in the judgment of the commission to determine whether a person is competent to act as a broker or salesperson in a manner that will protect the public.

(d) The examination for a salesperson license must be less exacting and less stringent than the broker examination.

(e) The commission shall provide each applicant with study material and references on which the examination is based.

(f) An applicant must satisfy the examination

FIGURE A.1

Texas Occupations Code (continued)

requirement not later than one year after the date the license application is filed.

Sec. 1101.402. WAIVER OF EXAMINATION. The commission shall waive the examination requirement for an applicant for:

(1) a broker license if:

(A) the applicant was previously licensed in this state as a broker; and

(B) the application is filed before the first anniversary of the expiration date of that license; and

(2) a salesperson license if:

(A) the applicant was previously licensed in this state as a broker or salesperson; and

(B) the application is filed before the first anniversary of the expiration date of that license.

Sec. 1101.403. ADMINISTRATION OF EXAMINATION; TESTING SERVICE. (a) The commission shall administer any examination required by this chapter or Chapter 1102 unless the commission enters into an agreement with a testing service to administer the examination.

(b) The commission may accept an examination administered by a testing service if the commission retains the authority to establish the scope and type of the examination.

(c) The commission may negotiate an agreement with a testing service relating to examination development, scheduling, site arrangements, administration, grading, reporting, and analysis.

(d) The commission may require a testing service to:

(1) correspond directly with license applicants regarding the administration of the examination;

(2) collect fees directly from applicants for administering the examination; or

(3) administer the examination at specific locations and specified frequencies.

(e) The commission shall adopt rules and standards as necessary to implement this section.

Sec. 1101.404. EXAMINATION RESULTS. (a) Not later than the 30th day after the date an examination is administered, the commission shall notify each examinee of the results of the examination. If an examination is graded or reviewed by a national testing service, the commission shall notify each examinee of the results of the examination not later than the 14th day after the date the commission receives the results from the testing service.

(b) If the notice of the results of an examination graded or reviewed by a national testing service will be delayed for more than 90 days after the examination date, the commission shall notify each examinee of the reason for the delay before the 90th day.

(c) If requested in writing by a person who fails an examination, the commission shall provide to the person an analysis of the person's performance on the examination.

Sec. 1101.405. REEXAMINATION. An applicant who fails an examination may apply for reexamination by filing a request accompanied by the proper fee.

SUBCHAPTER J.
LICENSE RENEWAL

Sec. 1101.451. LICENSE EXPIRATION AND RENEWAL. (a) The commission may issue or renew a license for a period not to exceed 24 months.

(b) The commission by rule may adopt a system under which licenses expire on various dates during the year. The commission shall adjust the date for payment of the renewal fees accordingly.

(c) For a year in which the license expiration date is changed, renewal fees payable shall be prorated on a monthly basis so that each license holder pays only that portion of the fee that is allocable to the number of months during which the license is valid. On renewal of the license on the new expiration date, the total renewal fee is payable.

(d) Except as provided by Subsection (e), a renewal fee for a license under this chapter may not exceed, calculated on an annual basis, the

FIGURE A.1

Texas Occupations Code (continued)

amount of the sum of the fees established under Sections 1101.152, 1101.154, and 1101.603.

(e) A person whose license has been expired for 90 days or less may renew the license by paying to the commission a fee equal to 1-1/2 times the required renewal fee. If a license has been expired for more than 90 days but less than six months, the person may renew the license by paying to the commission a fee equal to two times the required renewal fee.

(f) If a person's license has been expired for six months or longer, the person may not renew the license. The person may obtain a new license by submitting to reexamination and complying with the requirements and procedures for obtaining an original license.

Sec. 1101.452. INFORMATION REQUIRED FOR LICENSE RENEWAL. (a) To renew an active license that is not subject to the education requirements of Section 1101.454, the license holder must provide to the commission proof of compliance with the continuing education requirements of Section 1101.455.

(b) Each applicant for the renewal of a license must disclose in the license application whether the applicant has:

(1) entered a plea of guilty or nolo contendere to a felony; or

(2) been convicted of a felony and the time for appeal has elapsed or the judgment or conviction has been affirmed on appeal.

(c) The disclosure under Subsection (b) must be provided even if an order has granted community supervision suspending the imposition of the sentence.

Sec. 1101.4521. CRIMINAL HISTORY RECORD INFORMATION FOR RENEWAL. An applicant for the renewal of an unexpired license must comply with the criminal history record check requirements of Section 1101.3521.

Sec. 1101.453. ADDITIONAL RENEWAL REQUIREMENTS FOR BUSINESS ENTITIES. (a) To renew a license under this chapter, a business entity must:

(1) designate one of its managing officers as its agent for purposes of this chapter; and

(2) provide proof that the entity maintains errors and omissions insurance with a minimum annual limit of $1 million for each occurrence if the designated agent owns less than 10 percent of the business entity.

(b) A business entity may not act as a broker unless the entity's designated agent is a licensed broker in active status and good standing according to the commission's records.

Sec. 1101.454. SALESPERSON LICENSE RENEWAL. (a) An applicant applying for the first renewal of a salesperson license must provide to the commission satisfactory evidence of completion of at least 18 semester hours, or equivalent classroom hours, of postsecondary education, including 14 hours of core real estate courses.

(b) The commission may not waive the requirements for renewal under this section.

Sec. 1101.454. SALESPERSON LICENSE RENEWAL. (a) An applicant applying for the first renewal of a salesperson license must provide to the commission satisfactory evidence of completion of at least 18 semester hours, or equivalent classroom hours, of core real estate courses.

(b) The commission may not waive the requirements for renewal under this section.

Effective September 1, 2012.

Sec. 1101.455. CONTINUING EDUCATION REQUIREMENTS. (a) In this section, "property tax consulting laws and legal issues" includes the Tax Code, preparation of property tax reports, the unauthorized practice of law, agency law, tax law, law relating to property tax or property assessment, deceptive trade practices, contract forms and addendums, and other legal topics approved by the commission.

(b) A license holder who is not subject to the education requirements of Section 1101.454 must attend during the term of the current license at least 15 classroom hours of continuing education courses approved by the commission.

FIGURE A.1

Texas Occupations Code (continued)

(c) The commission by rule may:

(1) prescribe the title, content, and duration of continuing education courses that a license holder must attend to renew a license; and

(2) approve as a substitute for the classroom attendance required by Subsection (b):

(A) relevant educational experience; and

(B) correspondence courses.

(d) In addition, the commission may approve supervised video instruction as a course that may be applied toward satisfaction of the classroom hours of continuing education courses required by Subsection (b).

(e) At least six of the continuing education hours required by Subsection (b) must cover the following legal topics:

(1) commission rules;

(2) fair housing laws;

(3) Property Code issues, including landlord-tenant law;

(4) agency law;

(5) antitrust laws;

(6) Subchapter E, Chapter 17, Business & Commerce Code;

(7) disclosures to buyers, landlords, tenants, and sellers;

(8) current contract and addendum forms;

(9) unauthorized practice of law;

(10) case studies involving violations of laws and regulations;

(11) current Federal Housing Administration and Department of Veterans Affairs regulations;

(12) tax laws;

(13) property tax consulting laws and legal issues; or

(14) other legal topics approved by the commission.

(f) The remaining nine hours may be devoted to other real estate-related topics approved by the commission.

(g) The commission may consider courses equivalent to those described by Subsections (e) and (f) for continuing education credit.

(h) The commission shall automatically approve the following courses as courses that satisfy the mandatory continuing education requirements of Subsection (f) :

(1) core real estate courses; and

(2) real estate-related courses approved by the State Bar of Texas for minimum continuing legal education participatory credit.

(i) The commission may not require an examination for a course under this section unless the course is a correspondence course or a course offered by an alternative delivery system, including delivery by computer.

(j) Daily classroom course segments must be at least one hour and not more than 10 hours.

(k) An online course offered under this section may not be completed in less than 24 hours.

(l) Notwithstanding the number of hours required by Subsection (e), a member of the legislature licensed under this chapter is only required to complete three hours of continuing education on the legal topics under Subsection (e).

Sec. 1101.456. EXEMPTION FROM CONTINUING EDUCATION REQUIREMENTS FOR CERTAIN BROKERS. Notwithstanding any other provision of this chapter, a broker who, before October 31, 1991, qualified under former Section 7A(f), The Real Estate License Act (Article 6573a, Vernon's Texas Civil Statutes), as added by Section 1.041, Chapter 553, Acts of the 72nd Legislature, Regular Session, 1991, for an exemption from continuing education requirements is not required to comply with the mandatory continuing education requirements of this subchapter to renew the broker's license.

Sec. 1101.457. DEFERRAL OF CONTINUING EDUCATION REQUIREMENTS. (a) The commission by rule may establish procedures under which an applicant may have the applicant's license issued, renewed, or returned to active status before the applicant completes continuing education requirements.

(b) The commission may require an applicant under this section to:

FIGURE A.1

Texas Occupations Code (continued)

(1) pay a fee, not to exceed $200, in addition to any fee for late renewal of a license under this chapter; and

(2) complete the required continuing education not later than the 60th day after the date the license is issued, renewed, or returned to active status.

Sec. 1101.458. ADDITIONAL EDUCATION REQUIREMENTS FOR CERTAIN LICENSE HOLDERS. (a) A broker who sponsors a salesperson, or a license holder who supervises another license holder, must attend during the term of the current license at least six classroom hours of broker responsibility education courses approved by the commission.

(b) The commission by rule shall prescribe the title, content, and duration of broker responsibility education courses required under this section.

(c) Broker responsibility education course hours may be used to satisfy the hours described by Section 1101.455(f).

(d) This section does not apply to a broker who is exempt from continuing education requirements under Section 1101.456.

Effective September 1, 2012.

SUBCHAPTER K.
CERTIFICATE REQUIREMENTS

Sec. 1101.501. CERTIFICATE REQUIRED. A person may not sell, buy, lease, or transfer an easement or right-of-way for another, for compensation or with the expectation of receiving compensation, for use in connection with telecommunication, utility, railroad, or pipeline service unless the person:

(1) holds a license issued under this chapter; or

(2) holds a certificate of registration issued under this subchapter.

Sec. 1101.502. ELIGIBILITY REQUIREMENTS FOR CERTIFICATE. (a) To be eligible to receive a certificate of registration or a renewal certificate under this subchapter, a person must be:

(1) at least 18 years of age; and

(2) a citizen of the United States or a lawfully admitted alien.

(b) To be eligible to receive a certificate of registration or a renewal certificate under this subchapter, a business entity must designate as its agent one of its managing officers who is registered under this subchapter.

Amendments to Sec. 1101.502(b) effective December 1, 2011.

Sec. 1101.503. ISSUANCE OF CERTIFICATE. (a) The commission shall issue a certificate of registration to an applicant who meets the requirements for a certificate of registration.

(b) The certificate remains in effect for the period prescribed by the commission if the certificate holder complies with this chapter and pays the appropriate renewal fees.

Sec. 1101.504. CERTIFICATE EXPIRATION. The duration, expiration, and renewal of a certificate of registration are subject to the same provisions as are applicable under Section 1101.451 to the duration, expiration, and renewal of a license.

Sec. 1101.5041. CRIMINAL HISTORY RECORD INFORMATION REQUIREMENT FOR CERTIFICATE. An applicant for an original certificate of registration or renewal of a certificate of registration must comply with the criminal history record check requirements of Section 1101.3521.

Effective December 1, 2011.

Sec. 1101.505. DENIAL OF CERTIFICATE. The denial of a certificate of registration is subject to the same provisions as are applicable under Section 1101.364 to the denial of a license.

FIGURE A.1

Texas Occupations Code (continued)

Sec. 1101.506. CHANGE OF ADDRESS. Not later than the 10th day after the date a certificate holder moves its place of business from a previously designated address, the holder shall:

(1) notify the commission of the move; and

(2) obtain a new certificate of registration that reflects the address of the new place of business.

Sec. 1101.507. DISPLAY OF CERTIFICATE. A certificate holder shall prominently display at all times the holder's certificate of registration in the holder's place of business.

SUBCHAPTER L.
PRACTICE BY LICENSE HOLDER

Sec. 1101.551. DEFINITIONS. In this subchapter:

(1) "Intermediary" means a broker who is employed to negotiate a transaction between the parties to a transaction and for that purpose may act as an agent of the parties.

(2) "Party" means a prospective buyer, seller, landlord, or tenant or an authorized representative of a buyer, seller, landlord, or tenant, including a trustee, guardian, executor, administrator, receiver, or attorney-in-fact. The term does not include a license holder who represents a party.

Sec. 1101.552. FIXED OFFICE REQUIRED; CHANGE OF ADDRESS; BRANCH OFFICES. (a) A resident broker shall maintain a fixed office in this state. The address of the office shall be designated on the broker's license.

(b) Not later than the 10th day after the date a broker moves from the address designated on the broker's license, the broker shall submit an application, accompanied by the appropriate fee, for a license that designates the new location of the broker's office. The commission shall issue a license that designates the new location if the new location complies with the requirements of this section.

(c) A broker who maintains more than one place of business in this state shall obtain a branch office license for each additional office maintained by the broker by submitting an application, accompanied by the appropriate fee.

(d) A nonresident licensed broker is not required to maintain a place of business in this state.

(e) A license holder shall provide the commission with the license holder's current mailing address and telephone number, and e-mail address if available. A license holder shall notify the commission of a change in the license holder's mailing or e-mail address or telephone number.

Sec. 1101.553. DISPLAY OF LICENSE. A residential rental locator shall prominently display in a place accessible to clients and prospective clients:

(1) the locator's license;

(2) a statement that the locator is licensed by the commission; and

(3) the name, mailing address, and telephone number of the commission as provided by Section 1101.202(a).

Sec. 1101.554. COPY OF SALESPERSON LICENSE. The commission shall deliver or mail a copy of each salesperson license to the broker with whom the salesperson is associated.

Sec. 1101.555. NOTICE TO BUYER REGARDING ABSTRACT OR TITLE POLICY. When an offer to purchase real estate in this state is signed, a license holder shall advise each buyer, in writing, that the buyer should:

(1) have the abstract covering the real estate that is the subject of the contract examined by an attorney chosen by the buyer; or

(2) be provided with or obtain a title insurance policy.

Sec. 1101.556. DISCLOSURE OF CERTAIN INFORMATION RELATING TO OCCUPANTS. Notwithstanding other law, a license holder is not required to inquire about,

FIGURE A.1

Texas Occupations Code (continued)

disclose, or release information relating to whether:

(1) a previous or current occupant of real property had, may have had, has, or may have AIDS, an HIV-related illness, or an HIV infection as defined by the Centers for Disease Control and Prevention of the United States Public Health Service; or

(2) a death occurred on a property by natural causes, suicide, or accident unrelated to the condition of the property.

Sec. 1101.557. ACTING AS AGENT; REGULATION OF CERTAIN TRANSACTIONS. (a) A broker who represents a party in a real estate transaction or who lists real estate for sale under an exclusive agreement for a party is that party's agent.

(b) A broker described by Subsection (a):

(1) may not instruct another broker to directly or indirectly violate Section 1101.652(b)(22);

(2) must inform the party if the broker receives material information related to a transaction to list, buy, sell, or lease the party's real estate, including the receipt of an offer by the broker; and

(3) shall, at a minimum, answer the party's questions and present any offer to or from the party.

(c) For the purposes of this section:

(1) a license holder who has the authority to bind a party to a lease or sale under a power of attorney or a property management agreement is also a party to the lease or sale;

(2) an inquiry to a person described by Section 1101.005(6) about contract terms or forms required by the person's employer does not violate Section 1101.652(b)(22) if the person does not have the authority to bind the employer to the contract; and

(3) the sole delivery of an offer to a party does not violate Section 1101.652(b)(22) if:

(A) the party's broker consents to the delivery;

(B) a copy of the offer is sent to the party's broker, unless a governmental agency using a sealed bid process does not allow a copy to be sent; and

(C) the person delivering the offer does not engage in another activity that directly or indirectly violates Section 1101.652(b)(22).

Sec. 1101.558. REPRESENTATION DISCLOSURE. (a) In this section, "substantive dialogue" means a meeting or written communication that involves a substantive discussion relating to specific real property. The term does not include:

(1) a meeting that occurs at a property that is held open for any prospective buyer or tenant; or

(2) a meeting or written communication that occurs after the parties to a real estate transaction have signed a contract to sell, buy, or lease the real property concerned.

(b) A license holder who represents a party in a proposed real estate transaction shall disclose, orally or in writing, that representation at the time of the license holder's first contact with:

(1) another party to the transaction; or

(2) another license holder who represents another party to the transaction.

(c) A license holder shall provide to a party to a real estate transaction at the time of the first substantive dialogue with the party the written statement prescribed by Subsection (d) unless:

(1) the proposed transaction is for a residential lease for not more than one year and a sale is not being considered; or

(2) the license holder meets with a party who is represented by another license holder.

(d) The written statement required by Subsection (c) must be printed in a format that uses at least 10-point type and read as follows:

"Before working with a real estate broker, you should know that the duties of a broker depend on whom the broker represents. If you are a prospective seller or landlord (owner) or a prospective buyer or tenant (buyer), you should know that the broker who lists the property for sale or lease is the owner's agent. A broker who acts as a subagent represents the owner in cooperation with the listing broker. A broker who acts as a buyer's agent represents the buyer. A broker may act as an intermediary between the parties if the parties consent in

FIGURE A.1

Texas Occupations Code (continued)

writing. A broker can assist you in locating a property, preparing a contract or lease, or obtaining financing without representing you. A broker is obligated by law to treat you honestly.

"IF THE BROKER REPRESENTS THE OWNER: The broker becomes the owner's agent by entering into an agreement with the owner, usually through a written listing agreement, or by agreeing to act as a subagent by accepting an offer of subagency from the listing broker. A subagent may work in a different real estate office. A listing broker or subagent can assist the buyer but does not represent the buyer and must place the interests of the owner first. The buyer should not tell the owner's agent anything the buyer would not want the owner to know because an owner's agent must disclose to the owner any material information known to the agent.

"IF THE BROKER REPRESENTS THE BUYER: The broker becomes the buyer's agent by entering into an agreement to represent the buyer, usually through a written buyer representation agreement. A buyer's agent can assist the owner but does not represent the owner and must place the interests of the buyer first. The owner should not tell a buyer's agent anything the owner would not want the buyer to know because a buyer's agent must disclose to the buyer any material information known to the agent.

"IF THE BROKER ACTS AS AN INTERMEDIARY: A broker may act as an intermediary between the parties if the broker complies with The Texas Real Estate License Act. The broker must obtain the written consent of each party to the transaction to act as an intermediary. The written consent must state who will pay the broker and, in conspicuous bold or underlined print, set forth the broker's obligations as an intermediary. The broker is required to treat each party honestly and fairly and to comply with The Texas Real Estate License Act. A broker who acts as an intermediary in a transaction: (1) shall treat all parties honestly; (2) may not disclose that the owner will accept a price less than the asking price unless authorized in writing to do so by the owner; (3) may not disclose that the buyer will pay a price greater than the price submitted in a written offer unless authorized in writing to do so by the buyer; and (4) may not disclose any confidential information or any information that a party specifically instructs the broker in writing not to disclose unless authorized in writing to disclose the information or required to do so by The Texas Real Estate License Act or a court order or if the information materially relates to the condition of the property. With the parties' consent, a broker acting as an intermediary between the parties may appoint a person who is licensed under The Texas Real Estate License Act and associated with the broker to communicate with and carry out instructions of one party and another person who is licensed under that Act and associated with the broker to communicate with and carry out instructions of the other party.

"If you choose to have a broker represent you, you should enter into a written agreement with the broker that clearly establishes the broker's obligations and your obligations. The agreement should state how and by whom the broker will be paid. You have the right to choose the type of representation, if any, you wish to receive. Your payment of a fee to a broker does not necessarily establish that the broker represents you. If you have any questions regarding the duties and responsibilities of the broker, you should resolve those questions before proceeding."

(e) The license holder may substitute "buyer" for "tenant" and "seller" for "landlord" as appropriate in the written statement prescribed by Subsection (d).

Sec. 1101.559. BROKER ACTING AS INTERMEDIARY. (a) A broker may act as an intermediary between parties to a real estate transaction if:

(1) the broker obtains written consent from each party for the broker to act as an intermediary in the transaction; and

(2) the written consent of the parties states the source of any expected compensation to the broker.

(b) A written listing agreement to represent a seller or landlord or a written agreement to represent a buyer or tenant that authorizes a broker to act as an intermediary in a real estate transaction is sufficient to establish written consent of the party to the transaction if the written agreement specifies in conspicuous bold or underlined print the conduct that is prohibited under Section 1101.651(d).

(c) An intermediary shall act fairly and

FIGURE A.1

Texas Occupations Code (continued)

impartially. Appointment by a broker acting as an intermediary of an associated license holder under Section 1101.560 to communicate with, carry out the instructions of, and provide opinions and advice to the parties to whom that associated license holder is appointed is a fair and impartial act.

Sec. 1101.560. ASSOCIATED LICENSE HOLDER ACTING AS INTERMEDIARY. (a) A broker who complies with the written consent requirements of Section 1101.559 may appoint:

(1) a license holder associated with the broker to communicate with and carry out instructions of one party to a real estate transaction; and

(2) another license holder associated with the broker to communicate with and carry out instructions of any other party to the transaction.

(b) A license holder may be appointed under this section only if:

(1) the written consent of the parties under Section 1101.559 authorizes the broker to make the appointment; and

(2) the broker provides written notice of the appointment to all parties involved in the real estate transaction.

(c) A license holder appointed under this section may provide opinions and advice during negotiations to the party to whom the license holder is appointed.

Sec. 1101.561. DUTIES OF INTERMEDIARY PREVAIL. (a) The duties of a license holder acting as an intermediary under this subchapter supersede the duties of a license holder established under any other law, including common law.

(b) A broker must agree to act as an intermediary under this subchapter if the broker agrees to represent in a transaction:

(1) a buyer or tenant; and

(2) a seller or landlord.

SUBCHAPTER M.
REAL ESTATE RECOVERY TRUST ACCOUNT

Sec. 1101.601. REAL ESTATE RECOVERY TRUST ACCOUNT. (a) The commission shall maintain a real estate recovery trust account to reimburse aggrieved persons who suffer actual damages caused by an act described by Section 1101.602 committed by:

(1) a license holder;

(2) a certificate holder; or

(3) a person who does not hold a license or certificate and who is an employee or agent of a license or certificate holder.

(b) The license or certificate holder must have held the license or certificate at the time the act was committed.

Sec. 1101.602. ENTITLEMENT TO REIMBURSEMENT. An aggrieved person is entitled to reimbursement from the trust account if a person described by Section 1101.601 engages in conduct described by Section 1101.652(a)(3) or (b) or 1101.653(1), (2), (3), or (4).

Sec. 1101.603. PAYMENTS INTO TRUST ACCOUNT. (a) In addition to other fees required by this chapter, an applicant for an original license must pay a fee of $10.

(b) In addition to other fees required by this chapter, an applicant for an original certificate of registration or renewal certificate must pay a fee of $50.

(c) The commission shall deposit to the credit of the trust account:

(1) fees collected under Subsections (a) and (b); and

(2) an administrative penalty collected under Subchapter O for a violation by a person licensed as a broker or salesperson.

(d) A administrative penalty collected under Subchapter O for a violation by a person who is not licensed under this chapter or Chapter 1102 shall be deposited to the credit of the trust account or the real estate inspection recovery fund, as determined by the commission.

(e) On a determination by the commission at any time that the balance in the trust account is less than $1 million, each license holder at the next license renewal must pay, in addition to

FIGURE A.1

Texas Occupations Code (continued)

the renewal fee, a fee that is equal to the lesser of $10 or a pro rata share of the amount necessary to obtain a balance in the trust account of $1.7 million. The commission shall deposit the additional fee to the credit of the trust account.

(f) To ensure the availability of a sufficient amount to pay anticipated claims on the trust account, the commission by rule may provide for the collection of assessments at different times and under conditions other than those specified by this chapter.

Sec. 1101.604. MANAGEMENT OF TRUST ACCOUNT. (a) The commission shall hold money credited to the trust account in trust to carry out the purpose of the trust account.

(b) Money credited to the trust account may be invested in the same manner as money of the Employees Retirement System of Texas, except that an investment may not be made that would impair the liquidity necessary to make payments from the trust account as required by this subchapter.

(c) Interest from the investments shall be deposited to the credit of the trust account.

(d) If the balance in the trust account on December 31 of a year is more than the greater of $3.5 million or the total amount of claims paid from the trust account during the preceding four fiscal years, the commission shall transfer the excess amount of money in the trust account to the credit of the general revenue fund.

Sec. 1101.605. DEADLINE FOR ACTION; NOTICE TO COMMISSION. (a) An action for a judgment that may result in an order for payment from the trust account may not be brought after the second anniversary of the date the cause of action accrues.

(b) When an aggrieved person brings an action for a judgment that may result in an order for payment from the trust account, the license or certificate holder against whom the action is brought shall notify the commission in writing of the action.

Sec. 1101.606. CLAIM FOR PAYMENT FROM TRUST ACCOUNT. (a) Except as provided by Subsection (c), an aggrieved person who obtains a court judgment against a license or certificate holder for an act described by Section 1101.602 may, after final judgment is entered, execution returned nulla bona, and a judgment lien perfected, file a verified claim in the court that entered the judgment.

(b) After the 20th day after the date the aggrieved person gives written notice of the claim to the commission and judgment debtor, the person may apply to the court that entered the judgment for an order for payment from the trust account of the amount unpaid on the judgment. The court shall proceed promptly on the application.

(c) If an aggrieved person is precluded by action of a bankruptcy court from executing a judgment or perfecting a judgment lien as required by Subsection (a), the person shall verify to the commission that the person has made a good faith effort to protect the judgment from being discharged in bankruptcy.

(d) The commission by rule may prescribe the actions necessary for an aggrieved person to demonstrate that the person has made a good faith effort under Subsection (c) to protect a judgment from being discharged in bankruptcy.

Sec. 1101.607. ISSUES AT HEARING. At the hearing on the application for payment from the trust account, the aggrieved person must show:

(1) that the judgment is based on facts allowing recovery under this subchapter;

(2) that the person is not:

(A) the spouse of the judgment debtor or the personal representative of the spouse; or

(B) a license or certificate holder who is seeking to recover compensation, including a commission, in the real estate transaction that is the subject of the application for payment;

(3) that, according to the best information available, the judgment debtor does not have sufficient attachable assets in this or another state to satisfy the judgment;

(4) the amount that may be realized from the sale of assets liable to be sold or applied to satisfy the judgment; and

(5) the balance remaining due on the judgment after application of the amount under Subdivision (4).

FIGURE A.1

Texas Occupations Code (continued)

Sec. 1101.608. COMMISSION RESPONSE. (a) On receipt of notice under Section 1101.606 and the scheduling of a hearing, the commission may notify the attorney general of the commission's desire to enter an appearance, file a response, appear at the hearing, defend the action, or take any other action the commission considers appropriate.

(b) The commission and the attorney general may act under Subsection (a) only to:

(1) protect the trust account from spurious or unjust claims; or

(2) ensure compliance with the requirements for recovery under this subchapter.

(c) The commission may relitigate in the hearing any material and relevant issue that was determined in the action that resulted in the judgment in favor of the aggrieved person.

Sec. 1101.609. COURT ORDER FOR PAYMENT. The court shall order the commission to pay from the trust account the amount the court finds payable on the claim under this subchapter if at a hearing the court is satisfied:

(1) of the truth of each matter the aggrieved person is required by Section 1101.607 to show; and

(2) that the aggrieved person has satisfied each requirement of Sections 1101.606 and 1101.607.

Sec. 1101.610. PAYMENT LIMITS; ATTORNEY'S FEES. (a) Payments from the trust account for claims, including attorney's fees, interest, and court costs, arising out of a single transaction may not exceed a total of $50,000, regardless of the number of claimants.

(b) Payments from the trust account for claims based on judgments against a single license or certificate holder may not exceed a total of $100,000 until the license or certificate holder has reimbursed the trust account for all amounts paid.

(c) If the court finds that the total amount of claims against a license or certificate holder exceeds the limitations in this section, the court shall proportionately reduce the amount payable on each claim.

(d) A person receiving payment from the trust account is entitled to receive reasonable attorney's fees in the amount determined by the court, subject to the limitations prescribed by this section.

Sec. 1101.611. APPLICATION OF JUDGMENT RECOVERY. An aggrieved person who receives a recovery on a judgment against a single defendant before receiving a payment from the trust account must apply the recovery first to actual damages.

Sec. 1101.612. SUBROGATION. (a) The commission is subrogated to all rights of a judgment creditor to the extent of an amount paid from the trust account, and the judgment creditor shall assign to the commission all right, title, and interest in the judgment up to that amount.

(b) The commission has priority for repayment from any subsequent recovery on the judgment.

(c) The commission shall deposit any amount recovered on the judgment to the credit of the trust account.

Sec. 1101.613. EFFECT ON DISCIPLINARY PROCEEDINGS. (a) This subchapter does not limit the commission's authority to take disciplinary action against a license or certificate holder for a violation of this chapter or a commission rule.

(b) A license or certificate holder's repayment of all amounts owed to the trust account does not affect another disciplinary proceeding brought under this chapter.

Sec. 1101.614. WAIVER OF RIGHTS. An aggrieved person who does not comply with this subchapter waives the person's rights under this subchapter.

Sec. 1101.615. NOTICE TO CONSUMERS AND SERVICE RECIPIENTS. (a) Each license and certificate holder shall provide notice to consumers and service recipients of the availability of payment from the trust account for aggrieved persons:

FIGURE A.1

Texas Occupations Code (continued)

(1) in conjunction with the notice required by Section 1101.202;

(2) on a written contract for the license or certificate holder's services;

(3) on a brochure that the license or certificate holder distributes;

(4) on a sign prominently displayed in the license or certificate holder's place of business; or

(5) in a bill or receipt for the license or certificate holder's services ; or

(6) in a prominent display on the Internet website of a person regulated under this chapter.

(b) The notice must include:

(1) the commission's name, mailing address, and telephone number; and

(2) any other information required by commission rule.

SUBCHAPTER N.
PROHIBITED PRACTICES AND
DISCIPLINARY PROCEEDINGS

Sec. 1101.651. CERTAIN PRACTICES PROHIBITED. (a) A licensed broker may not pay a commission to or otherwise compensate a person directly or indirectly for performing an act of a broker unless the person is:

(1) a license holder; or

(2) a real estate broker licensed in another state who does not conduct in this state any of the negotiations for which the commission or other compensation is paid.

(b) A salesperson may not accept compensation for a real estate transaction from a person other than the broker with whom the salesperson is associated or was associated when the salesperson earned the compensation.

(c) A salesperson may not pay a commission to a person except through the broker with whom the salesperson is associated at that time.

(d) A broker and any broker or salesperson appointed under Section 1101.560 who acts as an intermediary under Subchapter L may not:

(1) disclose to the buyer or tenant that the seller or landlord will accept a price less than the asking price, unless otherwise instructed in a separate writing by the seller or landlord;

(2) disclose to the seller or landlord that the buyer or tenant will pay a price greater than the price submitted in a written offer to the seller or landlord, unless otherwise instructed in a separate writing by the buyer or tenant;

(3) disclose any confidential information or any information a party specifically instructs the broker or salesperson in writing not to disclose, unless:

(A) the broker or salesperson is otherwise instructed in a separate writing by the respective party;

(B) the broker or salesperson is required to disclose the information by this chapter or a court order; or

(C) the information materially relates to the condition of the property;

(4) treat a party to a transaction dishonestly; or

(5) violate this chapter.

Sec. 1101.652. GROUNDS FOR SUSPENSION OR REVOCATION OF LICENSE. (a) The commission may suspend or revoke a license issued under this chapter or take other disciplinary action authorized by this chapter if the license holder:

(1) enters a plea of guilty or nolo contendere to or is convicted of a felony or a criminal offense involving fraud, and the time for appeal has elapsed or the judgment or conviction has been affirmed on appeal, without regard to an order granting community supervision that suspends the imposition of the sentence;

(2) procures or attempts to procure a license under this chapter for the license holder or a salesperson by fraud, misrepresentation, or deceit or by making a material misstatement of fact in an application for a license;

(3) engages in misrepresentation, dishonesty, or fraud when selling, buying, trading, or leasing real property in the name of:

(A) the license holder;

FIGURE A.1

Texas Occupations Code (continued)

(B) the license holder's spouse; or

(C) a person related to the license holder within the first degree by consanguinity;

(4) fails to honor, within a reasonable time, a check issued to the commission after the commission has sent by certified mail a request for payment to the license holder's last known business address according to commission records;

(5) fails or refuses to produce on request, for inspection by the commission or a commission representative, a document, book, or record that is in the license holder's possession and relates to a real estate transaction conducted by the license holder;

(6) fails to provide, within a reasonable time, information requested by the commission that relates to a formal or informal complaint to the commission that would indicate a violation of this chapter;

(7) fails to surrender to the owner, without just cause, a document or instrument that is requested by the owner and that is in the license holder's possession;

(8) fails to use a contract form required by the commission under Section 1101.155;

(9) fails to notify the commission, not later than the 30th day after the date of a final conviction or the entry of a plea of guilty or nolo contendere, that the person has been convicted of or entered a plea of guilty or nolo contendere to a felony or a criminal offense involving fraud; or

(10) disregards or violates this chapter.

(b) The commission may suspend or revoke a license issued under this chapter or take other disciplinary action authorized by this chapter if the license holder, while acting as a broker or salesperson:

(1) acts negligently or incompetently;

(2) engages in conduct that is dishonest or in bad faith or that demonstrates untrustworthiness;

(3) Makes a material misrepresentation to a potential buyer concerning a significant defect, including a latent structural defect, known to the license holder that would be a significant factor to a reasonable and prudent buyer in making a decision to purchase real property;

(4) fails to disclose to a potential buyer a defect described by Subdivision (3) that is known to the license holder;

(5) makes a false promise that is likely to influence a person to enter into an agreement when the license holder is unable or does not intend to keep the promise;

(6) pursues a continued and flagrant course of misrepresentation or makes false promises through an agent or salesperson, through advertising, or otherwise;

(7) fails to make clear to all parties to a real estate transaction the party for whom the license holder is acting;

(8) receives compensation from more than one party to a real estate transaction without the full knowledge and consent of all parties to the transaction;

(9) fails within a reasonable time to properly account for or remit money that is received by the license holder and that belongs to another person;

(10) commingles money that belongs to another person with the license holder's own money;

(11) pays a commission or a fee to or divides a commission or a fee with a person other than a license holder or a real estate broker or salesperson licensed in another state for compensation for services as a real estate agent;

(12) fails to specify a definite termination date that is not subject to prior notice in a contract, other than a contract to perform property management services, in which the license holder agrees to perform services for which a license is required under this chapter;

(13) accepts, receives, or charges an undisclosed commission, rebate, or direct profit on an expenditure made for a principal;

(14) solicits, sells, or offers for sale real property by means of a lottery;

(15) solicits, sells, or offers for sale real property by means of a deceptive practice;

(16) acts in a dual capacity as broker and undisclosed principal in a real estate transaction;

(17) guarantees or authorizes or permits a person to guarantee that future profits will result from a resale of real property;

(18) places a sign on real property offering

FIGURE A.1

Texas Occupations Code (continued)

the real property for sale or lease without obtaining the written consent of the owner of the real property or the owner's authorized agent;

(19) offers to sell or lease real property without the knowledge and consent of the owner of the real property or the owner's authorized agent;

(20) offers to sell or lease real property on terms other than those authorized by the owner of the real property or the owner's authorized agent;

(21) induces or attempts to induce a party to a contract of sale or lease to break the contract for the purpose of substituting a new contract;

(22) negotiates or attempts to negotiate the sale, exchange, or lease of real property with an owner, landlord, buyer, or tenant with knowledge that that person is a party to an outstanding written contract that grants exclusive agency to another broker in connection with the transaction;

(23) publishes or causes to be published an advertisement, including an advertisement by newspaper, radio, television, the Internet or display, that misleads or is likely to deceive the public, tends to create a misleading impression, or fails to identify the person causing the advertisement to be published as a licensed broker or agent;

(24) withholds from or inserts into a statement of account or invoice a statement that the license holder knows makes the statement of account or invoice inaccurate in a material way;

(25) publishes or circulates an unjustified or unwarranted threat of a legal proceeding or other action;

(26) establishes an association by employment or otherwise with a person other than a license holder if the person is expected or required to act as a license holder;

(27) aids, abets, or conspires with another person to circumvent this chapter;

(28) fails or refuses to provide, on request, a copy of a document relating to a real estate transaction to a person who signed the document;

(29) fails to advise a buyer in writing before the closing of a real estate transaction that the buyer should:

(A) have the abstract covering the real estate that is the subject of the contract examined by an attorney chosen by the buyer; or

(B) be provided with or obtain a title insurance policy;

(30) fails to deposit, within a reasonable time, money the license holder receives as escrow agent in a real estate transaction:

(A) in trust with a title company authorized to do business in this state; or

(B) in a custodial, trust, or escrow account maintained for that purpose in a banking institution authorized to do business in this state;

(31) disburses money deposited in a custodial, trust, or escrow account, as provided in Subdivision (30), before the completion or termination of the real estate transaction;

(32) discriminates against an owner, potential buyer, landlord, or potential tenant on the basis of race, color, religion, sex, disability, familial status, national origin, or ancestry, including directing a prospective buyer or tenant interested in equivalent properties to a different area based on the race, color, religion, sex, disability familial status, national origin, or ancestry of the potential owner or tenant; or

(33) disregards or violates this chapter.

Sec. 1101.653. GROUNDS FOR SUSPENSION OR REVOCATION OF CERTIFICATE. The commission may suspend or revoke a certificate of registration issued under this chapter if the certificate holder:

(1) engages in dishonest dealing, fraud, unlawful discrimination, or a deceptive act;

(2) makes a misrepresentation;

(3) acts in bad faith;

(4) demonstrates untrustworthiness;

(5) fails to honor, within a reasonable time, a check issued to the commission after the commission has mailed a request for payment to the certificate holder's last known address according to the commission's records;

(6) fails to provide to a party to a transaction a written notice prescribed by the commission that:

(A) must be given before the party is obligated to sell, buy, lease, or transfer a right-

FIGURE A.1

Texas Occupations Code (continued)

of-way or easement; and

　(B) contains:

　　(i) the name of the certificate holder;

　　(ii) the certificate number;

　　(iii) the name of the person the certificate holder represents;

　　(iv) a statement advising the party that the party may seek representation from a lawyer or broker in the transaction; and

　　(v) a statement generally advising the party that the right-of-way or easement may affect the value of the property; or

　(7) disregards or violates this chapter or a commission rule relating to certificate holders.

　Sec. 1101.654. SUSPENSION OR REVOCATION OF LICENSE OR CERTIFICATE FOR UNAUTHORIZED PRACTICE OF LAW. (a) The commission shall suspend or revoke the license or certificate of registration of a license or certificate holder who is not a licensed attorney in this state and who, for consideration, a reward, or a pecuniary benefit, present or anticipated, direct or indirect, or in connection with the person's employment, agency, or fiduciary relationship as a license or certificate holder:

　(1) drafts an instrument, other than a form described by Section 1101.155, that transfers or otherwise affects an interest in real property; or

　(2) advises a person regarding the validity or legal sufficiency of an instrument or the validity of title to real property.

　(b) Notwithstanding any other law, a license or certificate holder who completes a contract form for the sale, exchange, option, or lease of an interest in real property incidental to acting as a broker is not engaged in the unauthorized or illegal practice of law in this state if the form was:

　(1) adopted by the commission for the type of transaction for which the form is used;

　(2) prepared by an attorney licensed in this state and approved by the attorney for the type of transaction for which the form is used; or

　(3) prepared by the property owner or by an attorney and required by the property owner.

　Sec. 1101.655. REVOCATION OF LICENSE OR CERTIFICATE FOR CLAIM ON ACCOUNT. (a) The commission may revoke a license, approval, or registration issued under this chapter or Chapter 1102 if the commission makes a payment from the real estate recovery trust account to satisfy all or part of a judgment against the license or certificate registration holder.

　(b) The commission may probate an order revoking a license under this section.

　(c) A person is not eligible for a license or certificate until the person has repaid in full the amount paid from the account for the person, plus interest at the legal rate.

　Sec. 1101.656. ADDITIONAL DISCIPLINARY AUTHORITY OF COMMISSION. (a) In addition to any other authority under this chapter, the commission may suspend or revoke a license, place on probation a person whose license has been suspended, or reprimand a license holder if the license holder violates this chapter or a commission rule.

　(b) The commission may probate a suspension, revocation, or cancellation of a license under reasonable terms determined by the commission.

　(c) The commission may require a license holder whose license suspension or revocation is probated to:

　(1) report regularly to the commission on matters that are the basis of the probation;

　(2) limit practice to an area prescribed by the commission; or

　(3) continue to renew professional education until the license holder attains a degree of skill satisfactory to the commission in the area that is the basis of the probation.

　Sec. 1101.6561. SUSPENSION OR REVOCATION OF EDUCATIONAL PROGRAM ACCREDITATION. The commission may suspend or revoke an accreditation issued under Subchapter G or take any other disciplinary action authorized by this chapter if the provider of an educational program or course of study violates this chapter or a rule adopted under this chapter.

FIGURE A.1

Texas Occupations Code (continued)

Sec. 1101.657. HEARING. (a) If the commission proposes to deny, suspend, or revoke a person's license or certificate of registration, the person is entitled to a hearing conducted by the State Office of Administrative Hearings.

(b) The commission shall adopt procedures by which all decisions to suspend or revoke a license or certificate are made by or are appealable to the commission.

(c) A hearing under this section is governed by the contested case procedures under Chapter 2001, Government Code.

Sec. 1101.658. APPEAL. (a) A person aggrieved by a ruling, order, or under this subchapter is entitled to appeal to a district court in the county in which the administrative hearing was held.

(b) An appeal is governed by the procedures under Chapter 2001, Government Code.

Sec. 1101.659. REFUND. (a) Subject to Subsection (b), the commission may order a person regulated by the commission to pay a refund to a consumer as provided in an agreement resulting from an informal settlement conference or an enforcement order instead of or in addition to imposing an administrative penalty or other sanctions.

(b) The amount of a refund ordered as provided in an agreement resulting from an informal settlement conference or an enforcement order may not exceed the amount the consumer paid to the person for a service or accommodation regulated by this commission. The commission may not require payment of other damages or estimate harm in a refund order.

Sec. 1101.660. INFORMAL PROCEEDINGS. (a) The commission by rule shall adopt procedures governing informal disposition of a contested case.

(b) Rules adopted under this section must:

(1) provide the complainant and the license holder, certificate holder, or regulated entity an opportunity to be heard; and

(2) require the presence of:

(A) a public member of the commission for a case involving a consumer complaint; and

(B) at least two staff members of the commission with experience in the regulatory area that is the subject of the proceeding.

Sec. 1101.661. FINAL ORDER. The commission may issue a final order in a proceeding under this subchapter or Subchapter O regarding a person whose license has expired during the course of an investigation or administrative proceeding.

Sec. 1101.662. TEMPORARY SUSPENSION. (a) The presiding officer of the commission shall appoint a disciplinary panel consisting of three commission members to determine whether a person's license to practice under this chapter should be temporarily suspended.

(b) If the disciplinary panel determines from the information presented to the panel that a person licensed to practice under this chapter would, by the person's continued practice, constitute a continuing threat to the public welfare, the panel shall temporarily suspend the license of that person.

(c) A license may be suspended under this section without notice or hearing on the complaint if:

(1) institution of proceedings for a hearing before the commission is initiated simultaneously with the temporary suspension; and

(2) a hearing is held under Chapter 2001, Government Code, and this chapter as soon as possible.

(d) Notwithstanding Chapter 551, Government Code, the disciplinary panel may hold a meeting by telephone conference call if immediate action is required and convening the panel at one location is inconvenient for any member of the panel.

SUBCHAPTER O.
ADMINISTRATIVE PENALTY

Sec. 1101.701. IMPOSITION OF ADMINISTRATIVE PENALTY. (a) The

FIGURE A.1

Texas Occupations Code (continued)

commission may impose an administrative penalty on a person who violates this chapter or a rule adopted or order issued by the commission under this chapter.

(b) The commission shall periodically review the commission's enforcement procedures and ensure that administrative penalty and disciplinary proceedings are combined into a single enforcement procedure.

(c) The commission may combine a proceeding to impose an administrative penalty with another disciplinary proceeding, including a proceeding to suspend or revoke a license.

Sec. 1101.7015. DELEGATION OF ADMINISTRATOR'S AUTHORITY. The commission may authorize the administrator to delegate to another commission employee the administrator's authority to act under this subchapter.

Sec. 1101.702. AMOUNT OF PENALTY. (a) The amount of an administrative penalty may not exceed $5,000 for each violation. Each day a violation continues or occurs may be considered a separate violation for purposes of imposing a penalty.

(b) In determining the amount of the penalty, the administrator shall consider:

(1) the seriousness of the violation, including the nature, circumstances, extent, and gravity of the prohibited acts;

(2) the history of previous violations;

(3) the amount necessary to deter a future violation;

(4) efforts to correct the violation; and

(5) any other matter that justice may require.

(c) The commission by rule shall adopt a schedule of administrative penalties based on the criteria listed in Subsection (b) for violations subject to an administrative penalty under this section to ensure that the amount of a penalty imposed is appropriate to the violation. The rules adopted under this subsection must provide authority for the commission to suspend or revoke a license in addition to or instead of imposing an administrative penalty.

Sec. 1101.703. NOTICE OF VIOLATION AND PENALTY. (a) If, after investigation of a possible violation and the facts relating to that violation, the administrator determines that a violation has occurred, the administrator may issue a notice of violation stating:

(1) a brief summary of the alleged violation;

(2) the administrator's recommendation on the imposition of the administrative penalty or another disciplinary sanction, including a recommendation on the amount of the penalty; and

(3) that the respondent has the right to a hearing to contest the alleged violation, the recommended penalty, or both.

(b) Not later than the 14th day after the date the report is issued, the administrator shall give written notice of the report to the person charged with the violation. The notice must:

(1) include a brief summary of the charges;

(2) state the amount of the recommended penalty; and

(3) inform the person of the person's right to a hearing on the occurrence of the violation, the amount of the penalty, or both.

Sec. 1101.704. PENALTY TO BE PAID OR HEARING REQUESTED. (a) Not later than the 20th day after the date the person receives the notice under Section 1101.703, the person may:

(1) accept the administrator's determination, including the recommended administrative penalty; or

(2) request in writing a hearing on the occurrence of the violation, the amount of the penalty, or both.

(b) If the person accepts the administrator's determination, or fails to respond in a timely manner to the notice, the commission by order shall approve the determination and order payment of the recommended penalty or impose the recommended action.

Sec. 1101.705. HEARING; DECISION. (a) If the person requests a hearing, the administrator shall set a hearing and give notice

FIGURE A.1

Texas Occupations Code (continued)

of the hearing to the person.

(b) An administrative law judge of the State Office of Administrative shall conduct the hearing. The administrative law judge shall:

(1) make findings of fact and conclusions of law; and

(2) promptly issue to the commission a proposal for decision regarding the occurrence of the violation and the amount of any proposed administrative penalty.

(c) Based on the findings of fact, conclusions of law, and proposal for decision of the administrative law judge, the commission by order may determine that:

(1) a violation occurred and impose an administrative penalty; or

(2) a violation did not occur.

(d) A proceeding under this section is subject to Chapter 2001, Government Code.

(e) The notice of the commission's order given to the person under Chapter 2001, Government Code, must include a statement of the person's right to judicial review of the order.

Sec. 1101.706. NOTICE OF ORDER. The administrator shall give notice of the commission's order to the person. The notice must:

(1) include the findings of fact and conclusions of law, separately stated;

(2) state the amount of any penalty imposed;

(3) inform the person of the person's right to judicial review of the order; and

(4) include other information required by law.

Sec. 1101.707. OPTIONS FOLLOWING DECISION: PAY OR APPEAL. (a) Not later than the 30th day after the date the commission's order becomes final, the person shall:

(1) pay the administrative penalty; or

(2) file a petition for judicial review contesting the occurrence of the violation, the amount of the penalty, or both.

(b) Within the 30-day period prescribed by Subsection (a), a person who files a petition for judicial review may;

(1) stay enforcement of the penalty by:

(A) paying the penalty to the court for placement in an escrow account; or

(B) giving the court a supersedeas bond in a form approved by the court that:

(i) is for the amount of the penalty; and

(ii) is effective until judicial review of the order is final; or

(2) request the court to stay enforcement by:

(A) filing with the court an affidavit of the person stating that the person is financially unable to pay the penalty and is financially unable to give the supersedeas bond; and

(B) giving a copy of the affidavit to the administrator by certified mail.

(c) If the administrator receives a copy of an affidavit under Subsection (b)(2), the administrator may file with the court, within five days after the date the copy is received, a contest to the affidavit.

(d) The court shall hold a hearing on the facts alleged in the affidavit as soon as practicable and shall stay the enforcement of the penalty on finding that the alleged facts are true. The person who files an affidavit has the burden of proving that the person is financially unable to pay the penalty and to give a supersedeas bond.

Sec. 1101.708. COLLECTION OF PENALTY. If the person does not pay the administrative penalty and the enforcement of the penalty is not stayed, the administrator may refer the matter to the attorney general for collection of the penalty.

Sec. 1101.7085. DETERMINATION BY COURT. (a) If the court sustains the determination that a violation occurred, the court may uphold or reduce the amount of the administrative penalty and order the person to pay the full or reduced amount of the penalty.

(b) If the court does not sustain the finding

FIGURE A.1

Texas Occupations Code (continued)

that a violation occurred, the court shall order that a penalty is not owed.

Sec. 1101.709. REMITTANCE OF PENALTY AND INTEREST. (a) If after judicial review the administrative penalty is reduced or is not upheld by the court, the court shall remit the appropriate amount, plus accrued interest, to the person if the person paid the penalty.

(b) The interest accrues at the rate charged on loans to depository institutions by the New York Federal Reserve Bank.

(c) The interest shall be paid for the period beginning on the date the penalty is paid and ending on the date the penalty is remitted.

(d) If the person gave a supersedeas bond and the penalty is not upheld by the court, the court shall order, when the court's judgment becomes final, the release of the bond.

(e) If the person gave a supersedeas bond and the amount of the penalty is reduced, the court shall order the release of the bond after the person pays the reduced amount.

Sec. 1101.710. ADMINISTRATIVE PROCEDURE. A proceeding under this subchapter is subject to Chapter 2001, Government Code.

SUBCHAPTER P.
OTHER PENALTIES AND ENFORCEMENT PROVISIONS

Sec. 1101.751. INJUNCTIVE ACTION BROUGHT BY COMMISSION. (a) In addition to any other action authorized by law, the commission may bring an action in its name to enjoin a violation of this chapter or a commission rule.

(b) To obtain an injunction under this section, the commission is not required to allege or prove that:

(1) an adequate remedy at law does not exist; or

(2) substantial or irreparable damage would result from the continued violation.

Sec. 1101.752. ADDITIONAL INJUNCTIVE AUTHORITY. (a) In addition to any other action authorized by law, the commission, acting through the attorney general, may bring an action to abate a violation or enjoin a violation or potential violation of this chapter or a commission rule if the commission determines that a person has violated or is about to violate this chapter.

(b) The action shall be brought in the name of the state in the district court in the county in which:

(1) the violation occurred or is about to occur; or

(2) the defendant resides.

(c) An injunctive action may be brought to abate or temporarily or permanently enjoin an act or to enforce this chapter.

(d) The commission is not required to give a bond in an action under Subsection (a), and court costs may not be recovered from the commission.

(e) If the commission determines that a person has violated or is about to violate this chapter, the attorney general or the county attorney or district attorney in the county in which the violation has occurred or is about to occur or in the county of the defendant's residence may bring an action in the name of the state in the district court of the county to abate or temporarily or permanently enjoin the violation or to enforce this chapter. The plaintiff in an action under this subsection is not required to give a bond, and court costs may not be recovered from the plaintiff.

Sec. 1101.753. CIVIL PENALTY FOR CERTAIN VIOLATIONS BY BROKER, SALESPERSON, OR CERTIFICATE HOLDER. (a) In addition to injunctive relief under Sections 1101.751 and 1101.752, a person who receives a commission or other consideration as a result of acting as a broker or salesperson without holding a license or certificate of registration under this chapter is liable to the state for a civil penalty of not less than the amount of money received or more than three times the amount of money received.

(b) The commission may recover the civil penalty, court costs, and reasonable attorney's

FIGURE A.1

Texas Occupations Code (continued)

fees on behalf of the state.

(c) The commission is not required to give a bond in an action under this section, and court costs may not be recovered from the commission.

Sec. 1101.754. PRIVATE CAUSE OF ACTION FOR CERTAIN VIOLATIONS BY BROKER, SALESPERSON, OR CERTIFICATE HOLDER. (a) A person who receives a commission or other consideration as a result of acting as a broker or salesperson without holding a license or certificate of registration under this chapter is liable to an aggrieved person for a penalty of not less than the amount of money received or more than three times the amount of money received.

(b) The aggrieved person may file suit to recover a penalty under this section.

Sec. 1101.755. APPEAL BOND EXEMPTION. The commission is not required to give an appeal bond in an action to enforce this chapter.

Sec. 1101.756. GENERAL CRIMINAL PENALTY. (a) A person commits an offense if the person willfully violates or fails to comply with this chapter or a commission order.

(b) An offense under this section is a Class A misdemeanor.

Sec. 1101.757. CRIMINAL PENALTY FOR CERTAIN VIOLATIONS BY RESIDENTIAL RENTAL LOCATOR. (a) A person commits an offense if the person engages in business as a residential rental locator in this state without a license issued under this chapter.

(b) An offense under this section is a Class A misdemeanor.

Sec. 1101.758. CRIMINAL PENALTY FOR CERTAIN VIOLATIONS BY BROKER, SALESPERSON, OR CERTIFICATE HOLDER. (a) A person commits an offense if the person acts as a broker or salesperson without holding a license under this chapter or engages in an activity for which a certificate of registration is required under this chapter without holding a certificate.

(b) An offense under this section is a Class A misdemeanor.

Sec. 1101.759. CEASE AND DESIST ORDER. (a) If it appears to the commission that a person is violating this chapter or Chapter 1102 or a rule adopted under this chapter or Chapter 1102, the commission, after notice and opportunity for a hearing, may issue a cease and desist order prohibiting the person from engaging in the activity.

(b) A violation of an order under this section constitutes grounds for imposing an administrative penalty under Subchapter O.

SUBCHAPTER Q.
GENERAL PROVISIONS RELATING TO LIABILITY ISSUES

Sec. 1101.801. EFFECT OF DISCIPLINARY ACTION ON LIABILITY. Disciplinary action taken against a person under Section 1101.652 does not relieve the person from civil or criminal liability.

Sec. 1101.802. LIABILITY RELATING TO HIV INFECTION OR AIDS. Notwithstanding Section 1101.801, a person is not civilly or criminally liable because the person failed to inquire about, make a disclosure relating to, or release information relating to whether a previous or current occupant of real property had, may have had, has, or may have AIDS, an HIV-related illness, or HIV infection as defined by the Centers for Disease Control and Prevention of the United States Public Health Service.

Sec. 1101.803. GENERAL LIABILITY OF BROKER. A licensed broker is liable to the commission, the public, and the broker's clients for any conduct engaged in under this chapter by the broker or by a salesperson associated with or acting for the broker.

FIGURE A.1

Texas Occupations Code (continued)

Sec. 1101.804. LIABILITY FOR PROVIDING CERTAIN INFORMATION. A license holder or nonprofit real estate board or association that provides information about real property sales prices or the terms of a sale for the purpose of facilitating the listing, selling, leasing, financing, or appraisal of real property is not liable to another person for providing that information unless the disclosure of that information is specifically prohibited by statute.

Sec. 1101.805. LIABILITY FOR MISREPRESENTATION OR CONCEALMENT. (a) In this section, "party" has the meaning assigned by Section 1101.551.

(b) This section prevails over any other law, including common law.

(c) This section does not diminish a broker's responsibility for the acts or omissions of a salesperson associated with or acting for the broker.

(d) A party is not liable for a misrepresentation or a concealment of a material fact made by a license holder in a real estate transaction unless the party:

(1) knew of the falsity of the misrepresentation or concealment; and

(2) failed to disclose the party's knowledge of the falsity of the misrepresentation or concealment.

(e) A license holder is not liable for a misrepresentation or a concealment of a material fact made by a party to a real estate transaction unless the license holder:

(1) knew of the falsity of the misrepresentation or concealment; and

(2) failed to disclose the license holder's knowledge of the falsity of the misrepresentation or concealment.

(f) A party or a license holder is not liable for a misrepresentation or a concealment of a material fact made by a subagent in a real estate transaction unless the party or license holder:

(1) knew of the falsity of the misrepresentation or concealment; and

(2) failed to disclose the party's or license holder's knowledge of the falsity of the misrepresentation or concealment.

Sec. 1101.806. LIABILITY FOR PAYMENT OF COMPENSATION OR COMMISSION. (a) This section does not:

(1) apply to an agreement to share compensation among license holders; or

(2) limit a cause of action among brokers for interference with business relationships.

(b) A person may not maintain an action to collect compensation for an act as a broker or salesperson that is performed in this state unless the person alleges and proves that the person was:

(1) a license holder at the time the act was commenced; or

(2) an attorney licensed in any state.

(c) A person may not maintain an action in this state to recover a commission for the sale or purchase of real estate unless the promise or agreement on which the action is based, or a memorandum, is in writing and signed by the party against whom the action is brought or by a person authorized by that party to sign the document.

(d) A license holder who fails to advise a buyer as provided by Section 1101.555 may not receive payment of or recover any commission agreed to be paid on the sale.

APPENDIX B

Questions and Answers Regarding Disclosure of Agency and Intermediary Practice

FIGURE B.1

Questions and Answers Regarding Disclosure of Agency and Intermediary Practice

QUESTIONS AND ANSWERS REGARDING DISCLOSURE OF AGENCY AND INTERMEDIARY PRACTICE

The following questions and answers have been developed to assist licensees in complying with the disclosure of agency and intermediary practice provisions (Representation Provisions) of The Real Estate License Act (TRELA or the Act). The provisions include §§1101.558-1101.561 and §1101.651(d) of the Occupations Code. These answers are intended to address general situations only and are not intended as legal opinions addressing the duties and obligations of licensees in specific transactions. What licensees say and do in a specific transaction may cause these general answers to be inapplicable or inaccurate. Licensees should consult their own attorneys for legal advice concerning the law's effect on their brokerage practices.

1. **Q: Explain how a typical intermediary relationship is created and how it would operate.**

   A: At the first substantive dialogue with a seller or a prospective buyer, the salespersons or brokers associated with a firm would provide the parties with a copy of the statutory information about agency required by TRELA. The statutory information includes an explanation of the intermediary relationship. The brokerage firm would negotiate a written listing contract with a seller and a written buyer representation agreement with a buyer. In those documents, the respective parties would authorize the broker to act as an intermediary and to appoint associated licensees to work with the parties in the event that the buyer wishes to purchase a property listed with the firm. At this point, the broker and associated licensees would be still functioning as exclusive agents of the individual parties. The listing contract and buyer representation agreement would contain in conspicuous bold or underlined print the broker's obligations set forth in Section 1101.651(d) of TRELA. When it becomes evident that the buyer represented by the firm wishes to purchase property listed with the firm, the intermediary status would come into play, and the intermediary may appoint different associates to work with the parties. The intermediary would notify both parties in writing of the appointments of licensees to work with the parties. The associates would provide advice and opinions to their respective parties during negotiations, and the intermediary broker would be careful not to favor one party over the other in any action taken by the intermediary.

2. **Q: What is an intermediary?**

   A: An intermediary is a broker who negotiates the transaction between the parties subject to the Representation Provisions of the Act. The intermediary may, with the written consent of the parties, appoint

FIGURE B.1

Questions and Answers Regarding Disclosure of Agency and Intermediary Practice (continued)

licensees associated with the intermediary to work with and advise the party to whom they have been appointed.

3. **Q: Is dual agency authorized by the Representation Provisions?**

   A: A licensee may not represent both parties as a dual agent under revisions to the Act under S.B. 810 79th Legislature (2005), effective September 1, 2005. Occupations Code Section 1101.561(b) provides that "a broker must agree to act as an intermediary under this subchapter if the broker agrees to represent in a transaction" a buyer or tenant, and a seller or landlord. Since a broker must act as an intermediary pursuant to this new provision, a licensee cannot act as a dual agent. To the extent a dual agency relationship is created by accident or otherwise, a licensee must resolve the matter by complying with the notice and consent requirements of the Representation Provisions to act as an intermediary, or by representing one of the parties only and working with the other party as a customer.

4. **Q: When must the broker act as an intermediary?**

   A: If the broker and associates are going to continue to work with parties they have been representing under listing contracts or buyer representation agreements, the intermediary role is the only way to handle "in-house" transactions, providing both parties the same level of service.

5. **Q: If a salesperson or associated broker lists a property and has also been working with a prospective buyer under a representation agreement, how can the salesperson or associated broker sell this listing under the Representation Provisions?**

   A: There are three alternatives for the brokerage firm and the parties to consider:

   (1) The firm, acting through the salesperson or associated broker, could represent one of the parties and work with the other party as a customer rather than as a client (realistically, this probably means working with the buyer as a customer and terminating the buyer representation agreement).

   (2) If the firm has obtained permission in writing from both parties to be an intermediary and to appoint licensees to work with the parties, the salesperson or associated broker could be appointed by the intermediary to work with one of the parties. Note: **Another licensee would have to be appointed to work with the other party under this alternative. The law does not permit an intermediary to appoint the same licensee to work with both parties.**

   (3) If the firm has obtained permission in writing from both parties to be an intermediary, but does not appoint different associates to work with the parties, the salesperson or broker associate could function as a representative of the firm. Since the firm is an intermediary, the

FIGURE B.1

Questions and Answers Regarding Disclosure of Agency and Intermediary Practice (continued)

salesperson and associated broker also would be subject to the requirement not to act so as to favor one party over the other.

6. **Q: If a salesperson may provide services to a party under the Representation Provisions without being appointed, why would a broker want to appoint a salesperson to work with a party?**

    A: Appointment following the procedures set out in the Representation Provisions would permit the salesperson to provide a higher level of service. The appointed salesperson may provide advice and opinions to the party to whom the salesperson is assigned and is not subject to the intermediary's statutory duty of not acting so as to favor one party over the other.

7. **Q: Is an intermediary an agent?**

    A: Yes, but the duties and obligations of an intermediary are different than for exclusive, or single, agents.

8. **Q: What are the duties and obligations of an intermediary?**

    A: The Representation Provisions require the intermediary to obtain written consent from both parties to act as an intermediary. A written listing agreement to represent a seller/landlord or a written buyer/tenant representation agreement which contains authorization for the broker to act as an intermediary between the parties is sufficient for the purposes of the Representation Provisions if the agreement sets forth, in conspicuous bold or underlined print, the broker's obligations under Section 1101.651(d), and the agreement states who will pay the broker.

    If the intermediary is to appoint associated licensees to work with the parties, the intermediary must obtain written permission from both parties and give written notice of the appointments to each party. The intermediary is also required to treat the parties fairly and honestly and to comply with TRELA. The intermediary is prohibited from acting so as to favor one party over the other, and may not reveal confidential information obtained from one party without the written instructions of that party, unless disclosure of that information is required by TRELA, court order, or the information materially relates to the condition of the property. The intermediary and any associated licensees appointed by the intermediary are prohibited from disclosing without written authorization that the seller will accept a price less than the asking price or that the buyer will pay a price greater than the price submitted in a written offer.

9. **Q: Can salespersons act as intermediaries?**

    A: Only a broker can contract with the parties to act as an intermediary between them.

    In that sense, only a broker can be an intermediary. If, however, the broker intermediary does not appoint associated licensees to work with

FIGURE B.1

Questions and Answers Regarding Disclosure of Agency and Intermediary Practice (continued)

the parties in a transaction, any salesperson or broker associates of the intermediary who function in that transaction would be required to act just as the intermediary does, not favoring one party over the other.

10. Q: Can there be two intermediaries in the same transaction?
    A: No.

11. Q: Can a broker representing only the buyer be an intermediary?
    A: Ordinarily, no; the listing broker will be the intermediary. In the case of a FSBO or other seller who is not already represented by a broker, the broker representing the buyer could secure the consent of both parties to act as an intermediary.

12. Q: May an intermediary appoint a subagent in another firm to work with one of the parties?
    A: Subagency is still permitted under the law, but a subagent in another firm cannot be appointed as one of the intermediary's associated licensees under the Representation Provisions of the Act.

13. Q: May the same salesperson be appointed by the intermediary to work with both parties in the same transaction?
    A: No; the law requires the intermediary to appoint different associated licensees to work with each party.

14. Q: May more than one associated licensee be appointed by the intermediary to work with the same party?
    A: Yes.

15. Q: What is the difference between an appointed licensee working with a party and a licensee associated with the intermediary who has not been appointed to work with one party?
    A: During negotiations the appointed licensee may advise the person to whom the licensee has been appointed. An associated licensee who has not been appointed must act in the same manner as the intermediary, that is, not giving opinions and advice and not favoring one party over the other.

16. Q: Who decides whether a broker will act as intermediary, the broker or the parties?
    A: Initially, the broker, in determining the policy of the firm. If the broker does not wish to act as an intermediary, nothing requires the broker to do so. If the broker's policy is to offer services as an intermediary, both

FIGURE B.1

Questions and Answers Regarding Disclosure of Agency and Intermediary Practice (continued)

parties must authorize the broker in writing before the broker may act as in intermediary or appoint licensees to work with each of the parties.

17. **Q: When must the intermediary appoint the licensees associated with the intermediary to work with the parties?**

    A: This is a judgment call for the intermediary. If appointments are going to be made, they should be made before the buyer begins to receive advice and opinions from an associated licensee in connection with the property listed with the broker. If the broker appoints the associates at the time the listing contract and buyer representation agreements are signed, it should be clear that the appointments are effective only when the intermediary relationship arises. **The intermediary relationship does not exist until the parties who have authorized it are beginning to deal with each other in a proposed real estate transaction; for example, the buyer begins to negotiate to purchase the seller's property.** Prior to the creation of the intermediary relationship, the broker will typically be acting as an exclusive agent of each party. It is important to remember that **both** parties must be notified in writing of **both** appointments. If, for example, the listing agent is "appointed" at the time the listing is taken, care must be taken to ensure that the buyer is ultimately also given written notice of the appointment. When a buyer client begins to show interest in a property listed with the firm and both parties have authorized the intermediary relationship, the seller must be notified in writing as to which associate has been appointed to work with the buyer.

18. **Q: Can the intermediary delegate to another person the authority to appoint licensees associated with the intermediary?**

    A: The intermediary may delegate to another licensee the authority to appoint associated licensees. **If the intermediary authorizes another licensee to appoint associated licensees to work with the parties, however, that person must not appoint himself or herself as one of the associated licensees, as this would be an improper combination of the different functions of intermediary and associated licensee. It is also important to remember that there will be a single intermediary even if another licensee has been authorized to make appointments.**

19. **Q: May a broker act as a dual agent?**

    A: A broker may not act as a dual agent under Occupations Code Section 1101.561(b), which provides that "a broker must agree to act as an intermediary under this subchapter if the broker agrees to represent in a transaction" a buyer or tenant, and a seller or landlord.

20. **Q: What are the agency disclosure requirements for real estate licensees?**

FIGURE B.1

Questions and Answers Regarding Disclosure of Agency and Intermediary Practice (continued)

    A: To disclose their representation of a party upon the first contact with a party or a licensee representing another party.

21. **Q: Is disclosure of agency required to be in writing?**

    A: The disclosure may be oral or in writing.

22. **Q: Are licensees required to provide parties with written information relating to agency?**

    A: Yes. The Representation Provisions require licensees to provide the parties with a copy of a written statement, the content of which is specified in the statute. The form of the statement may be varied, so long as the text of the statement is in at least 10 point type.

23. **Q: Are there exceptions when the statutory statement is not required?**

    A: Yes; the statement is required to be provided when the first substantive dialogue occurs between a party and the licensee at which discussion occurs with respect to specific real property. The statement is **not** required for either of the following:

    (1) a transaction which is a residential lease no longer than one year and no sale is being considered; or

    (2) a meeting with a party represented by another licensee.

24. **Q: Are the disclosure and statutory information requirements applicable to commercial transactions, new home sales, farm and ranch sales or transactions other than residential sales?**

    A: Except as noted above, the requirements are applicable to all real estate transactions. Licensees dealing with landlords and tenants are permitted by the law to modify their versions of the statutory statement to use the terms "landlord" and "tenant" in place of the terms "seller" and "buyer."

25. **Q: What are the penalties for licensees who fail to comply with the Representation Provisions?**

    A: Failure to comply is a violation of TRELA, punishable by reprimand, by suspension or revocation of a license, or by an administrative penalty (fine).

26. **Q: In what way do the Representation Provisions prohibit or permit disclosed dual agency?**

    A: The Representation Provisions prohibit disclosed dual agency.

FIGURE B.1

Questions and Answers Regarding Disclosure of Agency and Intermediary Practice (continued)

27. **Q:** Is the licensee required under any circumstance, to provide the "written statement" to buyer prospects at properties held open for prospective buyers?

    A: An encounter at an open house is not a meeting for the purposes of the Representation Provisions. A licensee would not be required to provide the statutory statement at the open house. However, at the first substantive dialogue thereafter with the buyer regarding a specific property and during which substantive discussions occur, the licensee will be required to provide the statement.

28. **Q:** When acting as an appointed licensee what "agency" limitations does the licensee have when communicating with a buyer/tenant or seller/landlord that an agent representing one party only doesn't have?

    A: The appointed licensee may not, except as permitted by Section 1101.651(d) of TRELA, disclose to either party confidential information received from the other party. A licensee representing one party would not be prohibited from revealing confidential information to the licensee's principal, and if the information were material to the principal's decision, would be required to reveal the information to the principal.

29. **Q:** If a buyer's agent is required to disclose that licensee's agency status to a listing broker when setting up an appointment showing, must the listing broker also disclose to the buyer's agent that the listing broker represents the seller?

    A: Yes, on the first contact with the licensee representing the buyer.

30. **Q:** Does the TREC encourage brokerage companies to act for more than one party in the same transaction?

    A: No.

31. **Q:** Must the intermediary broker furnish written notice to each party to a transaction when the broker designates the appointed licensees?

    A: Yes.

32. **Q:** How is a property "showing" different from a proposed transaction?

    A: The question appears to be "may an associate show property listed with the associate's broker while representing the buyer without first being appointed by the intermediary, and if so, why?" Yes. Only showing property does not require the associate to be appointed, because it does not require the licensee to give advice or opinions (only an appointed associate may offer opinions or advice to a party). If no appointments will

FIGURE B.1

Questions and Answers Regarding Disclosure of Agency and Intermediary Practice (continued)

be made, of course, the associate will be working with the party and will not be authorized to provide opinions or advice.

33. **Q: Does TREC recommend that licensees provide a written disclosure of agency?**

    A: It is the licensee's choice as to whether disclosure is in writing or oral, just as it is the licensee's choice as to whether proof of disclosure will be easy or difficult.

34. **Q: Our company policy requires all buyers and sellers to agree to the intermediary practice before commencing to work with them. Does the law permit a broker employment agreement to specify this practice only?**

    A: If by "broker employment agreement" you mean a listing contract or buyer representation agreement, yes.

35. **Q: What are the differences between the duties provided to the seller or landlord by the intermediary broker and the duties provided to the buyer or tenant by the appointed licensee?**

    A: The intermediary and the appointed licensees do not provide duties; they perform services under certain duties imposed by the law. The intermediary is authorized to negotiate a transaction between the parties, but not to give advice or opinions to them in negotiations. The appointed licensee may provide advice or opinions to the party to which the licensee has been appointed. Both intermediary and appointed licensee are obligated to treat the parties honestly and are prohibited from revealing confidential information or other information addressed in Section 1101.651(d) of TRELA.

36. **Q: Must each party's identity be revealed to the other party before an intermediary transaction can occur?**

    A: Yes. If associates are going to be appointed by the intermediary, the law provides that the appointments are made by giving written notice to both parties. To give notice, the intermediary must identify the party and the associate(s) appointed to that party. The law does not require notice if no appointments are going to be made. The law provides that the listing contract and buyer representation agreement are sufficient to establish the written consent of the party if the obligations of the broker under Section 1101.651(d) are set forth in conspicuous bold or underlined print.

37. **Q: As a listing agent I hold open houses. If a buyer prospect enters who desires to purchase the property at that time, can I represent that buyer and, if so, must my broker designate me as an appointed licensee and provide the parties with written notice before I prepare the purchase offer?**

FIGURE B.1

Questions and Answers Regarding Disclosure of Agency and Intermediary Practice (continued)

A: As a representative of the seller, you would be obligated to disclose your representation to the buyer at the first contact. The disclosure may be in writing or oral. As an associate of the listing broker, you can enter into a buyer representation agreement for your broker to act as an intermediary in a transaction involving this buyer and the owner of the property. If the owner has similarly authorized the broker to act as an intermediary, it will depend on the firm's policy whether appointments are to be made. If appointments are not going to be made, you may proceed in the transaction as an unappointed licensee with a duty of not favoring one party over the other. If appointments are going to be made, the parties must both be notified in writing before you may provide opinions or advice to the buyer in negotiations.

38. **Q: I have a salesperson's license through a broker and I also have a licensed assistant. Can that assistant be an appointed licensee under me as an intermediary?**

    A: Your broker, not you, will be the intermediary. The intermediary may appoint a licensed associate to work with a party. If the licensed assistant is an associate of the broker, the licensed assistant could be appointed by the intermediary to work with one of the parties. If the licensed assistant is not an associate of the broker, the licensed assistant cannot be appointed. NOTE: IF THE LICENSED ASSISTANT IS LICENSED AS A SALESPERSON, THE LICENSED ASSISTANT MUST BE SPONSORED BY, AND ACTING FOR, A BROKER TO BE AUTHORIZED TO PERFORM ANY ACT FOR WHICH A REAL ESTATE LICENSE IS REQUIRED. IF THE LICENSED ASSISTANT IS SPONSORED BY A BROKER WHO IS NOT ASSOCIATED WITH THE INTERMEDIARY, THE LICENSED ASSISTANT WOULD NOT BE CONSIDERED AN ASSOCIATE OF THE INTERMEDIARY EITHER.

39. **Q: I am a listing agent and a buyer prospect wants to buy the property I have listed. How can I sell my own listing?**

    A: See the three alternatives discussed in the related question on page 2. You could alter the agency relationships and only represent one party, you could be appointed to work with one party and another associate could be appointed to work with the other party, or no appointments would be made, or you could work with the parties being careful not to favor one over the other or provide advice or opinions to them.

40. **Q: Must the respective appointed licensees each provide an opinion of value to the respective buyer prospect and seller prospect?**

    A: At the time a property is listed, the licensee is obligated to advise the owner as to the licensee's opinion of the market value of the property. Once appointments have been made, the appointed associates are permitted, but not required, to provide the party to whom they have been appointed with opinions and advice during negotiations.

FIGURE B.1

Questions and Answers Regarding Disclosure of Agency and Intermediary Practice (continued)

41. **Q: How can the intermediary broker advise the seller or buyer on value, escrow deposit amount, repair expenses, or interest rates?**

    A: When the listing contract or buyer representation agreement has come into existence, and no intermediary status yet exists, the broker may advise the parties generally on such matters. Offers from or to parties not represented by the intermediary's firm may have made the parties knowledgeable on these matters. Once the intermediary status has been created, however, the intermediary broker may not express opinions or give advice during negotiations. Information about such matters which does not constitute an opinion or advice may be supplied in response to question. For example, the intermediary could tell the buyer what the prevailing interest rate is without expressing an opinion or giving advice. The seller's question about the amount of earnest money could be answered with the factual answer that in the broker's experience, the amount of the earnest money is usually $1,500 to $2,000, depending on the amount of the sales price. If the buyer asks what amount of money should be in the offer, the intermediary could respond with the factual statement that in the intermediary's experience, those offers closest to the listing price tend to be accepted by the seller. The intermediary also could refer the party to an attorney, accountant, loan officer or other professional for advice.

42. **Q: I was the listing agent for a property that didn't sell but was listed by another broker after the expiration of my agreement. I now have a buyer client who wants to see that same property. Must the new broker, or my broker, designate me as an appointed licensee or how may I otherwise act?**

    A: Assuming an agreement with the listing broker as regards cooperation and compensation, you may represent the buyer as an exclusive agent. You cannot be appointed by the intermediary because you are not an associate of the listing broker, and from the facts as you describe them, no intermediary status is going to arise. Confidential information obtained from the seller when you were acting as the seller's agent, of course, could not be disclosed to your new client, the buyer.

43. **Q: How is the intermediary broker responsible for the actions of appointed licensees when a difference of opinion of property value estimates is provided?**

    A: Brokers are responsible for the actions of their salespersons under TRELA. Opinions of property values may be different and yet not indicative of error or mistake by the salespersons. If a salesperson makes an error or mistake, the sponsoring broker is responsible to the public and to TREC under Section 1101.803 of TRELA.

44. **Q: Although both the buyer and the seller initially consented to the intermediary broker practice at the time each signed a broker**

FIGURE B.1

Questions and Answers Regarding Disclosure of Agency and Intermediary Practice (continued)

employment agreement, must each party consent again to a specific transaction to ensure there are not potential conflicts?

A: TRELA does not require a second written consent. TRELA does require written notice of any appointments, and the written notice would probably cause any objection to be resolved at that point. A broker would not be prohibited from obtaining a second consent as a business practice, so that potential conflicts are identified and resolved. The sales contract, of course, would typically identify the parties and show the intermediary relationship if the broker completes the "Broker Identification and Ratification of Fee" at the end of the TREC contract form.

45. **Q:** In the absence of the appointed licensees, can the intermediary broker actually negotiate a purchase offer between the parties?

A: Yes. See the answer to the question relating to the duties of an intermediary.

46. **Q:** May a licensee include the statutory statement in a listing agreement or buyer representation agreement, either in the text of the agreement, or as an exhibit?

A: Yes, but the licensee should provide the prospective party with a separate copy of the statutory statement as soon as is practicable at their first substantive dialogue.

APPENDIX C: Agency Cases from 50 States

Appendix C contains an annotation of 600 cases from all 50 states illustrating a number of the agency issues raised in the text.

■ CHAPTER 2. BASIC AGENCY RELATIONSHIPS, DISCLOSURE, AND DUTIES OF THE CLIENT

The Fiduciary Relationship

Fiduciary Duties. Persons dealing with a real estate licensee may naturally assume that the broker possesses the requisites of an honest and ethical person. *Ellis v. Flink*, 301 So.2d 493 (FL 1974); *Department of Employment v. Bake Young Realty*, 560 P.2d 504 (ID 1977); *Easton v. Strassburger*, 199 Cal.Rptr. 383 (CA App. 1984); *Zichlin v. Dill*, 25 So.2d 4 (FL 1946). Brokers hold themselves out to the public as having particular skills and knowledge in the real estate field. In essence, the law creates a public duty.

In any lawsuit alleging that the broker breached a fiduciary duty, the broker must prove no breach of duty occurred. *Vogt v. Town & Country Realty of Lincoln*, 231 N.W.2d 496 (NE 1975).

In a suit for negligence against a real estate broker, the Nebraska Supreme Court held that a special two-year statute of limitations for "professional negligence" was inapplicable because "real estate brokers are not professionals." *Tylle v. Zouche*, 412 N.W.2d 438 (NE 1987).

Duty of Loyalty. Of all the obligations imposed by the fiduciary duty, loyalty is the essential virtue required of a broker. *Rose v. Showalter*, 701 P.2d 251 (ID 1985); *Wegg v. Henry Broderick, Inc.*, 557 P.2d 861 (WA 1976); *Cogan v. Kidder, Mathews & Segner, Inc.*, 648 P.2d 875 (WA 1982).

Disclosure

1. Relationship. *Mersky v. Multiple Listing Bureau of Olympia, Inc.*, 437 P.2d 897 (WA 1968); *Kimmell v. Clark*, 520 P.2d 851 (AZ 1974); *Ross v. Perelli*, 538 P.2d 834 (WA 1975) (relationship between subagent and buyer); *Wilkinson v. Smith*,

639 P.2d 768 (WA 1982); *John J. Reynolds v. Snow,* 174 N.E.2d 753 (NY 1961); *Velten v. Robertson,* 671 P.2d 1011 (CO 1983); *Smith v. Zak,* 98 Cal.Rptr. 242 (CA 1971); *Jenkins v. Wise,* 574 P.2d 1337 (HI 1978); *Silva v. Bisbie,* 628 P.2d 214 (HI 1981); *Ramsey v. Sedlar,* 454 P.2d 416 (WA 1969); *Abell v. Watson,* 317 P.2d 159 (CA 1957) (buyer was broker's wife). See also *Handy v. Garmarker,* 324 N.W.2d 168 (MN 1982); *Christman v. Seymour,* 700 P.2d 898 (AZ 1985); *Drake v. Hasley,* 713 P.2d 1203 (AK 1986).

The broker must disclose any interest in a corporation offering to buy a listed property, even if the broker is a minority shareholder or is a director or an officer and has no stock ownership. *Bell v. Routh Robbins Real Estate Corp.,* 147 S.E.2d 277 (VA 1966); *McKinney v. Christmas,* 353 P.2d 373 (CO 1960); *Treat v. Schmidt,* 193 P.666 (CO 1920); *Newell-Murdoch Realty Co. v. Wickham,* 190 P. 359 (CA 1920); *Batson v. Strehlow,* 441 P.2d 101 (CA 1968); *Wendt v. Fischer,* 154 N.E. 303 (NY 1926); *Travagliante v. J. W. Wood Realty Company,* 425 S.W.2d 208 (MO 1968). Brokerage breached fiduciary duty owed seller by not disclosing that one of its general partners was part purchaser of listed property. *Designer Showrooms v. Kelley,* 405 S.E.2d 417 (SC 1991).

The fact that the broker is licensed or has an interest in the buyer does not preclude the broker from participating in the transaction and earning a commission, provided the seller receives full disclosure of the conflicting interests. In re *Estate of Baldwin,* 110 Cal.Rptr. 189 (CA App 1973); *Rosenfeld v. Glick Real Estate Co.,* 291 S.W.2d 863 (MO 1956); *Stevens v. Hutton,* 163 P.2d 479 (CA 1946). Failure to disclose broker's romance with divorce attorney of client's ex-spouse might influence complete loyalty to client. *Silverman v. Pitterman,* 574 So.2d 275 (FL 1991).

Note that a licensee acting as a principal in the sale or purchase of real estate should disclose to the other party the fact of licensure. An inactive licensee may have no duty of disclosure, although it would be preferable to disclose. *Gregory v. Selle,* 206 N.W.2d 147 (WI 1973). Upheld ruling that use of phrase by broker "for sale by owner" was misleading. *HelpSell v. Maine REC,* 611 A.2d 981 (ME 1992). Broker not liable for making repairs as personal guarantor when he signed agreement on line marked "witness." *McGinney v. Jackson,* 575 So.2d 1070 (ALA 1991).

2. Other Offers. The broker must present all offers as a matter of top priority. It is also advisable to inform the seller of facts that indicate another offer may be presented shortly and to present offers even after the seller has accepted an offer, in the event the seller wishes to have backup offers. The broker should tell the buyer that making a full-price offer does not mean the seller must accept such offer. The broker should avoid giving to the buyer "rights of first refusal" or assuring the buyer that the seller will accept a certain amount.

The broker must submit an offer even if the broker believes it is too low to warrant consideration. *E. A. Strout Realty Agency, Inc. v. Wooster,* 99 A.2d 689 (VT 1955).

The listing broker is under an affirmative duty to disclose a second offer to purchase and, by failing to disclose such offer, has made a representation that no other offer exists. Failure to disclose could result in loss of commission, loss of license, or even punitive damages. The buyer may sue the broker for money damages resulting from the broker's failure to present the buyer's offer. Such cases usually involve situations in which the broker purchases the property. *Simone v. McKee*, 298 P.2d 667 (CA 1956); *Cisco v. Van Lew*, 141 P.2d 433 (CA 1943); *Southern Cross Industries, Inc. v. Martin*, 604 S.W.2d 290 (TX 1980); *Hickman v. Colorado Real Estate Commission*, 534 P.2d 1220 (CO 1975); *Virginia Real Estate Commission v. Bias*, 308 S.E.2d 123 (VA 1983); *Githens v. Johnson*, 192 N.W. 270 (IA 1923); *Brown v. Carpenter*, 134 S.W. 1150 (KY 1911); *Barbat v. M.E. Arden Co.*, 254 N.W.2d 779 (MI 1977); *Harper v. Adametz*, 113 A.2d 136 (CT 1955); *Arnato v. Latter & Blum, Inc.*, 79 So.2d 873 (LA 1955); *Phillips v. Lynch*, 704 P.2d 1083 (NV 1985).

Brokers must respect the confidentiality of offers. The listing broker should not disclose to other salespersons in the broker's office the amount of a cooperating broker's offer. Nor should the listing broker reveal the amount of a previous counteroffer made by the seller. Likewise, the listing broker should not disclose the amounts of previously rejected offers unless the seller agrees to this strategy. Buyers should be encouraged to submit their best offers. Knowledge of other offers may result in a buyer submitting a lower offer than originally planned.

Brokers must also disclose any information that a prospective buyer may be willing to offer better terms or a higher price than the offer presented. *Carter v. Owens*, 50 So. 641 (FL 1909); *Gillespie v. Rosenbaum*, 173 N.Y.S.429 (NY 1918); *Raleigh Real Estate & Trust Co. v. Adams*, 58 S.E. 1008 (NC 1907); *Mason v. Bulleri*, 543 P.2d 478 (AZ 1975). Broker not liable to buyer for failure to convey purchase offer accurately to seller. *Andrie v. Crystal-Anderson*, 466 N.W.2d 393 (MI 1991).

3. Status of Deposit Money. *De St. Germain v. Watson*, 214 P.2d 99 (CA 1950) (failed to disclose payment in form of promissory note); *Nugent v. Scharff*, 476 S.W.2d 414 (TX 1971); *Roy H. Long Realty Company v. Vanderkolk*, 547 P.2d 497 (AZ 1976); *Merkeley v. MacPherson's Inc.*, 420 P.2d 205 (WA 1966); *Hughey v. Rainwater Partners*, 661 S.W.2d 690 (TN 1983) (seller awarded 100 percent of deposit); *Reich v. Christopulos*, 256 P.2d 238 (UT 1953); holding no violation of licensing law to fail to disclose postdated check is *Lowe v. State Dept. of Commerce, Real Estate Division*, 515 P.2d 388 (NV 1973); *Huizenga v. Withey Sheppard Associates*, 167 N.W.2d 120 (MI 1969); see *Wilson v. Lewis*, 165 Cal.Rptr. 396 (CA 1980).

A broker is liable for failure to disclose to the property owner that the broker did not collect the security deposits as indicated in the rental agreements. In *Murphy & Fritz's Place, Inc. v. Loretta*, 447 N.Y.S.2d 205 (NY 1982), the broker was held liable for failure to disclose that he had not received the initial or additional deposit the contract required the buyer to make. Broker liable for advising buyer to make a $50,000 down payment to person claiming falsely to be the owner of the property (rather than place money in escrow). *Keystone Realty v. Osterhus*, 807 P.2d 1385 (NV 1991).

4. Buyer's Financial Condition. *Miller v. Berkoski*, 297 N.W.2d 334 (IA 1980) (broker loaned buyer money for down payment); *McGarry v. McCrone*, 118 N.E.2d 195 (OH 1954); *Farrell v. Score*, 411 P.2d 146 (WA 1966); *Mason v. Bulleri*, 543 P.2d 178 (AZ 1975); *Alhino v. Starr*, 169 Cal.Rptr. 136 (CA 1980); *Banville v. Schmidt*, 112 Cal.Rptr. 126 (CA 1974); *R.A. Poff & Co. v. Ottaway*, 62 S.E.2d 865 (VA 1951). In *Fulsom v. Egner*, 79 N.W.2d 25 (MN 1956), the broker failed to disclose that the buyer's ability to pay was contingent on the outcome of a pending lawsuit.

When the broker makes a credit check of the buyer and discovers many negative features, the broker must disclose this information to the seller. Even though a failure to disclose may not amount to misrepresentation, it is still a breach of fiduciary duty sufficient to justify nonpayment of commission, as held in *White v. Boucher*, 322 N.W.2d 560 (MN 1982).

The seller is justified in relying on the broker's representation that the buyer is financially sound, without having to make an independent investigation of the buyer's finances. *Phillips v. JCM Development Corporation*, 666 P.2d 876 (UT 1983). But if the broker makes reasonable inquiry into the buyer's financial condition and discloses this to the seller, the broker is not liable if the buyer later defaults. *Zwick v. United Farm Agency, Inc.*, 556 P.2d. 508 (WY 1976).

Disclosure of financial condition is especially important when the buyer is a salesperson of the cooperating broker. *L.A. Grant Realty v. Cuomo*, 396 N.Y.S.2d 524 (NY 1977); *Hercules v. Robedeaux Inc.*, 329 N.W.2d 240 (WI App. 1982).

In *Prall v. Corum*, 403 So.2d 991 (FL 1981), the broker was held liable for failure to disclose the buyer's financial inability to purchase the property and the fact that the broker loaned the buyer money to close.

5. Property Value. The broker is liable for rendering a false opinion of value. *Eastburn v. Joseph Esphalla Jr. & Co.*, 112 So. 232 (AK 1927); *Moore v. Turner*, 71 S.E.2d 342 (WV 1952); *Iriart v. Johnson*, 411 P.2d 226 (NM 1966). In *Duhl v. Nash Realty, Inc.*, 429 N.E.2d 1267 (IL 1982), the seller bought another property, relying on the broker's assurance that the property would sell quickly. A mere mistake in judgment of value is not a breach. *Smith v. Fidelity & Columbia Trust Co.*, 12 S.W.2d 276 (KY 1928). No commission is owed a broker who withholds information that a property being taken by the broker's client in an exchange is overvalued due to faulty construction. The client may be justified in relying on the professional opinion of the broker without making an independent investigation. *Smith v. Carroll Realty Co.*, 335 P.2d 67 (UT 1959); *Frederick v. Sguillante*, 144 So.2d 848 (FL 1962). In some cases, the broker is liable for deliberately undervaluing the property and then attempting to buy it and resell it at a quick profit. *Barnard v. Gardner Inv. Corporation*, 106 S.E. 346 (VA 1921). Broker not liable for negligent misrepresentation of value of land. *1488, Inc. v. Philsec Inc.*, 939 F.2d 1281 (5th Cir. 1991).

When the broker learns of factors affecting the value of the property after the listing is signed, the broker must disclose such factors so the price can be adjusted in accordance with actual conditions. It is sometimes difficult, however, to pinpoint when a market is surging upward. *Holmes v. Cathcart*, 92 N.W. 956 (MN 1903). In *Ramsey v. Gordon*, 567 S.W.2d 868 (TX 1978), the broker-buyer was to be paid a commission by the seller. The seller was allowed to void the contract because the broker breached a fiduciary duty by not disclosing the increasing value of the property during the listing period. In *Ridgeway v. McGuire*, 158 P.2d 893 (OR 1945), the broker-buyer was held liable for failure to advise the seller that the property would be valued higher if it were subdivided. In *Schoenberg v. Benner*, 59 Cal.Rptr. 359 (CA 1967), the listing broker was held negligent for failing to verify the appraised value of property that secured the buyer's purchase money note carried back by the seller.

6. Commission Split. Failure to disclose a secret fee-splitting arrangement with the buyer's broker (as opposed to a subagent) can result in loss of commission by the listing broker. *Tracey v. Blake*, 118 N.E. 271 (MA 1918); *Devine v. Hudgins*, 163 A.83 (ME 1932); *Peaden v. Marler*, 189 P.741 (OK 1920). There is generally no prohibition against the listing broker dividing the commission with the buyer, as such a reduction in commission is a personal sacrifice on the broker's part to further the interests of the seller. *Banner v. Elm*, 248 A.2d 452 (MD 1968); *McCall v. Johns*, 294 S.W.2d 869 (TX 1956); *Douell v. Rosenstein*, 208 N.W. 651 (MN 1926); but see *Greenberg v. Meyer*, 363 N.E.2d 779 (OH 1977), in which broker was held to have breached duty of loyalty.

7. Contract Provisions. The broker must disclose important provisions of contracts that the client is expected to sign. Brokers have been held liable for not discussing with sellers the effect of accepting unsecured promissory notes or the fact that the sellers would receive minimal cash. *Morley v. J. Pagel Realty & Ins.*, 550 P.2d 1104 (AZ 1976); *Buffington v. Haas*, 601 P.2d 1320 (AZ 1979); *Wesco Realty, Inc. v. Drewry*, 515 P.2d 513 (WA 1973); *Reese v. Harper*, 329 P.2d 410 (UT 1958). While a listing broker clearly has a duty to advise the seller concerning tying up the seller's VA eligibility on an assumption by a nonveteran buyer, it has been held that a buyer's broker has no such duty. *Hurney v. Locke*, 308 N.W.2d 764 (SD 1981). The broker may be liable for failure to disclose that a listing agreement is an exclusive right to sell, *Lyle v. Moore*, 599 P.2d 336 (MT 1979), or the effect of an extender or a carryover clause, *Baird v. Madsen*, 134 P.2d 885 (CA 1943).

Some courts extend the duty of the broker to discuss with the buyer certain contract provisions, such as the seller's remedies upon default of the buyer. *Wegg v. Henry Broderick, Inc.*, 557 P.2d 861 (WA 1976); *Swift v. White*, 129 N.W.2d 748 (IA 1964); for a contrary result, see *Crawford v. Powers*, 419 F.Supp. 723 (D.S.C.), applying South Carolina law, *Kidd v. Maldonado*, 688 P.2d 461 (UT 1984). In an exchange, the broker was liable for failing to disclose that a second mortgage contained a due-on-sale clause, and the plaintiff lost the property through foreclosure, *Pepitone v. Russo*, 134 Cal.Rptr. 709 (CA 1976). In *Alhino v. Starr*, 169 Cal.Rptr.136 (CA 1980), the salesperson failed to disclose to the seller that the purchase money note was unsecured and did not contain the customary attorney fees and acceleration provisions. Broker acting as buyer owes duty of fair disclosure to seller (explain consequence of taking "subject to" as compared to "assumption of" loan). *Sigmen v. Arizona Dept. Real Estate*, 819 P.2d 969 (AZ 1991).

Sellers not required to pay commission when broker failed to comply with state disclosure law. *Huijers v. DeMarrais*, 12 Cal.App.4th 676 (CA December 1992).

Faithfulness

A broker who induces a buyer to believe that a property can be bought for less than the asking price may fail to discharge the duty of loyalty and, therefore, forfeit the commission. See *Beckwith v. Clevenger Realty Co.*, 360 P.2d 596 (AZ 1961), in which the broker told the buyer the seller was anxious to sell due to poor health; *Haymes v. Rogers*, 222 P.2d 789 (AZ 1950), in which the court held the broker liable only if done in bad faith. Likewise, the broker should not make an unauthorized statement that the property is listed at $195,000, but the seller yesterday countered another buyer's offer at $187,000.

Preparing two ascending offers for the buyer and presenting only the lower one without informing the seller that the buyer will go higher violates the broker's duty of loyalty. It is unfaithful for the broker to attempt to sell property well above the listing price to pocket the difference. *Mason v. Bulleri*, 543 P.2d 478 (AZ 1975); *Gillespie v. Rosenbaum*, 173 N.Y.S.429 (NY 1918); *Rattray v. Scudder*, 169 P.2d 371 (CA 1946); *Sankey v. Cramer*, 131 P. 288 (CO 1913). A broker who persuaded the buyer to buy elsewhere breached the fiduciary duty of good faith in *Lyon v. Giannoni*, 335 P.2d 690 (CA 1959). Broker breached duty of honesty to buyer of second home (former seller-client of broker). *Youngblood v. Wall*, 815 S.W.2d 512 (TN 1991).

Any collusion by the broker with the buyer will forfeit the broker's right to a commission, even though the seller obtains the full asking price. *Carter v. Owens*, 50 So. 641 (FL 1909); *Sternberger v. Young*, 75 A. 807 (NJ 1908). In *Greenfield v. Bausch*, 263 N.Y.S. 19 (NY 1933), the buyer agreed to pay the broker half of any amount by which the seller's listing price was reduced through the broker's efforts. The broker cannot suggest that the buyer offer terms less advantageous to the seller than the buyer had indicated the buyer would make. *Investment Exchange Realty, Inc. v. Hillcrest Bowl, Inc.*, 513 P.2d 282 (WA 1973); *Mitchell v. Gould*, 266 P. 565 (CA 1928).

Brokers cannot make false promises to induce their principals to enter into contracts, as in *Brown v. Coates*, 253 F.2d 36 (DC 1958). In *Jory v. Bennight*, 542 P.2d 1400 (NV 1975), the broker was held liable for the misconduct of its two salespersons, who falsely promised that the seller would receive additional monies outside of escrow.

Denial of commission due to conflict of interest when listing broker failed to disclose that salesperson in office was selling similar property to same buyer. *Reinhold v. Mallery*, 599 A.2d 126 (NH 1991).

Broker not liable to seller for damages caused as a result of buyer receiving inaccurate income financial information supplied by seller. *Burton v. Mackey*, 102 Or.App. 361 (OR 1990).

In *Moser v. Bertram*, No. 20692 (August 10, 1993), the New Mexico Supreme Court faced the issue of whether the listing salesperson was liable to a buyer client of the firm for breach of fiduciary duty. The buyer failed to close on an earlier contract with the listing salesperson's seller. The buyer subsequently arranged financing, expecting to consummate the sale, but was told the seller had accepted another offer. The buyer sued for loss of investment opportunity. The listing salesperson was the only one left with money. The court held that "although agency fiduciary obligations and liabilities may extend from a salesperson to the qualifying broker, the fiduciary duties of one real estate salesperson are not attributable to another salesperson operating under the same qualifying broker unless one salesperson is at fault in appointing, supervising, or cooperating with the to her." See *Restatement (Second) of Agency 358(1)* (1957).

The broker should not return deposit money to the buyer without first checking with the seller, as in *Kruger v. Soreide*, 246 N.W.2d 764 (ND 1976).

Many of the reported cases involve buyers' brokers who find the ideal properties for their clients, but first buy the properties themselves, then sell them to the buyers at a secret profit. *Des Fosses v. Notis*, 333 A.2d 822 (ME 1975); *Green v. Jones-Murphy Properties, Inc.*, 335 S.W. 2d 822 (AR 1960); *Hyman v. Burmeister*, 216 Ill.App. 98 (IL 1919); *Kurtz v. Farrington*, 132 A. 540 (CT 1926).

If the broker is not the agent of the buyer, however, the broker may owe no duty to disclose to the buyer the broker's interest in purchasing the property. *Fish v. Teninga*, 161 N.E. 515 (IL 1928); *Warren v. Mangels Realty*, 533 P.2d 78 (AZ 1975). Buyers' brokers cannot profit by their own unfaithfulness. *Hilbolt v. Wisconsin Real Estate Brokers' Board*, 137 N.W.2d 482 (WI 1965); *Neff v. Bud Lewis Company*, 548 P.2d 107 (NM 1976); *Pouppirt v. Greenwood*, 110 P. 195 (CO 1910); *Roquemore v. Ford Motor Company*, 290 F.Supp. 130 (TX 1967); *United Homes, Inc. v. Moss*, 154 So.2d 351 (FL 1963); *Kroeker v. Hurlbert*, 101 P.2d 101 (CA 1940); *Degner v. Moncel*, 93 N.W.2d 857 (WI 1959); *Smith v. Howard*, 322 P.2d 1034 (CA 1958).

In *Sawyer Realty Group, Inc. v. Jarvis Corp.*, 432 N.E.2d 849 (IL 1982), the seller's brokers breached a duty of good faith to the buyer by not disclosing the fact that after the buyer submitted an offer, the seller sold the property to the brokers. In *Funk v. Tiff*, 515 F.2d 23 (9th Cir. FL 1975), the buyer made an offer through the listing broker, who, in turn, submitted a similar offer for himself and his partner. The court held that the listing broker had a duty to deal fairly and honestly with the buyer and that outbidding the prospective buyer without adequate disclosure to the buyer was a breach. The listing broker held the property as a constructive trustee for the benefit of the buyer.

Self-Dealing

The real estate broker is brought by his calling into a relation of trust and confidence. Constant are the opportunities by concealment and collusion to extract illicit gains. We know from our judicial records that the opportunities have been not lost. *Roman v. Lobe*, 152 N.E. 461 (NY 1926) (Cardoza, J.)

Unfortunately, the casebooks are filled with lawsuits in which the real estate broker purchased property and was sued because either (1) the broker did not disclose to the seller that the broker or a relative was the real buyer or (2) the buyer's broker secretly purchased a property and then resold it to the buyer client at a profit in a double escrow or "flip" transaction. Some of the self-deal cases in which the broker is an undisclosed buyer are *Batson v. Strehlow*, 441 P.2d 101 (CA 1968); *Riley v. Powell*, 665 S.W. 2d 578 (TX 1984); *Rodes v. Shannon*, 35 Cal.Rptr. 339 (CA 1963); *Rosenfeld v. Glick Real Estate Co.*, 291 S.W.2d 863 (MO 1956); *Buckley v. Savage*, 7 Cal.Rptr. 328 (CA 1960). When the broker fully discloses the facts and takes no unfair advantage, no breach of fiduciary duty occurs, as in *Fisher v. Losey*, 177 P.2d 334 (CA 1947).

In some cases, the broker uses a dummy purchaser to buy and then sell at a secret profit. *Loughlin v. Idora Realty Company*, 66 Cal.Rptr. 747 (CA 1968); *Schepers v. Lautenschlager*, 112 N.W.2d 767 (NE 1962); *Alley v. Nevada Real Estate Division*, 575 P.2d 1334 (NV 1978) (double escrow); *Carluccio v. 607 Hudson Street Holding Co.*, 57 A.2d 452 (NJ 1948); *M.S.R., Inc. v. Lish*, 527 P.2d 912 (CO 1974); *Wendt v. Fischer*, 154 N.E. 303 (NY 1926); *Simone v. McKee*, 298 P.2d 667 (CA 1956).

Listing agent found out about seller's bid on a replacement home. Agent used the information to outbid seller. Court found no breach of fiduciary duty. *Walter v. Murphy*, 573 N.E.2d 677 (OH 1988). *Note:* In today's environment the result may have been considerably different.

Punitive damages awarded to buyer, whose offer was never presented by listing agent, who bought the property at a lower price from desperate seller. *Forbus v. City Realty*, Case No. 90-131 (AL 1992).

In *Thompson v. Searl*, 301 P.2d 804 (WY 1956), the seller broker breached its fiduciary obligation by accepting a commission from the buyer for selling the buyer's home that was used as part payment of the sales price, without first obtaining the seller's consent.

In some cases, the self-dealing broker is sued by the buyer who hired the broker to locate a property. *Henderson v. Hassur*, 594 P.2d 650 (KS 1979); *Quinn v. Phipps*, 113 So. 419 (FL 1927); *Rogers v. Genung*, 74 A.473 (NJ 1909); *Kurtz v. Farrington*, 132 A.540 (CT 1926); *Zichlin v. Dill*, 25 So.2d 4 (FL 1946); *Volz v. Burkeheimer, Inc.*, 21 P.2d 285 (WA 1933); *Barber's Super Markets, Inc. v. Stryker*, 500 P.2d 1304 (NM 1972); *Baskin v. Dam*, 239 A.2d 549 (CT 1967); *Spindler v. Krieger*, 147 N.E.2d 457 (IL 1958); *Jarvis v. O'Brien*, 305 P.2d 961 (CA 1957). Often, the buyer sues to impose a constructive trust in favor of the buyer. *Mitchell v. Allison*, 213 P.2d 231 (NM 1949); *Ward v. Taggart*, 336 P.2d 534 (CA 1959); *Antle v. Haas*, 251 S.W.2d 290 (KY 1952); *Green v. Jones-Murphy Properties, Inc.*, 335 S.W.2d 822 (AR 1960); *Burton v. Pet, Inc.*, 509 S.W.2d 95 (MO 1974); *Sierra Pacific Industries v. Carter*, 163 Cal.Rptr. 764 (CA 1980); *Hughes v. Miracle Ford, Inc.*, 676 S.W.2d 642 (TX 1984).

In cases where brokers act on their own behalf in a sale or purchase of property, they are generally held to a higher standard than nonlicensees. In *Mississippi Real Estate Commission v. Ruby Henessee*, Supreme Court 92 CC 1230 (April 1996), the broker maintained that she was not subject to the Mississippi license law because she was acting on her own behalf. The real estate commission suspended her license for 90 days for making misrepresentations in the sale of her property. She took her case to the circuit court who ruled in her favor, thus against the

Commission. The Commission appealed to the Supreme Court who ruled for the Commission saying, "To allow Ruby, or any other licensed broker, not to be held responsible for misrepresentations made during the course of the sale of property wholly owned by the broker, while simultaneously holding that a broker will be held responsible for making misrepresentations during the sale of another's property, would create logically inconsistent results."

Duty of Obedience

When the seller instructed the broker not to return the buyer's deposit money without first obtaining a written appraisal (confirming the buyer's contingency that the sales price be at or below fair market value), and the broker failed to obtain such appraisal, the broker could not recover the commission. The seller's instructions were reasonable and material and, if carried out, could have prevented litigation. *Jackson v. Williams*, 510 S.W.2d 645 (TX 1974). When the listing agreement stated that the broker was to lease a warehouse subject to the owner's approval of the tenant, and the broker allowed the tenant to move in without prior owner approval, the broker was not entitled to receive a commission. *Latter & Blum v. Richmond*, 388 So.2d 368 (LA 1980); *Owen v. Shelton*, 277 S.E.2d 189 (VA 1981).

The broker was held to have breached its fiduciary duty of obedience by failing to obey the seller's instruction to revoke a counteroffer prior to the buyer's acceptance. *Abboud v. State Real Estate Commission*, 316 N.W.2d 608 (NE 1982).

Duty to Use Reasonable Skill and Care

The broker's duties of care and disclosure are greater when the client is unsophisticated and unknowledgeable in real estate transactions. *Prall v. Gooden*, 360 P.2d 759 (OR 1961); *Bjornstad v. Perry*, 443 P.2d 999 (ID 1968); *Fairfield S&L v. Kroll*, 246 N.E.2d 327 (IL 1969).

The duties of reasonable skill and care are imposed not only by the common law of agency, but frequently also by the terms of the listing contract, and thus support a breach of contract action or defense. In most professional liability lawsuits, it is necessary to produce expert testimony regarding the standard of care required of the professional. This is not required in malpractice actions against a real estate broker. *Jorgensen v. Beach 'N' Bay Realty, Inc.*, 177 Cal.Rptr.882 (CA 1981); *Easton v. Strassburger*, 199 Cal.Rptr.383 (CA 1984). The complaining party's testimony may be sufficient to prove broker malpractice. Buyer's broker held to have fiduciary duties to discover and disclose material facts, such as existence of declaration of restriction against property prohibiting business use. *Lewis v. Long & Foster Real Estate*, 584 A.2d 1325 (MD 1991).

The broker should make a reasonable inquiry into the creditworthiness of a proposed buyer seeking to have the seller's carryback financing. The broker must exercise care in evaluating or preparing contract provisions and must use correct information, facts, and figures. Important facts, such as sewer connections and zoning, must be carefully researched and verified. The real estate broker is held to a standard of care that requires that the broker possess ordinary professional knowledge concerning the title and natural characteristics of the property being sold. *Brady v. Carman*, 3 Cal.Rptr. 612 (CA 1960). Broker not liable when buyer defaulted on seller carryback mortgage. *Garcia v. Unique Realty*, 92 FCDR 2162 (GA 1993).

The case of *Perkins v. Thorpe*, 676 P.2d 52 (ID 1984), involved the question of whether the broker breached a fiduciary duty owed to the seller by negligently misadvising the seller on the value of the listed property and failing to disclose that the broker represented the buyer in a separate but related transaction. The court stated:

> *The law imposes upon a real estate broker a fiduciary obligation of utmost good faith, integrity, honesty, and loyalty as well as a duty of due care and diligence. Breach of the fiduciary duty may result in the broker's loss of commission and in liability in damages. A broker ultimately is responsible to the public for the actions of real estate salespersons whom he employs.*
>
> *A broker is obligated to employ that degree of skill in his calling usually possessed by others in the same business. The broker's conduct is required to meet a standard of competence because he is issued a license and permitted to hold himself out to the public as qualified by training and experience to render a specialized service in the field of real estate transactions. The law requires that the broker perform [at] a certain level of skill; for if he failed to do so, instead of being the badge of competence and integrity it is supposed to be, the broker's license would serve only as a foil to lure the unsuspecting public in.*

The broker is liable to the seller whenever the broker's carelessness results in a buyer's successfully suing the seller for money damages or rescission. This is true even when the broker acts gratuitously, as in *Green v. Jones-Murphy Properties, Inc.*, 335 S.W.2d 822 (AR 1960). A gratuitous buyer's broker was held liable for failure to transfer the seller's insurance policy to the buyer as agreed in *Estes v. Lloyd Hammerstad, Inc.*, 503 P.2d 1149 (WA 1972). Consider the following:

- Broker innocently misstated the net operating income to indicate a positive cash flow.
- Broker failed to reveal that seller had only oral permission for a driveway access.
- Broker failed to ascertain that the property being sold was owned jointly, only one owner signed the acceptance, and the transaction failed; likewise, when the unsophisticated seller owned only a life estate.
- Broker failed to verify the issuance of a valid septic tank permit, a critical contingency to the sales contract. The broker is required to employ a reasonable degree of effort and professional expertise to confirm or refute important information obtained from the seller. *Tennant v. Lawton*, 615 P.2d 1305 (WA 1980).
- Broker assisted seller in preparing a financial statement based on a check register. Buyer canceled due to erroneous financial information supplied to buyer. Although brokers are not usually held to the standard of care of accountants, a broker must exercise extreme care when acting like an accountant in voluntarily assisting in the preparation of financial information for the broker's principal. *Lunden v. Smith*, 632 P.2d 1344 (OR 1981).

In some cases, the broker is liable to the seller for failing to properly advise and protect the seller's best interests. *Nolan v. Wisconsin Real Estate Brokers' Board*, 89 N.W.2d 317 (WI 1958). Suppose the broker allows the seller to carry back a

$50,000 note not secured by a mortgage or deed of trust without first making sure that the seller understands the consequences of taking an unsecured note. See *Morley v. J. Pagel Realty & Insurance*, 550 P.2d 1104 (AZ 1976), in which the court said the broker must use all of his professional ability and knowledge to make sure the client understands the facts. Or suppose, in a contemplated transaction, that (1) the broker promises the seller that a sale will occur by a date sufficient to have funds to purchase another property, (2) the broker fails to recommend protective contingency language in both contracts, and (3) the broker represents both ends of the transaction. Or suppose the broker advises the seller that the seller is entitled to keep the earnest money deposit on default, yet fails to mention that escrow usually requires mutual releases and deducts cancellation charges before paying out the deposit.

What if the broker fails to tell the seller about restrictions on VA and FHA financing, such as substitution of VA eligibility and the need to make repairs under minimum property requirements? See *Monty v. Peterson*, 540 P.2d 1377 (WA 1975); *Reese v. Harper*, 329 P.2d 410 (UT 1958). In *Jones v. Maestas*, 696 P.2d 920 (ID 1985), the court held that the broker was not required to communicate the meaning of an exclusive listing agreement that was unequivocally expressed by the instrument itself.

The broker was held liable when the broker wrote the purchase contract incorrectly and not according to specifications in *Mattieligh v. Poe*, 356 P.2d.328 (WA 1960). The broker is required to act with due diligence to inquire about an apparent discrepancy in property size. The broker must point out the desirable features of the seller's property. *Schackai v. Lagreco*, 350 So.2d 1244 (LA 1977); *Mallallieu-Golder, Inc. v. O'Neal*, 16 Pa. D & C 2d 594 (PA 1959).

The real estate broker is expected to do more than find a buyer for a seller's property. The broker must diligently exercise skill and care on behalf of the client. To illustrate the extent of the broker's obligation beyond matchmaking, refer to the checklist of listing broker responsibilities in the typical residential transaction.

Duty to Account

The broker must not commingle client funds with the broker's own funds. Brokers usually maintain separate client trust fund accounts. The broker should use one account for sales transactions and another for rental property management transactions.

State licensing law usually contains strict rules on trust fund accounting. The Texas Real Estate Commission can suspend or revoke a broker's license for not properly accounting for client funds. *Kilgore v. Texas Real Estate Commission*, 565 S.W.2d 114 (TX 1978). Brokers must deposit checks by the next business day after receipt unless special permission is obtained to hold the checks in uncashed form. Rather than use a client trust fund account, some brokers suggest the buyer's deposit check be payable directly to the escrow company or settlement agent.

Misrepresentation

Regarding the element of reliance, courts have held that the buyer is entitled to relief if the representations were a material inducement to the contract, even though the buyer may have made efforts to discover the truth thereof and did not rely wholly on the veracity of the representations. *Foxley Cattle Co. v. Bank of Mead*, 241 N.W.2d 495 (NE 1976); *Erickson v. Midgarden*, 31 N.W.2d 918 (MN 1948); *Schechter v. Brewer*, 344 S.W.2d 784 (MO 1961).

It is sometimes difficult to distinguish between fact and opinion. "Real property taxes are low" is different from "real property taxes are $1,000 per year." In *Foreman & Clark Corporation v. Fallon*, 479 P.2d 362 (CA 1961), the court found no breach because the statements as to the tenant's future sales in a percentage lease case were mere expressions of opinion, were not material, and were not relied on by the landlord. *Coleman v. Goran*, 168 N.E.2d 56 (IL 1960); *Lone Star Machinery Corporation v. Frankel*, 564 S.W.2d 135 (TX 1978). In *Peterson v. Auvel*, 552 P.2d 538 (OR 1976), the buyer relied on the broker's opinion that the earnest money contract was not enforceable. *Eyers v. Burbank Co.*, 166 P.656 (WA 1917). See *Gross v. Sussex, Inc.*, 630 A2d 1156 (MD 1993).

Examples of Misrepresentation

Even if a broker acts in good faith, he may still be liable for failure to exercise reasonable care or competence in obtaining or communicating information that the broker knew or should have known. The broker may be liable for (1) negligently failing to discover and disclose building defects that were discoverable upon exercising reasonable care, *Easton v. Strassburger*, 199 Cal.Rptr. 383 (CA 1984); *Gouveia v. Citicorp.*, 686 P.2d 262 (NM 1984); *Amato v. Rathbun Realty, Inc.*, 647 P.2d 433 (NM 1982); (2) making representations regarding title that the agent does not know to be true, *Hall v. Wright*, 156 N.W.2d 661 (IA 1968); or (3) representing the property as a "buildable site," *Tennant v. Lawton*, 615 P.2d 1305 (WA 1980).

It normally is no defense that the broker was simply passing on information received from the seller. *Dugan v. Jones*, 615 P.2d 1239 (UT 1980) (total acreage conveyed was 7 acres, not 23 acres, as represented); *Nordstrom v. Miller*, 605 P.2d 545 (KS 1980); *Gaurrky v. Rozga*, 332 N.W.2d 804 (WI 1983); *Hoffman v. Connall*, 718 P.2d 814 (WA 1986). For the broker to recover from the seller based on indemnity, the broker must show that the broker used due care and was justified in relying on the seller's representations. *Barnes v. Lopez*, 544 P.2d 694 (AZ 1976). Seller told broker the water well was "good" in *Bevins v. Ballard*, 655 P.2d 757 (AK 1982). See *Rach v. Kleiber*, 367 N.W.2d 824 (WI 1985).

The broker has been held liable for misrepresentation in the following types of cases:

- **Water leakage.** Broker should have known basement had a seepage problem. Broker knew of serious problems with leaking sewage from neighbor's yard and with drainage of water from property. *Sawyer v. Tildahl*, 148 N.W.2d 131 (MN 1967); *McGerr v. Beals*, 145 N.W.2d 579 (NE 1966); *McRae v. Bolstad*, 646 P.2d 771 (WA 1982); *Berryman v. Reigert*, 175 N.W.2d 438 (MN 1970); *Richmond v. Blair*, 488 N.E.2d 563 (IL 1985). Broker liable for misrepresentation regarding leaks and dampness. *Silva v. Stevens*, 589 A.2d 852 (VT 1991). Broker not liable when broker pointed out water stains and recommended buyer hire home inspector. *Connor v. Merrill Lynch Realty*, 581 N.E.2d 196 (IL 1991).

- **Operating expenses and income.** Broker showed that buyer falsified operating statements and promised to help run the restaurant. *Jennings v. Lee*, 461 P.2d 161 (AZ 1969). Broker incorrectly assured buyer that the property would generate monthly income of $900 without having checked available income records. *Ford v. Cournale*, 111 Cal.Rptr. 334 (CA 1974). Broker carelessly assured buyer that the property could be rented. *Emily v. Bayne*, 371 S.W.2d 663 (MO 1963).

- **Free of termites.** Seller's broker, who assured buyer that the property was free of termites, dry rot, and fungi, was held liable in *Johnson v. Sergeants*, 313 P.2d 41 (CA 1957), and *Saporta v. Barbagelata*, 33 Cal.Rptr. 661 (CA 1963). *Maples v. Porath*, 638 S.W.2d 337 (MO 1982); *Neveroski v. Blair*, 358 A.2d 473 (NJ 1976); *Miles v. McSwegin*, 388 N.E.2d 1367 (OH 1979); *Obde v. Schlemeyer*, 353 P.2d 672 (WA 1960). Broker with two termite reports intentionally concealed termite condition and was liable for punitive damages for intentionally inflicting emotional distress on buyer by concealing negative termite report and showing only the positive report in *Godfrey v. Steinpress*, 180 Cal.Rptr. 95 (CA 1982); *Lynn v. Taylor*, 642 P.2d 131 (KS 1982); and *Dicker v. Smith*, 523 P.2d 371 (KS 1974). Failure to disclose termites. *Wire v. Jackson*, 576 So.2d 1198 (LA 1991). Real estate broker acting as seller had plastered over the termite damage. In a subsequent sale, buyer not able to recover against original broker-seller. *Katz v. Schacter*, 251 N.J.Super. 467 (NJ 1991).

  The mere use of an "as is" clause without a more specific explanation of the defect may not eliminate a customary requirement of the seller to provide a termite clearance report or protect against claims for concealed termite damage. Seller liable for not disclosing known latent termite damage despite "as is" clause. *Stemple v. Dobson*, 400 S.E.2d 561 (WV 1990). Buyer denied recovery in *Van Gessel v. Fold*, 569 N.E.2d 141 (IL 1991). Fraudulent concealment of termite report despite "as is" clause. *Rayner v. Wise Realty*, 504 So.2d 1361 (FL 1987).

- **Free of liens and encumbrances.** Broker erroneously represented that seller owned the property free and clear of all encumbrances. *Floyd v. Myers*, 333 P.2d 654 (WA 1959); *Carl Needham, Inc. v. Camilleri*, 533 P.2d 765 (NV 1975); *Wilson v. Hisey*, 305 P.2d 686 (CA 1957); *Mayflower Mortgage Company v. Brown*, 530 P.2d 1298 (CO 1975); *Grandchamp v. Patzer*, 197 N.W.2d 537 (MI 1972). Minor encroachments sometimes do not render title unmarketable (free and clear of encumbrances) if the encroachment would not cause a prudent person to hesitate before buying.

- **Filled land.** Broker told buyer that the property listed was not a "filled lot." Buyer's house sank, and buyer successfully recovered against seller, who then sued broker for the loss caused by broker's unauthorized false representation. *Kruse v. Miller*, 300 P.2d 855 (CA 1956); *Sorrell v. Young*, 491 P.2d 1312 (WA 1971) (constructive fraud); *Thacker v. Tyree*, 297 S.E.2d 885 (WV 1982); *Ashburn v. Miller*, 326 P.2d 229 (CA 1958).

- **Property condition.** Salesperson stated the heater was in good working condition. Actually, seller had concealed the fact that the heater was broken. "Fraud includes the pretense of knowledge when there is none." *Spargnapani v. Wright*, 1 10 A.2d 82 (DC 1954). In *Fowler v. Benton*, 185 A.2d 344 (MD 1962), the broker failed to disclose that the house was built in a slide area. Silence is not golden when the broker has a duty to speak. Silence breaches an implied duty to warn of defects. *Henderson v. Johnson*, 403 P.2d 669 (WA 1965); *Easton v. Strassburger*, 199 Cal.Rptr. 383 (CA 1984); *Hunter v. Wilson*, 355 So.2d 39 (CA App. 1978) (leaking roof); *Berman v. Watergate West, Inc.*, 391 A.2d 1351 (DC 1978) (defective air-conditioning system); *Brown v. Pritchett*, 633 S.W.2d 294 (MO 1982); *Milliken v. Green*, 583 P.2d 548 (OR 1978); *Robert v. Estate of Barbagallo*, 531 A.2d 1125 (PA 1987). Faulty heating system was known to broker, who had managed the property for former owner. *Ne Bud v. Lewis Company*, 548 P.2d 107 (NM 1976); *Byrn v. Walker*, 267 S.E.2d 601 (SC 1980); *Sorensen v. Gardner*, 334 P.2d 471 (OR 1959) (misrepresented that plumbing complied with building code). Building in state of disrepair and had been placed for condemnation by city officials. *Lingsch v. Savage*, 29 Cal.Rptr. 201 (CA 1963); *Cooper v. Jevne*, 128 Cal.Rptr. 724 (CA 1976); *Merrill v. Buck*, 375 P.2d 304 (CA 1962). Cracked foundation. *Pinger v. Guaranty Investment Co.*, 307 S.W.2d 53 (MO 1957); *Josephs v. Austin*, 420 So.2d 1181 (LA 1982). Sewer not connected or backs up. *Kraft v. Lowe*, 77 A.2d 554 (DC 1950); *Shane v. Hoffman*, 324 A.2d 532 (PA 1974); *Crum v. McCoy*, 322 N.E.2d 161 (OH 1974). Broker misrepresented condition of foundation and past repairs. *Schechter v. Brewer*, 344 S.W.2d 784 (MO 1961). Relied on broker's advice to purchase a new house with substantial defects. *Menzel v. Morse*, 362 N.W.2d 465 (IA 1985).

No duty to warn buyer of readily observable condition (stepped on insulation and fell through attic). *Zaffiris v. O'Loughlin*, 585 NYS 2d 94 (NY 1992). Seller's agreement to repair faulty septic system not terminated by doctrine of merger. *Andreychak v. Lint*, 607 A.2d 1346 (NJ 1992). Seller liable for innocent misrepresentation regarding repairs to septic system. *Zimmerman v. Kent*, 575 N.E.2d 70 (MA 1991). Broker not liable for failure to disclose latent defect; seller normally has no duty to disclose defect in used property unless asked by buyer. *Commercial Credit Corp. v. Lisenby*, 579 So.2d 1291 (AL 1991). Broker held to have no duty to buyer to inspect property for defects beyond asking sellers if such defects existed. *Kubinsky v. Van Zandt Realtors*, 811 S.W.2d 711 (TX 1991). Former seller not liable to buyer for concealment of defects even though seller is now mortgagee and buyer defaulted under mortgage. *Kovach v. McLellan*, 564 So.2d 274 (FL 1990). Agent failed to disclose that "independent" property inspector had previously inspected home; house later found to be not structurally sound. *Johnson v. Beverly-Hanks*, 400 S.E.2d 38 (NC 1991). Seller-broker represented that house needed no repair. Both seller and appraiser held liable because house needed $23,000 of repairs to make it eligible for FHA financing. *Rene Lenoir v. Judy Hill Realty*, Case No. 5200 (2d District, MS 1990). Lead paint, see *Richwind v. Brunson*, 625 A2d 326 (MD 1993).

- **Easements.** When the buyer questioned the broker about an easement, the broker said not to worry. Three months after closing, the city used the easement to lay water pipes. The broker was held liable. *Brady v. Carman*, 3 Cal.Rptr. 612 (CA 1960); *Gilby v. Cooper*, 310 N.E.2d 268 (OH 1973); *Norgren v. Harwell*, 172 So.2d 723 (LA 1965); *Stone v. Lawyers Title Insurance Corp.*, 554 S.W.2d 183 (TX 1977).

- ■ ***Zoning.*** Broker disclosed zoning restrictions, but negligently failed to disclose private recorded restrictions that diminished the value of the lot, in *Monty v. Peterson*, 540 P.2d 1377 (WA 1975). Broker negligently misrepresented actual zoning. *Barnes v. Lopez*, 544 P.2d 694 (AZ 1976), in which broker merely affirmed the erroneous information given by seller. *Brandt v. Koepnick*, 469 P.2d 189 (WA 1970); *Asleson v. West Branch Land Co.*, 311 N.W.2d 533 (ND 1981); *Burien Motors, Inc. v. Balch*, 513 P.2d 582 (WA 1973); *Granberg v. Turnham*, 333 P.2d 423 (CA 1958). Broker represented that it would be easy to change the zoning. *Nantell v. Lim-Wick Construction Company*, 228 So.2d 634 (FL 1969). See *Blaine v. Jones Construction*, 841 SW2d 703 (MO 1992).

  Holding seller had no duty to disclose zoning problem in *City of Aurora v. Green*, 467 N.E.2d 1069 (IL 1984); *Denton v. Hood*, 461 N.E.2d 1069 (IL 1984); *O'Brien v. Noble*, 435 N.E.2d 554 (IL 1982); *Goldfarb v. Dietz*, 506 P.2d 1322 (WA 1973) (nonconforming use). Some courts distinguish statements of law from statements of fact and hold the seller liable only for misstatements of fact. Whether a statement was one of law or fact is not relevant in an equitable action for rescission based on mutual mistake. *Gartner v. Eikell*, 319 N.W.2d 397 (MN 1982); *Gardner Homes, Inc. v. Gaither*, 228 S.E.2d 525 (NC 1976). But see *Steinberg v. Bay Terrace Apt. Hotel Inc.*, 375 So.2d 1089 (FL 1979).

- ■ ***Size of property.*** Brokers frequently get into trouble because they say, "Here is the boundary line," when they're not sure, rather than, "I don't know; let's order a survey and find out." This is especially true with unintentional misrepresentations of square footage or acreage. *Alexander Myers & Company v. Hopke*, 565 P.2d 80 (WA 1977); *Nathanson v. Murphy*, 282 P.2d 174 (CA 1955); *Mikkelson v. Quail Valley Realty*, 641 P.2d 124 (UT 1982); *Carrel v. Lux*, 420 P.2d 564 (AZ 1966); *Dixon v. MacGillivray*, 185 P.2d 109 (WA 1947); *Cameron v. Terrell & Garrett, Inc.*, 618 S.W.2d 535 (TX 1981); *Shaffer v. Earl Thacker Co., Ltd.*, 716 P.2d 163 (HI 1986). Broker liable for misrepresentation of home's square footage even though buyer toured home. *John v. Robbins*, 764 F.Supp. 379 (NC 1991).

  Broker not liable for statement that boundary line "probably went to that stake." *Bischoff Realty v. Ledford*, 562 N.E.2d 1321 (IN 1990).

- ■ ***"As is" clause.*** Use of a general disclaimer clause does not protect against fraud. *Smith v. Rickards*, 308 P.2d 758 (CA 1957); *Wittenberg v. Robinov*, 173 N.E.2d 868 (NY 1961). An "as is" clause generally is sufficient to indicate that the seller will not make any repairs. *Lenawee County Bd. of Health v. Messerly*, 331 N.W.2d 203 (MI 1982). Selling a property "as is" does not relieve the broker from revealing known defects that are not readily observable to the buyer. *Lingsch v. Savage*, 29 Cal.Rptr. 201 (CA 1963); *Crawford v. Nastos*, 6 Cal.Rptr. 425 (CA 1960); *Katz v. Dept. of Real Estate*, 158 Cal. Rptr. 766 (CA 1979); *Weitzel v. Barnes*, 691 S.W.2d 598 (TX 1985); *Prichard v. Reitz*, 223 Cal. Rptr. 734 (CA 1986); *Davies v. Bradley*, 676 P.2d 1242 (CO 1983); *Prudential v. Jefferson Associates*, 839 S.W.2d 866 (TX 1992); *George v. Lumbrazo*, 584 NYS 2d 704 (1992); *Grube v. Thieol*, Wisconsin Ct.App. 91-2322 (WI 1992).

  Buyer could not recover for injuries to child from falling tree because buyer purchased property in "as is" condition. *Stonecipher v. Kornhaus & Moorman*, Miss. S.Ct. (MI June 17, 1993).

- ***Lawful use.*** The doctrine of caveat emptor continues to govern the disclosure of unlawful land usages. In many jurisdictions, the buyer is responsible for determining whether existing land uses are unlawful by checking zoning ordinances, building codes, occupancy rules, and restrictive covenants. These courts view the risk of illegal use as foreseeable and place that risk on the buyer. *Cousinea v. Walker*, 613 P.2d 608 (AK 1980) (caveat emptor in general); *Oates v. Jag, Inc.*, 311 S.E.2d 369 (NC 1984). Holding that the seller has no duty to disclose to the buyer a large increase in the assessed value of the property is *Lenzi v. Morkin*, 469 N.E.2d 178 (IL 1984). Once buyer asked broker why other homes were built on stilts, broker obligated to disclose material facts about building code violation and flood insurance. *Revitz v. Terrell*, 572 So.2d 996. See *Randels v. Best Real Estate*, 243 ILL App. 3d 801 (IL 1993).

    The recent trend is to interpret certain seller conduct as an implied representation of lawful use, which would support a buyer's claim for misrepresentation. *Iverson v. Solsbery*, 641 P.2d 314 (CO 1982); *Strickland v. Vescovi*, 484 A.2d 460 (CT 1984); *Kannavos v. Annino*, 247 N.E.2d 708 (MA 1969); *Dettler v. Santa Cruz*, 403 S.W.2d 651 (MO 1966).

- ***Miscellaneous.*** Concealed fact of prior grisly murder on the property, *Reed v. King*, 193 Cal.Rptr.130 (CA 1983); misrepresented location of lots, *Blanke v. Miller*, 268 S.W.2d 809 (MO 1954); misrepresented that property bounded on a river, *Carrington v. Graves*, 89 A. 237 (MD 1913). Broker intentionally inflated price of comparable sales in the area, *Miller v. Boeger*, 405 P.2d 573 (AZ 1965). Broker misrepresented the value of a property to be exchanged, *Quistgard v. Derby*, 250 P.2d 2 (CA 1952). Broker sent to jail for misrepresenting to lender existence of second mortgage on property purchased by broker in violation of 18 U.S.C.A. 1015, *U.S. v. Gregoria*, 956 F.2d 341 (1st CIR 1992).

    Broker misrepresented the duration of the lease because broker failed to read the lease completely; court also held that buyer had no independent duty to investigate because buyer had no reason to believe that the representations were false. *Hagar v. Mobley*, 638 P.2d 127 (WY 1981). Broker liable for failing to disclose to buyer that property was undergoing a foreclosure procedure. *Gray v. Boyle*, 803 S.W.2d 678 (TN 1990).

    Positive misrepresentations as to the asking price were held to go beyond the scope of "clever salesmanship." *Collins v. Philadelphia Oil Co.*, 125 S.E. 223 (WV 1924); *Booker v. Pelkey*, 180 N.W. 132 (WI 1920); *Huttig v. Nessy*, 130 So. 605 (FL 1930); *Stevens v. Reilly*, 156 P. 157 (OK 1916).

    In *Jerger v. Rubin*, 471 P.2d 726 (AZ 1970), the salesperson misrepresented that he was negotiating with a potential resale client, which would enable the plaintiff-buyer to sell off a portion of the property being purchased and thus afford the payoff of the additional financing. In *Foster v. Cross*, 650 P.2d 406 (AK 1982), the buyer's broker misrepresented the buyer's development experience and financial condition.

    Question of fact whether broker breached duty to homeowner to disclose recent "lock box burglaries" in area. *Moore v. Harry Norman Realtors*, 404 S.E.2d 793 (GA 1991). Suspicion of the presence of ghosts in residential property deemed a latent defect that must be disclosed to buyer. *Stambovsky v. Ackley*, 572 NYS 2d 672 (NY 1991). Broker held not liable for alleged negligent misrepresentation concerning railroad service to site. *Chicago*

Export Packing v. Teledyne, 566 N.E.2d 326 (IL 1990). Adequate circumstantial evidence to prove fraud and justify million-dollar punitive damage award. *Kuhnert v. Allison*, No. 14956 (HI Supreme Court 1993). Duty to disclose known pollution problem limited to residential properties; the rule is caveat emptor with commercial properties. *Futura Realty v. Lone Star*, 578 So.2d 363 (FL 1991). Tenant in shopping center sued broker for misrepresentation allegedly based on written material supplied by seller. *Henry S. Miller v. Bynum*, 797 S.W.2d 51 (TX 1990).

CHAPTER 4. CREATION AND TERMINATION OF AGENCY

Termination of Agency Relationship

Like marriage, an agency relationship is easy to create, but can be hard to terminate. The two main ways to terminate an agency are by acts of the parties and by operation of law.

An agency may end at the time stated in the listing agreement or, if no time is specified, within a reasonable period. A principal is justified in revoking the agency if the agent has breached any fiduciary duty. Also, the principal has the unilateral power to revoke the agency at any time, except in the rare case in which an agency is coupled with some interest of the broker in the property. Thus, the principal could revoke the agency and forbid the agent to show the property. Or a rental agent may be fired and asked to turn over keys and security deposits. The principal may have the power to terminate an agency, but not the legal right. If the principal wrongfully terminates the agency, the principal may be liable for the damages caused to the agent in revoking the agency prior to the termination date. *Roth v. Moeller*, 197 P.62 (CA 1921); *Sunshine v. Manos*, 496 S.W.2d 195 (TX 1973); *Chain v. Pye*, 429 S.W.2d 630 (TX 1968). Likewise, the agent can renounce the agency relationship, but only after adequate notice is given the principal. Fiduciary duty did not end when seller rejected a full-price offer. *Quechee Lakes v. Boggers*, No. 89-87 (Vermont S.C. 1992).

Courts are sometimes asked to determine when the agency relationship is ended, especially when the broker decides to become a principal in the transaction or decides to represent an adverse party. In cases in which the commission is earned only if the transaction closes, the broker's fiduciary duties continue throughout the entire closing and do not cease when the buyer is found and the purchase contract is signed. The broker's duty of disclosure as well as the other fiduciary duties continue until the transaction closes and the purpose of the agency comes to an end. *Cooke v. Iverson*, 500 P.2d 830 (ID 1972); *Zikratch v. Stillwell*, 16 Cal.Rptr. 660 (CA 1961); *Bate v. Marsteller*, 346 P.2d 903 (CA 1959); *Menzel v. Salka*, 4 Cal.Rptr. 78 (CA 1960); *Ramsey v. Sedlar*, 454 P.2d 416 (WA 1969); *Wesco Realty Inc. v. Drewry*, 515 P.2d 513 (WA 1973); *One Twenty Realty Co. v. Baer*, 272 A.2d 377 (MD 1971); *Pilling v. Eastern & Pacific Enterprises*, 702 P.2d 1232 (WA 1985), which held that a subagent has no duty to attend closing or perform services to the seller during closing.

In *Hardy v. Davis*, 164 A.2d 281 (MD 1960), the broker secretly loaned the buyer money to complete the purchase. The court held the agency terminated when the sale was made. Thus, the agent could properly deal with the other party if such dealing was not inconsistent with the broker's duty to the principal. *Sears v. Polans*, 243 A.2d 602 (MD 1968); *Olson v. Brickles*, 124 S.E.2d 895 (VA 1962).

The fiduciary relationship between a real estate broker and a principal may, under certain circumstances, exist even in the absence or after the expiration of a listing agreement. *Swallows v. Laney*, 691 P.2d 874 (NM 1984); *Wheeler v. Carl Rabe Inc.*, 599 P.2d 902 (CO 1979); *West v. Touchstone*, 620 S.W.2d 687 (TX 1981); *Cogan v. Kidder, Mathews & Segner, Inc.*, 600 P.2d 655 (WA 1979); *Harvey v. Tucker*, 12 P.2d 847 (ECS 1932). The burden of proving a termination of agency is on the party asserting it. In canceling an agency for an indefinite term, notice to the other party is generally required. *George v. Bolen*, 580 P.2d 1357 (KS 1978). Usually a broker can collect a commission after an exclusive listing agreement expires if an agreement between the seller and a buyer was reached before the listing expired. *Nicholson v. Myers*, 931 S.W. 2d 188 (MO App. 1996).

If state law requires that the agent's authority be express and in writing, the sales contract is unenforceable when one seller signs both sellers' names to a contract and that seller was not authorized in writing to act as the other's agent and when the nonsigning seller did not ratify the contract in writing. *Fejta v. GAF Companies, Inc.*, 800 F.2d 1395 (LA 1986).

The agency relationship may also be terminated through operation of law. Death of the agent or a principal prior to the broker finding a ready, willing, and able buyer will terminate the listing, as will insanity, destruction of the listed premises (or a taking by eminent domain), and bankruptcy of the principal, who loses all control of the property to the court. A broker who is decreed to be bankrupt may be required to surrender the license to the Texas Real Estate Commission.

Payment of Fee

A review of the legal cases reveals that the mere fact that the buyer undertakes to pay the commission does not itself create an agency relationship between buyer and broker. The courts have held that the establishment of an agency relationship does not stand or fall on the determination of whether a commission was to be paid. *Business Properties, Inc. v. Thomas*, 46 S.E.2d 337 (VA 1948); *Richardson v. DuPree*, 122 S.E. 707 (GA 1924); *Velten v. Robertson*, 671 P.2d 1011 (CO 1983). Broker is entitled to commission if licensed at time brokerage services were rendered, even if not licensed at closing. *Bersani v. Basset*, 585 NYS 2d 245 (NY 1992).

Even though the seller pays the fee, the broker may still be deemed to be the agent of the buyer. In *Brean v. North Campbell Professional Building*, 548 P.2d 1193 (AZ 1976), the broker first contacted the potential buyer with the idea of finding a desirable property and then searched for land and obtained a listing. *Mead v. Hummel*, 121 P.2d 423 (AZ 1942); *Wright v. Dutch*, 296 P.2d 34 (CA 1956); *Stephens v. Ahrens*, 178 P. 863 (CA 1919), holding that an agency is a consensual relationship and the broker is the agent of the person who first employs the broker. *Sands v. Eagle Oil & Refining Co.*, 188 P.2d 782 (CA 1948); *Norville v. Palant*, 545

P.2d 454 (AZ 1976); *Duffy v. Setchell*, 347 N.E.2d 218 (IL 1976); *Tanner Associates v. Ciralddo*, 161 A.2d 725 (NJ 1960); *Downing v. Buck*, 98 N.W.388 (MI 1904); *Walters v. Marler*, 147 Cal.Rptr.655 (CA 1978); *Pepper v. Underwood*, 122 Cal. Rptr. 343 (CA 1975).

As stated in *Wise v. Dawson*, 353 A.2d 267 (DE 1975), the splitting of fees between two brokers is not an indication of agency, but only a recognition of the mutual effort and cooperation used to effect the sale of the property. The splitting of fees frequently occurs in independent contractor situations. As held in *Banner v. Elm*, 248 A.2d 452 (MD 1968), it is not uncommon to provide in the purchase contract that the seller will pay the buyer's broker. *Dunatoo v. Home of the Good Shepherd of Omaha*, 228 N.W.2d 287 (NE 1975); *Antle v. Haas*, 251 S.W.2d 290 (KY 1952); *Price v. Martin*, 147 S.E.2d 716 (VA 1966).

Other cases hold that no compensation is necessary to create an agency relationship. A gratuitous agent may become an agent without compensation. *Kurtz v. Farrington*, 132 A. 540 (CT 1926). In *Walter v. Moore*, 700 P.2d 1219 (WY 1985), the court found that no agency was created with the buyer when the broker was doing a favor and not receiving any compensation. In *Canada v. Kearns*, 624 S.W.2d 755 (TX 1981), the broker unsuccessfully argued that the broker should not be responsible for the misrepresentation of one of the broker's salespersons selling the salesperson's own home through the broker for no fee.

Because agency is a consensual relationship, there is no legal barrier to having the seller authorize the listing broker to share fees with a buyer's broker. But consent is essential. Any secret agreement by a broker to split fees with the broker of the other principal is void as against public policy. *Sweeney & Moore Inc. v. Chapman*, 294 N.W. 711 (MI 1940); *Devine v. Hudgins*, 163 A. 83 (ME 1932); *Quinn v. Burton*, 81 N.E. 257 (MA 1907); *Corder v. O'Neill*, 106 S.W. 10 (MO 1907); *Ornamental and Structural Steel, Inc. v. BBG Inc.*, 509 P.2d 1053 (AZ 1973); *Greater Bloomfield Real Estate Co. v. Braun*, 235 N.W.2d 168 (MI 1975). Broker may compensate unlicensed finder who simply finds and introduces parties, but not someone who acts as a broker and is unlicensed. *Preach v. Monter Rainbow*, 12 Cal.App.4th 1441 (CA 1993).

Despite the fact that payment of the commission does not necessarily determine agency, the prudent broker will nevertheless document whom the broker represents. If no agency documentation exists, courts will likely use the commission payment as strong evidence of an agency relationship. *Price v. Eisan*, 15 Cal.Rptr. 202 (CA 1961); *St. James American Church of Los Angeles v. Kurkjian*, 121 Cal. Rptr. 214 (CA 1975); *Hickam v. Colorado Real Estate Commission*, 534 P.2d 1220 (CO 1975); *Standard Realty & Development Co. v. Ferrara*, 151 Cal.App.2d 514 (CA 1957); *Wilkie v. Abbott's Executrix*, 178 S.W.2d 210 (KY 1944); *Prichard v. Reitz*, 223 Cal.Rptr. 734 (CA 1986).

A finder is subject to licensing law and cannot qualify for a commission. *Cooney v. Ritter*, 939 F.2d 81 (3rd Cir. 1991). For special rules related to lawyers acting as brokers, see *Matter of Roth*, 577 A.2d 490 (NY 1990); *Lovett v. Estate of Lovett*, 593 A.2d 382 (NJ 1991).

Buyer's broker entitled to commission from buyer if the procuring cause of sale. *Douros Realty v. Kelley Properties*, 799 S.W.2D 179 (MO 1990). Buyer claimed that sales agent concealed facts about roof condition and about agent representing seller. Court held for agent because agency disclosure was made in sales contract prior to alleged concealment. *Magliaro v. Lewis*, Case No. A91A1912 (GA 1992). Broker entitled to commission from buyer based on oral agreement. *Weichert Co. Realtors v. Ryan*, 128 N.J. 427 (NJ 1992). Buyer's broker held not to have an enforceable agency agreement in commercial lease situation. *White & Associates v. Decker & Hallman*, Case No. A91A1595 (GA Ct. of Appeals Feb. 1992). Brokers successfully sued for commission on a contract not consummated. *Callaway v. Overholt*, 796 S.W.2d 828 (TX 1990).

CHAPTER 6. SUBAGENCY

The rules of the multiple listing service (MLS) usually create a system whereby members offer subagency to other members on behalf of the seller. *People ex rel. Woodard v. Colorado Springs Board of REALTORS®*, 692 P.2d 1055 (CO 1984); *United States v. Realty Multi-Lists*, 629 F.2d 1351 (5th Cir. 1980); *Iowa v. Cedar Rapids Board of REALTORS®*, 300 N.W.2d 127 (IA 1981); *Derish v. San Mateo-Burlingame Board of REALTORS®, et al.*, 186 Cal.Rptr. 390 (CA 1982). See also *1983-2 Trade Cas (CCH) Section 65,718; 1978-2 Trade Cas (CCH) Section 62,388; and 1977-1 Trade Cas (CCH) Section 61,435*. In *State v. Black*, 676 P.2d 963 (WA 1984), the court found no antitrust violation against certain brokers after they lowered their commission splits with alternative brokers who provided limited service to sellers at reduced fees. The MLS may be guilty of unlawful tie-in when it requires that participants belong to the Board of REALTORS®. *Fletcher Thomson v. Metropolitan Multi-List, Inc.*, 934 F.2d 1566 (11th Cir. 1991).

In *Wolfson v. Beris*, 295 N.W.2d 562 (MN 1980), the court held that the cooperating broker was the subagent of the seller. It was immaterial that the seller did not know the cooperating broker or authorize his actions. The cooperating broker did not become an agent of the buyer by merely preparing a purchase agreement with terms provided by the buyer. *First Church v. Dunton Realty, Inc.*, 574 P.2d 1211 (WA 1978); *Hale v. Wolfson*, 81 Cal.Rptr. 23 (CA 1969); *White v. Lobdell*, 638 P.2d 1057 (MT 1982); *Fred Tuke and Son v. Burkhardt*, 160 N.E.2d 283 (OH 1959); *Elliot v. Barnes*, 645 P.2d 1136 (WA 1982); *Granberg v. Turnham*, 333 P.2d 423 (CA 1958); *White v. Boucher*, 322 N.W.2d 560 (MN 1982); *Coons v. Gunn*, 69 Cal.Rptr. 876 (CA 1968); *Price v. Eisan*, 15 Cal.Rptr. 202 (CA 1961); *Timmerman v. Ankrom*, 487 S.W.2d 567 (MO 1972); *Hicks v. Wilson*, 240 P.289 (CA 1925); *Van Denberg v. Northside Realty Associates, Inc.*, 323 S.E.2d 839 (GA 1984); *Award Realty, Inc. v. Copeland*, 698 S.W.2d 337 (TN 1985); *Buzzard v. Bolger*, 453 N.E.2d 1129 (IL 1983).

In *Reich v. Christopulous*, 256 P.2d 238 (UT 1953), the agency relationship was created with the subagent by the MLS agreement and express language in the listing. In *Pilling v. Eastern & Pacific Enterprises*, 702 P.2d 1232 (WA 1985), the court held that the selling broker, in a multiple listing situation, is an authorized subagent of the listing broker and, therefore, owes the seller the same duties owed by the listing broker. In *Fennell v. Ross*, 711 S.W.2d 793 (AR 1986), the court was concerned with the issue of reliance on a misrepresentation when the cooperating broker knew the falsity of the statements about commercial use and a floodplain zone. The court concluded that the selling broker in an MLS listing is the subagent of the seller, even though the broker had worked with these buyers for a year before locating the property in question. Therefore, the knowledge of the cooperating broker was not imputed to the buyer.

Subagencies may be created even though the property is not listed in an MLS, as is frequently the case in commercial real estate transactions. *Marra v. Katz*, 347 N.Y.S.2d 143 (NY 1973).

Not all courts agree that the cooperating broker is the subagent of the seller. *Cashion v. Ahmadi*, 345 So.2d 268 (AL 1977); *Lester v. Marshall*, 352 P.2d 786 (CO 1960); *Lageschulte v. Steinbrecher*, 344 N.E.2d 750 (IL App. 1976). A participating member of an MLS was found to be the buyer's broker in *Gillen v. Stevens*, 330 S.W.2d 253 (TX 1959). Finding neither seller nor listing broker liable for the misrepresentation of the cooperating broker, the court in *Wise v. Dawson*, 353 A.2d 207 (DE 1975), found that no agency relationship existed between listing brokers and cooperating brokers in an MLS-type system. See *Pumphrey v. Quillen*, 141 N.E.2d 675 (OH 1955). The Supreme Court of Arizona ruled that the selling broker was not the agent of the seller in *Buffington v. Haas*, 601 P.2d 1320 (AZ 1979); *Brean v. North Campbell Professional Building*, 548 P.2d 1193 (AZ 1976); *Norville v. Palant*, 545 P.2d 454 (AZ 1976). The fact that the selling broker may share in the listing broker's fee does not necessarily create a subagency, *Hiller v. Real Estate Commission*, 627 P.2d 769 (CO 1981). In *Sullivan v. Jefferson*, 400 A.2d 836 (NJ 1979), the listing broker was held not liable for the wrongful act of an MLS cooperating broker who stole the buyer's earnest money deposit in a situation in which it was customary for the cooperating broker to hold the deposit check.

Imputed Notice

Notifying an agent is the same thing as notifying a principal. *Haislmaier v. Zache*, 130 N.W.2d 801 (WI 1964); 3 *Am.Jur.2d Agency* Section 152, page 543: "Notice to a subagent appointed by authority is imputable to, and is the equivalent of, notice to the principal." This imputed notice rule may make it critical in a lawsuit whether the cooperating broker is held to be a subagent of the seller or an agent of the buyer. Consider these situations:

- Purchase contract required buyer to give seller written notice of loan approval by May 8. Buyer notified cooperating broker on May 8, but broker did not tell seller, who then attempted to cancel on May 10. Court in *Grant v. Purdy*, 73 D & C 2d 42 (PA 1974), held that cooperating broker was, in reality, a subagent of the seller and, therefore, notice was imputed to seller by the May 8 deadline. Thus, seller could not cancel.
- Buyer notified cooperating broker with whom buyer was working that buyer accepted seller's counteroffer on a property listed in the MLS. Meanwhile, seller had received a higher offer, so seller attempted to revoke the counteroffer. If the cooperating broker is held to be a subagent of the seller, the revocation, coming after notice of acceptance to the seller's subagent, is too late and the contract is binding. If the cooperating broker is held to be the

buyer's broker, no binding contract exists because the seller's revocation was effective before the seller was notified of the acceptance. *Stortroen v. Beneficial Finance Co.*, No.85CA0548 (CO 1985); *Shriver v. Carter*, 6S I P.2d 436 (CO 1982); *Darling v. Nineteen-Eighty Corporation*, 176 N.W.2d 765 (IA 1970).

- Buyer Betty was working with salesperson Alice of South Side Realty, a large brokerage firm. Alice helped Betty prepare an offer on a property listed by South Side Realty salesperson Tom. The offer was contingent on Betty receiving a title report by July 10. Tom received the title report by July 10, but failed to tell Betty, who later attempted to cancel the contract. The trial court held that timely receipt of the report by South Side Realty, as agent of Betty, was imputed to Betty, and thus, the contract was binding. *Little v. Rohauer*, 707 P.2d 1015 (CO 1985).
- *Note:* To avoid the effect of the imputed notice rules, the seller could require that notice is not effective until delivered directly to the seller.

Good Faith

The subagent is under the same duty as the listing broker to exercise utmost good faith toward the principal and the listing broker. It is bad faith for the subagent to lead the buyer to believe the property could be bought for less than the listed price because this could "either force from the seller a lower price than that fixed or delay the sale, even if he finally buys at the price fixed, both detrimental to the interest of the seller." The subagent has a similar duty to disclose all material facts. In *re Sivert's Estate*, 135 N.W.2d 205 (MN 1965); *Kruse v. Miller*, 300 P.2d 855 (CA 1956); *Alford v. Creagh*, 62 So.254 (AL 1913); *Hughey v. Rainwater Partners*, 661 S.W.2d 690 (TN 1983); *Skopp v. Weaver*, 546 P.2d 307 (CA 1976).

The subagent may also be liable for the misrepresentations of the listing broker. In *First Church, etc. v. Cline J. Dunton Realty, Inc.*, 574 P.2d 1211 (WA 1978), the subagent was liable for not confirming the boundary description, even though the subagent relied on the information provided by the listing broker. Also, *Gauerke v. Rozga*, 332 N.W.2d 804 (WI 1983).

The listing broker must disclose any relationship between the proposed buyer and the subagent. This is true even if the MLS regulations do not create a seller subagency. *Frisell v. Newman*, 429 P.2d 864 (WA 1967). Even if the listing broker was unaware of the kinship ties between one of its subagents and the buyer, the seller may still have the right to rescind the sale and recover any profit gained by the broker or recoup the commission paid. *Mersky v. Multiple Listing Bureau of Olympia, Inc.*, 437 P.2d 897 (WA 1968). Also, *Kline v. Pyms Suchman Real Estate Company*, 303 So.2d 401 (FL 1974); *Ross v. Perelli*, 538 P.2d 834 (WA 1975).

Does a buyer who is a broker and also a member of the MLS have a fiduciary duty to the seller as a subagent? The cases holding no fiduciary duty of disclosure are *Case v. Business Centers, Inc.*, 357 N.E.2d 47 (OH 1976); *Cook v. Westersund*, 179 Cal.Rptr. 396 (CA App. 1981); *Blocklinger v. Schlegel*, 374 N.E.2d 491 (IL 1978); *Stout v. Edmonds*, 225 Cal.Rptr. 345 (CA 1986). When the prospective buyer was an MLS member, the listing broker owed a duty as agent to the seller only and not to the broker-buyer in *Carroll v. Action Enterprises, Inc.*, 292 N.W.2d 34 (NE 1980). Nor does the broker-buyer have a duty to discover listing mistakes made by the listing broker, even if the broker-buyer receives a commission split. *Asleson v. West Branch Land Co.*, 311 N.W.2d 533 (ND 1981); *Lageschute v. Steinbrecher*, 344 N.E.2d 750 (IL 1976).

Compensation

Many of the subagency cases are concerned with the cooperating broker seeking a commission. The majority of the cases hold that the cooperating broker and the listing broker are joint venturers who owe certain fiduciary duties between themselves, including the payment of fees, even under oral arrangements. *Nutter v. Bechtel*, 433 P.2d 993 (AZ 1967); *Moore v. Sussdorf*, 421 S.W.2d 460 (TX 1967) (even if the listing between seller and broker is not in writing, as required by law); *J.A. Cantor & Associates, Inc. v. Devore*, 281 So.2d 245 (FL 1973); *Sorenson v. Brice Realty Company*, 282 P.2d 1057 (OR 1955); *Hapsas Realty, Inc. v. McCoun*, 579 P.2d 785 (NM 1978); *Dean Vincent, Inc. v. Russell's Realty, Inc.*, 521 P.2d 334 (OR 1974). But in *Gray v. Fox*, 198 Cal.Rpts 720 (CA 1984), the buyer identified himself as a licensed real estate broker and received a share of the listing broker's commission. Unknown to anyone, the buyer immediately resold the property at a profit in a double escrow. The court found that the buyer was an agent for the seller and breached fiduciary duties owed to the seller by failing to disclose the resale and the secret profit.

While a fiduciary relationship exists between the cooperating broker and the seller, no contractual relationship does; therefore, the cooperating broker usually has no cause of action against the seller for payment of commission. *Gibson v. W.D. Parker Trust*, 527 P.2d 301 (AZ 1974); *Panorama of Homes v. Catholic Foreign Mission*, 404 N.E.2d 1104 (IL 1980); *Goodwin v. Glick*, 294 P.2d 192 (CA 1956); *Smith v. Wright*, 10 Cal.Rptr. 675 (CA 1961); *Philbrick v. Chase*, 58 A.2d 317 (NH 1948). In *Ju v. Jacoby*, 177 Cal.App.3rd 239 (CA 1986), the court held that the mere designation of a cooperating broker in a contract between buyer and seller did not give such a broker a right to enforce the contract in the absence of an intention on the part of the seller to personally secure for the cooperating broker the benefit of the contract. For a contrary result, see *Vanderschuct v. Christiana*, 198 N.Y.S.2d 768 (NY 1960); *Steve Schmidt & Co. v. Berry*, 228 Cal.Rptr. 689 (CA 1986), permitting recovery by the cooperating broker subagent on a third-party beneficiary theory.

A salesperson could sue the client for a commission, but could sue a creditor of the broker who had put a hold on all commission monies owed the broker. *Best-Morrison Properties v. Dennison*, 468 So.2d 483 (FL 1985).

In *Walters v. Marler*, 147 Cal.Rptr. 655 (CA 1978), the court held that a broker retained by the buyer is the agent of the buyer and owes the buyer a fiduciary duty, even though, as cooperating broker, his fee is paid by the seller.

In *Richard H. Huff Realty, Inc. v. Andrews*, 564 P.2d 93 (AZ 1977), the listing salesperson unsuccessfully sought to collect the selling agent's portion of the listing fee when the buyer was another salesperson in the listing broker's office. The court upheld the salesperson-buyer's claim to the selling commission. See *Fitzgerald v. Shannon & Luchs Co.*, 600 F. Supp.106 (DC 1984).

CHAPTER 8. REPRESENTING MORE THAN ONE PARTY IN A TRANSACTION: INTERMEDIARY BROKERAGE

A real estate broker cannot act as the agent for buyer and seller in the same transaction without the informed consents of both. When the broker assumes to act in a dual capacity without the intelligent consents of both parties, the transaction is voidable as a matter of law. *Taborsky v. Mathews*, 121 So.2d 61 (FL 1960); *Brockman v. Delta Mfg. Co.*, 87 P.2d 968 (OK 1939); *Darling v. Nineteen Eighty Corporation*, 176 N.W.2d 765 (IA 1970); *Shepley v. Green*, 243 S.W.2d 772 (MO 1951) (consent implied by failure to object); *Gordon v. Beck*, 239 P.309 (CA 1925); *Quest v. Barge*, 41 So.2d 158 (FL 1949); *Price v. Martin*, 147 S.E.2d 716 (VA 1966). Undisclosed dual agency has been held "a species of fraud." *Peyton v. Cly*, 7 Cal.Rptr. 504 (CA 1960); *Moore v. Mead*, 182 N.W. 29 (MI 1921); *Greater Bloomfield Realty Co. v. Brown*, 235 N.W.2d 168 (MI 1975). Listing broker breached duty to seller by actively participating in assisting buyer without informing seller of the dual capacity. *Gillmore v. Morelli*, 472 N.W.2d 738 (ND 1991).

In addition, the undisclosed dual agent cannot recover any commission. *Leno v. Stewart*, 95 A. 539 (VT 1915); *Spratlin et al. v. Hawn*, 156 S.E.2d 402 (GA 1967); *Investment Exchange Realty, Inc. v. Hillcrest Bowl, Inc.*, 513 P.2d 282 (WA 1973); *Panorama of Homes, Inc. v. Catholic Foreign Mission Society, Inc.*, 404 N.E. 2d 1104 (IL 1980); *Phillips v. Campbell*, 480 S.W.2d 250 (TX 1972); *Meerdink v. Kreiger*, 550 P.2d 42 (WA 1976); *Miller v. Berkoski*, 297 N.W.2d 334 (IA 1980). Even if the seller is not injured by the failure to disclose, the broker forfeits any right to a commission. A broker may act for both parties only if there is full disclosure to both principals, so that the principals may deal at arm's length. *Silverman v. Bresnahan*, 114 A.2d 307 (NJ 1955); *Lawton v. McHale Realty Co.*, 131 A.2d 679 (RI 1957). For want of proof that the parties consented to a dual commission arrangement, payments by one precluded recovery from the other. *Porter v. Striegler*, 533 S.W.2d 478 (TX 1976). No rule of law is better settled than the one that an agent cannot serve two masters. *McMichael v. Burnett*, 17 P.2d 932 (KS 1933); *Mortgage Bankers Assn. of New Jersey v. New Jersey Real Estate Commission*, 491 A.2d 1317 (NJ 1985).

Dual agency situations can also arise in real estate exchanges in which one broker represents both sides of the transaction. *Hays v. Ryker*, 118 So. 199 (MS 1928); *Rodenkirch v. Layton*, 176 N.W. 897 (IA 1920); *Hageman v. Colombet*, 198 P. 842 (CA 1921); *Hughes v. Robbins*, 164 N.E.2d 469 (OH 1959); *Homefinders v. Lawrence*, 335 P.2d 893 (ID 1959); *Galyen v. Voyager Inn, Inc.*, 328 F.Supp. 1299 (MO 1971).

Sometimes, the dual agency arises because of a prior long-standing relationship between the listing broker and the buyer. *Koller v. Belote*, 528 P.2d 1000 (WA 1974); *Adams v. Kerr*, 655 S.W.2d 49 (MO 1983) (listing broker also managed properties for buyer). Other times, the broker "adopts" the buyer prior to or during the closing process. The broker might reach an agreement with the buyer prior to presenting the offer that the broker will manage the property or sell it at a profit for the buyer, as in *Dickinson v. Tysen*, 103 N.E. 703 (NY 1913); or receive a percentage commission upon resale of the property at a profit, as in *Wilson v. Southern Pacific Land Company*, 215 P. 396 (CA 1923).

It may not be a breach of duty to reach an agency agreement with the buyer after the contract is signed, although the broker still should disclose this fact to the seller. *Currier v. Letourneau*, 373 A.2d 521 (VT 1977). It may not be a dual agency for the listing broker also to become the listing broker of the buyer's existing home, although the professional broker will disclose this fact to all parties. *Hall v. Williams*, 50 S.W.2d 138 (MO 1932); *Fred Tuke & Son v. Burkhardt*, 156 N.E.2d 490 (OH 1958). In *Harvey v. Tucker*, 12 P.2d 847 (KS 1932), the court held that fraud would not be presumed and dual agency would not apply when an agent immediately resells a property for the buyer, even if the transaction is near the "danger zone." In *Urban Investments, Inc. v. Branham*, 464 A.2d 93 (DC App. 1983), the court recognized that a broker can act as a dual agent when the buyer first engages the broker to sell the buyer's home and the broker subsequently represents the buyer in the purchase of a new home.

A broker may be the agent of two contracting parties in certain instances, but only on the fullest disclosure by the broker of the fact that the broker represents both parties, and the fullest comprehension of that fact by those contracting. *Quest v. Barge*, 41 Sa.2d 158 (FL 1949); *Barbat v. M.E. Arden Co.*, 254 N.W.2d 779 (MI 1977); *Napier v. Adams*, 158 S.E.18 (GA 1931); *Holley v. Jackson*, 158 A.2d 803 (DE 1954). The duty of care owed to each party by a dual agent is to exercise the same full and truthful disclosure of all known facts, or facts reasonably discoverable, in the exercise of due diligence, that are likely to affect either principal's interests and actions. *Brandt v. Koepnick*, 469 P.2d 189 (WA 1970); *Martin v. Hieken*, 340 S.W.2d 161 (MO 1960). For example, when a dual agent broker discovers an encumbrance and fails to further inquire whether the seller has marketable title, the broker has breached a fiduciary duty to the buyer and is liable for the loss of the buyer's down payment. *Garl v. Mihuta*, 361 N.E.2d 1065 (OH 1975). In *Wilson v. Lewis*, 165 Cal.Rptr. 396 (CA 1980), a cooperating broker retained by the buyer was held to also be the agent of the seller because the broker was receiving a 3 percent commission from the seller. The broker breached a duty by failing to disclose to the seller that the buyer's deposit check was postdated and could not be negotiated until after inspection of the property.

Dual agency was disclosed in an in-house sale, but the disclosure was inadequate because the broker intentionally misled the seller into thinking the buyer was an owner-occupant, whereas the buyer was an investor, and the broker had a substantial personal stake in retaining the buyer's continued business. *Jorgensen v. Beach 'N' Bay Realty*, 177 Cal.Rptr. 882 (CA 1981).

When several principals employ the same broker, misconduct of the broker cannot be imputed to any one of the principals who is not actually at fault, each of the principals being under an equal duty to supervise the broker and protect the principal's interests. *Whittlesey v. Spence*, 439 S.W.2d 195 (MO 1969).

In *Smith v. Sullivan*, 419 So.2d 184 (MS 1982), the broker breached its fiduciary duty to the seller by representing the buyer in a purchase from the seller after the listing had expired. The broker failed to disclose the identity and financial responsibility of the buyer. Buyer's agent obtained a one-time showing listing from seller. Held to be a dual agent. *Culver & Associates v. Jaoudi Industries*, 1 Cal.Rptr.2d 680 (CA 1991).

The dual agent has a duty to act with fairness to each party and to disclose to each all facts that the agent knows or should know would reasonably affect the judgment of each in permitting such dual agency. According to the *Restatement (Second) of Agency*, Section 392:

> *The agent's disclosure must include not only the fact that he is acting on behalf of the other party, but also all facts which are relevant in enabling the principal to make an intelligent determination. . . . The agent, however, is under no duty to disclose, and has a duty not to disclose to one principal, confidential information given to him by the other, such as the price he is willing to pay. If the information is of such a nature that he cannot fairly give advice to one without disclosing it, he cannot properly continue to act as advisor.*

In *Foster v. Blake Heights Corporation*, 530 P.2d 815 (UT 1974), the court held that a broker negotiating a transaction does not have to be exclusively the agent for either buyer or seller, but may be a go-between acting for both.

Consent must be knowing, intelligent, and obtained in such a way as to ensure that the client has had adequate time to reflect on the choice. Consent must not be forced on the client by the pressures of closing. *Matter of Dolan*, 384 A.2d 1076 (NJ 1978). In a complex commercial real estate transaction, an attorney may not represent both buyer and seller, even if both give their informed consents. *Baldasarre v. Butler*, A 49-50 N.J. S.C. 1993. *Bokusky v. Edina Realty*, Civ. 3-92-223 (D. Minn. 1993). Issue is the adequacy of informed consent to a dual agency. The only disclosure was a statement in the sales contract that the individual sales agent represented the buyer and the listing brokerage represented the seller. Certified as a class action suit with remedy sought being the disgorgement of all commissions earned on in-house sales.

Even though the broker acts as a dual agent, there will be no rescission and no forfeiture of commission if both parties intelligently consent to the common representation. *Nahn-Heberer Realty Co. v. Schrader*, 89 S.W.2d 142 (MO 1936), although the court still inquired whether the broker was disloyal to either party; *Panebianco v. Berger*, 199 N.W. 545 (NE 1924); *Lamb v. Milliken*, 243 P. 624 (CO 1926); *Cole v. Brundage*, 344 N.E.2d 583 (IL 1976); *Bonaccorso v. Kaplan*, 32 Cal. Rptr. 69 (CA 1963); *Lemons v. Barton*, 186 N.E.2d 426 (IN 1962); *Zimmerman v. Garvey*, 71 A. 780 (CT 1909); *Phillips v. Campbell*, 480 S.W.2d 250 (TX 1972); *Hladik v. Allen*, 147 P.474 (CA 1915); *Olson v. Brickles*, 124 S.E.2d 895 (VA 1962). As a general rule, dual agency does not apply to insurance agents, a rule some real estate agents may refer to. *Wright v. Providence Washington Ins. Co.*, 286 P.237 (KS 1930).

Broker breached fiduciary duty resulting in forfeiture of commission. *Wallace v. Odham*, 579 So.2d 171 (FL 1991). A buyer's broker who shows property listed in an MLS which offers subagency risks being a dual agent. *Stefani v. Baird & Warner*, 510 N.E.2D 65 (IL).

Appendix D: Web Site Resources

Association of Real Estate License Law Officials www.arello.com
Internal Revenue Service (IRS) www.irs.gov
National Do Not Call Registry www.donotcall.gov
Real Estate Center www.recenter.tamu.edu
Real Estate Information Sharing and Analysis Center www.reisac.org/report.html
Real Estate Settlement Procedures Act www.hud.gov/offices/hsg/sfh/res/respa_hm.cfm
Texas Appraiser Licensing and Certification Board www.talcb.texas.gov
Texas Attorney General www.oag.state.tx.us
Texas Department of Insurance www.tdi.texas.gov
Texas Legislature (bills) www.capitol.state.tx.us
Texas Real Estate Commission www.trec.texas.gov
Texas Workforce Commission Civil Rights Division www.twc.state.tx.us/crd/housing_fact.html
What is Agency Law? (video) www.ehow.com/video_4981789_what-agency-law.html

Glossary

accidental agency An unintended agency relationship that is created by actions or words.

agency relationship The fiduciary relationship that exists when one person (agent) represents the interests of another (principal) in dealings with others, with their consent and under their control.

agency by ratification Agency by ratification occurs when a principal gains some benefit from a previously unauthorized act of an agent, and the principal, on learning of the act, does not deny that the agent had authority to perform such an act on the principal's behalf. The principal ratifies the action of the agent by accepting the benefits that come from the action.

agent (1) A broker who represents a seller, a landlord, a buyer, or a tenant. (2) A salesperson or broker licensee who represents the broker with whom the agent is associated.

appraisal An estimate or opinion of the value of a piece of property as of a certain date.

appraiser An individual licensed under the Texas Occupation Code § 1103 to conduct appraisals that conform to those of the Uniform Standards of Practice of the Appraisal Foundation. Real estate brokers provide a broker price opinion or comparative market analysis.

arbitration A form of alternative dispute resolution whereby a neutral third party listens to each party's position and makes a final decision.

associate A salesperson or a broker licensee who is associated with a broker.

attorney in fact A person authorized to act for another under a power of attorney. This person is not necessarily a licensed attorney.

back-up offer An offer to purchase accepted by a seller who has already accepted an early primary offer to purchase the same property. The back up offer is contingent on the first offer failing to close.

blanket offer of subagency The offer made by the listing broker on behalf of the seller to all other participants in the multiple listing service (MLS) to act as a subagent for the seller. The seller has the option of making a blanket unilateral offer of subagency or making no offer of subagency; in either case, under MLS rules, an offer to cooperate must include an offer to compensate.

broker associate A broker associated with and conducting business, all or in part, as an agent of another broker.

Broker-Lawyer Committee A committee of six licensed brokers appointed by TREC, six licensed attorneys appointed by the State Bar of Texas, and one public member appointed by the governor. This committee is responsible for drafting and revising the standardized contract forms promulgated by TREC for public and licensee use.

broker licensee An individual holding a broker's license issued by the Texas Real Estate Commission (TREC). Brokers may act independently in conducting real estate transactions or may engage other broker licensees or salesperson licensees to represent them in the conduct of their real estate business. Under TRELA, a broker may also be a business entity such as a corporation, limited liability partnership company, or partnership authorized under the Texas Business Organizations Code.

business entity Any corporation, limited liability partnership company, partnership or similar entity authorized under the Texas Business Organizations Code. If the broker is a business entity, however, then one of its managing officers must be licensed as an individual broker in Texas, who then acts as the designated broker for the business entity.

buyer's agent A broker who is representing the buyer in a real estate transaction. Also called a buyer's broker, selling broker, or selling agent.

buyer's broker A real estate broker who is employed by and represents only the buyer in the transaction, whether the commission is paid by the buyer directly or by the seller through a commission split with the listing broker. To be distinguished from brokers who represent the seller but nevertheless "works with" the buyer; these brokers are not referred to as "buyers' brokers." They are subagents of the seller. Also, brokers acting as an intermediary for buyers and sellers are not called buyers' brokers. Buyer brokerage is one part of an exclusive or nonexclusive single agency real estate practice.

client A person, sometimes called a principal, who engages the professional advice or services of another, called an agent, and whose interests are protected by the specific duties and loyalties of an agency relationship.

commission split The sharing of the seller-paid commission between the listing broker and the selling broker. An MLS listing generally indicates the compensation being offered by the listing broker to the other MLS participants, either as a percentage of the gross selling price or as a definite dollar amount. Thus, MLS members know what they will earn on finding a suitable buyer.

common law Law that has evolved by custom or by court decisions (case law).

company policy A set of rules and principles that establishes how a brokerage company is to operate. Every firm should have a clear company policy on agency and take steps to ensure that the sales staff follows it.

consideration Anything of value given to induce another to enter into a contract, such as money, barter, promise, goods, or services.

contract A legally enforceable agreement between competent parties who agree to perform or refrain from performing certain acts for a consideration. In essence, a contract is an enforceable promise.

cooperating broker The real estate broker working with the prospective buyer on a property listed with another broker. The cooperating broker traditionally is compensated through a commission split with the listing broker. The cooperating broker, also called the selling broker, participating broker, outside broker, or other broker, may be either a subagent acting on behalf of the seller or a buyer's broker, both of whom cooperate to make a sale. In some states, the cooperating broker may act as a transaction broker or transaction coordinator.

customer A buyer or a seller in a real estate transaction being assisted by a broker, but without the benefits of an agency relationship.

dual agency The representation of two or more principals in the same transaction by the same agent. In Texas, the duties of a license holder acting as an intermediary supersede the previously accepted role of common law dual agent. Brokers in Texas are no longer permitted to act as dual agents when representing more than one party.

employee Someone who works under the control and direction of another. Compensation is generally based on time rather than results. *See* independent contractor.

ethics A system of accepted principles or standards of moral conduct.

exclusive single agency A type of agency business model adopted by a real estate broker who elects to represent only one side of a real estate transaction. That is, the broker and associates will only represent sellers in the capacity of listing broker or subagent of the listing broker; or the broker elects to only represent buyers (never sellers) in the roll of buyer's broker.

exclusive listing A written listing of real property in which the seller agrees to appoint only one broker to handle the transaction. Two types apply to the seller: (1) the exclusive-right-to-sell listing obligates the seller to pay a commission if anyone, including the seller, procures a ready, willing, and able buyer; and (2) the exclusive-agency listing reserves for the owner the right to sell the property directly without owing a commission. The exclusive agent is entitled to a commission if the buyer is procured by anyone other than the seller. A third type applies to the buyer: the exclusive-right-to-represent agreement obligates the buyer to pay a commission if the buyer agrees to buy a described type of property located by the broker, the buyer, or anyone else during the listing period.

express agency The agency relationship that is created when a principal engages or employs an agent to act for the principal by actually stating it in words, spoken or written. In legal terms, the word *express* means clear, definite, explicit, unmistakable, and unambiguous. *See* implied agency.

facilitator A person who assists the parties to a potential real estate transaction in communication and negotiation without being an advocate for any interest except the mutual interest of all parties to reach agreement. Also called a middleman, mediator, nonagent, or transaction broker.

fiduciary (1) A relationship of trust and confidence between principal and agent. The law imposes on the agent duties of loyalty, confidentiality, accounting, obedience, and full disclosure, as well as the duty to use skill, care, and diligence. A real estate agent owes complete fiduciary duties to the principal and must act in the best interests of the principal (the client) while also being competent with and honest to the other side (the customer, whether the seller or the buyer). (2) The agent is called the fiduciary—one who holds the faith, confidence, and trust of the client.

finder One who produces a buyer or locates a property—nothing more. The finder is not an agent and owes no fiduciary duties.

fraud A deceptive act practiced deliberately by one person in an attempt to gain an unfair advantage over another. There is always the intention to deceive.

FSBO For sale by owner; a property that is being offered for sale by the owner without the benefit of a real estate broker.

general agency The agent who is authorized to conduct an ongoing series of transactions for the principal and can obligate the principal to certain types of contractual agreements.

gratuitous agency The agency relationship that is created when the agent provides brokerage services and charges no fee.

implied agency An agency relationship created by the words or conduct of the agent or principal rather than by written agreement. For example, a listing agent who acts like a buyer's agent in negotiating for the buyer can become involved in an undisclosed dual agency relationship (express agent of seller and implied agent of buyer).

implied authority Not to be confused with implied agency, implied authority is a concept that is applicable to both express agency and implied agency. Implied authority is authority not specifically granted to the agent but necessary or customary if the agent is to perform the agency duties, and it is implied by the principal's actions.

independent contractor A person who contracts to do a job for another but maintains control over the task will be accomplished. Compensation is generally based on results rather than time. In real estate, brokers normally elect to subcontract with other licensees (either salespersons or broker associates) to assist in their real estate brokerage office. *See* employee.

informed consent A person's approval based on full disclosure of all the facts needed to make the decision intelligently. For example, to consent to an intermediary, the buyer and the seller need to understand the liability, the alternatives, and the roles that they and the real estate licensees will play once that relationship is established.

in-house sale A sale involving only one brokerage firm acting as both the listing and the selling agent; the listing agent is also the selling agent. Frequently, one real estate agent in the firm secures the listing and works for the seller, and a different member of the same firm finds and works either for or with the buyer (in which case, with written consent of both parties, the broker plays the role of intermediary). Assuming careful disclosure and conduct by the listing broker, however, there is nothing improper about selling a listing in-house; in fact, the seller lists the property so that the broker will find a qualified buyer.

intermediary A broker who is employed to negotiate a transaction between the parties subject to the obligations of § 1101.559 and § 1101.651(d).

landlord's agent A broker who is representing the landlord in a real estate transaction.

laundry list The enumerated acts in Section 17.46 of the Texas Deceptive Trade Practices Act (DTPA) that represent per se evidence of a false, misleading, or deceptive act or practice in the conduct of any trade or commerce.

liable Legally responsible.

licensee A person licensed by TREC to act as a broker or a salesperson in a real estate transaction.

license holder A broker or a salesperson licensed by TREC.

limited agency Limited agency authorizes the agent to perform only those acts permitted by the principal. Real estate agents are most frequently referred to as limited or special agents; their scope of authority usually does not extend beyond the terms of a listing agreement or a buyer-representation or tenant-representation agreement.

listing An agreement that establishes the rights and obligations between the seller and the broker or between the buyer and the broker. A salesperson usually obtains the listing of a seller's property in the name of the broker. The broker is called the listing broker; the salesperson is sometimes called the *listing agent*.

listing broker In this textbook, refers to the seller's agent. A buyer's agent can also list the buyer.

material fact Any fact that is relevant to a person making a decision.

mediation A type of alternative dispute resolution where a neutral third party works with parties to a dispute with the objective of assisting or facilitating the parties to come to a mutually acceptable resolution. The mediator does not make the decision for the parties. *See* arbitration.

middleman A person who facilitates a real estate transaction by introducing a buyer to a seller, both of whom negotiate their own transaction; a finder. Provided the middleman exercises no discretion in facilitating the transaction, the middleman, in some states, may be exempted from the traditional fiduciary duties owed by an agent to a principal. Very seldom does a real estate broker conform to this middleman concept. Middleman status could occur when a buyer works with a broker, but specifically refuses to authorize the broker to act as the buyer's agent; likewise, the seller does not authorize the broker to act as a subagent. *See also* facilitator.

misrepresentation A false statement made negligently or innocently that is a material factor in another's decision to contract. There does not have to be an intention to deceive.

MLS (multiple listing service) An information service, generally owned and operated by a local association of brokers, in which members pool their listings (primarily residential) and agree to share commissions with other member brokers who find purchasers. Most MLSs are affiliated with the National Association of REALTORS®, which considers the MLS to be a formal system of presenting listings in which blanket offers of cooperation and compensation are made to other MLS members.

Nonexclusive single agency The practice of representing either the buyer or the seller, but never both in the same transaction. The nonexclusive single-agency broker may be compensated indirectly through an authorized commission split or directly by the principal who employs the agent to represent him or her.

offer When one person proposes a contract to another. Once signed and accepted, the contract is binding on both parties.

one-time-showing agreement A one-time-showing agreement allows the terms of the agreement to apply to a specific buyer only.

open listing A listing in which the broker has the nonexclusive right to sell the property and receive a commission.

If the sale results through the efforts of the seller or another broker, the open listing broker receives no commission. Controversies may arise over which broker actually was the procuring cause of the sale.

optional offer of subagency The MLS policy that affords a seller represented by a participating member the option of whether to offer subagency. The seller can choose to make a blanket offer of subagency or to offer cooperation and compensation to buyer agents, subagents, and other licensed participants in the MLS. No mandatory offer of subagency exists.

ostensible agency Also known as agency by estoppel (when a court does not allow a principal to deny that agency existed), is based on a third party's being led to believe that a licensee was acting as an agent of another party. For example, if the buyer presumes the agent showing the buyer a property is the agent of the seller, then the agent is ostensibly the seller's agent, even though the agent never expressly self-identified as representing the seller in the transaction.

plaintiff The party who initiates the suit in civil court; the one who sues.

power of attorney A written authorization for one person (attorney in fact) to act as the agent of another.

principal (1) A person who employs an agent to represent him or her as a client, especially if referred to with the use of a pronoun: his or her principal. (2) One of the primary parties to a transaction, whether or not an agency relationship is involved (i.e., the buyer or the seller, especially if referred to as the principal).

representation To act on another's behalf (the principal) as an agent owing fiduciary duties to such principal. There is a definite distinction between working with a buyer (who is then a customer or prospect) and representing a buyer (who is then a client). Buyers often believe they are being represented when, in fact, they either are not represented or are represented by sellers' agents in undisclosed dual agencies. While a listing broker frequently works with buyers to encourage them to buy listed properties, the listing broker should be careful that the broker's words and actions do not lead the buyers to expect that the broker represents them. It is the broker's conduct that usually forms the basis for the reasonable expectations of a buyer or seller. If, in fact, the broker represents both buyer and seller, appropriate intermediary disclosures must be given and the informed consents of the buyer and the seller must be obtained to this form of limited representation.

promulgated contract form Forms that TREC has publically and officially announced that are mandatory for licensee use.

REALTOR® A real estate licensee who is an active member of the Texas and National Association of REALTORS® and usually a local board as well.

renunciation The giving up or rejecting of something that was originally accepted, such as when a broker unilaterally chooses to discontinue representation of a seller during the term of a listing or buyer representation contract.

rescission A mutual cancellation of a contract by all parties.

revocation The withdrawing of a permission that was previously given, such as when a seller or a buyer revokes the broker's authority to act as the agent prior to the expiration of the agency contract.

sales associate Salesperson licensee associated with and conducting business as an agent of his or her sponsoring broker.

salesperson A person who meets the state's requirements for a salesperson's or broker's license and who works for and is licensed under a broker or a brokerage firm. Salespersons are commonly called real estate agents, even though they are not the primary agents of sellers or buyers; in essence, they are agents of agents (brokers). This is an important concept to keep in mind when discussing the in-house intermediary situation in which, for example, salesperson Alice from Bay Realty is thought to represent the seller, and salesperson Sally, also from Bay Realty, is thought to represent the buyer. In this situation, both the buyer and the seller have the same agent (Bay Realty). Separate agents do not represent the buyer and the seller. Alice is not the seller's agent, and Sally is not the buyer's agent; rather, Bay Realty is the only agent of the two clients—in this case, acting as an intermediary. Bay Realty is the primary fiduciary that owns the listing. Bay Realty is obligated by TRELA to supervise its salespersons and is responsible for and bound by their actions.

salesperson licensee An individual holding a salesperson's license issued by TREC—an agent of the sponsoring broker. Salesperson licensees may conduct business only through their sponsoring brokers.

seller's agent A broker who is representing the seller in a real estate transaction. Also called seller's broker, listing broker, or listing agent.

selling broker The broker working with or representing the buyer in the purchase of a listed property. Also called the cooperating broker, participating broker, or other broker when the selling broker is a member of a firm other than the listing firm. The selling broker may be the listing broker or a cooperating broker (subagent or a buyer's agent).

special agency Sometimes known as limited agency, authorizes the agent to perform only those acts permitted by the principal. Real estate agents are most frequently referred to as limited or special agents; their scope of authority usually does not extend beyond the terms of a listing agreement or a buyer-representation or tenant-representation agreement.

statutory law Law that is enacted by legislatures (federal, state, county, or city council).

subagency A theory of agency law applicable to the agent of a person who already acts as an agent for a principal. In real estate, the client (usually the seller) lists with an agent, who, in turn, retains the services of subagents to find a buyer. A seller may limit the authority of the broker to appoint subagents. Cooperating broker members of the MLS may reject any blanket offer of subagency.

subagent A licensee holder not sponsored by or associated with the client's broker who is representing the client through a cooperative agreement with the client's broker. Also called the other broker.

tenant's agent A broker who is representing a tenant in a real estate transaction.

unintended dual representation Accidental representation of both the buyer and the seller by the same broker. This is especially prevalent when the broker does not expressly declare, and the principal does not expressly affirm, the agency status of the broker.

universal agency A type of agency in which the agent is empowered to conduct every type of transaction that may be legally delegated by a principal to an agent.

void Having no legal force or effect. A contract that one of the parties can make void without liability.

Index

A

Abstracts of title 44
Accomplishment, of the agency objective 71
Actions, of principals and agents 71
Adopting the buyer 176
Advice and opinions 96
    from appointed licensees 157
Agency 2, 14, 30, 59, 61, 75, 100, 222
    benefits to buyer or tenant 124
    benefits to seller or landlord 96
    by estoppel 63
    by ratification 64
    contract 54
    coupled with a broker's interest 70
    disclosure 8, 197
    is terminated 70
    objective 71
    office policy 204
    relationship(s) 5, 10, 14, 18, 30, 59, 65, 192
Agent 3
Agreements between brokers 217
AIDS-related illness 47
Alternate solution 244
Alvarado v. Bolton 268
Ambiguous situations 199
American Law Institute 18
Appointed licensees 157, 158, 165
Appointees 159
Appointment(s) 158
    process 157
Appraiser 26, 31
Asbestos 49
Assessments 141
Assignability 139
Authorization 59, 60

B

Bankruptcy 74
Black's Law Dictionary 224, 225
Boehl v. Boley 262
Breach of the agent's duty to the principal 73
Broad marketing 96
Broker
    as an intermediary 162
    as principal 173
    associate(s) 213
    licensee 3
Broker associate(s) 3, 215
Broker price opinion (BPO) 26
Brokers 1
    licensed in other states 218
Broker's services 154
Business consumer 256
Business entity 212
Buyer agency 112, 115
Buyer-agency relationships 124

Buyer brokerage 7, 144
Buyer Brokering 184
Buyer-paid fee 133
Buyer representation 114
    contracts 62
Buyer-representation 16
    agreements/contract 124, 144
Buyer's agent 4
Buyers' agents 127, 144
Buyers as customers 143
Buyer's broker disclosures 142
Buyer's financial condition 25

C

Cameron v. Terrell and Garrett, Inc. 265
Canons of Professional Ethics and Conduct 19, 47, 228, 229
Caravan tour 200
Checklist 142
Child molestation 50
Circumstances, of the sale or lease 97
Civil Rights Act (1866) 238
Client 4, 10, 75
Codes of ethics 227, 228
Commerce 255
Commercial leasing agent 169
Commission(s) 284, 290
    split 27, 131
Common-law
    dual agency (implied and express) 152
    fraud 254
Company policy 201, 240
    procedure 228
Comparative market analysis (CMA) 26, 126
Compensation 65, 215, 217, 219
    to broker 136
Complexity 6
Condition of property 126
Confidentiality 28, 75, 97, 125
Conflicting positions 152
Conflicts of interest 121, 187
Consequences of decision/policy reversal 243
Constructive or imputed notice 68
Consumer 255
    expectations 7, 243
    protection division 255
    services 198
Contingencies 127
Contract
    acceptance 140
    negotiations 96
    provisions 27
Contractual and promissory obligations 244
Cooperating brokers 108
Cooperating or other broker 172
Cooperative sales 99
Counseling 125, 186
Customer 4, 10, 75

D

Damages 266
Death 48
    of the agent or principal 73
Deceptive acts 256
Deceptive Trade Practices Act 275
Deceptive Trade Practices and Consumer Act 275
Deceptive Trade Practices and Consumer Protection Act 251, 252, 254
Decide 193
Default 284
Defenses 267
Destruction of property 74
Dialogues for brokerage situations 285
Disclose 194
Disclosure(s) 22, 36, 105
    of fee 134
    of seller's agent to buyer 106
    of seller's agent to seller 105
    of stigmatized properties 49
    policy 193
    to buyer 142
    to seller or listing broker 143
Do as you say 201
Document 201, 204
Documentary material 255
Dual agency 150, 152, 153
Dual representation 169
Duties 54
    of agency 74
    of the statutory dual agent 154

E

Earnest money 284, 289
    deposit(s) 25, 138
Economic damages 256
Educational requirement 8
Emotional aspects 6
Employee 214, 215
Employment 209
    agreements 218
    relationships between brokers and associates 211
    relationships between brokers and principals 210
    relationships between brokers and subagents 216
Erwin v. Smiley 261
Ethical and legal concerns 269
Ethical conduct 247
Ethical standards 246
Ethics 101, 222, 238, 240, 247, 248
    defined 224
Exchanges 168
Exclusive-agency listing 83, 93
Exclusive buyer agency 122

E

Exclusive-right-to-buy agreement 121
Exclusive right to purchase 116
Exclusive-right-to-sell listing 82, 84, 85, 86, 87, 88, 89, 90, 91, 92, 121
Exclusive seller agency 98, 104
    in practice 102
Exclusive seller representation 98
Exemption(s) 263, 270
Expiration, of the agency agreement 71
Express agency 61
Express and implied agreements 79
Expressed listing agreements 107
Extended closing 140

F

Fair Housing Act 238
Fair Housing Amendment Act (1988) 47
Fairness 36
Federal Housing Administration (FHA) 135
Federal law 226, 238
Federal Trade Commission (FTC) 7
Fee arrangements 129
Fiduciaries 18, 20
Fiduciary 3, 17, 19, 30, 75
    duty 101
    responsibility 125
Financing contingencies 141
First contact
    broker working for/with the buyer 280
    broker working for/with the seller 276
Fixtures 127
Flat fees (contingent or noncontingent) 133
Flow of authority 17, 18
Foreign brokers 218
For sale by owner (FSBO) 95, 96, 175
Fraud 253, 254
Full disclosure
    of buyer's financial condition 25
    of commission split 27
    of contract provisions 27
    of information 25
    of other offers 24
    of property value 26
    of relationships 24
    regarding status of earnest money deposits 25
    relating to the property 23

G

General agency 15, 30
Goods 255
Gratuitous agency 65
Gross price 135
Groundless lawsuits 269

H

Hoffman, Jennifer 49
Honesty 36
Hourly rate 133
Housing and Urban Development, Department of (HUD) 47

I

Implied agency 62
Implied agreement 79
Implied authority 62
Implied listing agreements 107
Imputed knowledge 69
Incapacity, of the agent or principal 73
Incentive, to market the property 97
Independent contractor 214, 215, 219
Individual ethics 228
Information About Brokerage Services 5, 195, 196
In-house listings 144, 173
In-house sale(s) 98, 171, 178
Inspection 140
Intentionally 256
Interests of immediate stakeholders 243
Intermediary 4, 280
    agency 98
    brokerage 149, 150, 155, 178, 200
    brokers 165
    broker with one associate and without appointments 163, 165
    broker with two associates and with appointments 164
    broker with two sales associates and without appointments 163
    practice 166
Intermediary Relationship Notice 160, 200
Internal Revenue Code 168
Inventory 127

J

Joseph v. James 16

K

Kelly v. Roussalis 66
Kennemore v. Bennett 268
Kessler v. Fanning 42
Knowingly 255

L

Landlord's agent 4
Language of Real Estate, The 43, 137
LA&N Interests, Inc. v. Fish 132
Lapse of time 70
Law(s) 222, 238, 244
    defined 224
Legal and ethical guidelines 225
Legal effect 67
Legality 244
Lenders 134
Liability 75, 101, 129
    for misrepresentation 52
Licensed associates buying properties 175
Licensee (active) 3
Licensee (inactive) 3
Licensee professionalism 7
Licensees' own property 176
License holder 3
Limited liability 97
Listing agreement(s) 79, 80, 81
Listing associate 102
Listing broker 7, 129
    and the buyer's broker 279
    or associate working with buyer-customer 277
    or associate working with seller 277
Listing contracts 62
Litigation 4
Long-term goals 243
Loss 74
Loyalty 22, 97, 127, 128

M

Madoff, Bernie 223
Marketplace 124
Material facts 43, 54
    relating to survey issues 46
    relating to title issues 44
Materiality 49
Maxwell, John C. 244
Megan's Law 50, 51
Minimum service requirements 29
Misrepresentation(s) 36, 52, 54, 253, 254
Morals, defined 225
Mortgagee's (lender's) title insurance 45
Multiple listing service (MLS) 93, 96, 108, 174
    subagency agreements 216
Multiple representation 153
Municipal codes and ordinances 226
Municipal ordinances 239
Mushtaha v. Kidd 17

N

National Association of REALTORS® (NAR) 5, 19, 47, 49, 55, 96
    Code of Ethics and Standards of Practice 143, 150, 228, 230, 231, 232, 233, 234, 235, 236, 237, 239
National Housing Act 135
Neary v. Mikob Properties, Inc. 211
Negligence 67
Negotiating position 125
Net listing 94
Net purchase price 134
Nonagency 177
Nonexclusive seller
    agency 105
    representation 98
Nonexclusive single agency 183, 184, 188, 189
Nonlicensee compensation 217
Non-MLS subagency agreements 216
Nonresidential intermediary applications 168
North, William D. 5
Notice 68
    and inspection 262
Notification, to the principals 158

O

Obedience 21
Offers to purchase 289
Ojeda de Toca v. Wise 268
OLD CAR 18, 30
Open house(s) 200, 203
Open listing 83, 93, 94
Operation of law 73
Oral agreement 80
Organizational commitment 243
Orkin Exterminating Co., Inc. v. LeSassier 259
Ostensible agency 63

Other broker
 as buyer's broker 280
 as subagent of seller 279

P

Percentage fee 133
Person 255
Personal assistants 216
Personal beliefs 228, 240
Pests 141
Physical material facts 43
Physical stigmas 48
Policies and procedures manual 202
"Practitioner's Quick Guide" 243, 244, 245
Presentation
 of multiple offers 282
 of offers by the listing broker 281
 of subsequent or backup offers 283
Preventive brokerage 275, 289
Price and appraised value 126
Prior relationships 170
Private morality 225
Procuring cause 137
Producing cause 265
Professional and ethical responsibility 70
Professional service 264
Prohibited disclosures 51
Properties, the buyer should see 278
Property condition 39, 40, 41, 140
Property Disclosures—What You Should Know 49
Prudential Insurance Company v. Jefferson Associates, Ltd. 260
Public morality 225
Public perceptions 6
Public scrutiny 244
Purchase agreement 137
Purely psychological stigmas 46

R

Real Estate License Act, The (TRELA) 8, 9, 15, 70, 150, 226, 227, 239
Real Estate Settlement Procedures Act 141
REALTOR®(s) 19
 Code of Ethics 19
 Code of Ethics and Standards of Practice 275
Reasonable care and diligence 19
Regulators 243
Rehearsed dialogue 285, 290
Reilly, John W. 43, 137
Renunciation, by the broker 72
Representation
 agreements 115
 of more than one party 150
Rescission, by the parties 71
Residence 256
Residential Buyer/Tenant Representation Agreement 116, 117, 118, 119, 120
Respondeat superior 212
Restatement (Second) of Agency 18
Retained earnest money in the event of a default 284
Retainer fee 129
Revocation, by the principal 72
Risk management 287

S

Sales associate 3, 215
Salesperson(s) 1, 212
 licensee 3
Sanchez v. Guerrero 50
Seller agency 107
 relationships 96
Seller financing 126, 139
Seller-paid fee 130
Seller pepresentation only 161
Seller's agent 4, 27
Seller's Disclosure of Property Condition 39, 40, 41, 42, 43, 54
Selling associate
 with no prior relationship with the buyer 103
 with prior relationship with buyer 103
Services 255
Short-term benefits 243
Single agency 178, 184, 185
Single property 123
Smith v. Levine 264
Special agency 16, 30
Sponsoring broker(s) 3, 218
Spradling v. Williams 251
Statements to consumers 53
Statutory dual agency 153
Statutory dual agent 154
Statutory fraud 254
Stigmas 54
Stigmatized properties 46, 49, 55
Stortroen v. Beneficial Finance Company 68
Subagency 98, 99, 100, 101, 108
Subagent(s) 3, 99, 107, 216
 of seller 279
Supervening law 73
Syndications 168

T

"Tax-Deferred Exchange Provisions" 168
Tenant-representation agreement 16
Tenant's agent 4
Termination date 121
Texas Administrative Code 9
Texas Association of REALTORS® 19, 50, 116, 131, 200, 228
Texas Board of Insurance 44
Texas Deceptive Practices Act 222
Texas Deceptive Trade Practices Act 22, 38, 50, 52, 53, 226
Texas Fair Housing Act 226
Texas Occupations Code 26
Texas Property Code 38, 275
Texas Real Estate Commission (TREC) 8, 9, 15, 150, 227
 Rules 239
Texas State Bar Association's Code of Ethics 28
Texas state law 226, 239
There's No Such Thing as Business Ethics 244
Third parties 36
Title defect 141
Title insurance 44, 45
Trade 255
Trammel Crow Company No. 60, et al. v. William Jefferson Harkinson 137

U

Unconscionable action 255, 264
Undisclosed agency relationship 108
Undisclosed relationships 5
Universal agency 14
Unlicensed brokerage owners 218
Unsuccessful defenses 268

V

Verbal and nonverbal communications 259
Veterans Affairs (VA) loan 135

W

"Waiver of Consumer Rights" 260
Waivers of rights, under the DTPA 259
Warkentin, James B. 184
Webster's Unabridged Dictionary 225
Weitzel v. Barnes 266
Wilson v. Donze 64, 174
Written agreements/contract 80, 285

Z

Zak v. Parks 267

Notes

Notes

Notes

Notes

Notes

Notes

Notes

Notes

Notes

Notes